Achieving Enterprise Agility through Innovative Software Development

Amitoj Singh
Chitkara University, Punjab, India

A volume in the Advances in Systems Analysis,
Software Engineering, and High Performance
Computing (ASASEHPC) Book Series

Managing Director:	Lindsay Johnston
Managing Editor:	Austin DeMarco
Director of Intellectual Property & Contracts:	Jan Travers
Acquisitions Editor:	Kayla Wolfe
Production Editor:	Christina Henning
Development Editor:	Caitlyn Martin
Cover Design:	Jason Mull

Published in the United States of America by
Information Science Reference (an imprint of IGI Global)
701 E. Chocolate Avenue
Hershey PA, USA 17033
Tel: 717-533-8845
Fax: 717-533-8661
E-mail: cust@igi-global.com
Web site: http://www.igi-global.com

Library of Congress Cataloging-in-Publication Data

Achieving enterprise agility through innovative software development / Amitoj Singh, editor.
    pages cm
 Includes bibliographical references and index.
 ISBN 978-1-4666-8510-9 (hardcover) -- ISBN 978-1-4666-8511-6 (ebook) 1. Organizational effectiveness. 2. Information technology--Management. 3. Business enterprises--Technological innovations--Management. I. Singh, Amitoj, editor.
 HD58.9.A275 2015
 658'.055--dc23
                        2015010289

This book is published in the IGI Global book series Advances in Systems Analysis, Software Engineering, and High Performance Computing (ASASEHPC) (ISSN: 2327-3453; eISSN: 2327-3461)

British Cataloguing in Publication Data
A Cataloguing in Publication record for this book is available from the British Library.

For electronic access to this publication, please contact: eresources@igi-global.com.

Advances in Systems Analysis, Software Engineering, and High Performance Computing (ASASEHPC) Book Series

Vijayan Sugumaran
Oakland University, USA

ISSN: 2327-3453
EISSN: 2327-3461

MISSION

The theory and practice of computing applications and distributed systems has emerged as one of the key areas of research driving innovations in business, engineering, and science. The fields of software engineering, systems analysis, and high performance computing offer a wide range of applications and solutions in solving computational problems for any modern organization.

The **Advances in Systems Analysis, Software Engineering, and High Performance Computing (ASASEHPC) Book Series** brings together research in the areas of distributed computing, systems and software engineering, high performance computing, and service science. This collection of publications is useful for academics, researchers, and practitioners seeking the latest practices and knowledge in this field.

COVERAGE

- Engineering Environments
- Enterprise Information Systems
- Distributed Cloud Computing
- Computer System Analysis
- Computer Networking
- Storage Systems
- Human-Computer Interaction
- Performance Modelling
- Network Management
- Parallel Architectures

IGI Global is currently accepting manuscripts for publication within this series. To submit a proposal for a volume in this series, please contact our Acquisition Editors at Acquisitions@igi-global.com or visit: http://www.igi-global.com/publish/.

Titles in this Series

For a list of additional titles in this series, please visit: www.igi-global.com

Delivery and Adoption of Cloud Computing Services in Contemporary Organizations
Victor Chang (Computing, Creative Technologies and Engineering, Leeds Beckett University, UK) Robert John Walters (Electronics and Computer Science, University of Southampton, UK) and Gary Wills (Electronics and Computer Science, University of Southampton, UK)
Information Science Reference • copyright 2015 • 519pp • H/C (ISBN: 9781466682108) • US $225.00 (our price)

Emerging Research in Cloud Distributed Computing Systems
Susmit Bagchi (Gyeongsang National University, South Korea)
Information Science Reference • copyright 2015 • 447pp • H/C (ISBN: 9781466682139) • US $200.00 (our price)

Resource Management of Mobile Cloud Computing Networks and Environments
George Mastorakis (Technological Educational Institute of Crete, Greece) Constandinos X. Mavromoustakis (University of Nicosia, Cyprus) and Evangelos Pallis (Technological Educational Institute of Crete, Greece)
Information Science Reference • copyright 2015 • 432pp • H/C (ISBN: 9781466682252) • US $215.00 (our price)

Research and Applications in Global Supercomputing
Richard S. Segall (Arkansas State University, USA) Jeffrey S. Cook (Independent Researcher, USA) and Qingyu Zhang (Shenzhen University, China)
Information Science Reference • copyright 2015 • 672pp • H/C (ISBN: 9781466674615) • US $265.00 (our price)

Challenges, Opportunities, and Dimensions of Cyber-Physical Systems
P. Venkata Krishna (VIT University, India) V. Saritha (VIT University, India) and H. P. Sultana (VIT University, India)
Information Science Reference • copyright 2015 • 328pp • H/C (ISBN: 9781466673120) • US $200.00 (our price)

Human Factors in Software Development and Design
Saqib Saeed (University of Dammam, Saudi Arabia) Imran Sarwar Bajwa (The Islamia University of Bahawalpur, Pakistan) and Zaigham Mahmood (University of Derby, UK & North West University, South Africa)
Information Science Reference • copyright 2015 • 354pp • H/C (ISBN: 9781466664852) • US $195.00 (our price)

Handbook of Research on Innovations in Systems and Software Engineering
Vicente García Díaz (University of Oviedo, Spain) Juan Manuel Cueva Lovelle (University of Oviedo, Spain) and B. Cristina Pelayo García-Bustelo (University of Oviedo, Spain)
Information Science Reference • copyright 2015 • 745pp • H/C (ISBN: 9781466663596) • US $515.00 (our price)

www.igi-global.com

701 E. Chocolate Ave., Hershey, PA 17033
Order online at www.igi-global.com or call 717-533-8845 x100
To place a standing order for titles released in this series, contact: cust@igi-global.com
Mon-Fri 8:00 am - 5:00 pm (est) or fax 24 hours a day 717-533-8661

Table of Contents

Detailed Table of Contents

Agile methods emphasize on team's collaboration and so does the requirements engineering process. But how do agile teams collaborate with their geographically distributed counter parts to accomplish requirements related activities? Although, proved to be flexible and dynamic it needs to conduct more empirical investigation to identify the collaboration patterns of distributed agile teams. Therefore, in this chapter collaboration patterns of geographically distributed agile teams are identified in terms of reported communication (defined as information exchange) among team members and their awareness (defined as knowledge about each other) of each other. A multiple case study method is used in this chapter to study the geographically distributed agile teams in four IT organizations. Though, some of the findings revealed several patterns are corroborating the previous results available in literature. However, some of the patterns identified in this chapter are specific to distributed agile teams. For instance, the chapter identifies that high awareness among agile teams leads to more communication. Implications for research and software industry are discussed and future research directions are also provided.

This chapter proposes the use of agile methodology in designing the innovation management system in young academic institutes. Technology innovations from most universities and research institutes originate out of chaos. As a result, it is difficult to associate structure to its management. While there have been many social science research methodology based studies on this subject under the broad umbrella of "Innovation and Technology Management", there is usually an absence of well defined process to help young academic institutions to manage their intellectual property better. There is a strongly desired need to associate a clearly articulated structure for translation of ideas into technology innovations that will help young academic institutes to inculcate research in students and faculties and would help identify the best commercial application of technology innovations. Agile methodologies are best suited to be adopted in the academic scenario as rapidly changing environment of academic institutes can be easily handled using agile methodology. The aim of this chapter is to produce an evolutionary advance practical innovation management process for academic institutes out of this chaos to inculcate research in students and faculties using agile methodologies.

To meet business demands, enterprise software systems are required to be more dynamic, flexible and adaptive. Business processes must often be context-aware. Things get complicated when enterprise software systems, after a decade of evolution, comprise heterogeneous platforms and different technological stacks. This chapter presents the design and implementation of a cross-platform architecture with intelligent agents for dynamic business rules, process flows and services composition. The architecture includes an Enterprise Service Bus for service integration. Service agents are used to handle services. A Central Intelligent Agent that contains a Prolog-style rule-based engine is designed to execute business rules and processes. These agents are implemented in both Java and COBOL. Business process flows are completely rule- and context-driven. The services and components for the business processes are dynamically constructed. The proposed architecture and programming model enables fast prototyping and rapid development in an agile development process across different platforms.

Chapter 4

Lean methodology is an improvement philosophy, an expansion of Lean manufacturing and lean principles to the management of Service and Information Technology industries. It articulates how waste can be minimal at Software Development Process (SDP) which begins from feasibility study and ends till the product is delivered to the customer. In today's competitive world throughout all the industries emphasis is on product's quality within the time constraints. To gear up with the market demand Lean improvement concepts is introduced in (information technology) IT industry. Lean IT is the translation of lean manufacturing practices applicable to the Software Development life cycle (SDLC). It works like a business model and oriented towards the principles that focuses on the non value added activities. This chapter will present how lean methodologies and principles works in service industries to deliver the best quality products. Although Lean concept is traditionally been used in manufacturing industries; but nowadays it is adapted by Services companies with the aim of improving their processes and enhance customer satisfaction.

This chapter reveals the role of business process reengineering (BPR) in the modern business world, thus illustrating the theoretical and practical concept of BPR, the applications of BPR, the drivers of BRR (in terms of internal drivers and external drivers), the critical success factors of BPR (i.e., egalitarian leadership, collaborative working environment, top management commitment, supportive management, information technology, change management, project management, and cross-functional coordination), the implementation of BPR, and BPR software tools. BPR is a systematic approach to helping an organization analyze and improve its processes in digital age. BPR is a continuum of change initiatives in order to deliver better business performance standards through establishing sustainable process capability in modern organizations. BPR has become a popular tool to dealing with rapid technological and business change in the global competitive environment. Applying BPR will greatly improve business performance and reach business goals in global business.

Chapter 6

Jonathan Bishop, Centre for Research into Online Communities and E-Learning Systems, UK

This chapter explores how a learning organisation differs from a teaching organisation, such as that each person holds responsibility for their own learning, yet are supported and guided by those who wish to help them further their personal development. This chapter aims to develop a software project management methodology, based on existing approaches, which can accommodate all people, regardless of ability. The model developed, called the C2-Tech-S2 approach, is specifically designed for projects that use crowd-funding and agile development, particularly in environments based around the Cloud. A pilot study is carried out to demonstrate the 'technology' stage of this model for assessment using the 'support' stage. This finds that all stages of the model need to be applied in a project, because on their own the stages may not produce the most effective outcomes in terms of increased participation.

Chapter 7

Karun Madan, SD College, India

Out of the many revolutions in software development methodologies over the past years, no new methodology withstands completely in one way or the other. The failure rate of projects is still very high in spite of so much of revolutionary methodologies come in existence. Unsuccessful projects not only mean the incomplete projects even after deadline or outdated projects but there may be several other scenarios like project did not meet up the real requirements or lack of ability to deal with the changing requirements etc. In this kind of circumstances, projects were never successfully utilized, and another high percentage of projects again required massive rework to be utilizable. Factors like changing requirements and late testing and integration are few of the main causes of this high percentage of failure.This paper reveals how agile development is a way out to the issues linked with traditional software development. Agile development primarily focuses on the rapid delivery of enterprise worth in the form of working software.

Chapter 8

Vinay Kukreja, Chitkara University, India
Amitoj Singh, Chitkara University, India

In the globalization of fast changing business and technology environment, it becomes very important to respond quickly to changing user requirements. Traditional methodologies are not appropriate for the projects where user requirements are not fixed. Agile methodologies have been developed to cope up with user changing requirements and emphasize more on working software and customer collaboration. Agile is an umbrella term and it is used for many software development methodologies which shares common characteristics. This chapter mainly focuses on the working methodology of agile development and the usage areas of industry where agile development is implemented. Agile software development is difficult in distributed environment as the team members are at distributed locations. This chapter discusses agile industry applicability enablers which are useful for agile software development in distributed environment.

Chapter 9
    Neila Rjaibi, Institut Supérieur de Gestion de Tunis, Tunisia
    Latifa Ben Arfa Rabai, Institut Supérieur de Gestion de Tunis, Tunisia
    Ali Mili, New Jersey Institute of Technology, USA

This chapter presents a quantitative security risk management cybersecurity measure namely the Mean Failure Cost (MFC). We illustrate it to quantify the security of an e-Learning application while taking account of its respective stakeholders, security requirements, architectural components and the complete list of security threats. Moreover, in the mean time, security requirements are considered as appropriate mechanisms for preventing, detecting and recovering security attacks, for this reason an extension of the MFC measure is presented in order to detect the most critical security requirements to support the quantitative decision-making. Our focus is widespread to offer a diagnostic of the non secure system's problems and a depth insight interpretation about critical requirements, critical threats and critical components. This extension is beneficial and opens a wide range of possibilities for further economics based analysis. Also this chapter highlights the security measures for controlling e-Learning security problems regarding the most critical security requirements.

Chapter 10
    Nisha Ratti, Rayat Institute of Engg. and Information Technology, India
    Parminder Kaur, Guru Nanak Dev University, India

Software evolution is the essential characteristic of the real world software as the user requirements changes software needs to change otherwise it becomes less useful. In order to be used for longer time period, software needs to evolve. The software evolution can be a result of software maintenance. In this chapter, a study has been conducted on 10 versions of GLE (Graphics Layout Engine) and FGS (Flight Gear Simulator) evolved over the period of eight years. An effort is made to find the applicability of Lehman Laws on different releases of two softwares developed in C++ using Object Oriented metrics. The laws of continuous change, growth and complexity are found applicable according to data collected.

Chapter 11
    Jose Carlos Martins Delgado, University of Lisbon, Portugal

The agility with which an Enterprise Information Systems (EIS) can be changed is of primordial importance in today's fast paced, competitive market. This depends on the changeability of the EIS software resources, which in turn is heavily influenced by the coupling between the services implemented by these resources. This chapter presents a solution to the coupling problem based on the concepts of structural compliance and conformance, in which compatibility between interacting services does not rely on a shared schema. Instead, it checks resources component by component, recursively, until primitive elements are reached. However, coupling is not a single-faceted issue and involves several aspects and slants. To help in understanding and systematizing them, the chapter proposes a multidimensional framework that caters for EIS lifecycle stages, concreteness (with various levels of abstraction), interoperability (based on structural compliance and conformance), and concerns (to deal with non-functional aspects such as security, reliability and quality of service).

Evolution and maintainability of legacy systems is all time attention drawing subject for researchers and especially practitioners. Discovering the crosscutting concerns and separating it from core functionalities of a software system may help in evolution of the legacy systems. Aspect-oriented software development (AOSD) tries to achieve the goal. AOSD is new programming paradigm which helps to bring in modularity in the program by writing the crosscutting concerns in the form of 'aspects'. Modularity brings comprehensibility and hence maintainability of the software system. Tools and techniques, which aid in identifying the crosscutting concerns in such systems and refactoring them into aspects, are needed to apply aspect-oriented techniques to legacy systems at use in industry. This chapter aims to identify issues, problems and approaches used in the migration from legacy systems to aspect-oriented software system.

Cloud computing environment is very much malicious intrusion prone hence cloud security is very vital. Existing network security mechanisms face new challenges in the cloud such as DDOS attacks, virtual machine intrusion attacks and malicious user activities. This chapter includes brief introduction about cloud computing, concept of virtualization, cloud security, various DDOS attacks, tools to run these attacks & various techniques to detect these attacks, review of threshold methods used for detection of DDOS attacks & abnormal network behavior and proposed dynamic threshold based algorithmic approach. Although various cloud security measures are prevailing to avoid virtual machine attacks and malicious user activities but these are not foolproof. Hence, new security methods are required to increase users' level of trust in clouds. By scrubbing traffic at major Internet points and backbone connection, a defense line is created for mitigation of DDOS attacks. Dynamic threshold algorithm based approach is proposed as a proactive approach to detect DDOS attacks for achieving secure cloud environment.

Preface

This is not a philosophical, theoretical or motivational book, but a practical one. Its purpose is to enable readers—software developers, managers involved in IT, and educators—to benefit from the good ideas and stay away from the bad ones. This book brings together a number of recent contributions to the domain of Software Engineering (CoSE) for achieving enterprise agility from a range of research groups and practitioners. Agility means the power of moving quickly and easily. These range from tools and techniques for managing discrete, low-level activities developers engage in when developing parts of software systems; knowledge, project and process management for large scale software engineering enterprises; and new ways of organizing software teams including outsourcing, open sourcing, highly distributed virtual teams and global software engineering. I believe that all practitioners engaging in or managing software engineering practices, researchers contributing to advancement in understanding and support for innovative software engineering, and students wishing to gain a deeper appreciation of the underpinning theories, issues and practices within this domain will benefit from most if not all of these contributions.

A large number of submissions have been received in response to our call for papers and invitations for this edited book from many leading research groups and well-known practitioners of leading collaborative software engineering techniques. After a rigorous review process 13 submissions were accepted for this publication. I tried to choose best work among the received lot. This book will enhance the learning about formation, management and evolution in domains such as agile teams, projects with substantive outsourcing, open source software, virtual software teams and global software engineering domains. Being an inter-personal and–often–inter-organizational activity, software engineering introduces a number of social and managerial challenges. Teams may be homogeneous or highly diverse in terms of culture, language and location. This introduces many challenges to supporting collaboration at high levels (process, project management) and low-levels (artefact sharing, consistency).Teams may be comprised of many generalist's e.g., agile methods or highly specialized individuals or sub-teams whose efforts must be coordinated. An organization needs to ensure appropriate management of teams and between teams. In particular, global software engineering domains introduce very new and challenging problems, such as in contracting and quality control in outsourcing, ownership and "group dynamics" in multi-site projects, and overall project direction and co-ordination in open source software projects.

The intended audience of this book will mainly consist of researchers, research students and practitioners in software engineering and allied fields; it can be in academic or industry. The book is also of interest to researchers and industrial practitioners in areas such as agile software methodologies, lean development, knowledge engineering, artificial intelligence, Legacy system, clod computing, software project management and component based software engineering.

The book has a simple structure and is intended for sequential reading. The opening chapter deals with the agile teams and challenges involves in distribution. Agile methods emphasize on team's collaboration, but how do agile teams collaborate with their geographically distributed counter parts to accomplish requirements related activities. In this chapter collaboration patterns of geographically distributed agile teams are identified in terms of reported communication among team members and their awareness of each other. A multiple case study method is used to study the geographically distributed agile teams in four IT organizations. The study identifies that high awareness among agile teams leads to more communication. Implications for research and software industry are discussed and future research directions are also provided.

The second chapter is a short foray into the style of agile description. This chapter proposes the use of agile methodology in designing the innovation management system in young academic institutes. Since process for technology innovations from most universities and research institutes originate out of chaos. There is a need to associate a clearly articulated method for translation of ideas into technology innovations that will certainly help young academic institutes to inculcate research in students and faculties and would help identify the best commercial application of technology innovations. This chapter presents a practical innovation management process for academic institutes to inculcate research in students and faculties using agile methodologies. Agile methodologies are best suited to adopt in the academic scenario due to rapidly changing environment of academic institutes that can be easily handled using SCRUM methodology.

Chapter 3 is a sketch that presents the design and implementation of a cross-platform architecture with intelligent agents for dynamic business rules, process flows and services composition. This architecture helps in meeting business demands. Things get complicated when enterprise software systems, after a decade of evolution, comprise heterogeneous platforms and different technological stacks. The architecture includes an Enterprise Service Bus for service integration. A Central Intelligent Agent that contains a Prolog-style rule-based engine is designed to execute business rules and processes. The services and components for the business processes are dynamically constructed. The proposed architecture and programming model enables fast prototyping and rapid development in an agile development process across different platforms.

Chapter 4 is about Lean methodology and expansion of Lean manufacturing and lean principles to the management of Service and Information Technology industries. It articulates how waste can be minimal at Software Development Process (SDP) which begins from feasibility study and ends till the product is delivered to the customer. To gear up with the market demand Lean improvement concepts is introduced in (information technology) IT industry. Lean IT is the translation of lean manufacturing practices applicable to the Software Development life cycle (SDLC). This chapter presents how lean methodologies and principles works in service industries to deliver the best quality products. Although Lean concept is traditionally been used in manufacturing industries; but nowadays it is adapted by Services companies with the aim of improving their processes and enhance customer satisfaction.

In chapter 5 role of business process reengineering (BPR) in the modern business world is talked about by illustrating the theoretical and practical concept of BPR, the applications of BPR, the drivers of BRR (in terms of internal drivers and external drivers), the critical success factors of BPR (i.e., egalitarian leadership, collaborative working environment, top management commitment, supportive management, information technology, change management, project management, and cross-functional coordination), the implementation of BPR, and BPR software tools. BPR is a continuum of change initiatives in order to deliver better business performance standards through establishing sustainable process capability in modern organizations. BPR has become a popular tool to dealing with rapid technological and business change in the global competitive environment. Applying BPR will greatly improve business performance and reach business goals in global business.

Chapter 6 take up the case study of a learning organisation. A learning organisation differs from a teaching organisation, such as a higher education institution, in that each person holds responsibility for their own learning, yet are supported and guided by those who wish to help them further in their personal development. This chapter aims to develop a software project management methodology, based on existing approaches, which can accommodate all people, regardless of ability. The model aims to be suited to those who require simplicity as well as those who want complexity, by integrating best practice from other models, such as PRINCE2, which it can work within. The model developed, called the C2-Tech-S2 approach, is specifically designed for projects that use crowd-funding and agile development, particularly in environments based around the Cloud.

In the seventh chapter high points of agile methodologies over traditional methodologies have been illustrated, Authors discussed about the high failure rates of projects in spite of so much of revolutionary methodologies. Factors like changing requirements and late testing and integration are few of the main causes of this high percentage of failure. Agile development is projected as a way out to the issues linked with traditional software development. Agile development focuses on the rapid delivery of enterprise worth in the form of working software. These methodologies reduces the overall risk linked with software as a result of continuous planning as well as feedback. In this way, agile development team can easily adapt to change requirements, which featured even late in the development process.

Chapter 8 examines about globalisation and its effects on business. Traditional methodologies are not appropriate for the projects where user requirements are not fixed. Agile methodologies have been developed to cope up with user changing requirements and emphasize more on working software & customer collaboration. This chapter mainly focuses on the working methodology of agile development and the usage areas of industry where agile development is implemented. Agile software development is difficult in distributed environment as the team members are at distributed locations. Authors discusses agile industry applicability enablers which are useful for agile software development in distributed environment.

Chapter 9 presents a quantitative security risk management cyber security measure namely the Mean Failure Cost (MFC) to quantify the security of an e-Learning application while taking account of its respective stakeholders, security requirements, architectural components and the complete list of security threats. Moreover, security requirements are considered as appropriate mechanisms for preventing, detecting and recovering security attacks, for this reason an extension of the MFC measure is presented in order to detect the most critical security requirements to support the quantitative decision-making. Chapter focuses on non secure system's problems and a depth insight interpretation about critical requirements, critical threats and critical components. This extension is beneficial and opens a wide range of possibilities for further economics based analysis. Also this chapter highlights the security measures for controlling e-Learning security problems regarding the most critical security requirements.

Tenth Chapter briefs about the evolution of software and factors involved in organisation agilty. In order to be used for longer time period, software needs to evolve. The software evolution can be a result of software maintenance. This chapter discussed 10 versions of GLE (Graphics Layout Engine) and FGS (Flight Gear Simulator) evolved over the period of eight years. An effort is made to find the applicability of Lehman Laws on different releases of two software developed in C++ using Object Oriented metrics. The laws of continuous change, growth and complexity are found applicable according to data collected.

Chapter 11 discusses the problems of coupling and interoperability in local and distributed applications. The former emphasize coupling, since interoperability is simply based on local pointers and on a type system with shared names. The latter had to solve the interoperability problem first and coupling became an afterthought. Chapter discuss both SOA- and REST-based solutions that depends on shared schema data description languages and as a result introduce a higher level of coupling than actually needed. This chapter contends that problems, interoperability and coupling, need to be dealt with in a balanced way. The fundamental problem of resource interaction is precisely satisfying the interoperability requirements of the interacting resources while reducing coupling to the minimum level possible. This way, changeability will be maximized and will significantly contribute to the agility of an enterprise when introducing the necessary changes in its EIS. To achieve these goals, this chapter has presented a multidimensional framework to describe the interoperability and coupling aspects of resources, in an orthogonal fashion, including lifecycle, levels of concreteness, levels of interoperability, and non-functional concerns. Coupling metrics have been defined, which show that these effects reinforce each other in the goal of coupling reduction

Chapter 12 inspect evolution and maintainability of legacy systems. Discovering the crosscutting concerns and separating it from core functionalities of a software system may help in evolution of the legacy systems. Aspect-oriented software development (AOSD) is new programming paradigm which helps to bring in modularity in the program by writing the crosscutting concerns in the form of 'aspects'. Modularity brings comprehensibility and hence maintainability of the software system. Tools and techniques, which aid in identifying the crosscutting concerns in such systems and refactoring them into aspects, are needed to apply aspect-oriented techniques to legacy systems at use in industry. This chapter aims to identify issues, problems and approaches used in the migration from legacy systems to aspect-oriented software system

Chapter 13 scrutinize about the malicious intrusion in cloud based systems. Chapter discuss about the existing network security mechanisms face new challenges in the cloud such as DDOS attacks, virtual machine intrusion attacks and malicious user activities. Although various cloud security measures are prevailing to avoid virtual machine attacks and malicious user activities but these are not foolproof. A new security method is proposed to increase users' level of trust in clouds. By scrubbing traffic at major Internet points and backbone connection, a defense line is created for mitigation of DDOS attacks. In this chapter Dynamic threshold algorithm based approach is proposed as a proactive approach to detect DDOS attacks for achieving secure cloud environment.

Software engineering has been a very heavily researched area and almost all practicing software teams will need to engage in it. However, many challenges still present both in terms of adopting collaboration practices, processes and tools and improving the state-of-the-art. Many of these challenges are long standing, and hence are fundamental to the act of working together to engineer shared artifacts. These include assembling teams, dividing work, social networking within and between teams, choosing best-practice processes, techniques and supporting tools, and effective project management. Others have arisen due to new organizational practices and technical advances, including open-sourced, out-sourced, multi-site and agile software engineering contexts. We still do not know the ideal way to share knowledge, facilitate the most effective communication, co-ordinate massively distributed work, and design and deploy support tools for these activities

At the end I would like to convey our appreciation to all contributors including the accepted chapters' authors, and many other participants who submitted their chapters that cannot be included in the book. In addition, I also appreciate all reviewers for their assistance in formatting the book.

Chapter 1
Communication and Awareness Patterns of Distributed Agile Teams

Irum Inayat
University of Malaya, Malaysia

Siti Salwah Salim
University of Malaya, Malaysia

Sabrina Marczak
Pontifícia Universidade Católica do Rio Grande do Sul (PUCRS), Brazil

ABSTRACT

Agile methods emphasize on team's collaboration and so does the requirements engineering process. But how do agile teams collaborate with their geographically distributed counter parts to accomplish requirements related activities? Although, proved to be flexible and dynamic it needs to conduct more empirical investigation to identify the collaboration patterns of distributed agile teams. Therefore, in this chapter collaboration patterns of geographically distributed agile teams are identified in terms of reported communication (defined as information exchange) among team members and their awareness (defined as knowledge about each other) of each other. A multiple case study method is used in this chapter to study the geographically distributed agile teams in four IT organizations. Though, some of the findings revealed several patterns are corroborating the previous results available in literature. However, some of the patterns identified in this chapter are specific to distributed agile teams. For instance, the chapter identifies that high awareness among agile teams leads to more communication. Implications for research and software industry are discussed and future research directions are also provided.

DOI: 10.4018/978-1-4666-8510-9.ch001

INTRODUCTION

Agile methods are iterative and incremental (Beck et al., 2001). Each iteration starts with a set of requirements, called user stories (Cohn, 2003, 2005). Therein, the refined list of user stories, called product backlog is formulated, discussed often in daily scrums and reprioritized for the next iterations. The flexibility and dynamic nature of agile methods offer benefits to the software development industry such as higher productivity (Eberlein & Julio Cesar, 2002), lesser rework (Bin, Xiaohu, Zhijun, & Maddineni, 2004), and efficient bug fixation (Lagerberg, Skude, Emanuelsson, & Sandahl, 2013).

Agile methods emphasize on collaboration of team members and entail dynamic management of requirements that evolve during the iteration, unlike traditional software development (Bang, 2007) (Beck et al., 2001). The dynamic yet flexible nature of agile methods makes it challenging to deal with ever changing-volatile requirements. The agile team members collaborate with each other to work on these interdependent user stories and their downstream artifacts i.e. code, design etc. The collaboration of agile teams widely depends upon their communication of changes in user stories and their awareness of each other's presence, professional expertise, work status and current task allocation. When the team members are geographically apart issue arises in frequent communication and awareness of each other. The major issues can be time zone difference, lousy means of communication, cultural and language barrier etc. Therefore, it is a challenge for distributed agile teams to maintain collaboration among each other while being geographically apart.

SOCIO TECHNICAL ASPECTS OF REQUIREMENTS-DRIVEN COLLABORATION AMONG AGILE TEAMS

This section presents the main underlying concepts required to develop an understanding of this study.

Requirements-Driven Collaboration

The Requirements-driven Collaboration (RDC) is defined as the collaboration among software development teams required to carry out requirements engineering activity by Damian and colleagues in (Damian, Kwan, & Marczak, 2010). This involves the team's collaboration with each other for the development and management of a certain set of interdependent requirements during the project development lifecycle. The authors have furthered studied RDC among traditional software development teams in terms of interaction of roles for shaping their communicating patterns (Marczak & Damian, 2011), measuring the impact of distance on awareness among distributed software development teams (Damian, Marczak, & Kwan, 2007), and for agile software development teams (Inayat, Marczak, & Salim, 2013; Inayat, Salim, Marczak, & Kasirun, 2014; Marczak, Inayat, & Salim, 2013)

Socio-Technical Aspects

The term socio-technical was defined by Trist and Bamforth (Trist & Bamforth, 1951) to describe a psychological view of workmen's relationship with their social structure and technical system for coal collection. These social and technical aspects are of great importance while analyzing an organization (Coombs, Knights, & Willmott, 1992).

Team members working on a certain set of interdependent requirements collaborate with other in order to get the user stories done, to share information, and to develop common understanding about shared goals. Therefore, working on interdependent requirements, team members tend to develop socio and technical dependencies giving rise to socio-technical relationships with one another as explained in Figure. 1. Social relationship means a people-to-people relationship, i.e. information sharing with one another (Cataldo, Wagstrom, & Carley, 2006). Technical relationship means work dependency among team members e.g. working on an interdependent user stories (Cataldo et al., 2006). These relationships generate dependencies among team members, namely people to task dependency (shown in Figure. 1(a)), task to task dependency (shown in Figure 1(b)) and social interaction among people working on interdependent requirements (shown in Figure 1(c)).

In this study the collaboration among agile teams is translated into two socio-technical aspects i.e. communication and awareness based on an online survey conducted with agile practitioners (Inayat et al., 2014). The survey was aimed to: (i) find out the perception of agile practitioners regarding collaboration while working on certain set of interdependent user stories; and (ii) to identify the most relevant socio-technical aspects of RDC. The findings revealed that the practitioners considered communication and awareness as the most relevant socio-technical aspects of collaboration among teams.

Communication

Communication is when team members to share information with each other regarding a certain issue related to the interdependent requirement under development. The communication among team members can be synchronous or asynchronous and possible through any means i.e. email, skype, face to face. In this study agile thirteen possible reasons of communication have been identified among agile teams i.e. User story clarification, user story negotiation, changes communication, code synchronization, code issues, code refactoring, code synchronization, quality issues, management issues support issues, sprint planning issues.. The communication reasons were recorded during the data collection phase by on-site observation of the team. Later, communication patterns for all of these thirteen reasons were studied for both of the iterations to find out the communication behavior of agile teams in relation to their awareness of each other.

Figure 1. Socio-technical relationships
(Kwan & Damian, 2011)

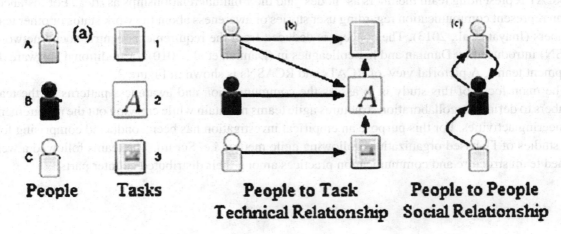

Awareness

Awareness is an individual's familiarity with other team members' presence, task status, professional background and interaction within the shared work space (Fuks, Rapsoso, Gerosa, Pimental, & Lucena, 2008)(Gutwin & Greenberg, 1996). Awareness is considered as an important aspect of collaboration among teams, both co-located and globally distributed. Awareness, as a socio-technical aspect of collaboration among teams has gained researcher's attention since 2006 (Steinmacher, Chaves, & Gerosa, 2012). However, most of the studies that discussed awareness focused on tools support for maintaining awareness among the team members (Steinmacher et al., 2012)(Steinmacher, Chaves, & Gerosa, 2010). Therefore, in this study awareness is explored further in the context of requirements-driven collaboration among agile teams. Based on literature, four kinds of awareness are taken into account in this study: (i) availability, accessibility of a person when one needs help about the project (Ehrlich & Chang, 2006); (ii) general awareness, awareness of a person's professional expertise and skills (Ehrlich & Chang, 2006); (iii) current awareness, awareness of the current set of tasks that a certain person is working on (Ehrlich & Chang, 2006); and (iv) work status awareness, awareness of a colleague's current progress of work. This fourth type of awareness has been defined for this study given the relevance of constant progress report in agile teams.

Requirements Centric Agile Teams

A requirements-centric agile team, in short RCAT, is defined as a group of cross-functional and self-managing people working on a certain set of interdependent user stories, broken down into tasks, as well as on downstream artifacts i.e. code, tests, design etc. (Inayat et al., 2013). This group of members includes anyone that is assigned to work on the project i.e. team members and the customer or customer representative. It also includes anyone that 'emerges' during the development life cycle, 'emergent members' (Inayat et al., 2013). The concept of RCATIs deduced from the requirements-centric teams (RCT) introduced by Damian and her colleagues in (Damian et al., 2010) for traditional software development teams.

Requirements Centric Agile Social networks

The requirements-centric agile social network, in short RCASN, is defined as a social network between the RCAT representing team members as 'nodes' and their mutual relationships as 'ties'. For instance a tie can represent communication regarding user stories or awareness about the work status or other team members (Inayat et al., 2013). The concept is deduced from the requirements-centric social networks (RCSN) introduced by Damian and her colleagues in (Damian et al., 2010) for traditional software development teams. A pictorial view of RCATs and RCASNs is shown in Figure 2.

The main focus of this study is to assess the communication and awareness patterns of the team members to define the collaboration structures agile teams maintain while carrying out the requirements engineering activities. For this purpose an empirical investigation has been conducted comprising four case studies of IT-based organizations following agile method i.e. Scrum. The teams followed a well-defined team structure and communication practices among their distributed counter parts.

Figure 2. Requirements Centric Agile Team (RCAT) and Requirements-Centric Agile Social Networks (RCASN)

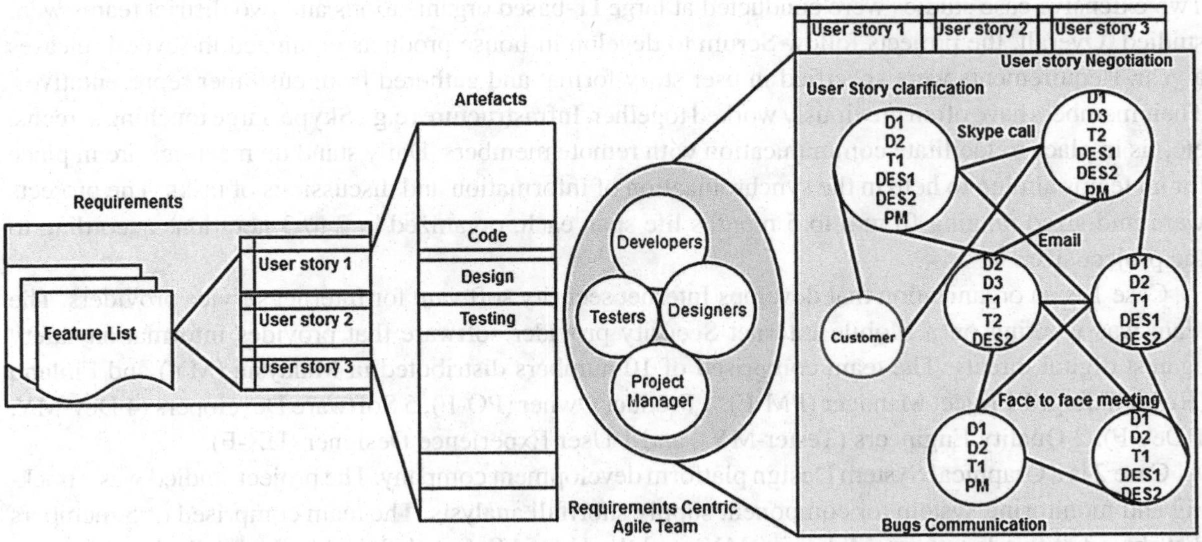

COMMUNICATION AND AWARENESS PATTERNS AMONG DISTRIBUTED AGILE TEAMS

The main focus of this chapter is to study the communication and awareness patterns of distributed agile teams and to find their interrelationship. This chapter aims to find out if agile teams have tendency to group or cluster with increase in communication and awareness. It explains: (i) who is involved in communication among distributed agile teams, (ii) are there any members involved else than the allocated ones, (iii) how dense are the communication and awareness networks for distributed agile teams, (iv) does the dense awareness networks affect the communication among distributed agile teams, (v) does the dense communication networks affects over all awareness of team members. This information is critical for the Project Managers and company's management to reorient their teams in order to achieve better collaboration among them. This helps to eradicate the communication gaps between team members due to any possible reason e.g. lack of awareness, broken communication link or several members holding all of the information. The managers can visualize the inside story of their teams and can make better decisions to achieve better performance and results. To achieve this purpose, teams' communication and awareness patterns are recorded and visualized in the form of networks or Sociograms. Literature supports the use of communication patterns to analyze the agile team performance (Cataldo & Ehrlich, 2011) (Ehrlich, Cataldo, & York, 2014) and development effort (Cataldo & Herbsleb, 2008). In this chapter, social network analysis, social network analysis (SNA) measures were applied on the networks to analyze the collaboration behaviors. The detailed discussion of the case studies and results is described below.

Case Studies

Two extensive case studies were conducted at large IT-based organizations and two district teams were studied. Overall, the projects follow Scrum to develop in-house products organized in several releases a year. Requirements were specified in user story format and gathered from customer representatives. Their members have often previously worked together. Infrastructure (e.g., Skype, large touching screens, etc.) is in place to facilitate communication with remote members. Daily stand up meetings are in place for all teams aiming to help in the synchronization of information and discussions of tasks. The projects were mid-sized ranging from 3 to 5 months life span each, organized in 2 to 3 iterations according to the project size.

Case 1 is an organization that develops Internet security software for Internet service providers. The team was working on a Mobile Internet Security provider software that provides information safety against digital threats. The team comprised of 10 numbers distributed in Malaysia (MY) and Finland (F), including: 1 Project Manager (PM-F), 1 Product Owner (PO-F), 5 Software Developers (4 Dev-MY, 1 Dev-F), 2 Quality Engineers (Tester-MY), and 1 User Experience Designer (UX-F).

Case 2 is a Graphical System Design platform development company. The project studied was a tracking and monitoring system for component supply shortfall analysis. The team comprised of 5 members distributed at two locations, Malaysia (MY) and the United States (US), including: 1 Project Manager (PM-US), 1 Technical Architect (Arch-US), and 3 Software Developers (2 Dev-MY, 1 Dev-US).

Data were gathered through multiple data collection methods including questionnaire, semi-structured interviews, observation and work diaries. These teams were studied for altogether a term of 9 months, almost 2-3 months spent at each company. The data was recorded for two iterations of the on-going projects to analyze the effect of elapsing time on team members' communication and awareness. Projects with life span not more than 6 months and iteration size of 2-4 weeks were chosen.

Construction of Communication and Awareness Networks (Sociograms)

The agile teams' collaboration data is recorded by physically deploying a questionnaire, on-site observations and semi-structured interviews with the team members. The semi-structured interviews helped to gather any missed out or confusing information in the questionnaires. The communication and awareness data retrieved from the aforementioned sources were recoded manually to create social networks or sociograms. The sociograms were used to represent the actors (team members) as "nodes" and their relationships i.e. communication and awareness as "links". The social network analysis measures specifically clustering coefficient and ties reciprocity were used to determine the traits of distributed agile teams' collaboration. The data for both communication and awareness were converted into node and edge tables and saved as excel spreadsheets. The node tables comprised of source, target, id, label of nodes. The edge table comprised of source, target, id, label, direction and weight of edges. All the possible communication and awareness links were manually transformed into tables called 'edge tables' in excel files. For each case study there were two iterations, 13 communication reasons and 4 awareness types for which total 34 edge and node tables were made. These tables were then loaded to Gephi, a network visualization and analysis tool to transform them into sociograms consisting actors as nodes and relationships as ties among them. Example of communication and awareness networks is shown in Figure 3.

Figure 3. Examples of (a) communication and (b) awareness sociograms

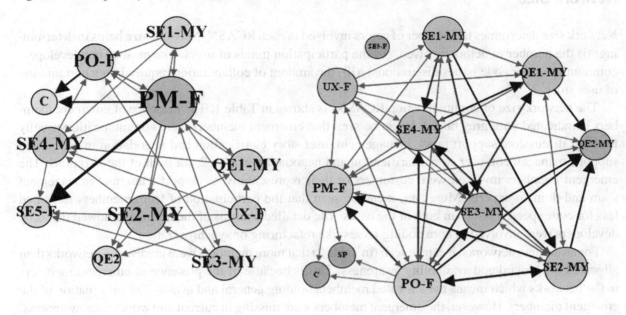

Social Network Analysis of the Communication and Awareness Networks (Sociograms)

The data were converted into square matrices for applying social network analysis measures and saved as separate excel spreadsheets. Each matrix comprised of actors (team members) on X and Y axis and populated with relationship between them. For instance if Project Manager communicated with Product owner '1' was placed in the respective row and '0' if otherwise. The diagonal was left empty to ensure no self-communication and awareness. These matrices were then loaded to the social network analysis tool (UCINET) to apply the measures.

RESULTS AND DISCUSSION

In this chapter the main focus was to define the patterns of RCATs regarding their mutual communication and awareness of each other. The network size and density were calculated for all of the RCASNs created for communication and awareness among the teams. As mentioned earlier, the communication RCASNs were built for thirteen possible reasons and four awareness types were taken into consideration. The description of size and density measures of the communication and awareness RCASNs is discussed below.

Network Size

Network size determines the number of actors involved in each RCASN. Network size helps in determining: (i) the number of actors involved, (ii) the participation trends of users (like most of the developers communicated for code issues discussions), (iii) the amount of collaboration required for a certain kind of user story.

The network size of communication RCASNs is shown in Table 1. The presence of emergent members is indicated with grey boxed. It can be seen that emergent members were communication usually for bugs discussion, support tasks, management, user story clarification and negotiation in case 1 and support, management, user story clarification and negotiation in case 2, for both of the iterations. The emergent members involved were customers or their representatives, support team, and management team and domain experts. Moreover, it can be seen that the participation of team members remained less for code specific issues in both of the cases. The detailed analysis of the networks showed that only developers were involved in core coding issues like refactoring or synchronization.

For awareness networks, it can be seen (in Table 2) that more members were involved in networks than allocated for general and availability awareness. This is because of the presence of emergent members in the networks which means the allocated members holding general and availability information of the emergent members. However, the emergent members were missing in current and work status awareness. Moreover, the number of members also decreased for both of these networks because the members like PM, PO and BA were not allocated any task.

Table 1. Communication RCASNs size for case 1 and 2, iteration 1 and 2

Communication Reasons	Case 1				Case 2			
	It 1		It 2		It 1		It 2	
	MY	F	MY	F	MY	US	MY	US
Bugs	5	6	6	5	2	3	2	3
Changes communication	6	4	6	4	2	5	2	3
Code issues	5	2	6	2	2	1	2	1
Code refactoring	4	2	4	2	2	1	2	1
Code reviews	6	3	6	2	2	1	2	1
Code synchronization	4	3	3	1	2	1	2	1
Coordination	6	4	6	4	2	2	2	3
Management	6	4	5	5	2	3	2	4
Quality	6	2	6	4	2	3	2	3
Sprint planning	4	3	6	4	2	1	1	2
Support	6	5	6	5	2	3	1	3
User story clarification	6	5	5	5	2	3	2	4
User story negotiation	6	5	5	5	2	4	2	4

Table 2. Awareness RCASNs size for case 1 and 2, iteration 1 and 2

Awareness Types	Case 1				Case 2			
	It 1		It 2		It 1		It 2	
	MY	F	MY	F	MY	US	MY	US
Availability	6	5	6	6	2	7	2	7
General	6	5	6	6	2	7	2	7
Current	6	4	6	4	2	3	2	3
Work Status	6	3	6	4	2	3	2	3

Network Density

Network density is defined as the proportion present ties with the total number of possible ties. Density helps to assess how tightly coupled the team is. If the density value is low it shows less communication happened between members than expected. The ideal network has density value 1. The networks with less participation eventually have low densities (closer to 0). The density of a communication network can be interpreted as the speed with which information travels in a network or as the social constraint of the actors (nodes). Similarly, for RCAT high density of change communication RCASN is interpreted as high communication of members with each other for communicating information about changes in user stories. On the other hand, low density for management related communication means that fewer actors participated in management related communication.

Density has been interpreted in several ways in literature such as: (i) high density indicates ease of coordination among geographically dispersed software development teams (Hinds & Mcgrath, 2006), volatility of requirements for traditional software development teams (Damian et al., 2010) etc.

For this study, density values equal or above 0.5 (50%) are considered as high-density values, meaning that more than half of the possible ties were reported as present and equal or lower than 0.3 (30%) are graded as low-density values. The density values for case 1, iteration 1 and 2 are reported in Table 1 below. The density values for both of the iterations are less than 50%. No network has shown more than 39% of total possible ties. This shows that the communication took place was much lesser than the possible number of ties expected. The density values close to the maximum value attained i.e. 39% are for bugs discussion (30%), user story clarification (31%) in iteration 1 and user story clarification (32%) and negotiation (39%) in iteration 2. The results show that only 15% of the networks reside in between the range of high and low density. However, rest of the 85% networks show lower density values. In low density cases (e.g. code issues, reviews, refactor and synchronization etc.) the communication took place between developers only which turned the density value lower when calculated in comparison with total number of nodes (which was higher). The code related communication happened mostly among the developers and sometimes with quality engineers. The rest of the roles remained out of touch for instance it was not a part of policy for this team to involve Project Manager or Owner in every slight code change. On the contrast it can be seen that for user stories clarification and negotiation whole team was communicating with each other so the density value is comparatively high. Therefore, we can say that low density does not depict low or no communication because even in low density networks adequate communication took place between same roles.

For case 2, Coordination and user story clarification had density values higher than 0.6 (60%) in iteration 1. In iteration 2, changes communication, coordination, user story clarification and negotiation had the high density values (above 50%), shown in grey in Table 3. This shows that most of the team members mutually communicated with each other for the communication reasons including coordination issues, changes communication, user story clarification and negotiation. The rest of the communication reasons had density index less than 0.5 and range from 0.1 to 0.54. The density results showed that 15% of the networks in iteration 1 and 30% in iteration 2 were dense networks.

Density values for awareness networks of case 1, are presented in Table 4. The density values for iteration 2 are greater than iteration 1 which shows increase in awareness with time. The high density awareness networks are availability awareness for iteration 1 and 2, general awareness, and task awareness for iteration 2. Almost 50% of the networks have density values in high density region (above 50%) and the rest of 50% reside in between high and low density region (above 30%).

Table 3. Density values for communication RCASNs Case 1 and 2, Iteration 1 and 2

Communication Reasons	Case 1		Case 2	
	It 1	It-2	It 1	It 2
Bugs	0.30	0.18	0.31	0.35
Changes communication	0.28	0.29	0.51	0.70
Code issues	0.09	0.13	0.3	0.3
Code refactoring	0.05	0.13	0.3	0.3
Code reviews	0.11	0.07	0.3	0.3
Code synchronization	0.08	0.07	0.3	0.3
Coordination	0.20	0.22	0.65	0.6
Management	0.12	0.12	0.3	0.35
Quality	0.12	0.15	0.5	0.5
Sprint planning	0.15	0.17	0.25	0.3
Support	0.12	0.16	0.1	0.4
User story clarification	0.31	0.32	0.7	0.7
User story negotiation	0.21	0.39	0.31	0.35
Mean	0.16	0.18	0.37	0.41

Table 4. Density values for communication RCASNs Case 1 and 2, Iteration 1 and 2

Awareness Types	Density			
	Case 1- It 1	Case 2-It 2	Case 1- It 1	Case 2-It 2
Availability	0.54	0.62	0.6	0.6
General	0.37	0.53	0.64	0.64
Current	0.38	0.46	0.65	0.65
Work Status	0.37	0.55	0.70	0.70
Mean	0.41	0.54	0.64	0.64

For case 2, the awareness density results show high density values for all four types of awareness in both of the iterations, except current awareness. This shows that team members were well aware of each other. In addition, the team had no newly hired member and thus all of the members already worked together. Therefore, dense awareness networks with high density index were seen in case 2.

Summary of Results

Summarizing the above discussion it can be seen that network size and density are two important aspects for studying the collaboration patterns of teams. Though, network size and network density are not correlated, since network density depends upon the number of ties between the nodes and network size is determined by the number of nodes or actors in a network. Therefore, if a network has large number of nodes yet less number of ties between them the density will be low (Scott, 2012). If the number of ties an actor can have is limited then the density will get low with the growth of network. So, for a social network with limited node size there is no correlation between network size and density.

The networks size results show the size of actual communication networks is slightly smaller than the planned networks. For instance the code related networks involved only the developers in Case 1 and 2. This finding is contrast to Damian et al.'s (2007) finding regarding the traditional software development teams that the communication RCSNs are larger than planned with one-third of the emergent members. However, the size of awareness networks is slightly larger due to the presence of emergent members in the networks.

The communication and awareness patterns of the distributed agile teams show that high density values for awareness contributed to high density values of communication networks (e.g. Case 2). In Case 2 density of availability, general, current and work status awareness is higher than 50% (0.5). The communication networks for Case 2 also showed four networks with density index more than 50%. It can be seen that dense awareness networks contributed to dense communication networks.

However, the networks having low density measures do not contribute to the fact that there was low or no communication among members. In low density cases (e.g. code issues, reviews, refactor in both cases) the communication took place between developers only which turned the density value lower (which is the ratio of actual edges with the possible edges) when calculated in comparison with number of nodes (total number of nodes). Therefore, it can be said that even in low density networks adequate communication took place between the team members.

FUTURE RESEARCH DIRECTIONS

This research can be further extended in a number of ways mentioned below.

1. Studying communication and awareness patterns of larger agile teams distributed at more than two locations.
2. Studying teams with larger number of requirements and requirements dependencies.
3. Studying teams working on new and innovative projects to examine the difference nature of work brings to the RDC patterns.
4. Studying teams having difference business domain and background, to find out its effects on RDC patterns.

5. Studying the communication and awareness patterns of agile teams in variable teams setting e.g. out sourcing teams, open sources software development teams etc.
6. Studying distributed agile teams following other variants of agile methods such as Kanban, Scrumban etc.
7. Studying other socio-technical aspects among distributed agile teams e.g. trust, organizational structure, knowledge management etc.
8. Developing approaches to study socio-technical aspects of RDC among software development teams.
9. Developing tools to facilitate the study of RDC among software development teams.

CONCLUSION

Agile methods encourage the team members to collaborate frequently with each other for completing the user stories and their downstream artifacts. In this chapter, the collaboration among agile teams is seen from the lens of team members' mutual communication and their awareness of each other. The communication and awareness of team members is recoded through a multiple data collection methods to avoid any missing details. The recoded data is then transformed into networks and social network measures are applied to analyze the real communication and awareness patterns within the teams in both of the iterations. The study results provide a longitudinal understanding of agile teams' communication and awareness behavior over the span of two iterations. The awareness of teams increases with time to facilitate more communication between members who were reluctant to talk to each other, earlier. Therefore, we identified agile teams' specific collaboration patterns in this chapter which can be used by the industry practitioners to orient their teams, mend broken links, assess the active members etc. on the other hand the researchers can expand the study by providing more empirical results for variable team settings for instance collaboration among agile teams in an out sourcing scenario.

REFERENCES

Bang, T. J. (2007). An Agile Approach to Requirement Specification. In *Proceedings of the 8th international conference on Agile processes in software engineering and extreme programming*. Como. Italy: Springer-Verlag Berlin, Heidelberg. doi:10.1007/978-3-540-73101-6_35

Beck, K., Beedle, M., van Bennekum, A., Cockburn, A., Cunningham, W., Fowler, M., & Thomas, D. (2001). *Manifesto for Agile Software Development*. Retrieved from http://agilemanifesto.org/

Bin, X., Xiaohu, Y., Zhijun, H., & Maddineni, S. R. (2004). Extreme Programming in reducing the reowrk of requirements change. In *Proceeding of Canadian Conference on Electrical and Computer Engineering*. Niagara Falls, Canada: IEEE.

Cataldo, M., & Ehrlich, K. (2011). The Impact of the Structure of Communication Patterns in Global Software Development: An Empirical Analysis of a Project Using Agile Methods. Pittsburgh, PA: Institute for Software. Retrieved from http://reports-archive.adm.cs.cmu.edu/anon/anon/home/ftp/isr2011/CMU-ISR-11-103.pdf

Cataldo, M., & Herbsleb, J. D. (2008). Communication patterns in geographically distributed software development and engineers' contributions to the development effort. In *Proceedings of the International Workshop on Cooperative and Human Aspects Of Software Engineering (CHASE'08)*. Leipzig,Germany: ACM.

Cataldo, M., Wagstrom, P. A., & Carley, K. M. (2006). Identification of Coordination Requirements : Implications for the Design of Collaboration and Awareness Tools. In *Proceedings of 20th anniversary conference on Computer supported cooperative work (CSCW'06)*. New York, US: ACM. doi:10.1145/1180875.1180929

Cohn, M. (2003). *User Stories Applied For Agile Software Development*. Addison Wesley.

Coombs, R., Knights, D., & Willmott, H. (1992). Culture, control, and competition: Towards a conceptual framework for study of information technology in organization. *Organization Studies*, *13*(1), 51–72. doi:10.1177/017084069201300106

Damian, D., Kwan, I., & Marczak, S. (2010). Requirements-Driven Collaboration : Leveraging the Invisible Relationships Between Requirements and People. In A. Finkelstein, J. Grundy, A. van der Hoek, I. Mistrik, & J. Whitehead (Eds.), *Collaborative Software Engineering, Computer Science Editorial Series* (pp. 1–24). Berlin, Germany: Springer-Verlag. doi:10.1007/978-3-642-10294-3_3

Damian, D., Marczak, S., & Kwan, I. (2007). Collaboration Patterns and the Impact of Distance on Awareness in Requirements-Centred Social Networks. In *Proceedings of 15th International Requirements Engineering Conference (RE'07)*. Delhi, India: IEEE. doi:10.1109/RE.2007.51

Eberlein, A., & Julio Cesar, S. do P. L. (2002). Agile Requirements Definition : A View from Requirements Engineering. In *Proceedings of the International Workshop on Time Constrained Requirements Engineering*. Essen, Germany: IEEE.

Ehrlich, K., Cataldo, M., & York, N. (2014). The Communication Patterns of Technical Leaders : Impact on Product Development Team Performance. In *Computer Supported Cooperative Work* (pp. 733–744). Baltimore, MD, US: ACM. doi:10.1145/2531602.2531671

Ehrlich, K., & Chang, K. (2006). Leveraging expertise in global software teams: Going outside boundaries. In *Proceedings of International Conference on Global Software Engineering (ICGSE'06)*. Florianopolis, Brazil: IEEE. doi:10.1109/ICGSE.2006.261228

Fuks, H., Rapsoso, A., Gerosa, M. A., Pimental, M., & Lucena, C. J. P. (2008). The 3C Collaboration Model. In K. K. K. Roth, J. N. S. Reed, & K. P. B. Shore (Eds.), Encyclopedia of E-Collaboration (pp. 637–344). UK: Information Science Reference (an imprint of IGI Global).

Gutwin, C., & Greenberg, S. (2004). The Importance of Awareness for Team Cognition in Distributed Collaboration. In E. Salas & S. Fiore (Eds.), *Team Cognition: Understanding the Factors That Drive Process and Performance* (pp. 177–201). doi:10.1037/10690-009

Hinds, P., & Mcgrath, C. (2006). Structures that Work : Social Structure, Work Structure and Coordination Ease in Geographically Distributed Teams. In *Proceedings of Computer Supported Cooperative Work (CSCW'06)*. Alberta, Canada: ACM. doi:10.1145/1180875.1180928

Inayat, I., Marczak, S., & Salim, S. S. (2013). Studying Relevant Socio-technical Aspects of Requirements-Driven Collaboration in Agile Teams. In *Proceedings of 3rd International Workshop on Empirical Requirements Engineering*. Rio de Janeiro, Brazil: IEEE. doi:10.1109/EmpiRE.2013.6615213

Inayat, I., Salim, S. S., Marczak, S., & Kasirun, Z. M. (2014). Identifying and Reviewing the Most Relevant Socio-technical Aspects of Requirements- Driven Collaboration in Agile Teams. In *Proceedings of International Conference on Advancements in Engineering and Technology (ICAET'14)*. Singapore: IIENG.

Kwan, I., & Damian, D. (2011). Extending Socio-technical Congruence with Awareness Relationships. In *Proceedings of 4th international workshop on Social Software Engineering*. Szeged, Hungary: ACM.

Lagerberg, L., Skude, T., Emanuelsson, P., & Sandahl, K. (2013). The Impact of Agile Principles and Practices on Large-Scale Software Development Projects: A Multiple-Case Study of Two Projects at Ericsson. In *International Symposium on Empirical Software Engineering and Measurement*. Baltimore, MD, US: IEEE. doi:10.1109/ESEM.2013.53

Marczak, S., & Damian, D. (2011). How interaction between roles shapes the communication structure in requirements-driven collaboration. *In Proceeding of 19th International Requirements Engineering Conference*. Trento, Italy: IEEE. doi:10.1109/RE.2011.6051643

Marczak, S., Inayat, I., & Salim, S. S. (2013). Expanding Empirical Studies to Better Understand Requirements-driven Collaboration. In *Proceedings of Requirements Engineering in Brazil*. Rio de Janerio, Brazil: Springer-Verlag.

Steinmacher, I., Chaves, A. P., & Gerosa, M. A. (2010). Awareness Support in Global Software Development : A Systematic Review Based on the 3C Collaboration Model. In L. G. Kolfschoten & T. Herrmann (Eds.), *Collaboration and Technology* (pp. 185–201). Berlin, Germany: Springer-Verlag. doi:10.1007/978-3-642-15714-1_15

Steinmacher, I., Chaves, A. P., & Gerosa, M. A. (2012). Awareness Support in Distributed Software Development: A Systematic Review and Mapping of the Literature. *Computer Supported Cooperative Work, 22*(3), 113–158.

Trist, E., & Bamforth, K. (1951). Some social and psychological consequences of the longwall method of coal getting. *Human Relations, 4*, 3–38. doi:10.1177/001872675100400101

ADDITIONAL READING

Al-Ani, B., Bietz, M. J., Wang, Y., Koehne, B., Marczak, S., Redmiles, D., & Prikladnicki, R. (2013). Globally Distributed System Developers : Their Trust Expectations and Processes. In Proceedings of Computer Supported Cooperative Work (CSCW'13). San Antonio, Texas, US.

De Souza, C. R., Quirk, S., Trainer, E., & Redmiles, D. F. (2007). Supporting collaborative software development through the visualization of socio-technical dependencies. In *Proceedings of International Conference on Supporting Group Work*, FL, USA. doi:10.1145/1316624.1316646

Dorairaj, S., & Noble, J. (2013). Understanding how agile teams manage knowledge. *Science International*, *25*(4), 1103–1109.

Dorairaj, S., Noble, J., & Malik, P. (2010). Understanding the Importance of Trust in Distributed Agile Projects : A Practical Perspective. In A. Sillitti, A. Martin, X. Wang, & E. Whitworth (Eds.), *Agile Processes in Software Engineering and Extreme Programming* (pp. 172–177). Berlin, Germany: Springer-Verlag.

Inayat, I., Salim, S. S., & Kasirun, Z. M. (2012). Socio-technical aspects of requirements-driven collaboration (RDC) in agile software development methods. *In Proceedings of IEEE Conference on Open Systems (ICOS'12)*, Kuala Lumpur, Malaysia. doi:10.1109/ICOS.2012.6417644

Inayat, I., Salim, S. S., Marczak, S., & Kasirun, Z. M. (2012). Viewing Collaborative Requirements Engineering Process from Social Actions Prespective. In *South Asian Conference (SAICON'12)*, Murree, Pakistan: AGBA.

Licorish, S., & MacDonell, S. (2013). What Can Developers' Messages Tell Us? A Psycholinguistic Analysis of Jazz Teams' Attitudes and Behavior Patterns. In *Proceedings of 22nd Australian Software Engineering Conference (ASWEC' 13)*, Melbourne, Australia.

Licorish, S. A., & Macdonell, S. G. (2013). The True Role of Active Communicators : An Empirical Study of Jazz Core Developers. In *Proceeding of 17th International Conference on Evaluation and Assessment in Software Engineering*. Porto de Galinhas, Brazil: ACM. doi:10.1145/2460999.2461034

Marczak, S., Al-Ani, B., Redmiles, D., & Prikladnicki, R. (2013). Designing Tools to Support Trust in Distributed Software Teams. In Proceeding of Computer Supported Cooperative Work (CSCW'13). San Antonio, US.

Marczak, S., Damian, D., Stege, U., & Schröter, A. (2008). Information Brokers in Requirement-Dependency Social Networks. In *Proceeding of 16th International Conference on Requirements Engineering (RE'08)*, Barcelona, Spain. doi:10.1109/RE.2008.26

Martakis, A., & Daneva, M. (2013). Handling Requirements Dependencies in Agile Projects : A Focus Group with Agile Software Development Practitioners. In *Proceeding of 7th International Conference on Research Challenges in Information Science*. Paris, France. doi:10.1109/RCIS.2013.6577679

Prikladnicki, R., Marczak, S., Carmel, E., & Ebert, C. (2012). Technologies to Support Collaboration across Time Zones. *IEEE Software*, *29*(3), 10–13. doi:10.1109/MS.2012.68

Sharp, H., Giuffrida, R., & Melnik, G. (2012). Information Flow within a Dispersed Agile Team. In C. Wohlin (Ed.), *Agile Processes in Software Engineering and Extreme Programming* (pp. 62–76). Berlin, Germany: Springer-Verlag. doi:10.1007/978-3-642-30350-0_5

KEY TERMS AND DEFINITIONS

Agile Teams: A group of 5-7 self-managing and cross-functional team members working together on certain set of interdependent requirements in fixed time slices called iterations in an iterative and incremental fashion.

Awareness: Awareness is defined as knowledge of team members about each other regarding their professional expertise, availability, current assignment and its status, etc.

Communication: Communication is information exchange among software development teams while working on interdependent tasks, requirements or other downstream artefacts.

Requirements Engineering: RE is about capturing the requirements of customers and analyzing, modeling and validating those requirements and presenting them in a software requirements specification, which is the final output within the RE process. The software is then developed based on these specified requirements.

Scrum: Scrum is an iterative and incremental variant of agile methods. The team members take major roles as project manager, scrum master and development team. The scrum master is responsible for the scrum process including the managerial tasks like holding daily meet up sessions, called daily scrum meetings. The self-organizing agile teams work in small time slices, called Sprints also known as iteration. The team works some of the user stories from the pre-decided items list, called product backlog and handover the committed snippet to customer at the end of each sprint.

Social Network Analysis: Social network analysis is used to study the network behaviors in order to determine the social phenomena among them. For instance a network comprising individuals on a social networking website can be studied using social network analysis to determine their friendship, tendency and frequency of social interaction with each other, and kinship etc.

Chapter 2

Designing and Implementing an Innovation Management System in Young Academic Institutions Using Agile Methodology

Sachin Ahuja
Chitkara University Research and Innovation Network, India

Archana Mantri
Chitkara University Research and Innovation Network, India

ABSTRACT

This chapter proposes the use of agile methodology in designing the innovation management system in young academic institutes. Technology innovations from most universities and research institutes originate out of chaos. As a result, it is difficult to associate structure to its management. While there have been many social science research methodology based studies on this subject under the broad umbrella of "Innovation and Technology Management", there is usually an absence of well defined process to help young academic institutions to manage their intellectual property better. There is a strongly desired need to associate a clearly articulated structure for translation of ideas into technology innovations that will help young academic institutes to inculcate research in students and faculties and would help identify the best commercial application of technology innovations. Agile methodologies are best suited to be adopted in the academic scenario as rapidly changing environment of academic institutes can be easily handled using agile methodology. The aim of this chapter is to produce an evolutionary advance practical innovation management process for academic institutes out of this chaos to inculcate research in students and faculties using agile methodologies.

INTRODUCTION

The working of academic institutions is changing at a rapid pace. The technological changes are taking place at a very high speed especially in comparatively new and emerging disciplines. The traditional disciplines are also applying the knowledge of emerging disciplines. The fast change in the computer

DOI: 10.4018/978-1-4666-8510-9.ch002

technology and information technology is affecting the way of life in the campus and off the campus. Apart from the technological changes, colossal transformation is taking place in various dimensions of the employer market such as competition, merger, collaboration, economic reform, adoption of new technology, way of functioning, corporate culture, continuously changing work practices, shifting in product services, and market. Continuous changes in the external environment are forcing the institution to change the way of functioning.

Besides academics, research has become essential for institutes to prove their excellence. The traditional system of teaching learning process is required to be changed in sync with the new scenario. The focus must be on research and innovation for developing a culture of knowledge sharing within the organization. Also, there is a need of evolving a robust support system that embeds the innovation management in academic institutions along with the existing academic teaching learning process. The system must be able to identify talent, provide direction and facilitate innovators to a nurturing bed. The rapid changing environment of academic institutes has seeded the way to use agile methodology for developing a system for innovation management since the very first need of adopting agility is defined as dynamic, context-specific, aggressively change embracing, and growth-oriented which aptly fits into the environment of academic institutes.

We are following agile methodology in this innovation management process. The focus is on delivering the conversion of patentable idea into patent application in shortest duration of time. The concept of Sprint in agile methodology best fits in this type of situation. Sprint refers to the duration in which agile project team has to develop working software. Sprint duration can be one week, two weeks or three weeks etc. The sprint duration can be negotiated and decided by taking consent of customer. Here the duration for conversion of patentable idea into filed patent application is been finalized after the discussion between the university authorities, coordinator and patent attorneys.

INNOVATION MANAGEMENT PROCESS

The term innovation comes from latin word *innovare*, which means 'to make something new'. The element of newness can be found in various definition of innovation which has been introduced into the literature. Khandwalla (1985), states that organizations are deemed excellent because of their uniqueness, their pioneering spirit and innovation. At different stages the excellence is something that makes the institution distinct than others. It is not necessary that all the institutions achieve excellence on all the dimensions of excellence but each institution achieves excellence in its core areas of performance. The parameters for excellence can be derived from the deployment of processes to achieve predefined objectives. The plans are implemented to achieve excellence at every stage of implementation and regular monitoring and feedback contributes a lot in achieving the excellence (Steen Hoyrup, 2012).

Innovation management is the management of innovation processes. It refers both to product and organizational innovation. Innovation management includes a set of tools that allow managers and engineers to cooperate with a common understanding of processes and goals. Innovation management allows the organization to respond to external or internal opportunities, and use its creativity to introduce new ideas, processes or products. It is not relegated to R&D; it involves workers at every level in contributing creatively to a company's product development, manufacturing and marketing.

By utilizing innovation management tools, management can trigger and deploy the creative capabilities of the work force for the continuous development of a company. Common tools include brainstorming, virtual prototyping, product lifecycle management, idea management, TRIZ, Phase–gate model, project management, product line planning and portfolio management. The process can be viewed as an evolutionary integration of organization, technology and market by iterating series of activities: search, select, implement and capture.

In academics the innovation management can be termed as management of innovation processes in terms of increasing the innovative index of the academic institution by means of increasing the patent index of the organization by helping innovators to provide an environment in which they can explore their innovative skills. Innovation management brings together collaboration and social software, with a clear focus on generating results and developing a culture of knowledge sharing and innovation. Innovation has always required those with different skills and expertise to come together and co-create [5]. Globalization ensures expertise exists in every corner of the world, no longer is it easy and cost effective to put the people we need in one room. Cloud based technology is a common way to bring together diverse opinions; it also allows many more people to share ideas and innovate together.

1. Examples from Industry

Kilbourne and Woodman (1999) have identified the numerous factors such as autonomy, the available information, the reward system, education or training, the system of authority, participation in decision-making, or the team cohesion on which any system of innovation depends besides creativity. He also stated that it is difficult to enumerate and include all the factors that affect creativity hence it is difficult to implement a innovation management system that addresses all the factors.

In October 2002, the world-renowned automobile manufacturer from Germany, BMW Group AG (BMW) was awarded the 'Outstanding Corporate Innovator (OCI)' title for 2002, by the Product Development & Management Association (PDMA).According to CaseStudy_BSTR060(2003) published online this award was given for BMW's 'demonstrated exceptional skill in constantly creating and capturing value, through its innovations and development of new products'. Commenting on BMW's selection for the award, the Chairman of the OCI Awards Selection Committee said that the company had shown a strong strategic commitment to innovation. The award came as a major recognition of the company's decision to let innovation be the driving force for its product development process throughout the late 1990s. Industry observers expected this development to further help BMW establish itself as one of the leading players in the premium segment of the global automobile market. According to analysts, BMW's innovation management system, developed in the late 1990s was the main reason behind the company winning the OCI title. This innovation management system enabled BMW to exploit various path breaking technological innovations, right from the idea generation stage to the market introduction stage. This system enabled BMW to develop a continuous stream of new products and brands. Company sources admitted that by focusing on new product development practices using the innovation approach, BMW successfully withstood competitive pressures and held on to its market position from source.

Fernando Cardoso de Sousa (2012) stated that it is easy to get ideas, but it is difficult to implement the system that may turn the creativity into profitable business. He also concluded that while individual creativity seems always to be the starting point, because it may exist even in the absence of innovation, the organization depends on it to innovate.

Sorin Cohn (2013) introduces the Value-Added Corporate Innovation Management (v-CIM) framework enabling a firm's leadership to undertake innovation activities strategically in a balanced approach across all the critical domains of competitiveness. The author outlines the importance of matching corporate vision and goals with a workable understanding of the competitive reality and developed a Firm-Level Innovation Management Framework and Assessment Tool. At the end she concludes that Industry needs adequate models for the management of innovation activities – models that are capable of tying the various aspects of the innovation domains: products, services, processes, the organization itself, people, and business strategies. The innovation model must enable meaningful, timely, and easy-to-use measurements of performance and capabilities to optimize the use of resources, to adjust the focus of activities, and to ensure that the competitive objectives are achieved.

Petra Andries and Dirk Czarnitzki (2013) in their research found that small firms rely mainly on the CEO's individual knowledge for developing innovations but this approach is inefficient since it under utilizes other employees' knowledge. They further study to which extent using CEOs, managers and non-managerial employees' ideas enhances small firms' innovation performance. They implemented Heckman selection model on 305 small firms and concluded that not only CEO's and managers', but also non-managerial employees' ideas contribute to innovation performance. However, contributions depend heavily on the individuals' area of expertise and on whether product or process innovation is desired. Their findings enrich the current view on the entrepreneurial team, but also warn against the implementation of one-size-fits-all employee involvement programs in small firms.

Jesper Bank, Adnan Raza (2014) explored the application of collaborative idea management to drive continuous innovation in large organizations based on experience at Waabii, an innovation software and consulting service provider. The software was implemented to create a collaborative and sustainable innovation environment in a large global telecommunications company. They describe the innovation model created at Waabii to help implement a sustainable innovation process, and present a case study of an innovation management software solution, Exago Idea Market. They concluded that despite the fact that innovation is most important factor contributing to companies' ongoing success, many organizations fail to develop sustainable innovation management processes.

Elke perl-vorbach (2014) concluded that R&D intensity is also an important influential factor in applying the open innovation approach. According to Gassmann et al . (2010), it is obvious that open innovation methods are mainly tied to the high- tech sector, even though there now appears to be a similar trend emerging in the low-tech sector. Anyhow, open research issues appear to be related mainly to the barriers and drivers for open innovation in the context of sustainable innovation. Thus, the different types of companies involved, as well as the differences between various branches need to be taken into account. The communication within the organization is required in innovation management system for addressing creativity needs.

According to Jens Hauglum(n.d.) the practice of reward is necessary to boost the innovative quotient. Hauglum presented a study in FINN.no, which is Norway's largest online marketplace. FINN.no is a story of disruption and innovation, with a goal of being one of the most innovative companies in the world. Once a year they organize a party called FINN Awards where prizes are given to teams or individuals in different categories, one being "Innovation of the year". The values are used as a part of the evaluation criteria in every category. The strategy of rewarding the creativity helps in inculcating the competitive environment within the organization that boost the morale of the person getting the reward and motivates others to perform well.

Jeff Dyer and Hal Gregersen(n.d.) suggests that innovation is a team game. Top executives must lead the innovation charge by understanding how innovation works, improving their own discovery skills, and sharpening their ability to foster the innovation of others.

2. Examples from Innovative Universities

Jean-Eric Aubert (2005) provided a conceptual framework for approaching the promotion of technological innovation and its diffusion in developing countries. Innovation climates in developing countries are, by nature, problematic, characterized by poor business and governance conditions, low educational levels, and mediocre infrastructure. This raises particular challenges for the promotion of innovation. Jean-Eric Aubert identifies the need to provide the necessary package of support to the innovators in terms of technical, financial, commercial, legal, and so on, with flexible, autonomous agencies adapting their support and operations to the different types of concerned enterprises.

Facilitating and responding to the emergence of grass-root needs at the local level is also essential. Support to entrepreneurs and local communities should be primarily provided in matching grant forms to facilitate the mobilization of local resources and ownership.

Bikas C. Sanyal, N.V. Varghese (2007) conducted a survey "Knowledge for the future: Research capacity in developing countries" in collaboration with UNESCO and International Institute of Education & Planning and found that in developing countries universities play a less significant role in funding and carrying out research but their role remains unchallenged in the area of research training. There is a need for reviving and strengthening the university system in developing countries to strengthen their research and innovation management system.

Bhushan Patwardhan (2014), an eminent professor at university of pune stated that India is the only country that slipped 10 ranks to the 76th place in Global Innovation Index(GII) 2014. India is also the only country among the BRICS nations to have witnessed a decline in the rankings. On the other hand, India also performed poorly in the GIPC IP Index released in January 2014. It has now become imperative to measure the country's poor performance against the global standards. There is a need to have an effective innovation ecosystem in order to unleash the country's full potential. The creation of a vibrant innovation ecosystem requires several things, with talent being the primary requirement. The present scenario of things in India requires a shift in mindset from the traditional paths to encouraging risk-taking and challenging status quo. Universities and colleges have a significant role to play in developing and shaping this kind of talent base. The effective ecosystem and a robust infrastructure would enhance skills and motivate budding entrepreneurs to scale up innovation efforts.

There is also a huge gap when it comes to providing a supporting environment for innovations and research. The scientists from developing countries are doing extremely well overseas, largely because of the infrastructure and support they receive. It is important that the government, the industry and the academia work in close coordination to leverage existing resources for nurturing manufacturing innovation, thereby creating a robust innovation ecosystem.

Also, developing countries like India have large pool of traditional knowledge and innovative prowess and there is a need to protect this intellectual property. Poor IP Protection is a major hurdle to innovation therefore there is a strong need for appropriate legislation, policies and legal decision to reaffirm stand on innovation and intellectual property. Hence we cannot ignore the importance of intellectual property rights from economic, social and legal standpoints as it is a critical driver of innovation and ensures creativity, growth and progress.

According to article published in India Today online (2014) the reasons behind the growth in IIT Bombay's patent filing are attributed to an in-house professional patent search facility. An extended panel of attorneys is available to help file IP patents, copyrights, designs and trademarks. Workshops and seminars are also expected to be conducted to improve the innovation portfolio.

Gupta V K, (2008) published a report in NISTADS which states that during the period from 1990-2007, Indian patent output was 26,250 patents wherein the patentees from industry sector contributed 57% of the total patents, from university sector 5% and from the government sector 21% of the total patents. Individual inventors contributed 17% of the total patents during this period.

According to an article by DNA correspondent (2013) published in DNA India magazine, consulting firm Zinnov found that universities in India, including the IISc, contribute about 5% of the total patents filed from India. Key areas where patents get filed by universities include robotics and embedded computing. Experts say filing of patent applications by universities reflects a trend wherein more and more innovation is under way in institutes, spearheaded by students under guidance from professors.

The need for innovation management system arises due to the fact that research and development functions experience problems with cohesion when their function reaches a certain size. When the function grows or expands past a certain level it is important to have a systematic and structured system in place to guide development efforts and to keep all stakeholders focused in the same direction. However, the adoption of a formalized system may conflict with the need to maintain responsiveness and flexibility. This is found to be particularly significant when team members are geographically distributed.

WHY TO USE AGILE TECHNOLOGY IN INNOVATION MANAGEMENT

What is the meaning of being agile? Jim Highsmith(2000) stated that being agile means being able to Deliver quickly, Change quickly, and Change often. In agile methods, people play a driving role in the success of the project, and lot of short time meetings are conducted for knowledge sharing and for the random change in the project, if required. Methodologists argue that working software without documentation is better than non-working software with a huge amount of documentation (Koskela and Teknillinen, 2003). There is no universally accepted definition of agility. "Agility is dynamic, context-specific, aggressively change embracing, and growth-oriented" (Goldman et al., 1995). The core concept in agile is quick response to change (Cockburn and Highsmith, 2001). Summary of some of the definitions of agility are given in Table 1.

Conboy and Fitzgerald (2004) carried out a review of the literature on agility across several disciplines and provide a broad definition of agility as "the continual readiness of an entity to rapidly or inherently, proactively or reactively, embrace change, through high quality, simplistic, economical components and relationships with its environment"(Conboy, K., and Fitzgerald, B. 2004) . Despite the differences, all definitions of ''agility'' emphasize the speed and flexibility as the primary attributes of an agile organization (Gunasekaran A 1999).

The concept of Knowledge management given by A. Singh (2013) is applicable in this academic context since agile methodologies employ short iterative cycles, and rely on tacit knowledge within a team. Knowledge Management (KM) can be easily accepted into agile software development environments. Following are two reasons in favor of this point of view (Singh A, 2012). First, the agile cultural infrastructure already encourages values such as cooperation, communication and knowledge sharing; specifically, agile software development processes include some practices that support KM, e.g. stand-up meetings, the planning game, pair programming and the informative workplace. Second, KM is about learning, and ASD set up an environment that supports learning processes. In this paper, attempt is made to find out specific agile practices which promote KM (Singh A, 2014).

Table 1. Agility Defined

Author	Definition
Iacocca Institute (1991)	A manufacturing system with capabilities (hard and soft technologies, human resources, educated management and information) to meet the rapidly changing needs of the marketplace (speed, flexibility, customers, competitors, suppliers, infrastructure and responsiveness).
Kidd (1994)	A quick and proactive adaptation of enterprise elements to unexpected and unpredicted changes.
Gunasekaran (1999)	Agile manufacturing (AM) is the ability of surviving and prospering in a competitive environment of continuous and unpredictable change by reacting quickly and effectively to changing markets, driven by customer-defined products and services.
Yusuf et al. (1999)	Successful application of competitive bases such as speed, flexibility, innovation, and quality by the means of the integration of reconfigurable resources and best practices of knowledge-rich environment to provide customer-driven products and services in a fast changing environment.
Kruchten (2001)	'Ability to adapt and react expeditiously and appropriately to changes in its environment and to demands imposed by this environment. An agile process is one that readily embraces and supports this degree of adaptability. So, it is not simply about the size of the process or speed of delivery; it is mainly about flexibility'.
Highsmith (2002)	'Quickness, lightness, and nimbleness – the ability to act rapidly, the ability to do the minimum necessary to get the job done, and the ability to adapt to changing conditions'.

The name "agile" came about in 2001, when seventeen process methodologists held a meeting to talk about the future trends in software development. The outcome to this meeting was the formation of "Agile Alliance" and its manifesto for agile software development which has the following features.

1. Individuals and interactions over processes and tools.
2. Working software over comprehensive documentation.
3. Customer collaboration over contract negotiation.
4. Responding to change over following a plan.

The contrast between Software development and Innovation management system using agile methodologies is made as follows:-

● As agile methodology defines the ability of surviving and prospering in a competitive environment of continuous and unpredictable change by reacting quickly and effectively to changing markets, driven by customer-defined products and services, In innovation management system we are working in a dynamically changing environment of academic institutions where there is a need of high level of adaptability that is provided by agile practices.
● The flow of incoming ideas is unpredictable and hence there is a need of quick and proactive system that easily adapts the change in input of ideas as in Agile we define quick and proactive adaptation of enterprise elements to unexpected and unpredicted changes.
● The raw ideas are refined at every stage of interaction between innovators, experts and professionals hence there is a need of agile methodology that advocates 'Quickness, lightness, and nimbleness – the ability to act rapidly, the ability to do the minimum necessary to get the job done, and the ability to adapt to changing conditions' hence are best suited in these conditions.

- The process of conversion of ideas to patents goes through various steps which needs involvement of innovators, experts, review team, patent attorneys, government organization and legal formalities therefore there is a need of ability to adapt and react expeditiously and appropriately to changes in this environment and to demands imposed by this environment. An agile process is one that readily embraces and supports this degree of adaptability. So, it is not simply about the size of the process or speed of delivery; it is mainly about flexibility.

'ANYBODY CAN INNOVATE' MODEL

1. Overview

As life finds its own way so is the innovation. The innovators never stop or stagnate but they are always flowing and continuously search the nurturing ground for their ideas. The most important is to build and sustain the innovation pool by providing the innovators with a conducive environment to innovate. The innovator requires an environment where ideas are welcomed and every possible opportunity is provided to convert ideas into product that may led to a tool for social welfare, commercialization or enhancement in existing technology.

There has been no method adopted till now in academic institutions to formalize the innovation management process in a well defined manner. We have adopted some of the concept of innovation management system from one of the earliest management system developed by William Denny at his shipyard in Dumbarton, Scotland called 'Rules for the awards committee to guide them in rewarding the workmen for the inventions and improvements' started in 1880 and, eventually was successfully adopted across England (Dabholkar V, Krishnan R T, 2013).

For facilitating the innovation management process a department very aptly named as office of patent facilitation & Licensing (OPFL) was established under Chitkara University Research & Innovation Network (CURIN). OPFL partnered with renowned patent attorneys for handling the commercial aspect of the ideas that can be patented. The overall process is supporting innovation process with social software and cloud based technologies and presents some significant benefits for innovators and institution as under:

- Find more ideas at a higher level of quality by expanding the innovation pool.
- Increase the visibility of ideas so that contributors with different skills and knowledge can help to identify and improve the best ideas.
- Manage complex innovation portfolio with greater governance and rigor using social software for key information.
- Ensure effective innovation resource management so that the best ideas make it to the patents and increase the intellectual property of the university
- Integrate innovation process with social software to ensure everyone can innovate wherever they are, whatever they're doing.

The Patent applications are kept as the basis of measurement for effectiveness of Innovation management system because Intellectual Property Rights (IPRs) are crucial for innovation. It is the foundation of any knowledge-based economy. It is the interface of - creations and rights. It pervades through all sectors of the economy and is increasingly becoming important for ensuring competitiveness of the enterprise. It is the original creation of human mind that has economic value and is protected by law. The extent to which countries protect their Intellectual property (IP) will determine how well they perform in the new economic environment. Role of IPR lay in providing a legal right to the inventor to protect his/her creation as well as preventing others from illegally exploiting the creation and thus avoid re-invention of the wheel. "Your ideas are your property and you have every right to benefit from it" - is the core ethos around which intellectual property rights have been formulated. These are the rights given to a person over the creation of his own mind. The chief purpose is to encourage inventiveness and research that leads to new ideas and the development of new technologies.

2. Objectives

The major identified objectives can be classified in Short term and long term objectives. The short term objectives are broadly classified as

- Building and sustaining incoming ideas,
- Managing the incoming ideas,
- Improving the idea flow,
- Improving the rate of ideas being accepted for taking further to implementation process.

The long term objectives can be classified as follows

- System must be able to identify talent, provide direction and facilitate innovators to a nurturing bed
- Support innovators with a combination of process, software, and best-practices to ensure that great ideas are captured, combined into concepts and brought to market
- Help innovators to open up steps in their innovation process to selected third parties, increasing the size of their innovation ecosystem without sacrificing the security of intellectual property and knowledge.

3. Process

We have devised an innovation management plan to help our innovators through the entire innovation lifecycle. The process outlines are as follows:

1. Sensitization of students and faculties through seminars and workshops conducted by experts,
2. Invitation of ideas by idea box or ERP system,
3. Collection of Ideas,
4. Expert review of ideas,
5. Concept enrichment by review committee,
6. Brainstorming session on the idea by innovator & expert committee,
7. Innovation management process,
8. Implementation of the top ideas.

Figure 1. Innovation Management Process

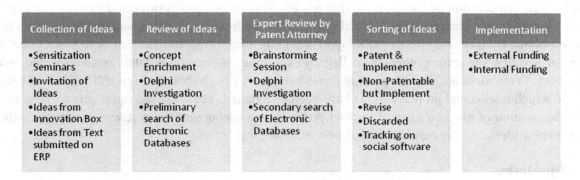

With the power of innovation management program, we can improve our ability to innovate, make it more reliable, and increase collaboration inside the university. The management of the university has been considerate enough to introduce an 'Easy Patent Policy' which is completely in accordance with our objective for providing a nurturing bed to the innovators in terms of financial support and the innovator is kept free from all legal formalities regarding patent filing and the commercial rights of the idea belongs to the innovator. Also, letter of appreciation is issued by university authorities for best idea of the month to encourage research & innovation in students and faculties.

A. Proposed Framework of 'Anybody can innovate'

We present here implemented framework of innovation management system, 'Anybody can innovate' implemented at Chitkara University, Chandigarh, India. The system can be adopted by other young academic institutes for managing innovation at starting phase. The innovation model enables meaningful, timely, and easy-to-use measurements of performance and capabilities to optimize the use of resources, to adjust the focus of activities, and to ensure that the competitive objectives are achieved. The implemented framework of 'anybody can innovate' in Chitkara University is shown in Figure 1.

The steps of innovation & review strategy are as under:

1. Collection of Ideas through Hand written form submitted in Innovation Box placed at different locations within the campus and in form of text messages entered on ERP system managed by university.
2. Acknowledge Mail to the innovator.
3. Expert Review team filters ideas on basis of scope and nature of the ideas shared on social software
4. Undertake Delphi investigations via Google spreadsheets/social software as shown in Table 1.
5. Preliminary search of electronic databases by the innovator
6. Develop analytic framework
7. Secondary search of electronic databases by expert committee (Third Party/Patent Attorney)
8. Content analysis of data set, sorting of ideas into patent and implement, non-patentable but implement, revision, discarded
9. Review measures against framework for gaps
10. Implementation of Ideas

This process of innovation is helping the innovators with an expert guidance at every step of the process. The innovators will be getting help from the experts even if they are not aware of all the dimensions of their innovation and are having a vague idea about how to implement it. The innovators are provided with financial support and guidance and also the academic resources and infrastructure of the organization at full perusal. A translational lab is also established to provide the innovators with the required interdisciplinary support for their ideas. All the ideas are taken up with equal fervor during each step of the innovation management process and the distinction is only made at the end of the innovation management process where the idea is classified as patentable or non-patentable on the basis of secondary search of electronic databases done by the professionals from the hired third party patent attorneys. The process is devised such that at every step innovator is provided with documented inputs to improvise his idea so that it can be patented and even if it is not patented the idea is not discarded. The innovators are motivated to take up the ideas and apply for funding under the guidance of experts available at university level.

'ANYBODY CAN INNOVATE' MODEL USING AGILE

One of the key methods in agile practices is scrum. A key principle of Scrum is its recognition that during a project the customers can change their minds about what they want and need (often called requirements churn), and that unpredicted challenges cannot be easily addressed in a traditional predictive or planned manner. As such, Scrum adopts an empirical approach—accepting that the problem cannot be fully understood or defined, focusing instead on maximizing the team's ability to deliver quickly and respond to emerging requirements. Scrum is built around the idea of a sprint, a short burst of activity. A sprint (or iteration) is the basic unit of development in Scrum. The sprint is a "time boxed" effort; that is, it is restricted to a specific duration. The duration is fixed in advance for each sprint and is normally between one week and one month, although two weeks is typical. Each sprint is started by a planning meeting, where the tasks for the sprint are identified and an estimated commitment for the sprint goal is made, and ended by a sprint review-and-retrospective meeting, where the progress is reviewed and lessons for the next sprint are identified. Scrum emphasizes working product at the end of the Sprint that is really "done"; in the case of software, this means a system that is integrated, fully tested, end-user documented, and potentially shippable. The emphasis is thus on highly dynamic, short cycles of work, and interaction between the team members and the customer to get the right product delivered by rapidly ensuring that the development team is on target. In Innovation management process we have effectively use the sprint in building the framework of an effective innovation management process which meets all the objectives of our support system.

1. Innovation Management using Sprint

We have designed an innovation management system using Sprint. Sprint refers to the duration in which agile project team has to develop working software. Sprint duration can be one week, 2 weeks and 3rd weeks etc. The sprint duration can be negotiated and decided by taking consent of customer .The overall system is divided into different sprints where each sprint is having a specific output. Each sprint is performing a time boxed activity and after every sprint we have a measureable output. Each day in sprint is called scrum. Scrum is time period in which developers sit in close locations (pair programming) and work together towards common goal. There would be a scrum meeting where developers and whole team sit and discuss on 3 key questions which are as below:-

1. What have you done yesterday?
2. What are you planning to do today?
3. Are they are any blocker issues?

Scrum meeting is generally time bound (15 minute) where scrum master coordinates the meeting and it's the responsibility of scrum master to adhere to the timings. Scrum master is one of the key persons. He coordinates the whole meeting and maintains impediment tracker and makes sure that the agile team is following process strictly.

In proposed innovation management process the sprint team consists of innovators, patent attorneys and coordinator. The sole aim of the process is to timeline all the activities that are performed during the process of conversion of an idea into patent application. The uncertainty of the process is that the innovators are from different departments having different background i.e. computer science, electronics, mechanical, pharmacy, nursing. The challenge is that in most of the cases the innovators are under graduate students who are still not well aware of the technological aspects themselves and generally come up with vague ideas that are not limited to their area of study or expertise and require lots of inputs and suggestion from peers, colleagues and faculties. For providing expert advice and views about their ideas a review committee is formed that consists of senior members from various departments and help innovator in concept enrichment. The working concept or modality of the ideas change frequently after every sprint meeting between the innovators and expert committee hence forming the basic background for adopting the agile methodology in innovation management process.

The coordinator of OPFL will act as scrum master. Scrum master is the key person that coordinates all the activities within a SCRUM.

Here the coordinator is the person responsible for all the activities under OPFL. The main activities of the coordinator are as listed below:-

1. Conduct sensitization seminar regarding IPR's for students and faculties for various departments in the university.
2. Invite ideas from innovators (Students & Faculties) through Department Head's and Dean's
3. Collection of Ideas from different departments
4. Filter them on the basis of preliminary prior art search of electronic databases
5. Arrange meetings of innovators of selected ideas with expert review committee for Concept enrichment
6. Arrange meetings of innovators with patent attorneys for discussion of idea for application for patents
7. Monitor and track the progress of innovators in implementing the suggestions given by patent attorneys for filing of patent application
8. Monitor and track the progress of patent attorneys in secondary search of electronic databases
9. Monitor and track the progress of patent attorneys in filing the application of patents

The above activities are divided into two different sprints namely Sensitization Sprint and Analysis Sprint as shown in Figure 2. All the monitoring and tracking of activities is done using cloud based technology and social software.

Figure 2. Sensitization Sprint-Analysis Sprint Cycle

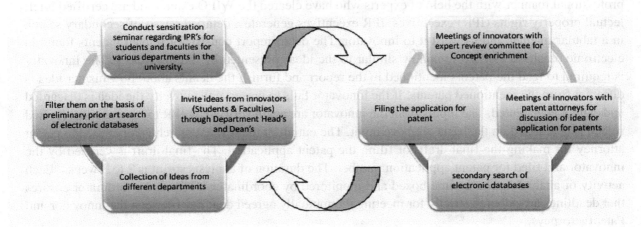

A. Sensitization Sprint

The activities from 1 to 4 are classified into sensitization sprint. The outcome of sensitization sprint is incoming flow of ideas that can be measured by the number of ideas flowing in after every sprint. The sensitization sprint is controlled by coordinator and follows the defined process each time with different audience of sensitization seminar. The coordinator talks with the Dean of Department and fixes a mutually decided date for the seminar. Each department is given equal priority in the process. The incoming ideas are collected at departmental level and handed over to coordinator by Dean of Departments. It is the responsibility of coordinator to filter ideas on the basis of prior art search of the electronic database. The prior art search is a well defined process that is followed in searching electronic databases of patent offices worldwide. The access to the patent office database is in public domain for general public viewing and is free of cost. The prior art search requires very basic level of expertise for performing search on basis of keywords with sole aim of destroying the novelty of ideas so that only those ideas are passed further to next level that have their novelty preserved. The sensitization sprint is of one week duration and there is no meeting between the innovators and coordinator during sensitization sprint.

B. Analysis Sprint

The analysis sprint comprise of activities from 5 to 9. The outcome of analysis sprint is applications filed for the patents. The output is measured by the number of application filed after each sprint. The analysis sprint is monitored by coordinator. The coordinator acts as Scrum Master and monitors all the activities during the sprint. The innovators of the ideas that have preserved their novelty are required to meet with expert committee comprising of Deans, Subject experts, faculties of respective departments and patent attorneys in a planned format defined by the coordinator for concept enrichment. Each innovator is provided with Patent Information Extraction (PIE) form after the meeting. The PIE form is so designed that it can be directly converted into patent application after incorporating changes that are suggested by expert committee and patent attorneys. Innovator is required to fill the PIE form in a specified time schedule generally one to two weeks and submit it to the patent attorneys for secondary search of electronic databases. The patent attorneys conduct secondary search of patent databases in a professional manner with the help of experts who have cleared the WIPO exams and are certified intellectual property rights (IPR) executives. IPR executives generate a detailed report of secondary search in a tabular manner and forward it to innovator. The detail report consists of related patents found in electronic database that are somehow similar to the ideas presented by the innovators. The innovator is required to read the patents mentioned in the report and furnish the details about how his/her idea is different from the mentioned patents. If the innovator fails to preserve the novelty the idea is discarded and cannot be patented. The inputs from the innovator are again verified by IPR executive and a revised search is conducted on the basis of above input. The output of the revised search is forwarded to patent attorney for making the final draft for filing the patent application. The final draft is verified by the innovator and filed for patent application number. The duration of analysis sprint is 2 to 3 weeks. Each activity of analysis sprint is time boxed and monitored by coordinator OPFL and coordinator ensures that deadlines are adhered strictly for meeting the mutually agreed deadline between the innovator and Patent attorneys.

CONCLUSION

Academic Institutions need adequate models for the management of innovation activities – models that are capable of binding the various aspects of the innovation domains: ideas, processes, products, services, the organization itself, people, and business strategies. The innovation model must enable timely and easy-to-use measurements to ensure that the innovative objectives are achieved.

Anybody can Innovate framework provides academic institutes with an effective methodology for innovation management. The methodology is straightforward and easy to apply. The application of agile provided the framework with required approach to incorporate the uncertainty factor of innovators and ideas which otherwise was difficult to handle. The sprint cycle are so designed that they clearly divide the process into two different but interrelated phases of innovation management which have clearly defined outputs that collectively contribute to the desired output for innovation management process as a whole. The application of SCRUM in innovation management provides means for measuring tangible output after every sprint. The SCRUM helps in managing unanticipated changes productively in a short period of time. The first thing we achieved by this innovation system is that it created a continuous stream of ideas to be tested and selectively implemented. The model provide an at-a- glance visual map capable of pointing the progress of ideas to innovation at any stage. Thus, enable the key stakeholders to act in an informed manner, with judicious innovation strategies and well-targeted activities to bring about tangible results most efficiently.

'Anybody can Innovate' model using agile methodology benefits academic institutes by enabling them to:

- Increase the thought process in terms of innovation by inception of new ideas hence achieved by the increased number of ideas.
- Clarify the ideas and research goals in a realistic, collaborative environment using social software
- Map the status on the evolutionary journey from ideas to inception under expert guidance
- Engage and mobilize all the stakeholders (innovator, experts, patent attorney & university management)

Table 2. List of Potential Ideas shortlisted after Sensitization Sprint

Sr No.	Date of Meeting	Date of Receiving PIE Form	Status
CKU01	14/8/2014	14/08/2014	Filed 5/9/2014
CKU02	14/08/2014	14/08/2014	Rejected
CKU03	14/08/2014	-	Pie form not received
CKU04	14/08/2014	20/08/2014	Filed 7/10/2014
CKU05	20/08/2014	20/08/2014	Rejected
CKU06	20/08/2014	18/12/2014	Pending
CKU07	20/08/2014	15/09/2014	Filed 18/10/2014
CKU08	28/08/2014	3/9/2014	Filed 24/09/2014
CKU09	28/08/2014	3/9/2014	Rejected
CKU10	28/08/2014	15/09/2014	Filed 8/10/2014
CKU11	28/08/2014	15/09/2014	Awaiting response from the inventor
CKU12	4/9/2014	8/9/2014	Rejected
CKU13	4/9/2014	-	Rejected
CKU14	4/9/2014	15/09/2014	Rejected
CKU15	4/9/2014	17/09/2014	Rejected
CKU16	28/08/2014	15/09/2014	Pending
CKU17	28/08/2014	15/09/2014	Filed 21/10/2014
CKU18	18/09/2014	22/09/2014	Filed 1/11/2014
CKU19	18/09/2014	5/10/2014	No response from inventor
CKU20	18/09/2014	21/09/2014	Filed 14/11/2014
CKU21	18/09/2014	-	Rejected
CKU22	18/09/2014	18/9/2014	Rejected
CKU23	18/09/2014	18/09/2014	No response from inventor
CKU24	18/09/2014	20/10/2014	Prior art done
CKU 25	18/09/2014	-	Rejected
CKU26	18/09/2014	20/09/2014	Prior art done
CKU27	25/09/2014	25/09/2014	Rejected
CKU28	9/10/2014	9/10/2014	Rejected
CKU29	16/10/2014	16/10/2014	Filed 28/10/2014
CKU30	16/10/2014	16/10/2014	Rejected
CKU31	16/10/2014	16/10/2014	No response from inventor
CKU32	16/10/2014	28/10/2014	Filed 26/11/2014
CKU33	30/10/2014	30/10/2014	Discussed suitable for copyright
CKU34	30/10/2014	30/10/2014	Discussed suitable for copyright
CKU35	30/10/2014	30/10/2014	Discussed suitable for copyright
CKU36	30/10/2014	3/11/2014	No response from inventor
CKU37	30/10/2014	30/10/2014	Rejected
CKU38	30/10/2014	30/10/2014	Rejected
CKU39	30/10/2014	30/10/2014	Rejected

continued on following page

Table 2. Continued

Sr No.	Date of Meeting	Date of Receiving PIE Form	Status
CKU40	30/10/2014	30/10/2014	Rejected
CKU41	30/10/2014	30/10/2014	Rejected
Sr no.	Date of Meeting	Date of receiving PIE form	Status
CKU42	30/10/2014	30/10/2014	Rejected
CKU43	30/10/2014	-	No response from inventor
CKU44	30/10/2014	-	No response from inventor
CKU45	30/10/2014	2/11/2014	Pending
CKU46	30/10/2014	-	No response from inventor
CKU47	30/10/2014	5/11/2014	Rejected
CKU48	7/11/2014	10/11/2014	Prior Art done. Awaiting inventors response
CKU49	7/11/2014	22/11/2014	Prior Art done
CKU50	7/11/2014	-	Already filed patent, wanted to be reviewed

Table 3. Uniformity of Innovation process for Patentable and Non-Patentable Ideas

CKU01	Idea submission by innovator	Keyword selection for patent database searching	Prior art search of patent Database by innovator	Meeting with patent attorneys and sharing of ideas and expert review	Prior art search of patent database by patent attorneys	Idea filtered on the basis of being Patentable	Patent filing of patentable idea
CKU14	Idea submission by innovator	Keyword selection for patent database searching	Prior art search of patent Database by innovator	Meeting with patent attorneys and sharing of ideas and expert review	Prior art search of patent database by patent attorneys	Idea filtered on the basis of being non patentable	Carried for implement-ation

- Enhance the research culture in accordance with innovation strategies by improvement in number of patents filed.
- Determine a series of actionable plans, with priorities to mobilize resources for implementation of ideas.

The effectiveness of above scenario is that after introducing the above innovation management system within first month we had more than 300 ideas at initial stage from the idea box and ERP system, out of which we nurtured potential ideas by following the innovation management process as shown in Table 2. All the ideas are taken up with same enthusiasm and anticipation until they reach the final level of distinguishing the ideas into patentable and non-patentable as shown in Table 3. Ten ideas have been patented within 4 weeks from the day of entrance in the innovation management process and more are in pipeline. Some of the ideas that cannot be patented are being implemented for the social cause. The process was successful to develope the research culture in the academic environment. Agile methodology provided the advantage of incorporating the risk factor related to uncertainty in ideas of upcoming innovators.

REFERENCES

Andries, P. & Dirk, C. (2013). *Working Paper Small firm innovation performance and employee involvement*. ZEW Discussion Papers, No. 12.

Aubert, J.-E. (2005). *Promoting Innovation in Developing Countries: A Conceptual Framework*. Retrieved October 14, 2014 from http://elibrary.worldbank.org/doi/pdf/10.1596/1813-9450-3554

Bank, J., & Raza, A. (2014). *Collaborative Idea Management: A Driver of Continuous Innovation, Technology Innovation Management Review*. CaseStudy_BSTR060(2003). Retrieved from http://www.icmrindia.org/casestudies/catalogue/Business%20Strategy1/BSTR060.htm

Cockburn, A., & Highsmith, J. (2001). Agile software development: The people factor. *IEEE Computer*, *34*(11), 131–133. doi:10.1109/2.963450

Cohn, S. (2013). *A Firm-Level Innovation Management Framework and Assessment Tool for Increasing Competitiveness*. Technology Innovation Management Review.

Conboy, K., & Fitzgerald, B. (2004). Toward a Conceptual Framework of Agile Methods. In *Proceedings of the 2004 ACM Workshop on Interdisciplinary Software Engineering Research*. Newport Beach, CA: ACM. doi:10.1145/1029997.1030005

Dabholka r, V., & Krishnan, R. T. (2013). *8 Steps to innovation: Going from jugaad to excellence*. Harper Collins Publishers.

DNA Correspondent. (2013). Retrieved from http://www.dnaindia.com/academy/report-indian-varsities-account-for-5-of-patents-1853811

Dyer, J., & Gregersen, H. (n.d.). *The secret of innovative companies isn't RD*. Retrieved from http://www.innovationmanagement.se/2013/04/18/the-secret-of-innovative-compa-nies-it-isnt-rd/

Fernando Cardoso de Sousa. (2012). Creativity, innovation and collaborative organizations. *The International Journal of Organization Innovation, 5*(1).

Goldman, S. L., Nagel, R. N., & Preiss, K. (1995). *Agile Competitors and Virtual Organizations: Strategies for Enriching the Customer*. Van Nostrand Reinhold.

Gunasekaran, A. (1999). Agile manufacturing: A framework for research and development. *International Journal of Production Economics*, *62*(1), 87–105. doi:10.1016/S0925-5273(98)00222-9

Gupta, V. K. (2008). Retrieved October 13, 2014 from http://www.nistads.res.in/indiasnt2008/t5output/t5out9.htm

Hauglum, J. (n.d.). Retrieved October 15, 2014 from http://www.mixprize.org/story/ensuring-innovation-through-autonomy-work

Highsmith. (2000). *Adaptive Software Development: A Collaborative Approach to Managing Complex Systems*. New York: Dorset House.

Hoyrup, S., Bonnafous-Boucher, M., Hasse, C., Lotz, M., & Moller, K. (2012). *Employee-Driven Innovation: A New Approach*. Palgrave Macmillan. doi:10.1057/9781137014764

Iacocca Institute. (1991). 21st Century Manufacturing Enterprise Strategy. An Industry-Led View (2 vols.). Iacocca Institute.

India Today Online. (2014). Retrieved from http://indiatoday.intoday.in/education/story/iit-bombay-leads-with-400-per-cent-growth-in%20patentfiling/1/341476.html

Khandwalla, P. A. (1985). *Management of Corporate Greatness: Blending Goodness with Greed*. Pearson Education in South Asia.

Koskela, teknillinen tutkimuskeskus, V. (2003). *Software configuration management in agile methods*. VTT Technical Research Centre of Finland.

Kruchten, P. (2001). *Common misconceptions about Software Architecture*. The Rational Edge.

Matthews, J. H. (2003). *Knowledge management and organizational learning: strategies and practices for innovation, Organizational Learning and Knowledge*. Paper presented at the 5th International Conference.

Patwardhan, B. (2014). *Fixing innovation ecosystem*. Retrieved October 10, 2014 from, http://www.financialexpress.com /news/fixing-innovation-ecosystem/1280202

Paul, T. (1994). *Kidd Manufacturing Knowledge Inc. Agile manufacturing: forging new frontiers*. Boston, MA: Addison-Wesley Longman Publishing Co., Inc.

Robinson, A., & Stern, S. (1998). *Corporate Creativity: How Innovation and Improvement Actually Happens*. Berret-Kohler Publishers.

Sanyal, B. C., & Varghese, N. V. (2007). *Knowledge for the future: Research capacity in developing countries*. Retrieved October 14, 2014 from www.unesco.org/iiep/en/publications/pubs.htm

Singh, A., Singh, K., & Sharma, N. (2012). Managing Knowledge in Agile Software Development. In *IJCA Proceedings on International Conference on Recent Advances and Future Trends in Information Technology* (iRAFIT 2012) (pp. 33-37). IJCA.

Singh, A., Singh, K., & Sharma, N. (2013). Knowledge Management: the agile way. Information and Knowledge Management, 3(3), 143-152.

Singh, A., Singh, K., & Sharma, N. (2014). Agile knowledge management: A survey of Indian perceptions. *Innovations in Systems and Software Engineering, 10*(4), 297–315. doi:10.1007/s11334-014-0237-z

Yusuf, Y., Sarhadi, M., & Gunasekaran, A. (1999). Agile manufacturing: The drivers, concepts and attributes. *International Journal of Production Economics, 62*(1/2), 33–43. doi:10.1016/S0925-5273(98)00219-9

KEY TERMS AND DEFINITIONS

Agile Practices: Agile development is supported by a bundle of concrete practices, covering areas like requirements, design, modeling, coding, testing, project management, process, quality, etc. Some notable agile practices include Acceptance test-driven development (ATDD) & Agile modeling, etc.

Chitkara University: Chitkara University is a non-profit private university in India with its campus in Punjab and Himachal Pradesh, India.

Cloud Based Technology: Cloud computing evolved in the late 1990s, based on utility and consumption of computer resources. Cloud based technology involves application systems which are executed within the cloud and operated through internet enabled devices.

Innovation Management: Innovation management is the management of innovation processes. It refers to both product and organizational innovation.

Intellectual Property Rights: Intellectual property rights are the rights given to persons for the creations of their minds. They usually give the creator an exclusive right over the use of his/her creation for a certain period of time.

Knowledge Management: Knowledge management (KM) is the process of capturing, developing, sharing, and effectively using organisational knowledge. It refers to a multi-disciplined approach to achieving organisational objectives by making the best use of knowledge.

Scrum: Scrum is an agile framework for completing complex projects. Scrum originally was formalized for software development projects, but it works well for any complex, innovative scope of work.

Sprint: In the Scrum method of agile software development, work is confined to a regular, repeatable work cycle, known as a sprint or iteration.

Chapter 3

A Cross–Platform Architecture with Intelligent Agents for Dynamic Processes and Services Composition

Chung-Yeung Pang
Seveco AG, Switzerland

ABSTRACT

To meet business demands, enterprise software systems are required to be more dynamic, flexible and adaptive. Business processes must often be context-aware. Things get complicated when enterprise software systems, after a decade of evolution, comprise heterogeneous platforms and different technological stacks. This chapter presents the design and implementation of a cross-platform architecture with intelligent agents for dynamic business rules, process flows and services composition. The architecture includes an Enterprise Service Bus for service integration. Service agents are used to handle services. A Central Intelligent Agent that contains a Prolog-style rule-based engine is designed to execute business rules and processes. These agents are implemented in both Java and COBOL. Business process flows are completely rule- and context-driven. The services and components for the business processes are dynamically constructed. The proposed architecture and programming model enables fast prototyping and rapid development in an agile development process across different platforms.

INTRODUCTION

Enterprise IT systems have typically undergone a long period of evolution since the 1960s. These decade-long projects have eventually produced some of the most complex software systems in existence. For large corporations, mainframe applications programmed in COBOL often form the backbone of their IT structures.

By the mid-1980s, the object-oriented programming paradigm had evolved and new programming languages, such as C++, Smalltalk and, later on, Java, were introduced. In the meantime, multi-tier and

DOI: 10.4018/978-1-4666-8510-9.ch003

client server architectures had become popular. Many corporations used these new architectures for their new lines of business applications. The front-end applications were programmed in OO languages while the backend applications were still in legacy languages, like COBOL. Applications for these new lines of business often formed silos in the whole enterprise IT.

With the advances in Web and mobile technology, corporations must consider integrating Web-based and mobile applications with their existing applications. Furthermore, applications of different lines of business cannot generally be isolated. Service-oriented architectures (SOAs) have become very popular for application integration in recent years. Enterprise IT systems consist of different systems, applications and architectures of different ages, as well as technologies that need to interoperate both within and across organizations. This heterogeneity in enterprise IT systems has become a big problem for many corporations - the operation and maintenance costs for these systems are usually very high and, worst of all, they lack business agility.

Contemporary businesses have placed heavy requirements on enterprise IT infrastructure to operate in highly stable yet flexible and fast environments, as well as to introduce new features and operation processes in order to meet their continual growth. Despite their obsolescence, legacy systems continue to provide a competitive advantage by supporting unique business processes and by storing invaluable knowledge and historical data. New features and applications can no longer be developed in an isolated manner. They must leverage the existing legacy software components within a heterogeneous environment. This is quite a challenge for software development.

Software systems are required to become more dynamic, flexible and adaptive. Business processes must often be context-aware. For example, in European banks, new rules have been imposed on transaction-processing for customers from the USA. The new regulations of Basel III have also resulted in deviations from standard business processes for transactions that involve deposits over a certain period of time. Traditional software engineering methodologies are inadequate in addressing the complexity and dynamic nature of these business requirements. On the other hand, there are serious consequences for companies when such requirements are not implemented responsively. In fact, some regional banks within Europe have ceased doing business with US customers because their systems cannot cope with the changes required.

In this chapter, I present a solution to the challenges mentioned above. The solution involves the design and implementation of a cross-platform architecture with intelligent agents for dynamic business rules, process flows and services composition. An agile approach to application development in a heterogeneous enterprise's IT system is also presented. Finally, the migration of legacy components to modern systems is also addressed.

BACKGROUND

Architecture, Programming Model, and Agile Development Process

Advances in software technologies have shown a lot of promise. Back in the late-1980s, software scientists claimed that OO languages were for programming in the large (Wegner, 1989). The OO paradigm, with polymorphism and inheritance, was a solution to resolve and control the complexity of enterprise applications. In practice, the OO approach has often been found inadequate in managing the complexity of real-world applications. Take, for example, the modeling of US customer objects - we can model a

US customer as a special case of a customer. Various questions arise: what if the customer has multiple nationalities? What if the customer is not an adult? What if the customer is not an adult and has multiple nationalities? Taking this example, it can be seen that a simple object can possess a wide-ranging combination of characteristics that can cause a significant deviation in the processing of the business object. Although one may be able to use decoration techniques for object modeling (Pang, 2001) in order to account for all the variations of objects, their combinations can easily result in large and complex software systems, which is hardly maintainable.

Despite the advances in recent software technologies, enterprise software development remains a challenge in general. The Standish Group's 2009 CHAOS report (Standish Group, 2009) notes that only 32% of software projects were completed successfully, 44% were late, over-budget and/or had fewer than the required features and functions, while 24% were cancelled prior to completion or else delivered and never used.

Agile software development processes have become very popular in the software industry in recent years. The agile manifesto (Agile Manifesto Group, 2001) places emphasis on individuals and interactions, working software, customer collaboration and responding to change. They are preferable over processes and tools, documentation, contract negotiation and planning. An agile development process takes an evolutionary and iterative approach to software development (Ambler, 2010). It focuses on adaptation to changes and continuous integration. The concept fits well with improving business and IT agility. Ambler challenged the CHAOS report in a LinkedIn debate and argued that the agile approach to software development had a far higher success rate (Saravanan, 2013). In a vote, many participants shared the view that their projects had been successful; however, most of them confronted significant challenges in their projects (Ambler, 2013). While the underlying idea of the agile concept can be beneficial to software development, carrying out the development process for enterprise applications combining different technology stacks is not straightforward.

With a proper architecture coupled with a model-driven approach, Pang (Pang, 2012) showed that it is possible to build flexible, maintainable and agile applications in a legacy platform with a language like COBOL. To enable an agile development process with continuous integration, Pang argued that the architecture must provide a plug-and-play mechanism for components and modules. The components, as well as individual modules, should be autonomous with well-defined contracts to fulfill. To ensure that the components and modules are decoupled, state data are kept in a context container. Each module would get its input from the context container. When the processing is completed, the output data is put into the context container. The collaboration between the components and modules is controlled by a central process controller. Components and modules can be plugged into the application at any time for continuous integration. The application architects must work out the process flow such that when a module is invoked, its required input is provided in the context container. This programming model conforms to the long-time software engineering principle of cohesion and coupling (Yourdon, 1979). It provides a way to manage the complexity of enterprise applications even in a legacy environment.

Enterprise Integration and Service-Oriented Architecture

The monolithic view does not really work for an enterprise application programmed for a business line. An application in general needs to interact with a lot of existing software components. For example, a banking application would require enterprise-shared data and business functions, like client and product information, and financial instruments, etc. Many of these business components comprise legacy

COBOL programs in mainframe host systems. Some of them may be in Java, running in decentralized UNIX platforms. Any software architecture must include enterprise integration. Enterprise integration has been discussed since the early days of the industry (Linthicum, 1999; Vernadat, 1996). Back in 1997, Nell and Kosanke identified the different requirements of enterprise integration (Nell & Kosanke, 1997). Hohpe and Woolf introduced various enterprise integration patterns, such as splitters and content-based routers, etc. (Hohpe & Woolf, 2004). Solution and architecture overviews for enterprise integration can be found in various publications in the literature (e.g., Spackman & Speaker, 2004; Shuster, 2013; Shankararaman & Megargel, 2013).

The modern form of enterprise integration is usually based on SOAs, particularly for the integration of legacy systems. Integrating legacy software objects with SOAs have been addressed by a number of authors (e.g., Bieberstein et al., 2008; Fuhr et al., 2012; Kooijmans et al., 2007; Laszenwski et al., 2008; Poduval & Todd, 2011; Pang, 2014; Roshen et al., 2007; Roshen, 2009; Sneed, 2012; Sweeny, 2010; Umar & Zordan, 2009). Large software vendors, like Oracle and IBM, also provide specific tools for legacy integration (Laszenwski, et al., 2008; Poduval & Todd, 2011; Kooijmans, et al., 2007). A detailed survey can be found in an article by Pang (Pang, 2014).

Existing software objects are generally wrapped with wrappers or adapters to form services. New applications or enhancements are implemented in the new SOA platform and they activate the existing software objects as service consumers. Communication between service providers and service consumers can be supported by an ESB. ESBs provide robust communication, intelligent routing and the translation and transformation of services (Christudas, 2008). They also provide a comprehensive and scalable way to connect a large number of service providers to their consumers, without the need to make direct connections between each other. There are many ESBs available on the market and as open source. A survey of the different ESB products can be found in an article by Wähner (2013).

Agents and Semantic Web Services

Currently, there are many tools and standards for service-oriented development. W3C has defined standards like the simple object access protocol (SOAP) (W3C) and Web services description languages (WSDLs) (W3C) for Web services. A normal application usually involves a business process that would invoke a number of services and interact with various software components. Services are autonomous but federated. The composition of services and the way in which the services collaborate from a global perspective of business processes is understood in terms of service choreography (Josuttis, 2007). Process flows with the invocation of components and services are termed 'orchestrations'. Description languages like BPEL (OASIS, 2007) and BPMN (Object Management Group, 2011) provide the standards for service choreography and orchestration. These standards require services used to be specified prior to the execution of the business process. This kind of static process specification does not lend itself to a dynamic or flexible approach to the context-aware composition of the components and services of a business process (Xiao et al., 2010). For dynamic composition, we need to use software agents and sematic Web services.

Semantic Web services use an ontology-based layer to achieve semantic matches for Web services (Dustdar, 2005). They are typically defined as self-contained, self-describing and semantically marked-up resources that can be published, discovered, choreographed and executed in an automated fashion (Hebeler et al., 2009). The vision is to enable both static and dynamic resources with semantics to facilitate context-based processing. The Resource Definition Framework (RDF) (W3C, 2004) and the

Web Ontology Language (OWL) (W3C, 2012) languages are two of the W3C standards designed for semantic Web services. The RDF is based on the idea that the things being described have properties that have values, and that resources can be described by making statements. OWL is designed to represent rich and complex knowledge about things, groups of things and relations between things.

Supplementary to the semantic matching of services, we can use software agents for goal-based requests (Stollberg & Strang, 2005). An agent is a piece of software that acts autonomously to perform tasks on behalf of requestors. The design of software agents is based on the idea that the requestors only need to specify their high-level goals, constraints and other relevant details, instead of issuing explicit and formal instructions, leaving the 'how and when' decisions to the agents (Erl et al., 2013). Effectively, an agent must be able to deduce rules and carry out processes to satisfy goals. The Prolog (Clocksin & Mellish, 2003) engine can be used as a base for agent implementation. Prolog is capable of capturing the semantics represented by RDF and OWL. In addition, it offers features like forward and backward chaining and back tracking, etc. We can build an expert system in Prolog (Merritt, 1989).

As mentioned in the previous section, legacy integration is generally done by wrapping existing software components with wrappers or adaptors to form services. Such a development process usually requires significant effort. Sneed (2012) has provided some experience reports in migrating legacy applications. In one of these, a team of 17 developers took three years to complete the wrapped versions of 990 online COBOL programs. An alternative approach is proposed by Pang (Pang, 2014). In his approach, a generic service is provided in the mainframe host system for all external service requests. Each service is associated with a set of rules and processing steps. An intelligent agent is used to parse the input message and carry out the business process according to the service rules and processing steps. Based on the context of the request and the service, it would deduce and invoke the COBOL modules that were required for the business process. The technique will further be elaborated in a future section in this chapter.

CROSS PLATFORM ENTERPRISE ARCHITECTURE AND FRAMEWORK

Architecture Design

Figure 1 shows the conceptual design of the cross-platform enterprise architecture. The architecture uses an ESB to glue different services and business components together. The ESB provides basic functions like routing, the caching of data, data transformation and extraction, message transportation and correlation, I/O, and DB access, etc.

Agents are used to provide points of communication between the services hosted within the ESB and the external systems. The service agents are the entry points for external service consumers. They can be servlets that provide Web services or endpoints for message-oriented middleware (MOM) for message communication using components such as ActiveMQ. A social media framework, like Drupal, can also be integrated as an agent for social media applications. The external service requestor agents are channels to consume services provided by external sources.

Business service components are pluggable, application-specific objects. They can be autonomous plain old Java objects (POJOs) or enterprise Java beans (EJBs). Each component has a well-defined interface and contract to fulfill. They carry out their processes independently of the other components

Figure 1. Design of an SOA-based enterprise architecture with an ESB

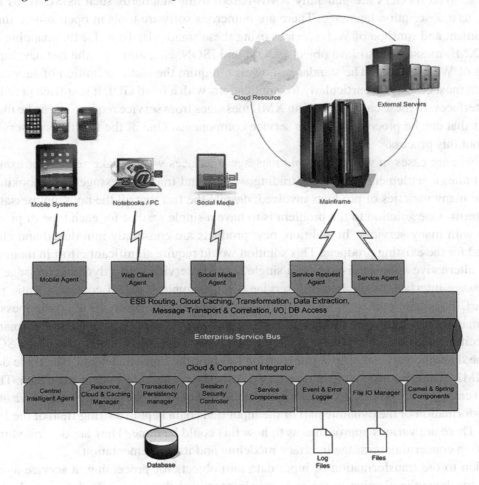

(i.e., they are completely decoupled from the other components). The various collaborations among the service components are orchestrated and controlled by a CIA, as presented in the next section.

Another set of components comprises infrastructure providers and managers, like file manager, session and security control, transaction and persistency manager, and resource and cache manager, etc. They provide the necessary functions for infrastructure and transparent abstractions of their usage so that developers can focus more on business logic instead of infrastructure-related logic.

Service Agent

In the proposed architecture, there are different types of agents. A service agent is a type of agent that facilitates external requestors in invoking services provided by the system. There is no restriction on the services that an agent can provide to the external world. As mentioned before, we can have a PHP-oriented Drupal framework as part of the agent for social media applications. However, in order to communicate with the central core of the architectural framework, the service agent must contain a standard Java service component that carries out a set of pre-defined operations, as explained below.

Enterprise Web services are generally XML-based, using standards such as SOAP as a protocol and WSDL as a description language. There are numerous software tools in open source that support the development and runtime of Web services using these standards. Tools for the mapping of incoming SOAP XML messages into Java objects, DOM and JSON, etc., allow for the fast development and prototyping of Web services. The standards, however, require the static definition of service message interfaces. In most cases, and particularly for applications with a fixed GUI, it is sufficient to have static message interfaces. In these cases, incoming XML messages from service requestors can be mapped into Java objects that can be processed by Java service components. One of the functions of service agents is to carry out this process.

Often, there are cases in which dynamic message interfaces would make sense. For example, in a finance institute, a settlement system for trading would send trading messages to a booking system. There are so many varieties of products involved, despite the fact that all the booking messages follow a set of patterns. One solution to the problem is to have a single service for each type of product. This can end up with many services. In addition, new products are constantly introduced and changes are also required for the existing products. This solution would require significant effort in maintaining the system. An alternative approach is to have a single booking service with a dynamic message interface.

The message interface of the booking service – for example – would contain a static part and a dynamic part. The static part would have all the information common to all the trade messages, like client information, product type and trade date, etc. The dynamic part would contain information about product-specific trade data. We can use standard WSDL to describe the static part of the SOAP message. For the dynamic part, we need a single string field for the input trade data. The trade data would also be in XML. Thus, we need a tag of type CDATA for the product-dependent trade data. The service agent would carry out the process to transform the static part of the input message into a Java object. The further transformation of the dynamic part of the input trade data kept in a string field of the Java object is required. There are various approaches as to how this could be done. They are described in detail in the sub-section concerning message interface modeling and its implementation.

In addition to the transformation of input data into objects for processing, a service agent is also responsible for the authentication of the requestor in accessing the service. It also controls the session for the lifecycle of the service.

Central Intelligent Agent Framework and Service Context

Most large corporations have well-established business processes and databases to support those processes. Data structures for base entities, such as client information, products, contracts, trade and booking information, and financial instruments, etc., are relatively standard and stable. When a new product-type is created, the information of the new type can be accommodated in the product database with no extension. The business rules and process logic, on the other hand, can be very different for the new product type. New components are usually developed to handle these rules and logic. In most cases, the components are very much tied to their specialized business logic.

Often, interactions between components are implemented within the business objects. As a result, most business objects cannot be reused. Developers usually start from scratch when a new line of business is required. An enterprise IT system usually contains many tens of thousands of business objects. It is very difficult to manage all these objects.

In my programming model, all the components for their respective business objects are autonomous with well-defined contracts to be fulfilled. A service context container is used to keep the state data. Each component gets its required data from the service context container. It will deposit its output data or else update the transformed data in the service context container. The collaboration of components is orchestrated by a CIA.

The CIA contains a Prolog-style rule engine. It uses Smalltalk (Lalonde, 1994) and the Java style for object-method invocations by sending messages to the objects. The business rules and process flow logic of the services are given in meta-information that is generated from rule scripts in the form of facts, clauses, predicates and actions. The rule scripts will be described in the next section.

An external service request is initially handled by a service agent. The service agent will carry out the following functions:

- Handle incoming external service requests with sessions and security controls
- Transform the input XML into objects
- Resolve rules and business processes for the service request
- Establish service context container
- Pass on the service context container to CIA
- Transform the output data from the objects in the service container into output XML
- Return the output XML to the service requestor

The functions of the CIA are listed in the following:

- Carry out the steps of goal-oriented business processes defined in clauses
- Carry out semantic matches for facts and clauses with predicates defined in the process
- Invoke components as needed
- Handle, route and dispatch service requests to other service providers using the service request agent
- Carry out data transformation using other components, like Camel and Spring
- Interact with other components for persistency and transaction management, etc.
- Return the service context container back to the service agent

The business rules and process control are handled by the CIA. The components can be designed to carry out generalized primitive functions that can be reused in multiple services. The CIA can also leverage existing legacy business objects whenever appropriate by treating them as black boxes for particular functions in a business process.

Enterprise Service Bus

There are many ESBs available on the market and in open source. We have been experimenting, first of all, with ServiceMix, an OSGI-based ESB (Apache, 2011), and later on with Mule (Mule, 2013). These two are the most popular open source ESBs. Our final choice was Mule because of its ease of use.

The Mule ESB is a lightweight Java-based ESB and integration platform. It provides the facilities of a normal ESB such as service creation and hosting, service mediation, message routing, and data transformation, etc. In addition, many components for transaction management, security control, database access, and so on, as well as a graphical design environment, 'Anypoint Studio', are included in the Mule ESB package. With Anypoint Studio, one can design the process flow of a service by dragging and dropping of components that make up the process flow.

There are many online tutorials on how to design the process flows of services and how to use and configure the Mule ESB components with Anypoint Studio (Mule, 2014; Middleware School, 2013). The studio enables fast prototyping for services. However, just like standard BPEL, message interfaces as well as the process flows with the components involved must be statically defined. For a dynamic message interface and the context-aware composition of components and services of a business process, we need to develop additional infrastructure with intelligent agents, as described before. This infrastructure should be composed of packages of Java classes that are integrated into the Mule ESB. Figure 2 shows the layout of a simple process flow of a Web service using Anypoint Studio. The flow consists of a standard HTTP component, a SOAP component which transforms the input SOAP XML into objects and the output objects into SOAP XML, and a Java component which is basically the implementation of our service agent.

The service agent is the entry point of the dynamic business processes of our services. Upon a service request, it will invoke the CIA and gather together the output objects when the business process is completed by the CIA. During the business process, external service requests might be required. For an external service request, the CIA will activate the service request agent. The service request agent will interact with the resource manager to look up the information concerning the service and its provider. It will then prepare input objects for the request. The service request agent will call a sub-flow configured in the Mule ESB for that service. An example of such a sub-flow for an external Web service request is shown in Figure 3. The Java code segment for activating the sub-flow is given in Listing 1.

Figure 2. Simple process flow of a Web service in Mule ESB Anypoint Studio.

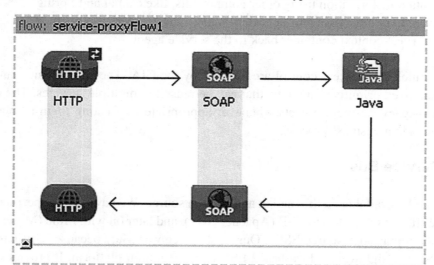

Figure 3. Sub- flow for an external Web service request in Mule ESB Anypoint Studio.

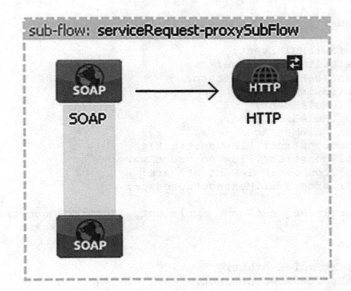

In addition to the Mule ESB components, we also use open source Java frameworks, like the Spring framework, Apache Camel and J2EE. Together, they form the basic infrastructure for enterprise service and component integration.

Legacy Integration

For the integration of legacy mainframe components, a single mainframe service gateway for service requests is used. All service requests are handled by one service agent. Again, a CIA is used for the execution of the business processes of the services. Both the service agent and the CIA are mirrors of the implementation of those running in the ESB. They are written in COBOL and contain a fully functional rule-based engine and process controller. The major difference is that they do not handle any Java-style objects but rather COBOL data records, like those defined in COBOL copy books. In a similar fashion to the Java object method for invocation, the CIA can call COBOL modules whenever required. In Java, the method for invocation can be done using reflection. This is not possible in COBOL. Hence, we need to write an assembler module as a part of the framework in order to do the job.

To call a module, the assembler module requires the following information:

- The name of the module
- Detailed information, such as the number of data records in the arguments as well as their sizes
- The input data records

It stacks input data into the registry, calls the module and returns the output data. The CIA is responsible for providing the module information, setting up a linked list of the input data records as well as retrieving the output data and moving them into the output data records.

Listing 1. Java code segment to activate a sub-flow in Mule ESB

```java
package ServiceRequestAgent;

import org.mule.DefaultMuleEvent;
import org.mule.DefaultMuleMessage;
import org.mule.MessageExchangePattern;
import org.mule.api.MuleContext;
import org.mule.api.MuleEvent;
import org.mule.api.MuleException;
import org.mule.api.MuleMessage;
import org.mule.api.construct.FlowConstruct;
import org.mule.api.construct.FlowConstructAware;
import org.mule.api.context.MuleContextAware;
import org.mule.api.processor.MessageProcessor;

public class ZOSServiceRequestAgent implements IServiceRequestAgent,
                                               MuleContextAware,
                                               FlowConstructAware {

  private MuleContext muleContext;
  private FlowConstruct flowConstruct;

  @Override
  public void setMuleContext(MuleContext context) {
    this.muleContext = context;
  }

  @Override
  public void setFlowConstruct(final FlowConstruct flowConstruct) {
    this.flowConstruct = flowConstruct;
  }

  @Override
  public ServiceResponse requestService(Object[] requestMessage,
      String proxySubFlow){
    MessageProcessor subFlow = muleContext.getRegistry().lookupObject(
      proxySubFlow);
    final MuleEvent muleEvent = new DefaultMuleEvent(
      new DefaultMuleMessage(requestMessage, muleContext),
      MessageExchangePattern.REQUEST_RESPONSE, flowConstruct);
    try {
      MuleEvent me = subFlow.process(muleEvent);
      MuleMessage msg = me.getMessage();
      Object payload = msg.getPayload();
      if (payload == null) {
        return null;
      } else {
        return new ServiceResponse(payload);
      }
    } catch (Exception e) {
      ....
    }
  }
}
```

Figure 4. Example of Message Interface Model in UML class diagram.

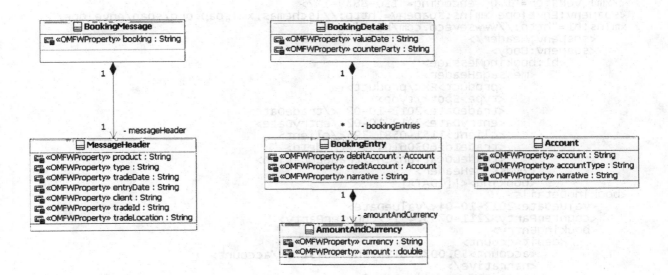

SERVICE MODELING

Message Interface Modeling and Implementation

Message interface modeling is one of the most important parts of service design. A message interface model in general contains the input and output data structure of the service. The data structure can be modeled using UML class diagrams. An example of such a UML class diagram is shown in Figure 4. The class structure usually mimics the XML tree structure. One can always specify the property of a class or an attribute to overwrite the default XML construct. For example, one can specify a field as an attribute or an element. One can also re-define an XML tag as a class or an attribute should it not be the same as the class or attribute name.

Most UML modeling tools come together with code generators that can generate a Java class, a XML schema as well as a WSDL direct from the class diagrams. Mule also provides a component to map XML to Java objects based on the description of a Java class or the WSDL. The corresponding Java classes of the model in Figure 4 are listed in Listing 2 and the XML in Figure 5.

Unfortunately, the Java classes generated by the code generators of many modeling tools do not always meet the requirements of XML-to-Java object mapping. For example, in order to map the dynamic list of BookingEntry, one needs to define a list for a variable BookingEntry, as given in Listing 2. Most code generators do not generate such constructs. Hence, some tailoring of the code generators from the modeling tools is required in order to generate the proper Java constructs for XML-to-Java object mapping.

Standard tools like XStream for XML-to-Java object transformation requires extra meta-information for the creation of objects from different classes and adding bookingEntry to the bookingEntries list. Our code generator is also extended to generate the XML-to-Java object transformation classes. Listing 3 shows the generated class for BookingDetails. Extra meta-information will also be generated if the

Figure 5. XML of the model in Figure 4

```
<?xml version="1.0" encoding="ISO-8859-1"?>
<soapenv:Envelope xmlns:soapenv="http://lschemas.xmlsoap.org/soap/envelope/"
xmlns:b1="http://wwwseveco.com/booking">
    <soapenv:Header/>
    <soapenv:Body>
        <b1:bookingMessage>
            <messageHeader>
                <product>FX</product>
                <type>Spot</type>
                <tradeDate>2012-10-02 </tradeDate>
                <entryDate>2012-10-02</entryDate>
                <client>1151-0581.395</client>
                <tradeId>6030610459</tradeId>
                <tradeLocation>CH</tradeLocation>
            </messageHeader>
            <booking><![CDATA[
<bookingDetails>
    <valueDate>2012-10-04</valueDate>
    <counterParty>2211-0735.451</counterParty>
    <bookingEntry>
        <debitAccount>
            <account>59.0070.0115.1007.8432.5</account>
            <narrative/>
            <accountType>clientAcc0unt</accountType>
        </debitAccount>
        <creditAccount>
            <account>52.0020.0216.1D03.2433.5</account>
            <narrative/>
            <accountType>profitAnd LossAccount</accountType>
        </creditAccount>
        <amountAndCurrency>
            <currency>GBP</currency>
            <amount>25600.00</amount>
        </amountAndCurrency>
        <narrative/>
    </bookingEntry>
    <bookingEntry>
        <debitAccount>
            <account>43.0032.0244.1o07.3453.5</account>
            <narrative/>
            <accountType>profitAndLossAccount</accountType>
        </debitAccount>
        <creditAccount>
            <account>59.0070.0115.2009.8543.5</account>
            <narrative/>
            <accountType>clientAccount</accountType>
        </creditAccount>
        <amountAndCurrency>
            <currency>USD</currency>
            <amount>24683.52</amount>
        </amountAndCurrency>
        <narrative/>
    </bookingEntry>
</bookingDetails>
]]></booking>
        </b1:bookingMessage>
    </soapenv:Body>
</soapenv:Envelope>
```

Listing 2. Java classes of the model in Figure 4

```
package com.seveco.booking;

public class Account {
        private String account;
        private String narrative;
        private String accountType;

        public String getAccount() {
                return account;
        }

        public void setAccount(String account) {
                this.account = account;
        }
....
}

public class AmountAndCurrency {
        private String currency;
        private double amount;
....
}

public class BookingEntry {
        private Account debitAccount;
        private Account creditAccount;
        private AmountAndCurrency amountAndCurrency;
        private String narrative;
....
}

import java.util.ArrayList;
import java.util.List;

public class BookingDetails {
        private String valueDate;
        private String counterParty;
        private List<BookingEntry> bookingEntries;
....
}

public class MessageHeader {
        private String product;
        private String type;
        private String tradeDate;
        private String entryDate;
        private String tradeId;
        private String tradeLocation;
        private String client;
....
}

public class BookingMessage {

        private String booking;
        private MessageHeader messageHeader;
....
}
```

Listing 3. Generated Java class for BookingDetails.

```
package com.seveco.booking;
import com.thoughtworks.xstream.XStream;
public class XMLToBookingDetails implements IXMLToObject {
    @Override
    public Object map(String xml) {
        XStream xStream = new XStream();
        xStream.alias("bookingDetails", BookingDetails.class);
        xStream.alias("bookingEntry", BookingEntry.class);
        xStream.alias("debitAccount", Account.class);
        xStream.alias("creditAccount", Account.class);
        xStream.alias("amountAndCurrency", AmountAndCurrency.class);
        xStream.addImplicitCollection(BookingDetails.class,
            "bookingEntries");
        return xStream.fromXML(xml);
    }
}
```

XML tag name is different to the attribute name of a class or if an attribute of a class should be mapped to an attribute in the XML.

In Figure 4, the class BookingMessage contains a single-string field booking. After the XML-to-Java object mapping in the service agent, this field will be filled with dynamic input data of a booking for a given product in the form of CDATA. The booking would contain raw XML data - it requires a second parsing. The easiest way is to activate the XML-to-Java object transformation for the booking of the particular product. It can be done by the service agent. The service agent can then forward the objects as input to the CIA, which carries out the business process. With this approach, however, if a new product should be integrated into the service, we need to modify the service agent.

An alternative approach to handle the dynamic interface is simply to pass the whole set of input objects together with the booking string to the CIA. Based on the rules defined, the CIA would activate the proper XML-to-object transformation. A third approach is to map the dynamic XML into a DOM. The CIA can extract individual data inside the DOM by navigating the tree structure or by using XPaths. This approach would be useful when the business process requires operations on individual data rather than complete objects. Mapping XML to objects is still better when objects are passed around for the business process.

For services running on a legacy platform with COBOL, we do not have objects. Rather, the XML data must be mapped onto COBOL data structures. We have developed tools that can generate meta-information from UML-class models. This meta-information attached to our COBOL service agent can carry out the conversion among XML-to-COBOL data. The meta-data will be discussed later.

Listing 4. Prolog style facts declaration

```
locationTradedCurrency(CH, USD, EUR);
locationTradedCurrency(CH, USD, AUD);
```

Rule and Process Flow Description Language

As mentioned before, the CIA contains a Prolog-style rule-based engine. The services and component invocations have a similar mechanism for sending messages to objects as in Smalltalk and Java. The rules and process flow logic are defined in a functional language-style script. Declarations of Prolog facts can take the form as shown in Listing 4.

CH, USD, EUR and AUD are all Prolog atoms but they are also considered to be objects. An object is dynamic in that it can be assigned with new properties and characteristics at any time. It can have attributes and methods. If there are no further declarations, it will remain as a Prolog atom. Each object inherits a base object that has some pre-defined properties and methods. These methods allow dynamic properties to be added to the object. Getters and setters are also pre-defined methods for object attributes and variables. Unfortunately, it is beyond the scope of this chapter to provide a full presentation of our entire script language with its syntax and semantics - only the relevant script that are required here will be presented further in the various examples below.

In contrast to Prolog, in our script language the first capital letter of an element does not represent a variable. Rather, we use '$' to represent a variable, like in PHP (Tatroe et al., 2013). Other symbols that we use are '@', to represent annotation, and '#' for logical names and default framework operations, as described later.

In our framework, with a Prolog-style rule-based engine, rules and processes are specified through facts, clauses, predicates and actions. Both predicates and actions form steps of rule-execution or operations within clauses. They can either be successful or else a failure. For example, taking the syntax of PHP, clauses for executing the booking process can be defined as in Listing 5.

The process is carried out by the clause executeBooking. This clause has two variables, $input and $output, as arguments. It also has an annotation of a cut pattern. The cut pattern has the same function as that in Prolog. It imposes a rule such that when the clause is executed successfully, the rule-based engine should cease seeking alternatives. If it fails, the engine will look for the next alternative clause. For executeBooking, the alternative clause is used to set a pre-defined service error object to the output variable. Error-handling will be described later on.

The first step in the booking process is to validate the booking input data with a standard predicate validateBooking. This predicate will activate the clause validateBooking. In the clause validateBooking, the service input dates are checked as to whether they are valid business dates via the validateDate clause.

The validateDate clause involves an action that invoke the static method validateDate() of a class BusinessCalendar (the Java class in our case). The return of this method is a Boolean value. The engine interprets 'true' as success and 'false' as failure. If the method returns another object or void, the action is always considered successful, unless an exception has been raised. The first validateDate clause also has an annotation of a cut pattern. If it fails, the second validateDate clause will be executed. This clause is used for error handling. It sets the message attribute of a pre-defined object in the framework

Listing 5. Example of clause definitions

```
@Pattern(cut)
validateDate($date, $dateType) {
  BusinessCalendar.validateDate($date);
}

@Pattern(fail)
validateDate($date, $dateType) {
  #serviceError.message($dateType + " with " + $date +
  " is incorrect business date!");
}

@Pattern(fail)
tradedCurrency($location, $currency1, $currency2) {
  #serviceError.message("Location " + $location + " Currencies " + $currency1
  + " and " + $currency2 + " cannot be traded!");
}

validateBooking($messageHeader, $bookingDetails) {
  validateDate($messageHeader.getEntryDate(), "entryDate");
  validateDate($messageHeader.getTradeDate(), "tradeDate");
  validateDate($bookingDetails.getValueDate(), "valueDate");
  $bookingEntry1.set($bookingDetails.getBookingEntry().get(0));
  $bookingEntry2.set($bookingDetails.getBookingEntry().get(1));
  @Pattern(cut)
  tradedCurrency($messageHeader.getLocation(),
    $bookingEntry1.getAmountAndcurrency().getCurrency(),
    $bookingEntry2.getAmountAndcurrency().getCurrency());
}

@Pattern(cut)
executeBooking($input, $output) {
  $bookingDetails.set($input.getBookingDetails())
  validateBooking($input.getMessageHeader(),$bookingDetails)
  #serviceDispatcher.addServiceRequest(validateClient,
    $messageHeader.getClient());
  #serviceDispatcher.addServiceRequest(doBooking,
    $messageHeader.getTradeId(), $bookingDetails.getBookingEntry().get(0));
  #serviceDispatcher.addServiceRequest(doBooking,
    $messageHeader.getTradeId(), $bookingDetails.getBookingEntry().get(1));
  #serviceDispatcher.dispatchService()
  @Pattern(final)
  #serviceDispatcher.clearServiceRequests();
  $ouput.set(#serviceSuccess);
}

executeBooking($input, $output) {
  $ouput.set(#serviceError);
}
```

with a logical name #serviceError. The annotation @Pattern(fail) forces the clause to fail even if it is executed successfully. This would trigger a ripple of failure among the clauses validateBooking and executeBooking. The second executeBooking clause will then be activated, setting the service error object into the output.

The next validation tradedCurrency($location, $input.currency1(), $input.currency2()) is a standard predicate. Valid traded currency can be declared as a fact, as in Listing 2. If the engine can match any of the declarations, the predicate will be successful or else it will fail. Note that the predicate has an annotation of a pattern cut. It imposes a rule such that once a fact is matched, the engine should not search for alternatives.

After validation, external service calls are required to carry out client validation and bookings for booking entries. Here, we use an object called #serviceDispatcher. This object is an instance of a class for service dispatching. This class is the service request agent part of the framework. An instance of this class is created whenever needed within a session for an external service request. The instance is associated with the logical name #serviceDispatcher. The symbol '#' tells the framework that the object name is a logical name in the context. The object is put into the service context container once it is created. It allows clients to add and dispatch requests to other services, and it can dispatch multiple requests at one time. In the case of dispatching service requests to the mainframe, it will put all the requests into a single XML message and send it to the mainframe. This avoids multiple transactions being triggered by the service requests. If the services should be executed locally, it will invoke each service request, one at a time, and pack the results into an array. At the end of the clause, we need to clear the requests in the cache of the service dispatcher. This action has an annotation of the pattern 'final'. This pattern imposes a rule similar to that of Java final, which means that the action is executed regardless of whether the clause is successful or not.

The examples given in this section show how the rules and business processes can be defined and executed. A business process can be defined in a clause, and there are more features within the framework for, e.g., iteration and parallel processing, etc., however, they are not within the scope of this chapter.

Modeling of Rules and Process Flows

Business rules and processes can be defined well through scripts with a functional language. However, for complicated process flows with many clauses, it is quite easy to lose the overview of the business processes and the rules they impose. Graphical models usually give a better picture of the processes than scripts.

To model the clauses involved in a business process, we simply use the normal activity diagrams of a standard UML modeling tool. Figure 6 illustrates the process flow of our executeBooking example. In this diagram, we have three clauses defined for executeBooking. The top diamond with the stereotype <<flow>> is a selection symbol. The difference between this and a normal selection in an activity diagram is that no condition to determine which flow should take place is specified. In our context, the flow on the left would be executed first. If the flow completes successfully, the other two will be ignored because of the cut pattern. If the flow fails to complete, the middle flow will be executed. The final flow for error handling will only be executed when the first two flows cannot be completed successfully.

With a code generator, the script in a functional language can be generated. The generated script for the middle and last clauses in the model will be the same as in Listing 5 for the executedBooking

Figure 6. Activity diagram of the business flow model of executeBooking clauses

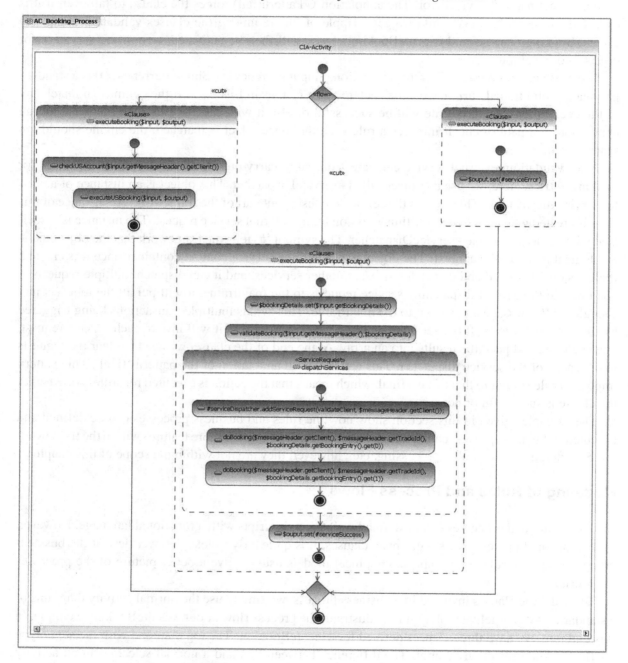

clauses. Note that we use a structural action dispatchServices with a stereotype <<service request>> to encapsulate the two doBooking service requests. This action, with its stereotype, has a predefined code pattern for generation such that the resulting generated code to dispatch the two service requests will be identical to what is shown in Listing 5. In addition to a functional language, the code generator can also generate scripts of meta-data, as described in the next sub-section.

Meta Data

The CIA running on the service bus is implemented in Java. The engine can interpret the functional language described previously and activate the required Java objects. The CIA running on the mainframe is implemented purely in COBOL. It requires different mechanisms to handle the objects declared in the functional language. The process to interpret the rule- and process descriptors based on the functional language can result in a substantial strain on performance. In our design, the functional language is parsed and translated into meta-data. The CIA can carry out its processes based on descriptors given in the meta-data. Meta-information derived from the message interface model is also provided for the service agent in order to carry out the conversion between XML and COBOL.

In the booking example described so far, we require a doBooking mainframe service which takes tradeId and bookingEntry as inputs. For a better illustration of the meta-data, I choose to use the booking details structure.

Listing 6 shows the COBOL records of some booking details and a booking entry. To carry out the conversion between the XML and COBOL structures, meta-information must be provided for each element in the COBOL record. Listing 7 shows the format of the meta-information script for an element using a ';' delimiter.

Listing 6. COBOL record for booking details

```
01 BookingDetails.
   05 ValueDate              PIC X(10).
   05 CounterParty           PIC X(13).
   05 BookingEntries         POINTER.


01 BookingEntry.
   05 DebitAccount.
      10 Account             PIC X(24).
      10 Narrative           PIC X(50).
      10 AccountType         PIC X(25).
   05 CreditAccount.
      10 Account             PIC X(24).
      10 Narrative           PIC X(50).
      10 AccountType         PIC X(25).
   05 AmountAndCurrency.
      10 Currency            PIC X(3).
      10 Amount              PIC 9(16)V9(4).
```

Listing 7. Meta-information script format of an element in a COBOL structure

```
;node;id;parentId;nodeName;valueType;relativeOffset;size;occurence;XMLType;
```

Both COBOL and XML essentially have a tree structure - each element can be considered as a node and each node is assigned with an id and has a parent. Further information included in the meta-data is explained in the following list:

- **nodeName:** the node name of the element in XML (the COBOL name is not needed)
- **valueType:** the type of the element, e.g., whether it is a structure, text, numerical, decimal, pointer or a linked list to handle the dynamic list in XML
- **relativeOffset:** the offset position of the element relative to its parent
- **Size:** the size of the element.
- **Occurrence:** the occurrence of the element.
- **XMLType:** XML type of the element (i.e., element, attribute or CDATA).

The meta-information script of the booking details example is shown in Listing 8.

As shown in the above listing, the COBOL record starts with struct. The first node has the same name as the struct itself, since it is the first element of the record, like bookingDetails. The first node also contains the size of the whole record.

After parsing the meta-information script, the service agent will create an internal meta-data record for each COBOL record. An internal linked list is included in the meta-data record. All existing or newly created COBOL records are linked to their meta-data records.

In order to support a dynamic list, a node can have the value-type of a dynamic list. For example, if there is more than one bookingEntry in our example, the node specification for the bookingEntries can take the form as shown in Listing 9. The service agent will build a linked list for all the booking entries needed. A new record structure for bookingEntry is required. Each time a bookingEntry is created, the service agent will look up the meta-data record for bookingEntry and allocate the memory for the bookingEntry record. The record is linked to the meta-data record.

The meta-data provides information for data conversions between COBOL and XML data structures. They also allow the service agent to handle the data records like objects. A COBOL data record can be created and used for data processing by the service agent. An example is given in Listing 10. In this example, the service agent allocates the memory required for the new instances of bookingEntry. BookingEntry is added to the corresponding linked list of bookingDetails. The data of the instances can be manipulated like standard objects. It shows that the rule and process scripts described previously can be applied for service definitions in the mainframe with few constraints. The major difference is that all the methods are pre-programmed in the framework. User-tailored methods must be programmed as standard COBOL modules and called by the framework.

At runtime, the CIA does not interpret the rule and process scripts in the functional language. Rather, it uses a similar kind of meta-data to those used for the COBOL data structure. Listing 11 shows the descriptor of a clause calling the COBOL module doBooking. Listing 12 shows the meta-data for this clause. A full description of the meta-data is not provided in this chapter for brevity.

Basically, the meta-data script captures the full information of the clause provided by the rule and process script. Each element (such as clause, predicate, fact, atom, variable, object, etc.) in the script is assigned with an ID - the first letter of the id indicates its type. Additional information that is not illustrated in the example is that a predicate script is tailored with all possible matches of facts and clauses. The tool which generates these meta-data scripts must carry out the pre-processing of the predicates and locate all the matched facts and clauses. This helps to push up the performance of the service agent at run-time.

Listing 8. COBOL structure meta-information script of booking entry example

```
;struct;bookingDetails;
;node;1;0;bookingDetails;s;0;39;1;e;
;node;2;1;valueDate;t;0;10;1;e;
;node;3;1;counterParty;t;10;13;1;e;
;node;4;1;bookingEntries;l;23;16;*;e;
```

Listing 9. Example of meta-data for handling the dynamic list

```
;node;4;1;bookingEntries;l;23;16;*;e;

;struct;bookingEntry;
;node;5;0;bookingEntry;s;0;110;1;e;
;node;6;5;debitAccount;s;0;99;1;e;
;node;7;6;account;t;0;24;1;e;
;node;8;6;narrative;t;24;50;1;e;
;node;9;6;accountType;t;74;25;1;e;
;node;10;5;creditAccount;s;99;99;1;e;
;node;11;10;account;t;0;24;1;e;
;node;12;10;narrative;t;24;50;1;e;
;node;13;10;accountType;t;74;25;1;e;
;node;14;5;amountAndCurrency;s;198;23;1;e;
;node;15;14;currency;t;0;3;1;e;
;node;16;14;amount;d;3;20;1;e;
```

Listing 10. Example of COBOL structure creation and manipulation

```
$bookingEntry.set(bookingEntry.newInstance());
$bookingEntry.getDebitAccount().setAccountType("clientAccount");
$bookingDetails.set(bookingDetails.newInstance());
$bookingDetails.getBookingEntries().addLink($bookingEntry);
```

Listing 11. Example of a clause for mainframe service

```
doBooking($tradeId, $bookingEntry, $output) {
  $moduleName.set(TBOOK215);
  $inputArguments.set(#linkList.newInstance());
  $inputArguments.addLink($tradeId);
  $inputArguments.addLink($bookingEntry);
  $outputArguments.set(#linkList.newInstance());
  $output.set(BookingOutput.newInstance());
  $outputArguments.addLink($output);
  #callModule($moduleName, $inputArguments, $outputArguments);
}
```

Listing 12. Meta-data of the clause shown in Listing 11

```
;a1;TBOOK215;
;v3;$tradeId;
;v4;$bookingEntry;
;v5;$output;
;v6;$moduleName;
;v7;$inputArguments;
;v9;$outputArguments;
....
;o1;set;v6;a1;;
;o2;newInstance;#3;r1;
;o3;set;v7;r1;
....
;#1;callModule;v6,v7,v8;
;c2;doBooking;v3,v4,v5;o1,o2,o3,o4,o5,o6,o7,o8,o9,o10,#1;;
....
;s2;doBooking;v3,v4,v5;c2;
```

Meta-data scripts of the mainframe services are generated based on activity models. They are stored in a resource management database. Upon a service request, the service request agent would retrieve the related script. Combined together with the input data, it would generate the SOAP XML for the service. Figure 7 shows an example of the skeleton of such a SOAP XML message.

APPLICATION DEVELOPMENT AND LEGACY MIGRATION

Development Tools

In the early history of programming, software artifacts consisted mainly of programs with very little documentation. Their maintenance was a particularly difficult task. Later on, with the development of the waterfall model, managers and developers began to place more emphasis on the software lifecycle. Heavy documentation, especially for requirement specifications, had become the trend. It was often difficult to find the right information among so many documents - they were often out of date and not updated when the software evolved. The new trend of the agile software development approach stresses running code to documentation. Again, we find projects that contain mainly programs with some user stories as software artifacts.

Some sort of document that reflects the up-to-date implementation are always needed. Software models together with some descriptions can be useful documents. As mentioned in the sub-section *Message Interface Modeling*, message interfaces can be modeled through UML class diagrams. These diagrams can be used to generate XML schemas, WSDL, a base XML structure and Java classes, etc. For mainframe services, they are used to generate the meta-information for the XML and COBOL structure-conversion as well as the COBOL copy books (if they do not exist yet). For our development, we have extended the code generator of a commercial UML case tool to fit our purpose.

Figure 7. Example of the skeleton of a SOAP XML message for mainframe service

```
<?xml version="1.0" encoding="ISO-8859-1"?>
<soapenv:Envelope xmlns:soapenv="http://lschemas.xmlsoap.org/soap/envelope/"
xmlns:m1="http://www.seveco.com/meta"  xmlns:i1"http://www.seveco.com/seviceinput">
    <soapenv:Header/>
    <soapenv:Body>
        <m1:metaData><![CDATA[
;struct;bookingEntry;
;node;5;0;bookingEntry;s;0;110;1;e;
;node;6;5;debitAccount;s;0;99;1;e;
;node;7;6;account;t;0;24;1;e;
;node;8;6;narrative;t;24;50;1;e;
;node;9;6;accountType;t;74;25;1;e;

...
;a1;TBOOK215;
;v3;$tradeId;
;v4;$bookingEntry;
;v5;$output;
;v6;$moduleName;
;v7;$inputArguments;
;v9;$outputArguments;

;o1;set;v6;a1;;
;o2;newInstance;#3;r1;
;o3;set;v7;r1;

;#1;callModule;v6,v7,v8;
;c2;doBooking;v3,v4,v5;o1,o2,o3,o4,o5,o6,o7,o8,o9,o10,#1;;

...
;s1;validateClient;v1;c1;
;s2;doBooking;v3,v4,v5;c2;
;s3;doBooking;v3,v4,v5;c2;
]]></m1:metaData>
        <i1:input>
            <client>1151-0581.395</client>
        </i1:input>
        <i1:input>
            <tradeId>6030610459</tradeId>
            <bookingEntry>
                <debitAccount>
                    <account>59.0070.0115.1007.8432.5</account>
                    <narrative/>
                    <accountType>clientAcc0unt</accountType>
                </debitAccount>
                <creditAccount>
                    <account>52.0020.0216.1003.2433.5</account>
                    <narrative/>
                    <accountType>profitAndLossAccount</accountType>
                </creditAccount>
                <amountAndCurrency>
                    <currency>GBP</currency>
                    <am0unt>25600.00</am0unt>
                </amountAndCurrency>
                <narrative/>
            </bookingEntry>
        </i1:input>
        <i1:input>
            <tradeId>6030610459</tradeId>
            <bookingEntry>
....
            </bookingEntry>
        </i1:input>
    </soapenv:Body>
</soapenv:Envelope>
```

Other generators have also been built to parse the rule and process descriptions in a functional language and activity diagrams. Scripts of the meta-data that can be interpreted by service agents and the CIA are generated by these generators.

What is lacking in our development environment is a full IDE. There is also no interactive debugger for rule and process descriptors. What we have implemented is a tracing facility in the CIA. This produces traces of the rules as they are executed, the result of each execution step, and the argument and variable contents. Together with the interactive debuggers for Java and COBOL, we have managed to debug the services quite well.

Agile Enterprise Application Development

The agile development process is an iterative and incremental approach. Iterations generally cover a two-week period. Carrying out such an approach is rather challenging for cross-platform enterprise application development. For the different platforms, we need teams with different skill sets. If a legacy system is involved, the development of applications and maintenance is generally lengthy and costly. Fast prototyping and rapid development within a two-week iteration period is not feasible.

Many corporations look to avoid further development in their legacy systems. However, there are always new requirements and one must leverage existing legacy software modules. A standard approach is to wrap legacy software modules with service adaptors. The new rules and business processes are carried out on a modern platform but access the functions provided by the legacy mainframe system via services. Such an approach, as mentioned before, requires a significant development effort to wrap legacy modules with adaptors. In addition, a business process may involve the invoking of a large number of mainframe services. In the mainframe, each service invocation would involve a transaction. Transactions are expensive to run. To give an example, a re-engineering project was carried out in a corporation for its trading platform. The software architecture was based on the approach just described. After the project was completed, the final trading services turned out to have high performance degradation. The client advisors had problems at peak times of trading and the production costs also increased substantially.

With the architecture proposed in this chapter, we can develop an intelligent service with scripts that runs in the mainframe without writing any COBOL modules. Wrappers and adaptors for the COBOL modules in order to form services are not needed. New services that leverage existing COBOL modules can be developed using the script language described above. Complex rules and process flows can be combined with COBOL modules to form a sophisticated service. The composition of the COBOL modules is fully and dynamically driven by the service context and the business rules in the scripts.

The same programming model is applied to the Java objects hosted in decentralized platforms. The Java components are autonomous entities with well-defined signatures and contracts to fulfill. The collaborations between components are governed by the business rules in the scripts executed by the CIA.

To build complex rules and process flows using a functional language, however, is far from easy. It requires special skills and it is certainly not attainable for just any programmer. On the other hand, when one is familiar with the language, one can easily build services for prototyping and experiments. A service can be developed within hours. Even when legacy COBOL modules are involved in the service, there is no need for developers to have deep COBOL or mainframe knowledge. Some basic understanding of COBOL data structures and its module-calling mechanism would be sufficient. When new Java components are required, they are relatively easy to develop when they are cohesive, with no coupling with other components. Thus, application development does not require teams with different skills. Services can be developed and enhanced incrementally with a short iteration period. The agile development processes is very well supported.

Our architecture with the rule-based control approach enhances the flexibilities of business processes. The Prolog-style engine provides for a goal-oriented search and semantic matching mechanism for the business processes. Going back to our executeBooking example, we might have a new booking mechanism for trades made for accounts of US citizens. What we need to do is to add a new clause for executeBooking. This has already been considered in the executeBooking model in Figure 6. This new clause is set up to be processed, first of all. If the predicate checkUSAccount succeeds, the executeUSBooking clause will be invoked. If it fails, the original process will be carried out. Note that executeUSBooking must have its own error handling clause and executeBooking must be successful once it has passed through the predicate checkUSAccount. The booking service thus becomes context-aware with new processing behaviors by adding new rules. The old rules are still intact in their original form.

Legacy Migration

The proposed architecture allows for system migration to be done successively, in an iterative manner. New services can be created out of current legacy applications. There is, in general, no dependency between services. They can be developed in an iterative and incremental process. We can start extracting the business rules and processes from the legacy applications and model them as clauses, predicates and actions in new services. The new services would use more primitive modules (e.g., modules to access the database). The whole service will be able to run in the new platform with little modification when the data is migrated. Since service invocations are transparent to the service consumers, the applications that act as service consumers need no extension or modification.

FUTURE RESEARCH DIRECTIONS

The current project for a cross-platform architecture with intelligent agents is still in the prototyping stage. However, we have already verified the concept and the architectural design. Various prototypes have been built with a Mule ESB, service agents, a CIA, and mainframe services. The mainframe services were implemented without using the native mainframe programming language COBOL. The main consideration, at the moment, is that the rule-based-style script language is rather advanced for many developers. Even with our modeling technique, developers must understand how logical programming works. We are looking into improving our development approach with techniques and tools that would enable developers to specify rules and process flows more easily.

In the booking example described in this chapter, two bookings are made in the mainframe. These bookings require data inserts into the mainframe database. The two service requests plus the client validation service are packed into one input XML and handled by the mainframe CIA within one transaction. When client validation and both bookings are completed successfully, the transaction will be committed. If client validation or any one booking fails, the transaction will roll back. Hence, we fulfill the ACID requirement of our booking service. There are, on the other hand, services that require multiple transactions and database updates in different platforms. This is a general problem for SOAs across different platforms, since there is seldom the support of a two-phase commit protocol for services. We have developed a concept of how to support two-phase commit when a database update is required in multiple platforms. The concept is being tested and will be published if it is proved to work.

The code generators we have developed for a UML modeling tool so far are good enough for prototyping. They are insufficient for large-scale software development. Our goal is to develop a complete IDE with a repository. The IDE would support the full development lifecycle. Given the agent framework - IDE - we also need to combine the agile approach into our development process. This is another area for research.

The architectural framework thus far supports Java and COBOL. It could also be extended to other programming languages when needed.

CONCLUSION

This chapter presented the design and implementation of a cross-platform architecture with an ESB and intelligent agents. The service agents are used to handle incoming service requests. A CIA is responsible for carrying out the execution of business rules and processes. It contains a Prolog-style rule-based engine with object activation in Smalltalk and Java styles. Rules and process flows are defined through a functional language. They can also be modeled using UML activity diagrams. We also use UML class diagrams to model service message interfaces.

A Mule ESB is used in our implementation of the architectural framework. The agents are implemented in both Java and COBOL. A COBOL service agent and CIA are used in the mainframe to enable the integration of legacy COBOL applications as services. The underlying framework also provides a full set of functions to convert data between COBOL data records and XML, as well as manipulations of COBOL data records. Dynamic lists are also supported in the conversion.

Message interfaces can be modeled using UML class diagrams. Code generators are used to generate Java classes as well as the meta-data required for COBOL and XML mapping. They are also used to transform scripts or models of business processes into meta-data. The CIA uses this meta-data to execute the business rules and processes. Messages in the SOAP XML format are used for communication between the mainframe and the ESB. The meta-data are included together with the service request data in the SOAP XML messages.

The proposed architecture and programming model enables fast prototyping and rapid development in an agile development process across different platforms. It also allows for legacy migration through successive and iterative processes. Our approach to SOAs represents a different paradigm. Services can be (but not necessarily) statically defined. The service provider offers a number of reusable components. Services are modeled according to their rules and the business processes incorporated with the components. Services are dynamic and flexible. They are goal-oriented with a semantic matching mechanism. New rules can be added to a service at any time. The technique proposed for application development does not require multiple teams with different skill sets for different platforms. Rather, developers who are capable of logical programming and modeling are required.

REFERENCES

W3C. (2012). *Web Ontology Language (OWL) Primer* (2nd Ed.). W3C. Retrieved September 28, 2113, from http://www.w3.org/TR/owl2-primer/

W3C. (2004). *Resource Description Framework Primer*. Retrieved September 28, 2113, from http://www.w3.org/TR/rdf-primer/

Agile Manifesto Group. (2001). *Manifesto for Agile Software Development*. Retrieved from http://agilemanifesto.org

Ambler, S. W. (2010). *Agile Modeling. Ambysoft*. Retrieved July 26, 2010, from http://www.agilemodeling.com/

Ambler, S. W. (2013). *What Was Final Status*. Retrieved March 20, 2013, from http://www.linkedin.com/groups/What-was-final-status-most-1523.S.222770182

Apache. (2011). *Apache ServiceMix*. Retrieved September 20, 2111, from http://servicemix.apache.org

Bieberstein, N., Laird, R. G., Jones, K., & Mitra, T. (2008). *Executing SOA: A Practical Guide for the Service-Oriented Architect*. Upper Saddle River, NJ: IBM Press.

Christudas, B. A. (2008). *Service Oriented Java Business Integration: Enterprise Service Bus integration solutions for Java developer*. Birmingham, UK: Packt Publishing.

Clocksin, F. W., & Mellish, C. S. (2003). *Programming in Prolog*. Berlin: Springer-Verlag. doi:10.1007/978-3-642-55481-0

Dustdar, S., & Schreiner, W. (2005). A survey on web services composition. *International Journal of Web and Grid Services, 1*(1), 1–30. doi:.10.1504/IJWGS.2005.007545

Erl, T., Utschig, C., Maier, B., Normann, H., & Trops, B. (2013). *Next Generation SOA: A Real-World Guide to Modern Service-Oriented Computing*. Upper Saddle River, NJ: Prentice Hall PTR.

Fuhr, A., Winter, A., Erdmenger, U., Horn, T., Kaiser, U., Riediger, V., & Teppe, W. (2012). Model-Driven Software Migration: Process Model, Tool Support, and Application. In A. D. Ionita, M. Litoiu, & G. Lewis (Eds.), *Migrating Legacy Applications: Challenges in Service Oriented Architecture and Cloud Computing Environments*. Hershey, PA: Information Science Publishing.

Hebeler, J., Fisher, M., Blace, R., Perez-Lopez, A., & Dean, M. (2009). *Semantic Web Programming*. New Jersey: John Wiley & Son.

Hohpe, G., & Woolfe, B. (2004). *Enterprise Integration Patterns: Designing, Building, and Deploying Messaging Solutions*. Reading, MA: Addison-Wesley.

Josuttis, N. M. (2007). SOA in Pratice. Sebastopol, CA: O'Reilly Media.

Kooijmans, A. L., Chiang, R., Litman, I., Pettersson, M., Seubert, B., & Wendelboe, J. E. (2007). *SOA Transition Scenarios for the IBM z/OS Platform*. Upper Saddle River, NJ: IBM Redbooks.

Lalonde, W. (1994). *Discovering Smalltalk*. Redwood City, CA: Benjamin Cummings.

Laszenwski, T., & Williamson, J. (2008). *Oracle Modernization Solutions*. Birmingham, UK: Packt Publishing.

Linthicum, D. (1999). *Enterprise application integration*. Massachusetts, USA: Addison-Wesley.

Merritt, D. (1989). *Building Expert Systems in Prolog*. New York, NY: Springer-Verlag. doi:10.1007/978-1-4613-8911-8

Middleware School. (2013) *Mule ESB*. Retrieved July 23, 2114, from http://training.middlewareschool.com/mule/category/mule/mule-esb/

Mule, E. S. B. (2013). Retrieved September 28, 2113, from http://www.mulesoft.org

Mule, E. S. B. (2014). *Basic Studio and Tutorial*. Retrieved July 23, 2114, from http://www.mulesoft.org/documentation/display/current/Basic+Studio+Tutorial

Nell, J. G., & Kosanke, K. (1997). Enterprise engineering and integration: building international consensus. *Proceedings of ICEIMT 97, International Conference on Enterprise Integration and Modeling Technology*. Springer.

OASIS. (2007). *Web Services Business Process Execution Language Primer Version 2.0*. Retrieved September 28, 2113, from https://www.oasis-open.org/committees/download.php/23964/

Object Management Group. (2011). *Business Process Model and Notation Version 2.0*. Retrieved September 28, 2113, from http://www.omg.org/spec/BPMN/2.0/PDF

Pang, C.Y. (2001). A Design Pattern Type Extension with Facets and Decorators. *Journal of Object-Oriented Programming, 13*.

Pang, C. Y. (2012). Improve Business Agility of Legacy IT System. In V. Valverde & M. R. Talla (Eds.), *Information Systems Reengineering for Modern Business Systems: ERP, SCM, CRM, E-Commerce Management Solutions* (pp. 1–29). Hershey, PA: Information Science Publishing. doi:10.4018/978-1-4666-0155-0.ch001

Pang, C. Y. (2014). Legacy Software Integration in Service-driven Ecosystems: An Intelligent Agent-based Approach. In R. Ramanathan & K. Raja (Eds.), *Handbook of Research on Architectural Trends in Service-driven Computing*. Hershey, PA: Information Science Publishing.

Poduval, A., & Todd, D. (2011). *Do More with SOA Integration*. Birmingham, UK: Packt Publishing.

Roshen, M., Lublinsky, B., Smith, K. T., & Balcer, M. J. (2008). *Applied SOA: Service-Oriented Architecture and Design Strategies*. New Jersey: John Wiley & Son.

Roshen, W. (2009). *SOA-Based Enterprise Integration*. New York, NY: McGraw-Hill.

Saravanan, G. (2013). *Why Software Engineering Fails! (Most of the Time)*. Retrieved March 9, 2013 from https://www.linkedin.com/groups/Why-Software-Engineering-Fails-Most-1523.S.221165656

Shankararaman, V., & Megargel, A. (2013). Enterprise Integration: Architectural Approaches. In R. Ramanathan & K. Raja (Eds.), *Service-Driven Approaches to Architecture and Enterprise Integration*. Hershey, PA: Information Science Publishing. doi:10.4018/978-1-4666-4193-8.ch003

Shuster, L. (2013). Enterprise Integration: Challenges and Solution Architecture. In R. Ramanathan & K. Raja (Eds.), *Service-Driven Approaches to Architecture and Enterprise Integration*. Hershey, PA: Information Science Publishing. doi:10.4018/978-1-4666-4193-8.ch002

Sneed, H. M. (2012). Reengineering and Wrapping Legacy Modules for Reuse as Web Services: Motivation, Method, Tools, and Case Studies. In A. D. Ionita, M. Litoiu, & G. Lewis (Eds.), *Migrating Legacy Applications: Challenges in Service Oriented Architecture and Cloud Computing Environments*. Hershey, PA: Information Science Publishing.

Spackman, D., & Speaker, M. (2004). *Enterprise Integration Solution*. Microsoft Press.

Stollberg, M., & Strang, T. (2005). Integrating Agents, Ontologies, and Semantic Web Services for Collaboration on the Semantic Web. In *Proc. of the First International Symposium on Agents and the Semantic Web*. AAAI.

Sweeny, R. (2010). *Achieving Service-Oriented Architecture*. Hoboken, NJ: John Wiley & Son.

Tatroe, K., MacIntyre, P., & Lerdorf, R. (2013). *Programming PHP* (3rd ed.). Sebastopol, CA: O'Reilly.

Umar, A., & Zordan, A. (2009). Reengineering for service oriented architectures: A strategic decision model for integration versus migration. *Journal of Systems and Software*, 82(3), 448–462. doi:10.1016/j.jss.2008.07.047

Vernadat, F. (1996). *Enterprise Modeling and Integration: Principles and Applications*. London: Chapman & Hall.

Wähner, K. (2013). Choosing the Right ESB for Your Integration Needs. *InfoQ Articles*. Retrieved June 11, 2014, from http://www.infoq.com/articles/ESB-Integration

Wegner, P. (1989). *Concepts and Paradigms of Object-Oriented Programming*. Expansion of Oct. 4 OOPSLA-89 Keynote Talk.

Xiao, H., Zou, Y., Ng, J., & Nigul, L. (2010). An Approach for Context-Aware Service Discovery and Recommendation. In *Proceedings of the IEEE International Conference on Web Services* (pp. 63-170). IEEE. doi:10.1109/ICWS.2010.95

Yourdon, E., & Contantine, L. (1979). *Structured Design: Fundamentals of a Discipline of Computer Program and Systems Design*. Yourdon Press.

ADDITIONAL READING

Chappell, D. A. (2004). *Enterprise Service Bus*. Sebastopol, CA: O'Reilly.

Ebbers, M. (2009). *Introduction to the New Mainframe: z/OS*. Upper Saddle River, NJ: IBM Press.

Erl, T. (2008). *SOA Principle of Service Design*. Upper Saddle River, NJ: Prentice Hall PTR.

Hunt, J. (2006). *Agile Software Construct*. London, UK: Springer.

Ignatiadis, I., Svirskas, A., Vokrinek, J., & Briggs, J. (2008). Towards Combining SOA, Web 2.0 and Intelligent Agents Virtual Organizations. In *Proceedings of the European and Mediterranean Conference on Information Systems*, Dubai.

Lee, S., Choi, K., Shin, H., & Shin, D. (2007). Ag Webs: Web Services based on Intelligent Agent Platform. In *Proceedings of the 9th International Conference on Advanced Communication Technology* Volume 1, pp. 353-356. IEEE. doi:10.1109/ICACT.2007.358371

McGovern, J., Ambler, S. W., Stevens, M. E., Linn, J., Sharan, V., & Jo, E. K. (2003). *A Practical Guide To Enterprise Architecture*. Upper Saddle River, NJ: Prentice Hall PTR.

Trajkovski, G. (2010). *Developments in Intelligent Agent Technology and Multi-Agent Systems*. Hershey, PA: Information Science Publishing.

KEY TERMS AND DEFINITIONS

ACID: Atomicity, Consistency, Isolation, Durability, is a set of properties that guarantee that database transactions are processed reliably.

Agile Software Development Process: An evolutionary and iterative approach to software development with focuses on adaptation to changes.

COBOL: The programming language designed for commercial business data processing used for applications that often form the backbone of the IT structure in many corporations since 1960.

Context Aware Services: A technique which incorporates information about current situation to activate more relevant service.

Enterprise Service Bus (ESB): A software architecture model used for designing and implementing the interaction and communication between mutually interacting software applications in service oriented architecture (SOA).

Intelligent Agent: An autonomous entity which acts upon the circumstances and direct its activities towards achieving goals.

Legacy Integration: The integration and Web extension of existing (legacy) systems, especially mission-critical mainframe systems, in order to leverage existing IT assets.

Mainframe: Mainframe computer systems like IBM z/OS.

Prolog: A logical programming language used in artificial intelligence for building of expert systems.

Service Oriented Architecture (SOA): A technical software architecture that allows client applications to request services from service provider type applications in a host system.

SOAP: Simple Object Access Protocol, a standard from W3C.

Software Component: A software unit of functionality that manages a single abstraction.

WSDL: Web Service Description Language, a standard from W3C.

Chapter 4
Lean Manufacturing to Lean IT:
An Emerging Quality Assurance Methodology in IT

Deepinder Kaur
IBM India Pvt. Ltd., India

ABSTRACT

Lean methodology is an improvement philosophy, an expansion of Lean manufacturing and lean principles to the management of Service and Information Technology industries. It articulates how waste can be minimal at Software Development Process (SDP) which begins from feasibility study and ends till the product is delivered to the customer. In today's competitive world throughout all the industries emphasis is on product's quality within the time constraints. To gear up with the market demand Lean improvement concepts is introduced in (information technology) IT industry. Lean IT is the translation of lean manufacturing practices applicable to the Software Development life cycle (SDLC). It works like a business model and oriented towards the principles that focuses on the non value added activities. This chapter will present how lean methodologies and principles works in service industries to deliver the best quality products. Although Lean concept is traditionally been used in manufacturing industries; but nowadays it is adapted by Services companies with the aim of improving their processes and enhance customer satisfaction.

INTRODUCTION

Quality product is the demand of today's customer. So to attain the quality of Software products; thousands of service organizations are adapting Lean to achieve higher levels of performance. A lean operating system alters the way a company learns through changes in problem solving, coordination through connections, pathways and consistency.

Lean is all about standardizing work processes to make problem visible and developing your team member's critical thinking ability so that they can solve the various problems and improve development processes. With its focus on standardization, quality improvement, cost reduction, and efficiency, lean's influence continues to grow by providing a realistic and experience-based overview. This chapter will focus on Lean Basics, Lean Principles, and Various Lean Tools and also define how lean is related to Six Sigma.

DOI: 10.4018/978-1-4666-8510-9.ch004

What Is Lean

Lean is a systematic method, tool based philosophy focuses on eliminating waste so that all activities add value from the customer's perspective. Value here in industry is any action or process that a customer would be willing to pay for. Lean manufacturing emphasis on Just in Time (JIT) production. JIT is assumed to decrease the cost and to highlight problems at different phases. This can be achieved by reducing the resources in the system, so that buffers do not cover up the problems that arise. In the short-term perspective, the reduction of resources implies a direct reduction of cost. The same concepts are ejaculated in service companies to provide the best services within specified time limits.

BACKGROUND

Lean Production

There are many referenced origins regarding the founding concepts behind lean production. Lean thinking concepts were publicized by James Womack and Daniel Jones in their research done during the International Motor Vehicle Program (IMVP) at the Massachusetts Institute of Technology in the late 1980's. (Womack, J., 2004). This research highlighted the production system used by Toyota Motor Company in Japan from the 1960's to 1980's which gave them a competitive edge over their U.S. counterparts, Ford and General Motors. Their research highlighted that the Lean producer, by contrast, combines the advantages of craft and mass production, while avoiding the high cost of the former and the rigidity of the latter.

Figure 1 portrays the progress of quality techniques from Production flow by Henry Ford to Lean Six Sigma successfully implemented throughout the industries. Lean production changed the understanding of organization by bringing together all of the essential ingredients or principles required to implement a complete lean manufacturing process. It initialized new structures for assembly plants to promote teamwork, multi functionality, worker satisfaction, continuous improvement and waste elimination. Lean Production particularly pays attention to customer with flexible processes, which respond to demand variations and create value for the customer. This continued success has over the past two decades formed an enormous demand for greater knowledge about lean thinking. There are literally hundreds of books and papers, thousands of media articles exploring the subject, and numerous other resources available to this growing audience. As lean thinking continues to spread to every country in the world, leaders are also adapting the tools and principles beyond manufacturing, to logistics and distribution, services, retail, healthcare, construction, maintenance, and even government. Indeed, lean consciousness and methods are only beginning to take root among senior managers and leaders in all sectors today.

LEAN PRINCIPLES

Lean Thinking provides a way to specify value, line up value-creating actions in the best sequence, conduct these activities without interruption whenever someone requests them and perform them more and more effectively.

Figure 1. Lean Journey

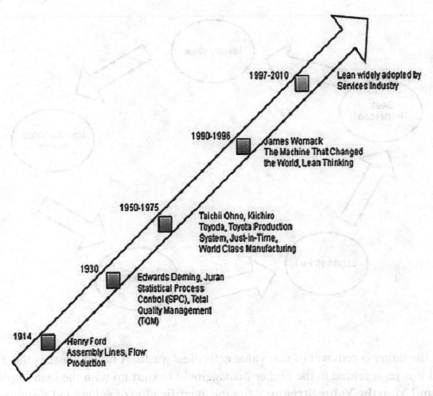

There ar-e several key lean manufacturing principles that need to be understood in order to implement lean. Failure to understand and apply these principles will most likely result to be a lack of commitment of an organization (Lean Manufacturing Junction, 2014). Without commitment the process becomes ineffective. One most important factor in production is touch time—the amount of time the product is actually being worked on or touched by the worker (Pettersen, J., 2009).

There are five Principles in lean:

1. Identify what features creates value from the customer's perspective.
2. Identify the sequence of activities along the process chain called the value stream.
3. Make the activities flow.
4. Make only what the customer pull; product or service through the process.
5. Perfect the process by continuing eliminating waste.

1. **Identify Value:** The first principle/step is to determine the features which create value in the product from the customer's perspective.The initiative for this is to recognize customer's needs, with time constraints and money value (how much money customer wants to invest in a particular project). Specific products or services are evaluated to find out the value added and non-value added activi-

Figure 2. Five Principles of Lean

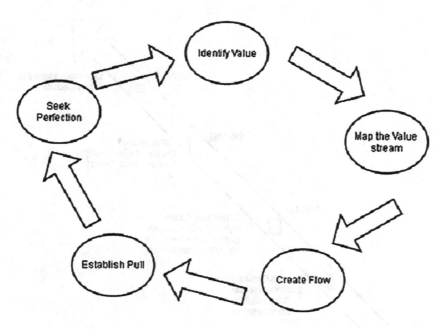

ties. Now the target is removal of non value activities/ waste. A list of waste is the outcome of this phase and it is represented to the higher management to start up with the lean implementation.

2. **Identify and Map the Value Stream:** After the identification of values and activities a sequence is generated. The entire set of activities across all parts of the organization involved jointly in delivering the product or service. This sequence is called Value Stream. This represents the end-to-end process that delivers the value to the customer.

Once you understand what your customer wants to implement. A categorization of value added activities and non-value added activities are done by understanding customer's views on implementation start up. . But some non values also contribute to the product or services are necessary. Necessary operations are defined as being a prerequisite to other value added activities or being an essential part of the business. An example of a non value added but necessary process is payroll. After all, people need to be paid. Finally the impact of non-value added activities on the process is reduced to a minimum. All other non value added activities are transitioned out of the process. The final step under this section will be how you are delivering valued activities and necessary non value activities to the customer.

3. **Improve Flow by Eliminating Waste:** Typically when value added activities and necessary non value activities are recognized, efforts are directed toward creating the improved activities flow. By eliminating the waste we can ensures the customer that your product or service can flow without any interruption or waiting. Flow is the uninterrupted movement of product or service through the system to the customer. Major inhibitors of flow are work in queue, batch processing and transportation. These buffers slow the time from product or service initiation to delivery. Buffers also strap the money that can be used elsewhere in the organization and cover up the effects of system restraints and other wasted activities.

This improvement must be continuous at organization level because continuous improvement promotes constant, necessary change toward achievement of a desired state. The changes can be big or small but must lend itself toward improvement.

4. **Allow Customer Pull:** This is about understanding the customer's demand on your service and then creating your process to respond to this. After waste is removed and established flow, efforts turn to letting the customer pull product or service through the process. The company must make the process responsive to provide the product or service what and when the customer needs it.

5. **Seek Perfection:** Improved flow and successful customer pull initializes the re organizing of individual process steps and this gain becomes truly significant as all the steps link together. It is continuous throughout the product development so that more and more layers of waste become visible. This process leads to theoretical end point of perfection, where every asset and action adds value for the end customer. The ultimate results improved Quality products with less processing time and less damage or obsolescence. Simplification of processes results in reduction of variation, the system constraints are removed and performance is improved.

WASTE IN LEAN METHODOLOGY

In full lean cycle elimination of waste is the highest priority task. In order to eliminate waste, first need is to recognize it. Partially done coding eventually discarded during the development process is waste. (LS-7FormsOfWaste.pdf)Extra processes and features not often used by customers are waste. Waiting for other activities, teams, processes and defects are waste. Managerial overhead not producing real value is waste. So the ultimate goal of Lean is to make the process waste free.

Various techniques are used to identify waste. For this first step is to point out sources of waste and to eliminate them. Waste-removal should take place iteratively until the essential processes and procedures are executed. We will discuss this later in the chapter.There are 7 basic types of waste in Lean IT:

- Defects,
- Transportation,
- Delays,
- Over Provisioning,
- Inventory,
- Motion (Excess),
- Extra Processing.

Defects

Defects come into the scene when are when products or service stray from what the customer actually requires or the defined specifications. Defects are the easiest waste to detect and can be the costliest of all the wastes. In the cycle of the development cost of defect removal increases on daily basis as a small error of earlier phase can leads to a big defect in the final product. It may even cost you a customer, which will result in lost future sales. There are costs associated with problem solving, materials, rework, rescheduling materials, setups, transport, paperwork, increased lead times, delivery failures and potentially lost customers who will take their customer elsewhere. . This is a major reason why lean promotes building quality into your process as one of its main principles.

Waste of Defects

- Misunderstanding of customer requirements and specifications.
- Lack of proper template documents to gather different types of data at various levels.
- Application level bugs.
- Design flaws or unstable designed applications
- Fail to maintain our tools with the up growing technology.
- Unauthorized changes to software and systems.
- No proper helpdesk or lack of knowledgeable information for users.
- Lack of proper training.
- Emphasis on quantity rather than quality.
- Free text field instead of check boxes or dropdowns that allows bad data entries and user errors.

Transportation

Transportation is the unnecessary movement and handling of work. This happens when work is passing between multiple teams, multiple companies and locations. To see this type of waste we have to take a step back and map activities.

Waste of Transportation

- Lack of clear process and poor coordination.
- Excessive email attachments rather than link.
- Distributing unnecessary copies to people who don't really need to know.
- Frequent onsite visits instead of using remote technology to resolve issues.
- Poor user interfaces.
- Physical software/security and compliance audits.

Delays

Waste of waiting/Delays can be found in many forms. In IT delays happens in areas like user signoff, requirements definition, testing, and other areas. Waiting comes from multi-tasking that often comes from trying to fully-allocate IT resources. In some situations it is easy to identify and remove this waste, yet very difficult to find in others. By removal of this waste efficiency can be greatly boosted, response time is reduced, together with balanced workflow and pulls production.

Waste of Delays

- Time and resources consumed in between major steps in a process.
- Delays from excessive review and approval steps

- Slow application response
- Downtime of applications, network delays
- Manual Service escalation procedures
- Delays between coding and testing
- Reports that take a long time to run
- Long helpdesk hold and call back times
- Slow speed devices and peripherals.
- Waiting for customer information or waiting for clarification or correction of work received from upstream process create much waste in office and business systems.
- Long synchronization/replication cycles between application platforms.

Over Provisioning

Developing something that is not required or needed is definitely a waste. Over provisioning is the waste which comes when IT builds solutions or provides capacity that is in excess of the business requirements. Cost of idle services like resources, depreciation floor space etc comes under over provisioning. By managing availability, capacity and Pull production systems this waste is reduced.

Waste of Over Provisioning

- Deployment of scripts which are not Vital Business Functions
- Help desk troubleshooting that address symptoms but not root causes
- Misunderstanding of root causes.
- Lack of technicality in resources.
- Requirements are not clear so extra coding is done.
- Producing and distributing reports that are not used.
- Unused functionality in software.
- Workflow routings that is not necessary.
- Over-dimensioned systems.
- Ineffective and repetitive meetings.
- Mirroring of file servers that do not contain business critical data.

Inventory

Inventory comes under one of the worst waste as it leads to many other types of wastes. Inventory issues are not so visible in our daily work environment but it impacts the whole work system. Likewise at a point of time if we have total of ten active projects and all the projects are in running state (Roy, S., 2014). It leads to increased inventory with no output. Inventory issues can lead to delays, overproduction, and defects from expiries etc. The ideal thing of having exact material with zero inventories is impossible to achieve in real time situations due to variation and uncertainty. Excess of inventory increases project cost because of follow up, maintenance and coordination of inventory. This waste can often be improved with supply chain optimization, capability studies, variation studies and inventory modeling.

Waste of Inventory

- Batch Processing, unread emails create inventory
- Risk of server collapse, un utilized hardware
- Excess information on local and shared drives
- Work waiting to be reviewed/approved/forwarded
- Problem tickets waiting for resolution
- Software purchased but not deployed
- Backlog accumulating in software development
- Risk of outdated services and materials.
- Unused/unnecessary software licenses
- Excessive inventory of printer cartridges and consumables
- Multiple repositories or backup servers to handle risk and control.
- Change requests waiting for decision/ implementation
- Benched application development teams.

Motion (Excess)

Excess motion is also one type of waste which deviate people from performing their actual jobs but these motions are also unavoidable. The waste of motion is usually one of the hardest to reduce significantly and does not provide as big an impact to the total value stream as removal of the other wastes. We can reduce the time and energy needed for a process by making limits of the motion while doing that process.

Waste of Motion (Excess)

- People looking for parts/tools/supplies
- Walking between offices
- People looking for files/paperwork
- Higher resource occupation
- People going to a meeting, not prepared
- People going to a room down the hall to retrieve printouts from their computer
- People walking to another room or building to process documents.

Extra Processing

In IT and service organizations there are many non value added processes are overflowing in the system. The challenge is to identify these in office environment as these are easy to find out in manufacturing culture. Improvement can be done by looking at current processes. The three main things to consider with waste of processing are whether or not the work is actually necessary, if it adds value to the product and if there is a better method to perform the work. Value stream mapping and root cause analysis can help in reducing this waste.

Waste of Extra Processing

- Over dependencies on inspections, so no emphasis on error eliminating techniques.
- Generating unused reports, entering data into multiple information systems.
- Processing of sales invoices.
- Ordering of training materials.
- Unused applications in standardized software loads.
- Storing of materials.
- Having staff meetings to discuss a product or service.
- IT portfolio elements that are not requested.
- Printing and assembling work books for training class.

LEAN TOOLS AND TECHNIQUES

Lean thinking and its application transforms an organization towards a Lean enterprise. These principles can only work as an orientation if the tools are intended, managed and applied appropriately. The Lean and project management goals are almost the same as delivering customer values in an expected time period. To implement Lean tools in a service organization demands standardization of all processes. To standardize the service processes first divide these into two categories:

- Identify the primary processes, the processes serving an external customer.
- Identify the secondary processes supporting the primary processes.

With this categorization an estimate can be done to determine which processes are most important for the customer and why, (Pettersen, J., 2009). After this consideration from the customer's viewpoint, it should be explored which processes are vital for the organization in terms of affecting the bottom line or providing a unique value proposal. Following section describes some of the most popular Lean management tools and techniques used in service organization:

1. Value Stream Mapping

One of the most important Lean tools for getting aware of the business processes is Value Stream Mapping (VSM). The purpose of VSM is to provide optimum value to the customer through a complete value creation process with minimum waste in all the three phases:

- Design (concept to customer)
- Build (order to delivery)
- Sustain (in-use through life cycle to service).

It also transfers the current employees' perspective and let them see the current processes with a new mindset focused on value and its flow (Green Suplier Netwrok, 2014). For this VSM divides the overall work in two phases:

- In the first phase of VSM it should focus on mapping the current processes in the service organization.
- In the second phase the map of the current processes will be used as a base of improvement operations.

VSM highlights both Value Added & Non Value Added activities. It works upon end-to-end activities. Identification of waste sources becomes easy after mapping of all processes' activities and a better plan can be executed to eliminate this waste. Following are the key points of Value stream mapping:

- It provides a graphical flow of the process.
- It supports the related value stream analysis tool.
- It also provides the scope for the project by defining the current and future states of the system.
- It includes time diagrams and identifies process steps of both value added and necessary non-value added features.
- It assists a communication flow from customer to supplier and a resource flow from supplier to customer.

2. 5S

5S is an organized and basic fundamental approach for productivity, quality and safety improvement in all types of business. It is a method to make workplace a highly systematic and efficient business place. An organization needs to be structured according to 5S principles to apply 5S at micro and macro level to reduce wasted time and motion(http://leanmanufacturingtools.org/5s/)The 5S program focuses on:

- Visual workplace,
- Organization,
- Cleanliness,
- Standardization.

The expectations from 5S are improved profitability, efficiency and appropriate services. It is a system designed to make your job easier, through organization, when done correctly. For a successful application of the 5S (c.f. Table 1) in a service organization a cross-functional team of service operators should consider following:

5S Example: Shared Drive Arrangement

Problem Statement:

- Available space – 14.6 GB
- Searching for a file was tedious and time-taking

Table 1. 5s explained

	Definition	Example	Benefits
SORT (Seiri)	Arrange or prioritize as per the requirements	• Storing information on your PC • Managing your wardrobe • Managing your kitchen items • Managing your workplace	• Create more space • Eliminates clustering • Focus on important items • Quick Retrieval
SET IN ORDER (Seiton)	Have a dedicated place for everything and arrange so that it is easy to find, remove, return, and change	• Storing imp documents; Are they on a local server, your PC, in the portal, the Internet, in the 3rd drawer of your desk, your car boot • Managing your Mail box	• Quick Retrieval • Better space utilization • Reduction in safety hazards • Reduces loss and damage • Helps manage inventory
SHINE (Seisō)	Keep everything spotlessly clean	• Think about where you work – are all areas clean & tidy? • Document versioning	• Increased office morale • Pride in the workplace • Less frustration with tools • Improved quality by using the correct version of a procedure
STANDARDIZE (Seiketsu)	Determine best practices and ensure everybody does things the same best way	• Use of coding standards • Use of QMS processes	• Communicates what is expected • Exposes non-compliance • Ensures consistency • Forms the basis for continuous improvement
SUSTAIN (Shitsuke)	Continue to look for opportunities to make further improvements	• Conduct Audits • Conduct Reviews	• Prevents back sliding • Introduces a culture of discipline and teamwork • Provides the basis for further best practice initiatives

Solution Approach:

- Sort: All the files were named appropriately with version controls, month and date details and process wise (c.f. Fig. 3,4)
- Set in Order: Folders were created for frequently used files
- Shine: All the unnecessary files like old picture files, duplicate files etc., are deleted.
- Standardize: Clear instructions were given to all the members who have access to the folder about the need for maintaining the folder.
- Sustain: Constant efforts are in place to ensure that we don't fall back to the previous model thereby sustaining the improvement

Impact:

- Available space increased to 17.2 GB

3. Poka-Yoke (Mistake Proofing)

Poka Yoke, also called mistake proofing, is a simple method to prevent defects to occur in business processes. Error proofing uses some procedures to avoid defects or equipment malfunction during normal

Figure 3. Space before implementing Lean

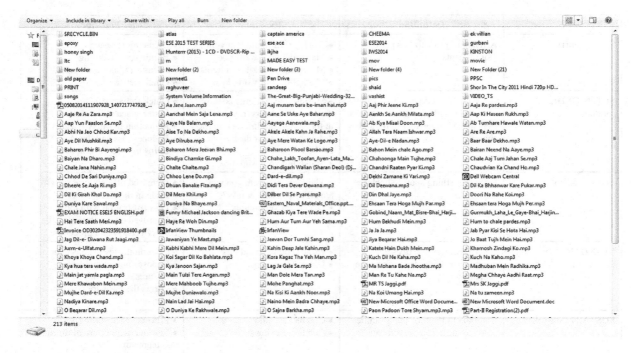

Figure 4. Space after implementing Lean

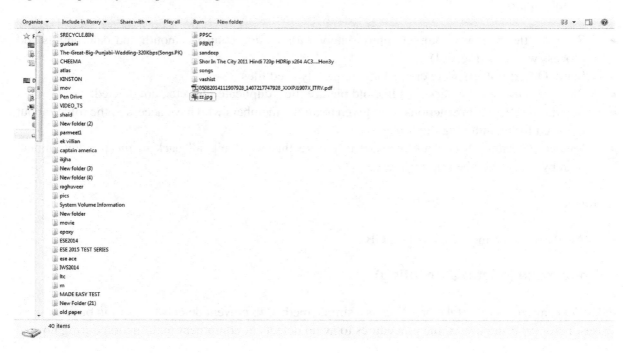

processing. An error-proofing device enforces the adequate execution of the activity by eliminating choices that could lead to incorrect actions, which may cause equipment or product damage. It works in 2 ways:

Preventive Approach:

- Implement methods that do not permit the production of a defect
- 100% elimination of defects (zero defects)

Detective Approach:

- Stop the process or signal the occurrence of a defect to the employee
- Fix the defective part when a process step is incomplete
- Stop the process when irregularities occur

Examples:

- Checklists to ensure that all fields in a claim are filled
- Drop-down lists in data entry to ensure that invalid option cannot be selected
- Automating data entry steps to avoid typo errors
- Conditional formatting in MS-Excel

4. Visual Management

Visual management is plain view of all indicators of operations (targets vs. actual) and system performance, so that the status can be understood at a glance by everyone involved. It helps us to eliminate the wasteful motion involved in searching for information or items that should be in place when required. It highlights potential abnormality and our jobs easier.

Examples:

- Control charts
- Productivity graphs
- Make the current performance visible against customer requirements.
- Dashboards published online.

5. Standardize Processes

Standardizing the processes leads to establishment of the best methods and practices to optimize performance and minimize non value added activities (i.e. waste). It also forms a baseline for future improvement activities. Documented procedures in an organization capture best practices and completion time and it must work as living documentation that is easy to change. Through standards in activities execution the Lean enterprise gains consistency in it processes.

IMPLEMENTING LEAN

Lean transformation is a change from both cultural and organizational perspectives. Implementing lean is a never ending process; this is what continuous improvement is all about. When you get one aspect of lean implementation, it can always be improved. There will always be time to go back and refine some of the processes (Womack, J. P. (2004). To implement lean a solid plan and some attainable targets are prerequisites of Lean. Don't be unrealistic with your target dates. As with any major project, people will want to see that whether you are progressing and reaching your milestones as planned. If you continually miss your deadlines due to overly aggressive target dates, you will lose support from upper management and delivery is also affected. Perform an initial lean assessment. Following are basic steps of Lean implementation:

1. **A Basic Lean Assessment:** With basic lean assessment we can identify organizational strengths and weaknesses in the various projects. It determines up to what extent organization is Lean in different areas and projects. This assessment can be done by some senior person in the organization who has already worked on lean projects or a consultant with Lean experience can be hired to conduct this. Financial and operational analysis will also be the part of this assessment.
2. **Tracking of Metrics:** After the lean assessment now the question comes how we will track the progress of lean implementation on daily basis. For this we need to develop a set of metrics which track the everyday progress and status that where we stand till the date in lean implementation and transformation. These metrics must be apparent and accessible to everyone in the project premises. It is important to select a reasonably small number of metrics and post them.
3. **Develop a Short Term thorough Execution Plan and a Long Term Plan:** From the lean assessment and metrics selected we can develop two types of lean implementation plans on the basis of timeline. One a short term plan of 6 months to 1 year and a long term plan for three to five years. But still at organization level Lean implementation time deadly depends on the number of resources of the project. It should include goals and milestones in the specified duration.
4. **Create an Appropriate Training Plan:** The training plan must be concur with the implementation plans and steps. When a new resource joins he can able to grasp the progress of the lean thoroughly. Training can be provided parallel while implementing Lean to do it in perfect manner. Some template documents also can be shown to the trainees to make the things practically clear. Training material should be precise and clear from the aspect that how to prioritize different processes of an organization while implementing Lean.
5. **Develop a Communication and Performance/Reward Plan:** Communicating the plan to go lean to everyone in the organization and letting them know how this will affect them is critical to success. Part of the communication plan should include a plan to reward both teams and individuals for their successful participation in the Lean implementation.

CHALLENGES IN IMPLEMENTING LEAN

1. **Conflicts in Changing the Existing System:** Implementation of Lean IT stipulates organizational, operational and behavioral changes to staff. This can lead to be met with resistance throughout

the organization. Whether driven by a fear of job losses, a belief that existing work practices are superior, or some other concern, such changes may encounter resistance.

2. **Value-Stream Visualization:** As Lean IT is derived from lean manufacturing so various basic things are articulated from the perspective of Lean manufacturing. Lean IT is often dependent on value streams that are digital and fuzzy, rather than physical and tangible as of manufacturing. This makes it difficult to visualize IT value streams and apply Lean IT.

3. **Fragmented IT Departments:** IT organizations are usually managed in a series of operational or technology techniques, each with its own management tools and methods to address particular aspect of waste. Sadly, fragmented efforts at Lean IT contribute little benefit because they lack the integration necessary to manage cumulative waste across the value chain.

4. **Integration of Lean Production and Lean Consumption:** As above mentioned due to issue of fragmented IT departments there is a lack of integration across the entire supply chain, including business partners as well as consumers. To overcome from this a new technique called lean consumption is proposed and it treats as a complement to lean production. In this regard, the processes of prerequisite and utilization are tightly integrated and efficient to minimize total cost and waste and to create new sources of value.

RELATION BETWEEN LEAN AND SIX SIGMA

Both the Lean and Six Sigma have the same objectives. But the way an organization achieve the same goal is different. Basically these both methodologies apply different ways to find out the root causes of waste. Lean and Six Sigma enable and provide the right tools, the right projects, and the right processes to drive sustainable breakthrough improvements resulting in improved quality, lower costs, improved dashboard metrics, and culture change. In Lean methodology Improvement teams focused on dramatically improving process speed and the elimination of the deadly wastes. In Six Sigma breakthrough process Improvement teams focus on eliminating chronic problems and reducing variation in processes.

In an organization Lean takes things from the cultural perspective as well by its mantra of "doing things better" (Villanova University, 2014), Lean intends at continuous improvement across the entire value-stream of operations by encouraging and empowering the entire workforce to identify and eliminate waste in their sphere of activity. It is an on-going process embedded to operations of the company, and requires adoption by the entire employees and in all aspects of the operations of company for effectiveness.

The biggest strength of Lean is its fast implementation. This results both immediate and long term benefits to the organization. Immediate benefits are related to productivity, client lead times and error reduction. Long-term benefits comprise improvements to staff morale, financial performance and customer satisfaction.

On the other hand Six Sigma is a comprehensive methodology that aims to eliminate variations in a specific project or area of operations, and the results remain confined to such specific area instead of permeating to the entire organization. Its goals vary for each employee based on their level in the hierarchy of an organization. For example for a statistical engineer in manufacturing, it can be a simple production quality metric, but to a CEO of an organization or for customer service employee, it might represent the corporate culture. The implementation of Six Sigma rests on a dedicated enhancement team divided into hierarchies based on a belt accreditation system. The team leverages advanced statistical

Table 2. Comparing Lean and Six Sigma

	Lean	Six Sigma
Goal	Create flow and eliminate waste	Improve process capability and reduce variation
Approach	Teaching principles and "cookbook style" implementation based on best practice	Teaching a generic problem solving approach relying on statistics
Length of Projects	2 weeks – 2 months	2 months – 6 months
Training	½ day- 1day training	1 day – 15 days trainings
Focus Area	• Lean focuses on eliminating waste in a process to improve Speed & reduce effort to deliver same Value. • It is Flow focused.	• Six Sigma focuses on reducing Variance in the process to improve Process Capability • It is problem focused.
Theory	Remove waste	Reduce variation
Steps to Apply on a Project	• Identify Value • Identify Stream • Flow • Pull • Perfection	• Define • Measure • Analyze • Improve • Control

techniques such as pareto charts and root cause analysis to reach quantified value targets In short Its a quality improvement methodology that provides a framework for a company to train its employees in key performance areas, shape strategy, align its services with customer needs, and to measure and improve the effectiveness of business processes. Table 2 shows the basic differences between Lean and Six Sigma.

INTEGRATION OF LEAN AND SIX SIGMA

After discussing about Lean and Six Sigma individually now we explore Lean Six Sigma and how it is replacing both. To get the quality products today many organizations are moving towards the combination of both Lean and Six sigma. This integrated term is called Lean Six Sigma (LSS) and it tries to reap the advantages of both methodologies and minimize the weaknesses. Roy, S., (2014) Many organizations that emphasis on quality programmes within a company now prefer to use Lean Six Sigma rather than just one or the other methodology to get better results out of the business.

All companies and organizations must have the following basic characteristics of their processes:

- Quicker and receptive to customers.
- Accomplish Six Sigma competency.
- Manage at global rates.

If an organization applies the combination of Six Sigma and Lean; it can accomplish all three goals in less time as well. In this integration lean methodology is used to identify and remove non-value adding activities within processes, and after it Six Sigma is applied to identify and eliminate process variation. Lean Six Sigma builds a value stream map of the process by categorize value add and non-value add costs, and captures the Voice of the customer to define the criticality of quality issues to the customer. Projects within the process are then prioritized based on the delay time they inject. With this prioritization process the activities are divided to be handled by Six Sigma tools or Lean Tools.

Implementation of Lean Six Sigma has a large impact on the existing culture of an organization. Improvement proposals can be chosen using a top down or bottom up approach, either way has its advantages and limitations. Whichever is chosen, it is essential for management to communicate clearly with the improvement specialists in order to line up them with the organization's policies and goals. A basic training must be given to all the employees as the prerequisites of Lean Six Sigma regarding problem recognition and to tackle with different requirements of the customer. In addition to it some resources can be trained with improvement specialist's specific training regarding the methods and tools of Lean Six Sigma. For effective implementation of Lean Six Sigma throughout all the levels of organization worker motivation is also one of the factors.

Following are the key Characteristics of combining these two methodologies:

- Both methods take emphasis on customer perspectives and can support each other to achieve a high level of customer focus that delivers value to both the customer and the organization
- An improved team
- A comprehensive tool set to increase the speed and effectiveness of all the process
- Customer retention and loyalty.
- Waste creates an unnecessary cost. By targeting waste directly Lean eliminates waste more effectively.
- All types and sizes of problems can be brought to limelight; root causes are identified; and the problems are solved in an effective and efficient manner.
- Increased revenue
- Reduced costs
- Waste elimination, error elimination and a customer focus will become the vital part of an organization's culture.
- Management can take decisions based on data and facts
- Proper use of human resources as cross functional teamwork is the demand of LSS.

A CASE STUDY

Challenge

In the IT department of a major Health Product company XYZ two-thirds of the projects deal in application production support. 24X7 support is required in this type of work environment. This support can be tool based or manually done by human resources. The basic challenges/questions while working for Support Projects are.

- Is there any tool installed to check if all the applications are up and working.
- Is checking process runs after some intervals?
- What is the priority of that error (in how much time it will be resolved)?
- To which team error belongs?
- What reports need to retrieve from the systems to deal with the problem?
- What result documents need to share with customer or third party people?
- What types of changes are required to resolve the issue like code enhancement or with existing database?

If processes are not managed or pre-determined in this type of environment the human resources were constantly abstracted from high-value preventative work to deal with urgent requests, resulting in a constantly growing backlog.

As far as internal customers were concerned, the entire change-request process appeared mournfully incompetent. The IT support function appeared to be poor value for money and far from transparent. With this type of working style the main problem is Staff morale remains low. "It is often the storm, but we never get the calm," said one IT manager.

Discovery

In the first phase of the work, team conducted a lean analytics to understand the performance of the IT support, monitoring functions and also tried to find how much Lean is the organization. In the result of these analyses it was found that exchange of best practices across the group was almost missing, and interaction with outside IT departments was cumbersome as if some problem was found then to which department it must go to find out the solution was totally disappeared in the system. Up to 15 percent of time was spent on value-adding activities rest all the time went in managing the request from customers. Sometime it takes more than month to resolve an issue. The situation was flawed and destructive which leads to loss of organization's loyal customers.

From this situation it was cleared that a just-in-time lean approach would be more accurate and effective, and if it were implemented correctly, the whole IT maintenance team would feel ownership of the new process.

As part of the transformation, the Lean Certified and Quality department people worked with the IT Support team to determine the steps to resolve a problem and to remove the waste / non value added activities. First of all a sequence of steps is made to tackle the request from the customer end. A proper documentation is also done from the future perspective. Following are some steps:

- As per the Service level Agreement (SLA) priority of request is determined. It can be P1, P2, and P3 etc. On the basis of this priority the completion time is calculated. SLA is an agreement document between the development team and customer which defines some basics of the deal like time frame, SMEs.
- Template and standard documents for different tools were created. It was really helpful to gather requirements from the customer. These vary according to tool.
- A lean whiteboard was introduced, enabling best-practice sharing and making capacity and achievements transparent for the whole team. The board clarified ownership of any given request and was used to check on estimated time to complete vs. time taken.
- Vital Business functionalities are identified on basis of which priority and completion time was decided.
- If customer wants to resolve an issue with an immediate action then a meeting (conference call) is arranged. Customer, Support team and the development team of the application will be the part of that call.
- Knowledge Transfer (KT Docs) documents were generated to handle all type of request by using different tools. So resources can refer to these documents to find out the solution.
- Some technical and domain based trainings are provided to the resources.

- This process encouraged best-practice sharing and built commitment from the whole team to stick to the agreed timeframes.
- Another part of the solution was a major shift in how staff capacity was used. Rather than turning to new projects when they had time, staff instead helped their colleagues complete change requests already underway.

As with all lean conversion, these process improvements alone were not sufficient. Moving forward with this culture of continuous improvement, managers were trained to see themselves as coaches.

Impact

After a great effort of 2 to 2.5 months a managed working environment is there in which resources can deal with customer request and prioritize them. The new processes and more collegial way of working gives free time to the staff. So they start to work on preventative methodologies or working on tools so that some alarm emails can directly go to the associated teams whom application is down for that time period. When some new resource joins the team KT documents helps him to work upon tools and to handle the issues. This saved the time of senior resource and cut the cost of company to train the resources. Almost half of the time saved came from standardizing operations and sharing best practices. The rest came from better planning, better use of management time, and other adjustments to the entire process. It ultimately leads to the satisfied customer and confident resources.

CONCLUSION

Implementing Lean in IT is not about to develop a tool or technique to wok upon, it is all about the processes and procedures used in any project. Lean requires a full framework with domain experts and process optimization experts. Domain experts understand and can develop ideas for how to eradicate waste and process optimization experts can analyze work, understand cost-benefits and can plan and execute the proposed improvements. Lean implementation in IT and Services industries starts with understanding what assets an organization has and how they are used. For the majority organizations, usage will be measured on a cost and value basis, but they should measure anything that is meaningful to the organization. The objective of lean is to eliminate waste and to make IT as efficient as possible, but efficiency is only one dimension that organizations have to consider, there is also risk and sustainability, which ensures that IT services will be delivered to match the organization's future demands and customer satisfaction.

REFERENCES

Aitken, A. (2014). *Lean: Concepts and Realities*. Lanner Group. Retrieved on 18.09.2014 from http://www.lanner.com/en/pdf/lean_and_lanner.pdf

FDRsafty. (2014). *Seven forms of Waste*. Retrieved on 21.11.2014 from http://www.fdrsafety.com/LS-7FormsOfWaste.pdf

Green Suplier Netwrok. (2014). *Lean and clean value stream mapping*. Retrieved on 10.06.2014 from http://gsn.nist.gov/pubs/VSM.pdf

Infosys Lodestone. (2014). *Using Lean IT to do more with less*. Retrieved on 11.11.2014 from http://www.lodestonemc.com/files/pdf/white%20papers/WP_LeanIT_web_271112.pdf

Lean Manufacturing Junction. (2014).*Key Lean Manufacturing Principle*. Retrieved on 15.10.2014 from http://www.lean-manufacturing-junction.com/lean-manufacturing-principles.html

Pettersen, J. (2009). Defining lean production: Some conceptual and practical issues. *The TQM Journal, 21*(2), 127–142. doi:10.1108/17542730910938137

Roy, S. (2014). *5 Lean Tools and Principles to Integrate into Six Sigma*. Retrieved on 16.10.2014 from http://www.isixsigma.com/methodology/lean-methodology/5-lean-tools-and-principles-integrate-six-sigma/

Villanova University. (2014). *Six Sigma vs. Lean Six Sigma*. Retrived on 12.10.2014 from http://www.villanovau.com/resources/six-sigma/six-sigma-vs-lean-six-sigma/

Wolak, R., Kalafatis, S., & Harris, P. (1998). An investigation into four characteristics of services. *Journal of Empirical Generalisations in Marketing Science, 3*(2), 22–43.

Womack, J. (2005). *A Lean Walk Through History*. Saatavissa. Retrieved from http://www. superfactory. com/articles/featured/2005/pdf/0501-womack-lean-walkhistory. pdf

Womack, J. P. (2004). *An action plan for Lean services*. Amsterdam: Lean Service Summit.

Womack, J. P., & Jones, D. T. (2010). *Lean thinking: Banish waste and create wealth in your corporation*. Simon and Schuster.

KEY TERMS AND DEFINITIONS

5S: It is a basic fundamental, systematic approach for productivity, quality and safety improvement in all types of business.

Benched Applications: Applications which are just proposed. But no planning is done to develop these. If the number of these applications increases it become an inventory waste at industry level.

JIT Production: It refers to the production of goods to meet customer demand exactly in time, quality and quantity.

Lean Production: It is a systematic methodology used to eliminate various types of wastes within manufacturing Process.

Poke Yoke: It is a mistake proofing mechanism designed to improve quality while reducing cost.

Six Sigma: It can be defined as set of techniques and tools used in process improvement. It consists of data driven methods for achieving near perfect quality.

Waste: It can be anything that does not contribute to the value of product or Service that is being provided to customer.

Chapter 5
The Role of Business Process Reengineering in the Modern Business World

Kijpokin Kasemsap
Suan Sunandha Rajabhat University, Thailand

ABSTRACT

This chapter reveals the role of business process reengineering (BPR) in the modern business world, thus illustrating the theoretical and practical concept of BPR, the applications of BPR, the drivers of BRR (in terms of internal drivers and external drivers), the critical success factors of BPR (i.e., egalitarian leadership, collaborative working environment, top management commitment, supportive management, information technology, change management, project management, and cross-functional coordination), the implementation of BPR, and BPR software tools. BPR is a systematic approach to helping an organization analyze and improve its processes in digital age. BPR is a continuum of change initiatives in order to deliver better business performance standards through establishing sustainable process capability in modern organizations. BPR has become a popular tool to dealing with rapid technological and business change in the global competitive environment. Applying BPR will greatly improve business performance and reach business goals in global business.

INTRODUCTION

As the basis of competition in modern business, many organizations consider BPR project, which lead to changes from cost and quality to flexibility and responsiveness (Darmani & Hanafizadeh, 2013). Organizations are different in design compared to some years back (Sungau, Ndunguru, & Kimeme, 2013). Business processes are considered as critical corporate assets (Seethamraju, 2012). BPR is a common practice for a continuous improvement of the organization and the operations of an enterprise (De Nicola, Missikoff, & Smith, 2012).

BPR projects force companies to follow a sequential methodology for changing and implementing new processes in modern organizations (Guimaraes & Paranjape, 2013). BPR targets to achieve quantum improvements by rethinking and redesigning the way that business processes are carried out with the

DOI: 10.4018/978-1-4666-8510-9.ch005

help of information technology (IT) as the primary facilitator (Jain, Chandrasekaran, & Gunasekaran, 2010). Pérez-Castillo et al. (2012) stated that business processes have become one of the key assets of organization, since these processes allow them to discover and control what occurs in their environments, with information systems automating most of an organization's processes.

The strength of this chapter is on the thorough literature consolidation of BPR in modern organizations. The extant literature of BPR in modern organizations provides a contribution to practitioners and researchers by describing a comprehensive view of the functional applications of BPR in modern organizations to appeal to different segments of BPR in modern organizations in order to maximize the business impact of BPR in the modern business world.

BACKGROUND

BPR has been studied since the 1990s (Davenport & Short, 1990; Hammer, 1990), and continues to be one of the top five management aspects for IT executives (Luftman & Ben-Zvi, 2009; Luftman & Zadeh, 2011). Hammer (1990) introduced the concept of reengineering as a radical redesign of business processes to achieve dramatic improvements on critical measures of performance. Davenport and Short (1990) defined BPR as analyzing and designing work flows and processes within and between organizations. Davenport (1993) changed the BPR definition to a procedure which interferes with organizational boundaries.

Talwar (1993) defined BPR as a procedure in which organizational value is created and delivered by focusing on reconsideration and concentration of business structures, processes, methods of working, management systems and external relationships. BPR became as popular as in mid-1990s (Rigby & Bilodeau, 2005). BPR involves business process-based thinking and innovation, fundamental rethinking, radical redesign, dramatic improvement, and technology enablement (Hammer & Champy, 1993) have largely been adopted by the private sector and remain to be still valid (Harmon, 2010). Various techniques and tools have been exploited to speed up and enhance the process (Chan & Spedding, 2003; MacIntosh, 2003). Rethinking and redesigning business processes tend to obtain dramatic and sustainable improvements (Revere, 2004).

ROLE OF BUSINESS PROCESS REENGINEERING IN THE MODERN BUSINESS WORLD

This section illustrates the theoretical and practical concept of BPR, the applications of BPR, the drivers of BRR (in terms of internal drivers and external drivers), the critical success factors of BPR (i.e., egalitarian leadership, collaborative working environment, top management commitment, supportive management, IT, change management, project management, and cross-functional coordination), the implementation of BPR, and BPR software tools.

Concept of Business Process Reengineering

In a global economy that competes on knowledge and time, organizations have been embarking on BPR as a way of removing inefficiencies or sharpening their strategic perspectives (Sia & Neo, 2008).

Organizations may change from time to time due to changes in technology and customers' demands (Banham, 2010; Hesson, 2007). The fundamental philosophy of BPR is an innovative approach to change management, resulting in best practices (Yung & Chan, 2003). BPR is primarily recognized because of its resonance with the enterprise culture (Green, 2011). BPR has been viewed as a cross-functional and enterprise-wide effort (Davenport, 1993; Hammer & Champy, 1993).

Quality continues to be one of the top ranking strategic issues in all major organizations (Moonsamy & Singh, 2014). Quality is critical to achieving long-term competitive advantages (Zhang & Xia, 2013). BPR integrates methods from total quality management (TQM), technology and innovation management, strategic planning, systems engineering, and organizational design (Winter, 2002). TQM has been recognized as a successful management philosophy (Sarathy, 2013) for improving customer satisfaction and organizational performance (Asif, Awan, Khan, & Ahmad, 2013). Executives should focus their efforts on implementing TQM practices for building competitive knowledge sharing competencies (Ooi, Cheah, Lin, & Teh, 2012).

Regarding TQM, competitive capabilities have been defined as a manufacturing plant's actual performance related to its competitors with the most commonly investigated capabilities being quality, delivery, flexibility, and cost (Schoenherr, Power, Narasimhan, & Samson, 2012). TQM is positively related to performance for cost leaders (Zatzick, Moliterno, & Fang, 2012). Organizational cultural values influence the success of quality initiatives (Kull, Narasimhan, & Schroeder, 2012). The management accounting practice of TQM positively impacts on the financial performance of small and medium enterprises (SMEs) (Kober, Subraamanniam, & Watson, 2012).

BPR is a management tool, in which business processes are examined and redesigned to improve cost efficiency and service effectiveness (Lindsay, Downs, & Lunn, 2003). Enterprises need to adopt both linear and non-linear improvement schemes continuously to enhance their quality, flexibility and agility (Ng, Ip, & Lee, 1999). In order to accelerate the effectiveness and efficiency of the changes, the best of positioning, and continuous learning and improvement should be employed with BPR (Altinkemer, Chaturvedi, & Kondareddy, 1999; Bae, Jeong, Seo, Kim, & Kang, 1999).

Business processes constitute a significant portion of organizational costs, and managing business processes offers significant opportunities for improving market share, managerial decision making, and performance (Seethamraju, 2012). To remain competitive in today's global economy, there is an urgent need to rethink and transform the existing business processes for improved quality and efficiency, reduced costs, and increased profitability (Jain et al., 2010). The perspective of BPR systems focuses on looking at a set of problems as a whole and the context that creates the holistic view rather than looking at a set of problems as individually isolated events (Jain, Erol, & Chandrasekaran, 2007).

Business processes are dynamic and unpredictable (Verginadis & Mentzas, 2008). BPR is a new concept, used to describe the process redesign (Heygate, 1993; Rigby, 1993), process innovation (Davenport, 1993), business process redesign (Davenport & Short, 1990), organizational reengineering (Lowenthal, 1994), breakpoint business process redesign (Johansson, McHugh, Pendlebury, & Wheeler, 1993), and business restructuring (Talwar, 1993). BPR involves critical changes in many parts in the organization, such as adoption of technologies, organizational structures, job designs, and human resources (Kamhawi, 2008). Organizations should work hard to improve their business processes in order to improve or maintain their services and to retain customers (Sungau et al., 2013).

The advancement in new technology forces organizations to modernize their processes, thus promoting their competitive advantages (Laudon & Laudon, 2006). Customers' demands cause organization to change to gain sustainable competitive advantage. Organizational failure to meet customers' demand

and/or expectations forces customers to shift to other service providers (Heizer & Render, 2011). While technological advancement leads to competitive global business, awareness and education on consumerism leads to complexity of customers' tastes. Organizations are urged to improve their business processes in order to cope with business competition while meeting customers' demands, need, and desire (Heizer & Render, 2011; Laudon & Laudon, 2006).

BPR is a mature concept, which has evolved over a period of time (Jain, Gunasekaran, & Chandrasekaran, 2009). Most organizations that have undertaken BPR can improve their business processes performance (Kassahun & Molla, 2013). BPR is enabled by business process modeling (Groznik & Maslaric, 2012). BPR is a meaningful device for organizations that seek improvement in current organizational performance (Adeyemi & Aremu, 2008).

Development of inter-organizational relationships and significant increases in the business integration has made BPR even more important (Abdolvand, Albadvi, & Ferdowsi, 2008). BPR literature advances a comprehensive view encompassing both the radical and incremental process improvement approaches (Hammer, 2010). The utilization of BPR in improving productivity and lowering operational cost is on the rise for modern organizations (Adeyemi & Aremu, 2008; Xiaoli, 2011).

BPR is an organizational initiative to fundamentally re-examine and redesign business processes with the objectives of achieving competitive breakthrough in quality, responsiveness, cost, satisfaction and other critical process performance measures (Doomun & Jungum, 2008). BPR can be implemented at different scopes and levels. These range from narrow processes to changes that go beyond the organization's boundaries concerning business partners, customers and suppliers. Many authors propose different models to explain the degree and scope of BPR-related organizational change (Andreu, Ricart, & Valor, 1997; Venkatraman, 1994).

BPR is considered as a new concept for business improvement, its methods and approaches are still developing. As the application of BPR concepts can take different forms, methodologies that have been developed are often distinct from each other, as emphasis varies from one BPR project to another. Several approaches and methodologies have been introduced by a number of researchers (Kettinger, Teng, & Guha, 1997; Yu & Wright, 1997). BPR focuses on the key concept of business process rather than on function, product or service. Davenport and Short (1990) defined a business process as a set of logically-related tasks performed to achieve a business outcome.

Business process as a set of integrated and coordinated activities required for producing products or offering services (Hinterhuber, 1995). Business process is a distinguished characteristic among organizations (Venkatraman, 1994), and is a significant factor leading to competitive edge (Hinterhuber, 1995). The elimination of functional bias can be done by adopting process orientation to gain substantial business improvement (Andreu et al., 1997).

BPR emerges as a high priority area of interest in modern business (Al-Mashari & Zairi, 2000). BPR is the technique that can be used to perfect the business processes (Sungau et al., 2013). BPR involves discovering how business processes currently operates, how to redesign these processes to eliminate the wasted or redundant effort and improve efficiency and how to implement the process change in order to gain competitiveness. The improved business processes facilitated organizations to minimize the time taken to service the customers (Heizer & Render, 2011; Slack, Chambers, & Johnston, 2007). BPR enables the service organization to improve its service delivering speed (Gunasekaran, Chung, & Kan, 2000).

Cypress (1994) categorized BPR efforts into two generations. The first generation is customer value-oriented, where redesign covers a narrow business process, and the business comprises a number of processes which bring value to customers. The second generation is shareholder value-oriented, and the redesign covers an enterprise-wide process. Cypress (1994) identified four enterprise-wide processes (i.e., innovation, social, technical and enabling processes) to represent the second generation. Davidson (1993) defined levels of change for BPR projects as comprising three phases. The first automates processes to achieve a level of excellence in operations, the second extends services and products offered to customers by exploiting capabilities that phase one brings about, and the third introduces new business units to offer new products or services (Davidson, 1993).

Andreu et al. (1997) identified the three levels (i.e., elementary tasks, sub-processes, and business processes) where improvement efforts can take place. Venkatraman (1994) developed a complex model that demonstrates relationships between IT developments and business processes. The model represents a hierarchy of five levels of IT-induced business transformation (i.e., localized exploitation, internal integration, business process redesign, business network redesign, and business scope redefinition). These five levels describe the degree of business transformation and the benefits introduced by a more integrated use of IT. The higher levels of business transformation offer greater benefits but require more corresponding change in organizational structure and in the role that IT has to play within the business process (Venkatraman, 1994).

Applications of Business Process Reengineering

Reengineering project in the business process has been introduced as a managerial tool of today to accomplish the effectiveness, responsiveness and competition of processes (MacIntosh, 2003; Terziovski, Fitzpatrick, & O'Neill, 2003). Governments of both the developed and developing economy have embraced BPR as an essential reform tool to meet the ever increasing demands for efficient, transparent and effective public service delivery (Ongaro, 2004). There are many viewpoints of BPR adoption and implementation in the public sector (Sia & Neo, 2008) and public sector of developing economies (Debela, 2010; Tarokh, Sharifi, & Nazemi, 2008).

The value of BPR can be viewed at both process such as cost and time reduction (Grover, Jeong, Kettinger, & Teng, 1995), and overall organizational performance such as productivity, profitability and market advantages levels (Ozcelik, 2009). BPR plays important roles of making continuity of progression of work activities (Debela, 2010; Shin & Jemella, 2002), automating business processes (Hammer, 1990; Laudon & Laudon, 2006), keeping the sections with high to-from movement close (Al-Mashari, Irani, & Zairi, 2001; Magutu, Nyamwange, & Kaptoge, 2010), and facilitating the communication between employees or employees and customers (Al-Mashari et al., 2001; Attaran, 2004; He, 2005).

A business process has structure, inputs, outputs, customers (internal and external) and owners (Hinterhuber, 1995), and is built up by integrating fragmented functions that contribute to its operations and internal and external flows (Hammer, 1990). BPR involves radical and fundamental changes, and it evolves from the need to recognize that the long-established ways of doing business are designed for customers, services, and products that are different in the competitive environment (Al-Mashari & Zairi, 2000). There has been a shift in organizational focus toward improving quality, the customer, and innovation, rather than emphasizing control and cost cutting (Hammer, 1990).

Organizations are moving to manage the old business processes by introducing new structures and procedures, and are including new ways of doing business. IT is considered as a major tool and a fundamental enabler of BPR efforts (Grover, Teng, & Fiedler, 1993). IT reshapes business processes in that it has the potential to facilitate the flow of information between globally-distributed processes, and ensures the availability of consistent information across the business (Tapscott & Caston, 1993). Davenport and

Short (1990) defined the relationship between IT capabilities and BPR as a periodic loop within which both the IT components and BPR continually refine each other. In addition, the greatest advantage resulting from IT can be attained by exploiting its capabilities to create new business processes, rather than only automating outdated functions (Hammer, 1990).

Management techniques related to the principles of the quality, such as TQM, are often confused with BPR. Several studies have attempted to distinguish the two practices in terms of the differences and similarities between them (Green & Wayhan, 1996; Zairi & Sinclair, 1995). TQM and BPR share common features, such as the principle of process (Green & Wayhan, 1996; Zairi & Sinclair, 1995), the requirement for organizational and cultural change (Zairi & Sinclair, 1995), the use of benchmarking (Zairi & Sinclair, 1995), the focus on customer needs (Green & Wayhan, 1996), the importance of process measurement (Zairi & Sinclair, 1995), and their purpose of improving business performance for competitive gains (Zairi & Sinclair, 1995).

TQM practices are related to better quality performance (Kasemsap, 2015a). While TQM is incremental, evolutionary and continuous in nature, BPR is radical and revolutionary as a one-time approach (Green & Wayhan, 1996; Zairi & Sinclair, 1995). TQM addresses narrow processes within departments; BPR is wider in scope and addresses one or more processes that cross multiple functions (Gulden & Reck, 1992; Wells, O'Connell, & Hochman, 1993). Quality is commonly applied to products and processes (Melé, 2014). While quality is desired in BPR projects, benefits such as quick cost and cycle-time reduction are the major targets (Kelada, 1994). While IT has a major role in BPR, and understanding its potential and using it is a major ingredient of BPR projects, its role is less important in TQM (Wells et al., 1993).

Drivers of Business Process Reengineering

BPR is motivated by external drivers, internal drivers, or both (Al-Mashari & Zairi, 2000). External drivers are related mainly to the increased level of competition, the changes in customers' needs, IT changes, and changes in regulations (Grover et al., 1993). Internal drivers are mainly related to changes in both organizational strategies and structures. The applications of external drivers and internal drivers are described.

External Drivers of BPR

The increasing level of competition in the global market has emphasized the need for organizational innovation to cope with global standards of products and services. Increasing knowledge and co-ordination of the organization's processes that cross its distributed functions become the main desire of many organizations seeking competitive advantage (Ovenden, 1994). BPR is considered as a tool to improve their business performance and lead them to a competitive position (Schnitt, 1993). Ovenden (1994) stated that BPR is driven by the never-ending needs of customers to look for better services and products.

Technology is used to develop databases of information systems (Grachev, Esin, Polukhina, & Rassomakhin, 2014). The importance of IT increases as it becomes involved in each task in modern business. This is a result of its growing ability to bring new business opportunities, and facilitate the development of the new organizational forms and structures needed to meet the continuously emerging changes in business imperatives. Rapid changes in IT development force organizations to be updated in their use of advanced technologies regarding the delivery of speedy and high-quality information, as well as facilitating greater degrees of communication and integration across business units and external partners (Grover et al., 1993).

Internal Drivers of BPR

Many organizational strategic and structural changes are centered on IT-enabled BPR. Changes in organizational strategy may involve some BPR efforts to bring about the new business desires. Changes in organizational structure may necessitate a change in underlying business processes as IT infrastructure is adjusted to enable such a change. One example of internal factors which motivate the launching of BPR efforts is the need for simplification to achieve better levels of performance, and to highlight inefficiencies which have increased as a result of outmoded ways of conducting business and accumulating complexities (Keen, 1991). Changes of capability in terms of processes, methods, skills competencies, attitudes and behaviors can be considered as internal drivers. Business transformation is a journey driven by a strategy that links short-term changes to capability in terms of processes, skills, and style, with long-term changes to manage business among its competitors and customers.

Critical Success Factors of Business Process Reengineering

Crowe et al. (2002) categorized the success factors of BPR into four groups (i.e., egalitarian leadership, collaborative working environment, top management commitment, and supportive management). The IT and change management are two more critical success factors of BPR (Guimaraes, 1999; Motwani, Subramanian, & Gopalakrishna, 2005; Terziovski et al., 2003). Project management, strategic planning for BPR projects, change management, competitive pressures, resources availability, IT capabilities, and top management support are examples of some success factors that have shown influence on success of the implementation of BPR projects (Terziovski et al., 2003; Wells, 2000).

Some critical success factors for successful implementation of BPR are teamwork and quality culture, quality management system and satisfactory rewards, effective change management, less bureaucratic and participative, IT, information system, effective project management, and adequate financial resources (Ahmad, Francis, & Zairi, 2007). Below are the details of egalitarian leadership, collaborative working environment, top management commitment, supportive management, IT, change management, project management, and cross-functional coordination.

1. Egalitarian Leadership

Motwani et al. (2005) stated that key constructs in managements are employee involvement. Top managers should drive the changes by providing vision (shared vision). Employees should become more responsive. Other members in the BPR team should understand the process. Top management should provide employees with channels of communication and improve their ability of understanding each other (Abdolvand et al., 2008). Effective communication is necessary toward better organizational decision making (Grant, 2002; Tatsiopoulos & Panayiotou, 2000).

To empower employee and cooperate in a new system, top management should establish inter- and intra-organizational confidence and trust. The chains' interactions reflect the organizational ability in adapting changes (Crowe et al., 2002). Groupware techniques significantly decrease the time required for performing the analysis phases of BPR (effective use of subordinates' idea). Involving employees and effective use of their idea enable top management to achieve optimal process operation (Maull, Tranfield, & Maull, 2003; Terziovski et al., 2003).

Egalitarian culture makes the positive changes take place with little resistance (Crowe et al., 2002). It is important to share information, democratically interact with employees, and increase confidence and creativity to make egalitarian society practically successful (Abdolvand et al., 2008).

2. Collaborative Working Environment

Cooperation is one of the critical success factors in BPR projects (Crowe et al., 2002). Employees should work together in the same organization and interact with each other in a friendly way (Tatsiopoulos & Panayiotou, 2000). In order to work in a cooperative environment, and interact in a friendly way, employees should trust each other to ensure that the top management recognizes their role (Crowe et al., 2002; Maull et al., 2003). A cooperative environment has a chance of improving performance (Green & Roseman, 2000; Marir & Mansar, 2004).

Cultural intelligence on the organizational level is an organization's capacity to reconfigure its capability to function and manage effectively in culturally diverse environments and to gain and sustain its competitive advantages (Yitmen, 2013). Working seminars and cultural training can facilitate the structural change (Abdolvand et al., 2008). Participation in high-involvement work practices is positively correlated with the promotion opportunities for individuals, especially for those in lower hierarchical levels and for the supervisors of these levels in modern organizations (Bonet, 2014).

High-performance work practices are frequently considered to have positive effects on corporate performance (Cristini, Eriksson, & Pozzoli, 2013). Business strategy and the use of other complementary human resource policies affect the dynamics of employee involvement use in the United States-based manufacturing establishments (Chi, Freeman, & Kleiner, 2011). Practical implications include the selection and training of team leaders in managerial coaching and the development of challenging projects in situations where team learning is greatly important in modern business (Hagen & Gavrilova Aguilar, 2012).

3. Top Management Commitment

A clearly defined strategic mission is necessary for reengineering (Maull et al., 2003). Strategic management is the highest level of management where top officials determine the strategic direction of the organization (Grant, 2002). Top management should have a clear knowledge about the current situation of the organization (Abdolvand et al., 2008). It is necessary to have a sufficient knowledge about the BPR projects and realistic expectation of BPR results. The process of strategic learning, through its intraorganizational elements that enable the dissemination, interpretation, and implementation of strategic knowledge, enables firms to capitalize on the benefits of both exploration and exploitation strategies (Sirén, Kohtamäki, & Kuckertz, 2012).

In order to have a successful BPR, top management should communicate with employees in order to motivate the movement, control the BPR team and users (Crowe et al., 2002). Communication is crucial to show support to the process change project and effective leadership to coordinate deployment of the resources to accomplish the strategic objectives (Smith, 2003). Communication management principles, such as stakeholder relationship management, can promote modern organizations in achieving its objectives (de Beer & Rensburg, 2011).

In strategic opportunity pursuit, decision incongruence (the gap between the decision-making rationale that an individual conveys to others and the rationale that informs his/her actual decisions) can lead to difficulties achieving the commitment necessary to grow a venture (Robert Mitchell & Shepherd, 2012). Top management's support of the corporate venture, as well as the level of initial strategic assets endowed to the venture, increases the subsequent performance of the internal corporate venture (Garrett & Neubaum, 2013). The ways managers use strategic actions to leverage resources has important influences on firms' resulting competitive advantages (Combs, Ketchen, Ireland, & Webb, 2011).

Top management team (TMT) shared leadership is recognized as an important enabler of organizational ambidexterity (Mihalache, Jansen, Van den Bosch, & Volberda, 2014). Confidence is necessary for effective TMT functioning (Clark & Maggitti, 2012). Managers with greater metacognitive experience make less erratic strategic decisions (Robert Mitchell, Shepherd, & Sharfman, 2011). Top managers' corporate governance orientation can be an important antecedent of strategic renewal and of organizational ambidexterity, both of which influence corporate longevity (Kwee, Van Den Bosch, & Volberda, 2011).

4. Supportive Management

Financial resources are important to move the initiatives, since without enough funding any efforts would end meaningless and stagnant (Ahmad, Francis, & Zairi, 2007). Budget allocations to BPR should be viewed as a long-term investment to get favorable results which would give profit to the organization (Kotnour, 2001). To make radical process change a success, the concern for people is important (Ahmad et al., 2007). Firms create such process definitions through iterative trial-and-error processes, in which experiments, environmental scanning, and administrative planning constitute key methods for uncertainty reduction (Frishammar, Lichtenthaler, & Richtnér, 2013).

Human resources play an important role in organizational process improvement (Abdolvand et al., 2008) as the essential ingredients of any human activity system (Grant, 2002). In performing reengineering, the human resources architecture should be reengineered to support information sharing and decision making (Mansar, Marir, & Reijers, 2003; Vakola & Rezgui, 2000). Employees should be assisted in the transition period to new working environment (Crowe et al., 2002). The adoption of a strategic business partner role by human resources has considerable potential to contribute to the strategic agility that firms require to globally compete (Ananthram & Nankervis, 2013). The line management development moderates the relationship between the human resources strategic role and high-performance human resource practices (Mitchell, Obeidat, & Bray, 2013).

Strategic human resource management is necessary for directors and experts in the field of human resources in order to lead their organizations toward becoming competitive in a dynamic environment (Esmaeili, 2012). Strategic human resource management literature emphasizes the potential of pay to secure strategically desirable employee outcomes for the employer (Trevor & Brown, 2014). Strategic alignment is broadly accepted as a prerequisite for a firm's success (Acur, Kandemir, & Boer, 2012). Discrepancies between the organization's intended and implemented human resources practices are essential to understanding employees' perceptions of and reactions to human resources management (Piening, Baluch, & Ridder, 2014).

Human resource management, organizational learning, knowledge management (KM) capability leads to improved organizational performance (Kasemsap, 2015b). Human resource professionals have long realized the value of learning from the experiences of other leading organizations toward taking the best practices approach to the human resource function can drive the high performance necessary to survive and thrive in a competitive market (Suttapong, Srimai, & Pitchayadol, 2014). Human resource practices and corporate ethics enhance employees' work attitudes (Valentine, Hollingworth, & Francis, 2013).

5. Information Technology

IT is widely recognized as a critical component and a natural partner of BPR, which has a continuous and important role in projects (Attaran, 2003). Khalil (1997) defined IT as an enabler for radical BPR, but it needed proper management. The role of IT is a key enabler of BPR re-emergence in modern business (Ahadi, 2004). Successful application of IT is effective in BPR success (Abdolvand et al., 2008). IT is needed to achieve the best results in BPR implementation, and its integration in processes could aid in redesign activities (Bhatt, 2000; Vakola, Rezgui, & Wood-Harper, 2000). Overlooking the role of IT can result in failure (Motwani et al., 2005; Shin & Jemella, 2002).

IT covers the areas of hardware, information system, and communication technology, which provide individuals with the required information (Al-Mashari & Zairi, 2000; Attaran, 2003). These perspectives bring effectiveness in realizing the critical success factors by pulling human, business, and organization together (Grant, 2002; Motwani et al., 2005). The aims of IT are to make open communication, share information, and create collaborative team working (Attaran, 2003; Tatsiopoulos & Panayiotou, 2000).

Regarding the IT application, utilizing data mining methods for business intelligence makes it easier for the users to promote its overall contribution to the KM process (Kasemsap, 2015c). Organizations aiming to improve business performance within enterprise architecture should create and develop IT, technical alignment, and information system capabilities (Kasemsap, 2015d). The advancement of Web technology like Web 2.0 drives many organizations to adjust their marketing strategy since it affects the way customers control the flow of information (Almunawar, Anshari, & Susanto, 2013).

Utilizing IT makes open communication and facilitates performance measurement in an accurate way (Abdolvand et al., 2008). Technology allows the rapid development of business process, thus facilitating the smooth flow of information in the digital age (Sungau et al., 2013). The high-tech IT company is characterized by a path dependency of the generative learning, which must be recognized by managers concerned with managing the entirety of service quality operations (Soltani, Chau, & Liao, 2012). Supporting information system requires both thought and action (Loonam, McDonagh, Kumar, & O'Regan, 2014).

Regarding IT, management innovation relates to the firm's organizational form, practices and processes in a way that is new to the firm and/or industry, and results in leveraging the firm's technological knowledge base and its performance in terms of innovation, productivity and competitiveness (Volberda, Van Den Bosch, & Heij, 2013).

6. Change Management

Major changes to business processes have a direct impact on processes, technology, job roles, and workplace culture. Change management is another element that has been referred to as a critical success factor for the success of BPR implementation (Tennant & Wu, 2005; Wells, 2000). The organization should know very well about how to manage the impact of change in the organization (Ahmad et al., 2007). Effective change management should consider soft issues around the human, and would avoid resistance to change among employees (Mabin, Forgeson, & Green, 2001; Moran & Brightman, 2000). Change management relates to how a manager or leader manages the potential impact of change to make people accept it in order to implement change (Ahmad et al., 2007).

Mabin et al. (2001) explained the importance of training and development in the change management to make people well equipped with all sorts of knowledge and skills, which would reduce the fear of uncertainty. Grieves (2000) stated that the right way of managing people for adapting to and adopting change will make change successful and a benefit in the long term. BPR fosters change and human being resists change (Abdolvand et al., 2008). This resistance is the most common barrier of BPR and renders success difficult (Guimaraes, 1999; Schniederjans & Kim, 2003).

Employees resist changes because of uncertain future initiated by BPR changes regarding job loss, and authority loss (Crowe et al., 2002; Palmer, 2004). BPR needs to change the culture and behavior of human in each organizational level. Regarding change management, an action plan can be extracted based on the strategy plan to specify required pre-executing phases to make an organization in accepting radical changes in organizations (Abdolvand et al., 2008). To make BPR successfully work, it must be executed by people within the organization (Campbell & Kleiner, 2001; Maull, Weaver, Childe, Smart, & Bennet, 1995).

7. Project Management

Before any BPR project can be implemented successfully, there must be a commitment to the project by the management of the organization, and strong leadership must be provided. Projects are expected to bring value to their constituents (Martinsuo & Killen, 2014). BPR projects implementations could be complicated and risky projects (Kamhawi, 2008). BPR projects require the effective arrangements for managing contributions from different functional departments, consultants, and/or even business partners. All these requirements and more magnify project management challenges for such undertakings, making them failure-prone (Al-Mashari et al., 2001; Box & Platts, 2005).

Organizations view sustainable development principles as a key tool in aligning their strategic plans with specific objectives and procedures used for managing projects (Herazo, Lizarralde, & Paquin, 2012). A project manager needs both production and product-related competence, including customers' processes in order to gain competitive advantage in modern organizations (Chronéer & Bergquist, 2012).

8. Cross-Functional Coordination

Cross-functional coordination is an important enabler for an innovative BPR environment (Malhotra, Grover, & Desilvio, 1996). This factor is especially critical in reengineering processes that cross-functional boundaries (Grover & Malhotra, 1997). An integration of cross-functions based on a process perspective is expected to increase organizational efficiency (Kamhawi, 2008). The practice of cross-functional teams facilitates the opportunity to have a more process perspective, which is parallel to the BPR concept (Ahmad et al., 2007).

Team members who are selected from each work group within the organization will have an impact on the outcome of the reengineered process according to their desired requirements The most effective BPR teams include active representatives from the following work groups: top management, business area responsible for the process being addressed, technology groups, finance, and members of all ultimate process users' groups

Implementation of Business Process Reengineering

There are various methodologies proposed for the implementation of BPR (Davenport, 1993; Kettinger et al., 1997). Radhakrishnan and Balasubramanian (2008) stated that BPR literature summarizes BPR methodologies include three main phases (i.e., pre-BPR implementation, BPR implementation and post-BPR implementation). The pre-BPR implementation phase involves envisioning (planning), initiating (establishing steering teams, select projects and teams), and diagnosing (mapping and analyzing existing processes). The BPR implementation phase involves redesigning processes and prototyping, implementing and managing the redesigned processes. The post-BPR implementation phase involves on-going activity of process adaptation, acceptance, alignment of the information system to the information needs of the redesigned business processes and the management support system (Kassahun & Molla, 2013).

Kettinger et al. (1997) developed a comprehensive stage-activity framework consisting of six stages, each stage containing a number of activities. The stages of their framework are to envision, initiate, diagnose, redesign, reconstruct and evaluate. This stage-activity framework is valuable in viewing a BPR project as a set of integrated and coordinated tasks to alter different organizational subsystems through business process change. It can be a useful starting point for those who want to establish an understanding of various alternatives to BPR project approaches.

The four major project characteristics are critical in customization (i.e., project radicalness to determine the level of emphasis on change management; structuredness of the process to determine level of emphasis on process mapping; level of customer focus to determine level of emphasis on benchmarking and understanding customer requirements; and the potential for IT enablement to determine level of emphasis on IT-related activities) (Kettinger et al., 1997). Determination of project radicalness is considered a prerequisite for assessing the three other critical factors (Al-Mashari & Zairi, 2000). Successful adoption and implementation of BPR requires organizations to develop and exploit essential skills, systems, and technologies in the three phases (Kassahun & Molla, 2013).

Organizations that manage to develop and institutionalize continuous process improvement through integrating the BPR project with a continuous process improvement program achieve better performance than others (Al-Mashari et al., 2001; Lee & Asllani, 1997). The significance of linking BPR with continuous process improvement and developing the corresponding skills, systems and technologies is recognized in public sector BPR context (Ongaro, 2004). Many researchers stated that the following items enhance the organizational value of the BPR: BPR-information system alignment (Davenport, 2008; Eardley, Shah, & Radman, 2008); building enabling IT infrastructure (Ahadi, 2004; Al-Mashari & Zairi, 1999); and an effective information system service delivery to all process owners (Attaran, 2004; Herzog, Polajnar, & Tonchia, 2007).

An organizational capability is critical for realizing organizational benefits from a BPR undertaking in order to build BPR-enabling IT infrastructure and to deliver information that meets the needs of various process owners (Abdolvand et al., 2008; Hesson, 2007). Another area of post-BPR associated skills, systems, and technologies that has BPR role relates to top-management's ability to craft a strategy that integrates and leverages the outcomes of the BPR and establish a management system and practices that nurture new organizational beliefs and business values (Sia & Neo, 2008). Pre-BPR organizational culture and management systems and practices contain beliefs and values that might no longer be appropriate for the redesigned business processes (Hammer, 2010; Linden, 1994).

During the stage of post-BPR, the top-management needs to integrate the BPR with organizational strategy, establish and deploy new process measurement and management systems that go with the re-engineered business process (Abdolvand et al., 2008), and empower process owners and process teams with knowledge, skill, and decision making power (Herzog et al., 2007; Sia & Neo, 2008). The public sector-related BPR literature realizes information system service delivery (Ranganathan & Dhaliwal, 2001) and BPR-enabling IT infrastructure (Ongaro, 2004) as critical to sustain the impact of BPR in modern business.

Business Process Reengineering Software Tools

Research efforts in the technical treatment of BPR have introduced many management tools (Mertins & Jochem, 2005); software solutions (Ha, Bae, Park, & Kang, 2006), better approaches for modeling (Clegg, 2006; Giaglis, Hlupic, de Vreede, & Verbraeck, 2005; Hwang & Yang, 2002), software design (Baldwin, Eldabi, & Paul, 2005; Mansar & Reijers, 2005), and the implementation of BPR tools (Reijers, 2006). The role of IT in BPR has drawn much attention of research (Akhavan, Jafari, & Ali-Ahmadi, 2006; Wu, 2003), from the beginning of introducing BPR as a strategic enabler of BPR projects (Davenport, 1993).

BPR software tools are used to support the techniques through a set of automated applications (Al-Mashari & Zairi, 2000). Klein (1994) stated that software tools are used more for methodological-based BPR projects than for intuitive ones. The aims of using tools in BPR projects are to improve productivity (Klein, 1994), finish projects faster (Kettinger et al., 1997), produce higher quality results, and eliminate non-value-added work. Carr and Johansson (1995) indicated that taking advantage of modern modeling and simulation tools is an element of BPR best practice.

Carr and Johansson (1995) stated that BPR tools help in providing visions as well as measuring process costs. Manganelli and Klein (1994) stated that common office tools, such as project management tools and spreadsheets, are usually enough for BPR efforts. Klein (1994) stated that BPR software tool should have specific features, such as being usable by non-technical people, enhancing the clarity of the BPR team's vision, enforcing consistency in analysis and design, permitting iterative and top-down refinement from BPR project goal to its solution, and producing an acceptable return on investment.

FUTURE RESEARCH DIRECTIONS

The strength of this chapter is on the thorough literature consolidation of BPR in modern organizations. The extant literature of BPR in modern organizations provides a contribution to practitioners and researchers by describing a comprehensive view of the functional applications of BPR in modern organizations to appeal to different segments of BPR in modern organizations in order to maximize the business impact of BPR in the modern business world. The classification of the extant literature in the domain of BPR will provide the potential opportunities for future research. Future research direction should broaden the perspectives in the implementation of BPR to be utilized in the knowledge-based organizations.

Practitioners and researchers should recognize the applicability of a more multidisciplinary approach toward research activities in implementing BPR in terms of KM-related variables (i.e., knowledge-sharing behavior, knowledge creation, organizational learning, learning orientation, and motivation to learn). It will be useful to bring additional disciplines together (i.e., strategic management, marketing, finance, and human resources) to support a more holistic examination of BPR in order to combine or transfer existing theories and approaches to inquiry in this area. An examination of linkages between BPR and information architecture would seem to be viable for future research efforts.

CONCLUSION

This chapter revealed the role of BPR in the modern business world, thus illustrating the theoretical and practical concept of BPR, the applications of BPR, the drivers of BRR (in terms of internal drivers and external drivers), the critical success factors of BPR (i.e., egalitarian leadership, collaborative working environment, top management commitment, supportive management, IT, change management, project management, and cross-functional coordination), the implementation of BPR, and BPR software tools. This chapter also provided a comprehensive review of literature, bringing together different groups of thought on various BPR aspects.

BPR is an important business approach that is practically used for transforming organizations in modern business. BPR becomes embedded in the strategic planning of organizational departments and approaches. When met with high levels of competition and pressures from the industry, most organizations turn to radical approaches for transforming themselves to help gain sustainable competitive advantage in the global marketplace by performing better internally through saving organizational resources and through becoming functionally adept in responding to these challenges from the modern business world. Concerning the development of BPR, efforts may be directed to speeding-up the cycle time for BPR by focusing on rapid implementation of improvements in the context of longer-term and more radical process change.

The practices of BPR are described in terms of scope, development, application, and integration. Regarding BPR, a shift is likely to be toward changes in the business network for an organization rather than toward internal business processes. Process management is likely to be institutionalized in other management domains like performance measurement, information architecture, enterprise architecture, and organizational structure. BPR may be combined with incremental process changes within the same initiatives or integrated into process management by pulling tools from a wide variety of business process change approaches to build hybrid process design and implementation techniques.

The fulfillment of BPR is necessary for modern organizations that seek to serve suppliers and customers, increase business performance, strengthen competitiveness, and achieve continuous success in the modern business world. Therefore, it is vital for modern organizations to explore their BPR applications, promote a strategic plan to systematically evaluate their practical advancements, and urgently respond to the BPR needs of organizational members in modern organizations. Applying BPR will effectively enhance business performance and gain sustainable competitive advantage in the digital age.

REFERENCES

Abdolvand, N., Albadvi, A., & Ferdowsi, Z. (2008). Assessing readiness for business process reengineering. *Business Process Management Journal*, *14*(4), 497–511. doi:10.1108/14637150810888046

Acur, N., Kandemir, D., & Boer, H. (2012). Strategic alignment and new product development: Drivers and performance effects. *Journal of Product Innovation Management*, *29*(2), 304–318. doi:10.1111/j.1540-5885.2011.00897.x

Adeyemi, S., & Aremu, M. A. (2008). Impact assessment of business process reengineering on organizational performance. *European Journal of Soil Science*, *7*(1), 115–125.

Ahadi, H. (2004). An examination of the role of organizational enablers in business process reengineering and the impact of information technology. *Information Resources Management Journal*, *17*(4), 1–19. doi:10.4018/irmj.2004100101

Ahmad, H., Francis, A., & Zairi, M. (2007). Business process reengineering: Critical success factors in higher education. *Business Process Management Journal*, *13*(3), 451–469. doi:10.1108/14637150710752344

Akhavan, P., Jafari, M., & Ali-Ahmadi, A. R. (2006). Exploring the interdependency between reengineering and information technology by developing a conceptual model. *Business Process Management Journal*, *12*(4), 517–534. doi:10.1108/14637150610678104

Al-Mashari, M., Irani, Z., & Zairi, M. (2001). Business process reengineering: A survey of international experience. *Business Process Management Journal*, *7*(5), 437–455. doi:10.1108/14637150110406812

Al-Mashari, M., & Zairi, M. (1999). BPR implementation process: An analysis of key success and failure factors. *Business Process Management Journal*, *5*(1), 87–112. doi:10.1108/14637159910249108

Al-Mashari, M., & Zairi, M. (2000). Revisiting BPR: A holistic review of practice and development. *Business Process Management Journal*, *6*(1), 10–42. doi:10.1108/14637150010283045

Almunawar, M. N., Anshari, M., & Susanto, H. (2013). Crafting strategies for sustainability: How travel agents should react in facing a disintermediation. *Operations Research*, *13*(3), 317–342. doi:10.1007/s12351-012-0129-7

Altinkemer, K., Chaturvedi, A., & Kondareddy, S. (1999). Business process reengineering and organizational performance: An exploration of issues. *International Journal of Information Management*, *18*(6), 381–392. doi:10.1016/S0268-4012(98)00030-9

Ananthram, S., & Nankervis, A. (2013). Strategic agility and the role of HR as a strategic business partner: An Indian perspective. *Asia Pacific Journal of Human Resources*, *51*(4), 454–470.

Andreu, R., Ricart, J., & Valor, J. (1997). Process innovation: Changing boxes or revolutionizing organizations? *Knowledge and Process Management*, *4*(2), 114–125. doi:10.1002/(SICI)1099-1441(199706)4:2<114::AID-KPM90>3.0.CO;2-S

Asif, M., Awan, M. U., Khan, M. K., & Ahmad, N. (2013). A model for total quality management in higher education. *Quality & Quantity*, *47*(4), 1883–1904. doi:10.1007/s11135-011-9632-9

Attaran, M. (2003). Information technology and business-process redesign. *Business Process Management Journal*, *9*(4), 440–458. doi:10.1108/14637150310484508

Attaran, M. (2004). Exploring the relationship between information technology and business process reengineering. *Information & Management*, *41*(5), 585–596. doi:10.1016/S0378-7206(03)00098-3

Bae, J. S., Jeong, S. C., Seo, Y., Kim, Y., & Kang, S. H. (1999). Integration of workflow management and simulation. *Computers & Industrial Engineering*, *37*(1-2), 203–206. doi:10.1016/S0360-8352(99)00055-8

Baldwin, L. P., Eldabi, T., & Paul, R. J. (2005). Business process design: Flexible modeling with multiple levels of detail. *Business Process Management Journal*, *11*(1), 22–36. doi:10.1108/14637150510578700

Bhatt, G. D. (2000). Exploring the relationship between information technology, infrastructure and business process re-engineering. *Business Process Management, 6*(2), 139–163. doi:10.1108/14637150010324085

Bonet, R. (2014). High-involvement work practices and the opportunities for promotion in the organization. *Industrial Relations, 53*(2), 295–324. doi:10.1111/irel.12057

Box, S., & Platts, K. (2005). Business process management: Establishing and maintaining project alignment. *Business Process Management Journal, 11*(4), 370–387. doi:10.1108/14637150510609408

Campbell, S., & Kleiner, B. H. (2001). New developments in re-engineering organizations. *Management Research News, 24*(3–4), 5–8. doi:10.1108/01409170110782531

Carr, D., & Johansson. (1995). *Best practices in reengineering: What works and what doesn't in the reengineering process.* New York, NY: McGraw–Hill.

Chan, K. K., & Spedding, T. A. (2003). An integrated multidimensional process improvement methodology for manufacturing systems. *Computers & Industrial Engineering, 44*(4), 673–693. doi:10.1016/S0360-8352(03)00002-0

Chi, W., Freeman, R. B., & Kleiner, M. M. (2011). Adoption and termination of employee involvement programs. *LABOUR, 25*(1), 45–62. doi:10.1111/j.1467-9914.2010.00510.x

Chronéer, D., & Bergquist, B. (2012). Managerial complexity in process industrial R&D projects: A Swedish study. *Project Management Journal, 43*(2), 21–36. doi:10.1002/pmj.21257

Clark, K. D., & Maggitti, P. G. (2012). TMT potency and strategic decision-making in high technology firms. *Journal of Management Studies, 49*(7), 1168–1193. doi:10.1111/j.1467-6486.2012.01060.x

Clegg, B. (2006). Business process orientated holonic (PrOH) modeling. *Business Process Management Journal, 12*(4), 410–432. doi:10.1108/14637150610678050

Combs, J. G., Ketchen, D. J. Jr, Ireland, R. D., & Webb, J. W. (2011). The role of resource flexibility in leveraging strategic resources. *Journal of Management Studies, 48*(5), 1098–1125. doi:10.1111/j.1467-6486.2009.00912.x

Cristini, A., Eriksson, T., & Pozzoli, D. (2013). High-performance management practices and employee outcomes in Denmark. *Scottish Journal of Political Economy, 60*(3), 232–266. doi:10.1111/sjpe.12010

Crowe, T. J., Fong, P. M., & Zayas-Castro, J. L. (2002). Quantitative risk level estimation of business process reengineering efforts. *Business Process Management Journal, 8*(5), 490–511. doi:10.1108/14637150210449148

Cypress, H. (1994). Reengineering. *OR/MS Today, 21*(1), 18–29.

Darmani, A., & Hanafizadeh, P. (2013). Business process portfolio selection in re-engineering projects. *Business Process Management Journal, 19*(6), 892–916. doi:10.1108/BPMJ-08-2011-0052

Davenport, T. H. (1993). Need radical innovation and continuous improvement? Integrated process reengineering and TQM. *Planning Review, 21*(3), 6–12. doi:10.1108/eb054413

Davenport, T. H. (2008). Business process management-foreword. In V. Grover & M. L. Markus (Eds.), *Business process transformation* (pp. 41–46). Armonk, NY: M.E. Sharpe.

Davenport, T. H., & Short, J. (1990). The new industrial engineering: Information technology and business process redesign. *Sloan Management Review, 31*(4), 11–27.

Davidson, W. (1993). Beyond re-engineering: The three phases of business transformation. *IBM Systems Journal, 32*(1), 65–79. doi:10.1147/sj.321.0065

de Beer, E., & Rensburg, R. (2011). Towards a theoretical framework for the governing of stakeholder relationships: A perspective from South Africa. *Journal of Public Affairs, 11*(4), 208–225. doi:10.1002/pa.414

De Nicola, A., Missikoff, M., & Smith, F. (2012). Towards a method for business process and informal business rules compliance. *Journal of Software: Evolution and Process, 24*(3), 341–360.

Debela, T. (2010). Business process reengineering in Ethiopian public organizations: The relationship between theory and practice. *Journal of Business and Administrative Studies, 1*(2), 20–59. doi:10.4314/jbas.v1i2.57348

Doomun, R., & Jungum, N. V. (2008). Business process modelling, simulation and reengineering: Call centres. *Business Process Management Journal, 14*(6), 838–848. doi:10.1108/14637150810916017

Eardley, A., Shah, H., & Radman, A. (2008). A model for improving the role of IT in BPR. *Business Process Management Journal, 14*(5), 629–653. doi:10.1108/14637150810903039

Esmaeili, A. (2012). Strategic human-resource management in a dynamic environment. *Scientific and Technical Information Processing, 39*(2), 85–89. doi:10.3103/S0147688212020037

Frishammar, J., Lichtenthaler, U., & Richtnér, A. (2013). Managing process development: Key issues and dimensions in the front end. *R & D Management, 43*(3), 213–226. doi:10.1111/radm.12011

Garrett, R. P. Jr, & Neubaum, D. O. (2013). Top management support and initial strategic assets: A dependency model for internal corporate venture performance. *Journal of Product Innovation Management, 30*(5), 896–915. doi:10.1111/jpim.12036

Giaglis, G. M., Hlupic, V., de Vreede, G. J., & Verbraeck, A. (2005). Synchronous design of business processes and information systems using dynamic process modeling. *Business Process Management Journal, 11*(5), 488–500. doi:10.1108/14637150510619849

Grachev, V. M., Esin, V. I., Polukhina, N. G., & Rassomakhin, S. G. (2014). Technology for developing databases of information systems. *Bulletin of the Lebedev Physics Institute, 41*(5), 119–122. doi:10.3103/S1068335614050017

Grant, D. (2002). A wider view of business process reengineering. *Communications of the ACM, 45*(2), 84–92. doi:10.1145/503124.503128

Green, F., & Wayhan, V. (1996). Reengineering: Clarifying the confusion. *SAM Advanced Management Journal, 61*(3), 37–40.

Green, P., & Roseman, M. (2000). Integrated process modeling: An ontological evaluation. *Information Systems*, *25*(2), 73–87. doi:10.1016/S0306-4379(00)00010-7

Green, S. D. (2011). *From business process re-engineering to partnering, in making sense of construction improvement.* Oxford, UK: Wiley-Blackwell. doi:10.1002/9781444341102

Grieves, J. (2000). Introductions: The origins of organizational development. *Journal of Management Development*, *19*(5), 345–447. doi:10.1108/02621710010371865

Grover, V., Jeong, S. R., Kettinger, W., & Teng, J. T. (1995). The implementation of business process reengineering. *Journal of Management Information Systems*, *12*(1), 109–144.

Grover, V., & Malhotra, M. (1997). Business process re-engineering: A tutorial on the concept, evolution, method, technology and application. *Journal of Operations Management*, *15*(3), 193–213. doi:10.1016/S0272-6963(96)00104-0

Grover, V., Teng, J., & Fiedler, K. (1993). Information technology enabled business process redesign: An integrated planning framework. *Omega: The International Journal of Management Science*, *21*(4), 433–447. doi:10.1016/0305-0483(93)90076-W

Groznik, A., & Maslaric, M. (2012). A process approach to distribution channel re-engineering. *Journal of Enterprise Information Management*, *25*(2), 123–135. doi:10.1108/17410391211204383

Guimaraes, T. (1999). Field testing of the proposed predictors of BPR success in manufacturing firms. *Journal of Manufacturing Systems*, *18*(1), 53–65. doi:10.1016/S0278-6125(99)80012-0

Guimaraes, T., & Paranjape, K. (2013). Testing success factors for manufacturing BPR project phases. *International Journal of Advanced Manufacturing Technology*, *68*(9–12), 1937–1947. doi:10.1007/s00170-013-4809-0

Gulden, G., & Reck, R. (1992). Combining quality and re-engineering efforts for process excellence. *Information Strategy: The Executive's Journal*, *10*(1), 10–16.

Gunasekaran, A., Chung, W. W. C., & Kan, K. (2000). Business process reengineering in British company: A case study. *Logistics Information Management*, *13*(5), 271–285. doi:10.1108/09576050010378496

Ha, B. H., Bae, J., Park, Y. T., & Kang, S. H. (2006). Development of process execution rules for workload balancing on agents. *Data & Knowledge Engineering*, *56*(1), 64–84. doi:10.1016/j.datak.2005.02.007

Hagen, M., & Gavrilova Aguilar, M. (2012). The impact of managerial coaching on learning outcomes within the team context: An analysis. *Human Resource Development Quarterly*, *23*(3), 363–388. doi:10.1002/hrdq.21140

Hammer, M. (1990). Reengineering work: Don't automate, obliterate. *Harvard Business Review*, *68*(4), 104–112.

Hammer, M. (2010). What is business process management? In J. vom Brocke & M. Rosemann (Eds.), *Handbook on business process management 1: Introduction, methods, and information systems* (pp. 3–16). Berlin, Germany: Springer–Verlag. doi:10.1007/978-3-642-00416-2_1

Hammer, M., & Champy, J. (1993). *Reengineering the corporation: A manifesto for business revolution.* New York, NY: HarperBusiness.

Harmon, P. (2010). The scope and evolution of business process management? In J. vom Brocke & M. Rosemann (Eds.), *Handbook on business process management 1: Introduction, methods, and information systems* (pp. 37–81). Berlin, Germany: Springer–Verlag. doi:10.1007/978-3-642-00416-2_3

He, X. J. (2005). A comparative study of business process reengineering in China. *Communication of the IIMA, 5*(2), 25–30.

Heizer, J., & Render, B. (2011). *Operations management.* Upper Saddle River, NJ: Printice–Hall.

Herazo, B., Lizarralde, G., & Paquin, R. (2012). Sustainable development in the building sector: A Canadian case study on the alignment of strategic and tactical management. *Project Management Journal, 43*(2), 84–100. doi:10.1002/pmj.21258

Herzog, N. V., Polajnar, A., & Tonchia, S. (2007). Development and validation of business process reengineering (BPR) variables: A survey research in Slovenian companies. *International Journal of Production Research, 45*(24), 5811–5834. doi:10.1080/00207540600854992

Hesson, M. (2007). Business process reengineering in UAE public sector: A naturalization and residency case study. *Business Process Management Journal, 13*(5), 707–727. doi:10.1108/14637150710823174

Heygate, R. (1993). Immoderate redesign. *The McKinsey Quarterly,* (1): 73–87.

Hinterhuber, H. (1995). Business process management: The European approach. *Business Change & Re-engineering, 2*(4), 63–73.

Hwang, S., & Yang, W. (2002). On the discovery of process models from their instances. *Decision Support Systems, 31*(1), 41–57. doi:10.1016/S0167-9236(02)00008-8

Jain, R., Chandrasekaran, A., & Gunasekaran, A. (2010). Benchmarking the redesign of "business process reengineering" curriculum: A continuous process improvement (CPI). *Benchmarking: An International Journal, 17*(1), 77–94. doi:10.1108/14635771011022325

Jain, R., Erol, O., & Chandrasekaran, A. (2007). *Designing a course on business process reengineering (BPR): Bridging the gap between business operations and engineering of systems.* Paper presented at the 2007 ASEE Annual Conference, Honolulu, HI.

Jain, R., Gunasekaran, A., & Chandrasekaran, A. (2009). Evolving role of business process reengineering: A perspective of employers. *Industrial and Commercial Training, 41*(7), 382–390. doi:10.1108/00197850910995782

Johansson, H., McHugh, P., Pendlebury, J., & Wheeler, W. (1993). *Business process reengineering: Break point strategies for market dominance.* Chichester, UK: John Wiley & Sons.

Kamhawi, E. M. (2008). Determinants of Bahraini managers' acceptance of business process reengineering. *Business Process Management Journal, 14*(2), 166–187. doi:10.1108/14637150810864916

Kasemsap, K. (2015a). The role of total quality management practices on quality performance. In A. Moumtzoglou, A. Kastania, & S. Archondakis (Eds.), *Laboratory management information systems: Current requirements and future perspectives* (pp. 1–31). Hershey, PA: IGI Global. doi:10.4018/978-1-4666-6320-6.ch001

Kasemsap, K. (2015b). Developing a framework of human resource management, organizational learning, knowledge management capability, and organizational performance. In P. Ordoñez de Pablos, L. Turró, R. Tennyson, & J. Zhao (Eds.), *Knowledge management for competitive advantage during economic crisis* (pp. 164–193). Hershey, PA: IGI Global. doi:10.4018/978-1-4666-6457-9.ch010

Kasemsap, K. (2015c). The role of data mining for business intelligence in knowledge management. In A. Azevedo & M. Santos (Eds.), *Integration of data mining in business intelligence systems* (pp. 12–33). Hershey, PA: IGI Global. doi:10.4018/978-1-4666-6477-7.ch002

Kasemsap, K. (2015d). The role of information system within enterprise architecture and their impact on business performance. In M. Wadhwa & A. Harper (Eds.), *Technology, innovation, and enterprise transformation* (pp. 262–284). Hershey, PA: IGI Global. doi:10.4018/978-1-4666-6473-9.ch012

Kassahun, A. E., & Molla, A. (2013). BPR complementary competence: Definition, model and measurement. *Business Process Management Journal*, *19*(3), 575–596. doi:10.1108/14637151311319950

Keen, P. (1991). *Shaping the future: Business design through information technology*. Boston, MA: Harvard Business School Press.

Kelada, J. (1994). Is reengineering replacing total quality? *Quality Progress*, *27*(12), 79–85.

Kettinger, W., Teng, J., & Guha, S. (1997). Business process change: A study of methodologies, techniques, and tools. *Management Information Systems Quarterly*, *21*(1), 55–80. doi:10.2307/249742

Khalil, O. E. M. (1997). Implications for the role of information systems in a business process reengineering environment. *Information Resources Management Journal*, *10*(1), 36–42. doi:10.4018/irmj.1997010103

Klein, M. (1994). Reengineering methodologies and tools: A prescription for enhancing success. *Information Systems Management*, *11*(2), 30–35. doi:10.1080/10580539408964633

Kober, R., Subraamanniam, T., & Watson, J. (2012). The impact of total quality management adoption on small and medium enterprises' financial performance. *Accounting and Finance*, *52*(2), 421–438. doi:10.1111/j.1467-629X.2011.00402.x

Kotnour, T. (2001). Building knowledge for and about large-scale organizational transformations. *International Journal of Operations & Production Management*, *21*(8), 1053–1075. doi:10.1108/EUM0000000005585

Kull, T. J., Narasimhan, R., & Schroeder, R. (2012). Sustaining the benefits of a quality initiative through cooperative values: A longitudinal study. *Decision Sciences*, *43*(4), 553–588. doi:10.1111/j.1540-5915.2012.00359.x

Kwee, Z., Van Den Bosch, F. A. J., & Volberda, H. W. (2011). The influence of top management team's corporate governance orientation on strategic renewal trajectories: A longitudinal analysis of Royal Dutch Shell plc, 1907–2004. *Journal of Management Studies*, *48*(5), 984–1014. doi:10.1111/j.1467-6486.2010.00961.x

Laudon, K. C., & Laudon, J. P. (2006). *Management information system: Managing the digital firm.* Upper Saddle River, NJ: Prentice–Hall.

Lee, S. M., & Asllani, A. (1997). TQM and BPR: Symbiosis and a new approach for integration. *Management Decision, 35*(6), 409–416. doi:10.1108/00251749710173788

Linden, R. M. (1994). *Seamless government: A practical guide to re-engineering in the public sector.* San Francisco, CA: Jossey–Bass.

Lindsay, A., Downs, D., & Lunn, K. (2003). Business processes: Attempts to find a definition. *Information and Software Technology, 45*(15), 1015–1019. doi:10.1016/S0950-5849(03)00129-0

Loonam, J., McDonagh, J., Kumar, V., & O'Regan, N. (2014). Top managers and information systems: "Crossing the Rubicon! *Strategic Change, 23*(3–4), 205–224. doi:10.1002/jsc.1971

Lowenthal, J. (1994). Reengineering the organization: A step-by-step approach to corporate revitalization. *Quality Progress, 27*(2), 61–63.

Luftman, J., & Ben-Zvi, T. (2009). Key issues for IT executives 2009: Difficult economy's impact on IT. *MIS Quarterly Executive, 9*(1), 203–213.

Luftman, J., & Zadeh, H. S. (2011). Key information technology and management issues 2010–11: An international study. *Journal of Information Technology, 26*(3), 193–204. doi:10.1057/jit.2011.3

Mabin, V. J., Forgeson, S., & Green, L. (2001). Harnessing resistance: Using the theory of constraints to assist change management. *Journal of European Industrial Training, 25*(2–4), 168–191. doi:10.1108/EUM0000000005446

MacIntosh, R. (2003). BPR: Alive and well in the public sector. *International Journal of Operations & Production Management, 23*(3), 327–344. doi:10.1108/01443570310462794

Magutu, P. O., Nyamwange, S. O., & Kaptoge, G. K. (2010). Business process reengineering for competitive advantage: Key factors that may lead to the success or failure of the BPR implementation (The Wrigley Company). *African Journal of Business & Management, 1,* 135–150.

Malhotra, M., Grover, V., & Desilvio, M. (1996). Reengineering the new product development process: A framework for innovation and flexibility in high technology firms. *Omega: International Journal of Management Science, 24*(4), 425–441. doi:10.1016/0305-0483(96)00007-2

Manganelli, R. L., & Klein, M. M. (1994). Your reengineering toolkit. *Management Review, 83*(8), 26–29.

Mansar, S. L., Marir, F., & Reijers, H. A. (2003). Case-based reasoning as a technique for knowledge management in business process redesign. *Electronic Journal of Knowledge Management, 1*(2), 113–124.

Mansar, S. L., & Reijers, H. A. (2005). Best practices in business process redesign: Validation of a redesign framework. *Computers in Industry, 56*(5), 457–471. doi:10.1016/j.compind.2005.01.001

Marir, F., & Mansar, S. L. (2004). *An adapted framework and case-based reasoning for business process redesign.* Paper presented at the IEEE 2nd International Conference on Information Technology: Research and Education, London, UK. doi:10.1109/ITRE.2004.1393671

Martinsuo, M., & Killen, C. P. (2014). Value management in project portfolios: Identifying and assessing strategic value. *Project Management Journal, 45*(5), 56–70. doi:10.1002/pmj.21452

Maull, R. S., Tranfield, D. R., & Maull, W. (2003). Factors characterizing the maturity of BPR programmes. *International Journal of Operations & Production Management, 23*(6), 596–624. doi:10.1108/01443570310476645

Maull, R. S., Weaver, A. M., Childe, S. J., Smart, P. A., & Bennet, J. (1995). Current issues in business process re-engineering. *International Journal of Operations & Production Management, 15*(11), 37–52. doi:10.1108/01443579510102882

Melé, D. (2014). "Human quality treatment": Five organizational levels. *Journal of Business Ethics, 120*(4), 457–471. doi:10.1007/s10551-013-1999-1

Mertins, K., & Jochem, R. (2005). Architectures, methods and tools for enterprise engineering. *International Journal of Production Economics, 98*(2), 179–188. doi:10.1016/j.ijpe.2004.05.024

Mihalache, O. R., Jansen, J. J. P., Van den Bosch, F. A. J., & Volberda, H. W. (2014). Top management team shared leadership and organizational ambidexterity: A moderated mediation framework. *Strategic Entrepreneurship Journal, 8*(2), 128–148. doi:10.1002/sej.1168

Mitchell, R., Obeidat, S., & Bray, M. (2013). The effect of strategic human resource management on organizational performance: The mediating role of high-performance human resource practices. *Human Resource Management, 52*(6), 899–921. doi:10.1002/hrm.21587

Moonsamy, V., & Singh, S. (2014). Using factor analysis to explore principal components for quality management implementation. *Quality & Quantity, 48*(2), 605–622. doi:10.1007/s11135-012-9790-4

Moran, J. W., & Brightman, B. K. (2000). Leading organizational change. *Journal of Workplace Learning, 12*(2), 66–74. doi:10.1108/13665620010316226

Motwani, J., Subramanian, R., & Gopalakrishna, P. (2005). Critical factors for successful ERP implementation: Exploratory findings from four case studies. *Computers in Industry, 56*(6), 529–544. doi:10.1016/j.compind.2005.02.005

Ng, J. K. C., Ip, W. H., & Lee, T. C. (1999). A paradigm for ERP and BPR integration. *International Journal of Production Research, 37*(9), 2093–2108. doi:10.1080/002075499190923

Ongaro, E. (2004). Process management in the public sector: The experience of one-stop shops in Italy. *International Journal of Public Sector Management, 17*(1), 81–107. doi:10.1108/09513550410515592

Ooi, K. B., Cheah, W. C., Lin, B., & Teh, P. L. (2012). TQM practices and knowledge sharing: An empirical study of Malaysia's manufacturing organizations. *Asia Pacific Journal of Management, 29*(1), 59–78. doi:10.1007/s10490-009-9185-9

Ovenden, T. (1994). Business process reengineering: Definitely worth considering. *The TQM Magazine, 6*(3), 56–61. doi:10.1108/09544789410057917

Ozcelik, Y. (2009). Do business process reengineering projects payoff? Evidence from the United States. *International Journal of Project Management, 28*(1), 7–13. doi:10.1016/j.ijproman.2009.03.004

Palmer, B. (2004). Overcoming resistance to change. *Quality Progress*, *37*(4), 35–40.

Pérez-Castillo, R., García-Rodríguez de Guzmán, I., Piattini, M., & Places, Á. S. (2012). A case study on business process recovery using an e-government system. *Software, Practice & Experience*, *42*(2), 159–189. doi:10.1002/spe.1057

Piening, E. P., Baluch, A. M., & Ridder, H. G. (2014). Mind the intended-implemented gap: Understanding employees' perceptions of HRM. *Human Resource Management*, *53*(4), 545–567. doi:10.1002/hrm.21605

Radhakrishnan, R., & Balasubramanian, S. (2008). *Business process reengineering: Text and cases*. New Delhi, India: Phi Learning.

Ranganathan, C., & Dhaliwal, J. (2001). A survey of business process reengineering practices in Singapore. *Information & Management*, *39*(2), 125–134. doi:10.1016/S0378-7206(01)00087-8

Reijers, H. A. (2006). Implementing BPM systems: The role of process orientation. *Business Process Management Journal*, *12*(4), 389–409. doi:10.1108/14637150610678041

Revere, L. (2004). Re-engineering proves effective for reducing courier costs. *Business Process Management Journal*, *10*(4), 400–414. doi:10.1108/14637150410548074

Rigby, D. (1993). The secret history of process reengineering. *Planning Review*, *21*(2), 24–27. doi:10.1108/eb054408

Rigby, D., & Bilodeau, B. (2005). The Bain 2005 management tool survey. *Strategy and Leadership*, *33*(4), 4–12. doi:10.1108/10878570510607997

Robert Mitchell, J., & Shepherd, D. A. (2012). Capability development and decision incongruence in strategic opportunity pursuit. *Strategic Entrepreneurship Journal*, *6*(4), 355–381. doi:10.1002/sej.1145

Robert Mitchell, J., Shepherd, D. A., & Sharfman, M. P. (2011). Erratic strategic decisions: When and why managers are inconsistent in strategic decision making. *Strategic Management Journal*, *32*(7), 683–704. doi:10.1002/smj.905

Sarathy, P. S. (2013). TQM practice in real-estate industry using AHP. *Quality & Quantity*, *47*(4), 2049–2063. doi:10.1007/s11135-011-9641-8

Schniederjans, M. J., & Kim, G. C. (2003). Implementing enterprise resource planning systems with total quality control and business process reengineering: Survey results. *International Journal of Operations & Production Management*, *23*(4), 418–429. doi:10.1108/01443570310467339

Schnitt, D. (1993). Reengineering the organization using information technology. *Journal of Systems Management*, *44*(1), 14–20.

Schoenherr, T., Power, D., Narasimhan, R., & Samson, D. (2012). Competitive capabilities among manufacturing plants in developing, emerging, and industrialized countries: A comparative analysis. *Decision Sciences*, *43*(1), 37–72. doi:10.1111/j.1540-5915.2011.00341.x

Seethamraju, R. (2012). Business process management: A missing link in business education. *Business Process Management Journal*, *18*(3), 532–547. doi:10.1108/14637151211232696

Shin, N., & Jemella, D. F. (2002). Business process reengineering and performance improvements: The case of Chase Manhattan Bank. *Business Process Management Journal, 8*(4), 351–363. doi:10.1108/14637150210435008

Sia, S. K., & Neo, B. S. (2008). Business process reengineering, empowerment and work monitoring: An empirical analysis through the Panopticon. *Business Process Management Journal, 14*(5), 609–628. doi:10.1108/14637150810903020

Sirén, C. A., Kohtamäki, M., & Kuckertz, A. (2012). Exploration and exploitation strategies, profit performance, and the mediating role of strategic learning: Escaping the exploitation trap. *Strategic Entrepreneurship Journal, 6*(1), 18–41. doi:10.1002/sej.1126

Slack, N., Chambers, S., & Johnston, R. (2007). *Operations management.* Harlow, UK: Financial Times/ Prentice–Hall.

Smith, M. (2003). Business process design: Correlates of success and failure. *The Quality Management Journal, 10*(2), 38–49.

Soltani, E., Chau, V. S., & Liao, Y. Y. (2012). A learning organization perspective of service quality operations in the IT industry. *Strategic Change, 21*(5-6), 275–284. doi:10.1002/jsc.1909

Sungau, J., Ndunguru, P. C., & Kimeme, J. (2013). Business process re-engineering: The technique to improve delivering speed of service industry in Tanzania. *Independent Journal of Management & Production, 4*(1), 208–227. doi:10.14807/ijmp.v4i1.68

Suttapong, K., Srimai, S., & Pitchayadol, P. (2014). Best practices for building high performance in human resource management. *Global Business and Organizational Excellence, 33*(2), 39–50. doi:10.1002/ joe.21532

Talwar, R. (1993). Business reengineering: A strategy-driven approach. *Long Range Planning, 26*(6), 22–40. doi:10.1016/0024-6301(93)90204-S

Tapscott, D., & Caston, A. (1993). *Paradigm shift: The new promise of information technology.* New York, NY: McGraw–Hill.

Tarokh, M., Sharifi, E., & Nazemi, E. (2008). Survey of BPR experiences in Iran: Reasons for success and failure. *Journal of Business and Industrial Marketing, 23*(5), 350–362. doi:10.1108/08858620810881629

Tatsiopoulos, I. P., & Panayiotou, N. (2000). The integration of activity based costing and enterprise modeling for reengineering purposes. *International Journal of Production Economics, 66*(1), 33–44. doi:10.1016/S0925-5273(99)00080-8

Tennant, C., & Wu, Y. C. (2005). The application of business process reengineering in the UK. *The TQM Magazine, 17*(6), 537–545. doi:10.1108/09544780510627633

Terziovski, M. E., Fitzpatrick, P., & O'Neill, P. (2003). Successful predictors of business process reengineering (BPR) in financial services. *International Journal of Production Economics, 84*(1), 35–50. doi:10.1016/S0925-5273(02)00378-X

Trevor, J., & Brown, W. (2014). The limits on pay as a strategic tool: Obstacles to alignment in non-union environments. *British Journal of Industrial Relations*, *52*(3), 553–578. doi:10.1111/bjir.12004

Vakola, M., & Rezgui, Y. (2000). Critique of existing business process re-engineering methodologies: The development and implementation of a new methodology. *Business Process Management Journal*, *6*(3), 238–250. doi:10.1108/14637150010325453

Vakola, M., Rezgui, Y., & Wood-Harper, T. (2000). The Condor business process re-engineering model. *Managerial Auditing Journal*, *15*(1–2), 42–46. doi:10.1108/02686900010304623

Valentine, S., Hollingworth, D., & Francis, C. A. (2013). Quality-related HR practices, organizational ethics, and positive work attitudes: Implications for HRD. *Human Resource Development Quarterly*, *24*(4), 493–523. doi:10.1002/hrdq.21169

Venkatraman, N. (1994). IT-enabled business transformation: From automation to business scope re-definition. *Sloan Management Review*, *35*(2), 73–87.

Verginadis, Y., & Mentzas, G. (2008). Agents and workflow engines for inter-organizational workflows in e-government cases. *Business Process Management Journal*, *14*(2), 188–203. doi:10.1108/14637150810864925

Volberda, H. W., Van Den Bosch, F. A. J., & Heij, C. V. (2013). Management innovation: Management as fertile ground for innovation. *European Management Review*, *10*(1), 1–15. doi:10.1111/emre.12007

Wells, M. G. (2000). Business process re-engineering implementations using Internet technology. *Business Process Management Journal*, *6*(2), 164–184. doi:10.1108/14637150010321303

Wells, R., O'Connell, P., & Hochman, S. (1993). What's the difference between reengineering and TQEM? *Total Quality Environmental Management*, *2*(3), 273–282. doi:10.1002/tqem.3310020307

Winter, R. (2002). An executive MBA program in business engineering: A curriculum focusing on change. *Journal of Information Technology Education*, *1*(4), 279–288.

Wu, I. (2003). Understanding senior management's behavior in promoting the strategic role of IT in process reengineering: Use of the theory of reasoned action. *Information & Management*, *41*(1), 1–11. doi:10.1016/S0378-7206(02)00115-5

Xiaoli, L. (2011). Correlation between business process reengineering and operation performance of National Commercial Banks. *Journal of Innovation and Management*, *7*, 981–985.

Yitmen, I. (2013). Organizational cultural intelligence: A competitive capability for strategic alliances in the international construction industry. *Project Management Journal*, *44*(4), 5–25. doi:10.1002/pmj.21356

Yung, W. K. C., & Chan, D. T. H. (2003). Application of value delivery system (VDS) and performance benchmarking in flexible business process reengineering. *International Journal of Operations & Production Management*, *23*(3), 300–315. doi:10.1108/01443570310462776

Zairi, M., & Sinclair, D. (1995). Business process reengineering and process management: A survey of current practice and future trends in integrated management. *Management Decision*, *33*(3), 3–16. doi:10.1108/00251749510085021

Zatzick, C. D., Moliterno, T. P., & Fang, T. (2012). Strategic (MIS)FIT: The implementation of TQM in manufacturing organizations. *Strategic Management Journal, 33*(11), 1321–1330. doi:10.1002/smj.1988

Zhang, G. P., & Xia, Y. (2013). Does quality still pay? A reexamination of the relationship between effective quality management and firm performance. *Production and Operations Management, 22*(1), 120–136. doi:10.1111/j.1937-5956.2012.01341.x

ADDITIONAL READING

Abu Rub, F. A., & Issa, A. A. (2012). A business process modeling-based approach to investigate complex processes: Software development case study. *Business Process Management Journal, 18*(1), 122–137. doi:10.1108/14637151211215046

Antonucci, Y. L., & Goeke, R. J. (2011). Identification of appropriate responsibilities and positions for business process management success. *Business Process Management Journal, 17*(1), 127–146. doi:10.1108/14637151111105616

Blasini, J., & Leist, S. (2013). Success factors in process performance management. *Business Process Management Journal, 19*(3), 477–495. doi:10.1108/14637151311319914

Bouchbout, K., Akoka, J., & Alimazighi, Z. (2012). An MDA-based framework for collaborative business process modeling. *Business Process Management Journal, 18*(6), 919–948. doi:10.1108/14637151211283357

Cheung, M., & Hidders, J. (2011). Round-trip iterative business process modeling between BPA and BPMS tools. *Business Process Management Journal, 17*(3), 461–494. doi:10.1108/14637151111136379

Fady, R., & Abd El Aziz, R. (2012). Process architecture and process modeling in the Egyptian industry: The case of Incom. *International Journal of Enterprise Network Management, 5*(1), 33–42. doi:10.1504/IJENM.2012.045593

Fuente, M. V., Ros, L., & Ortiz, A. (2010). Enterprise modeling methodology for forward and reverse supply chain flows integration. *Computers in Industry, 61*(7), 702–710. doi:10.1016/j.compind.2010.05.010

Hanafizadeh, P., & Osouli, E. (2011). Process selection in re-engineering by measuring degree of change. *Business Process Management Journal, 17*(2), 284–310. doi:10.1108/14637151111122356

Hernaus, T., Bach, M. P., & Vuksic, V. B. (2012). Influence of strategic approach to BPM on financial and non-financial performance. *Baltic Journal of Management, 7*(4), 376–396. doi:10.1108/17465261211272148

Iden, J. (2012). Investigating process management in firms with quality systems: A multi-case study. *Business Process Management Journal, 18*(1), 104–121. doi:10.1108/14637151211215037

Isik, O., Mertens, W., & Van den Bergh, J. (2013). Practices of knowledge intensive process management: Quantitative insights. *Business Process Management Journal, 19*(3), 515–534. doi:10.1108/14637151311319932

Kang, B., Kim, D., & Kang, S. H. (2012). Periodic performance prediction for real-time business process monitoring. *Industrial Management & Data Systems, 112*(1), 4–23. doi:10.1108/02635571211193617

Kohlbacher, M. (2010). The effects of process orientation: A literature review. *Business Process Management Journal, 16*(1), 135–152. doi:10.1108/14637151011017985

Kohlbacher, M., & Gruenwald, S. (2011). Process orientation: Conceptualization and measurement. *Business Process Management Journal, 17*(2), 267–283. doi:10.1108/14637151111122347

Lin, H. F. (2013). The effects of knowledge management capabilities and partnership attributes on the stage-based e-business diffusion. *Internet Research, 23*(4), 439–464. doi:10.1108/IntR-11-2012-0233

Lin, L. M., & Hsia, T. L. (2011). Core capabilities for practitioners in achieving e-business innovation. *Computers in Human Behavior, 27*(5), 1884–1891. doi:10.1016/j.chb.2011.04.012

Liu, C., Li, Q., & Zhao, X. (2009). Challenges and opportunities in collaborative business process management: Overview of recent advances and introduction to the special issue. *Information Systems Frontiers, 11*(3), 201–209. doi:10.1007/s10796-008-9089-0

Magal, S. R., & Word, J. (2012). *Integrated business processes with ERP systems*. Hoboken, NJ: John Wiley & Sons.

Niehaves, B., & Plattfaut, R. (2011). Collaborative business process management: Status quo and quo vadis. *Business Process Management Journal, 17*(3), 384–402. doi:10.1108/14637151111136342

Ofner, M. H., Otto, B., & Osterle, H. (2012). Integrating a data quality perspective into business process management. *Business Process Management Journal, 18*(6), 1036–1067. doi:10.1108/14637151211283401

Recker, J. C., & Rosemann, M. (2010). A measurement instrument for process modeling research: Development, test and procedural model. *Scandinavian Journal of Information Systems, 22*(2), 3–30.

Sidorova, A., & Isik, O. (2010). Business process research: A cross-disciplinary review. *Business Process Management Journal, 16*(4), 566–597. doi:10.1108/14637151011065928

Solaimani, S., & Bouwman, H. (2012). A framework for the alignment of business model and business processes: A generic model for trans-sector innovation. *Business Process Management Journal, 18*(4), 655–679. doi:10.1108/14637151211253783

Trkman, P. (2010). The critical success factors of business process management. *International Journal of Information Management, 30*(2), 125–134. doi:10.1016/j.ijinfomgt.2009.07.003

Vom Brocke, J., & Sinnl, T. (2011). Culture in business process management: A literature review. *Business Process Management Journal, 17*(2), 357–378. doi:10.1108/14637151111122383

Zellner, G. (2011). A structured evaluation of business process improvement approaches. *Business Process Management Journal, 17*(2), 203–237. doi:10.1108/14637151111122329

KEY TERMS AND DEFINITIONS

Business: An organization or economic system where goods and services are exchanged for one another or for money.

Business Process: A series of logically related activities (i.e., planning, production, and sales) performed together to produce a defined set of results.

Business Process Reengineering: A viewpoint of business processes, job definitions, management systems, organizational structure, work flow, and underlying assumptions and beliefs.

Human Resource Management: The process of hiring and developing employees so that they become more valuable to the organization.

Information Technology: A set of tools, processes, and associated equipment employed to collect, process, and present information.

Leadership: The activity of leading a group of people or an organization or the ability to do this.

Process: A sequence of interdependent procedures which consume one or more resources (i.e., employee time, energy, machines, and money) to convert inputs (i.e., data, material, and parts) into outputs.

Project Management: The body of knowledge related to the principles, techniques, and tools used in planning, control, monitoring, and review of projects.

Reengineering: An application of technology and management science to the modification of existing systems, organizations, processes, and products in order to make them more effective, efficient, and responsive.

Chapter 6
A Learning Organisation Approach to Software Project Management:
Promoting Knowledge Transformation and Interprofessionalism through Crowd-Funded Agile Development

Jonathan Bishop
Centre for Research into Online Communities and E-Learning Systems, UK

ABSTRACT

This chapter explores how a learning organisation differs from a teaching organisation, such as that each person holds responsibility for their own learning, yet are supported and guided by those who wish to help them further their personal development. This chapter aims to develop a software project management methodology, based on existing approaches, which can accommodate all people, regardless of ability. The model developed, called the C2-Tech-S2 approach, is specifically designed for projects that use crowd-funding and agile development, particularly in environments based around the Cloud. A pilot study is carried out to demonstrate the 'technology' stage of this model for assessment using the 'support' stage. This finds that all stages of the model need to be applied in a project, because on their own the stages may not produce the most effective outcomes in terms of increased participation.

INTRODUCTION

Tight budgets for some software projects, where income can be sporadic is leading to the need for a significant rethink of how such initiatives are approached. The use of crowd-funding is often suggested as a means to gain interest in and capital for software production, and is in fact one of the means recommended by the Welsh Government. Such projects, however, pose challenges for existing project management methods, as the development cycle does not simply go from start to finish, but is somewhat a

DOI: 10.4018/978-1-4666-8510-9.ch006

sporadic form of iterative development. This chapter therefore suggests that adopting an agile approach to software development that it will be possible for innovative software projects where finance is scarce to get off the ground without a hugely uncertain development model where it would not be known whether there would be anything at the end should funds cease to exist. It is therefore necessary for existing software development models to be rethought to take account of crowd-funding and agile development approaches – something this chapter attempts to achieve. Agile development is a successful method for project management, evolving with the same alacrity, but organisational culture also needs to change (Berger, 2007). This chapter shows how to address such change.

The Learning Organisation

A learning organisation is a place where people are continually discovering how they create their reality (Gibb, 1997). Many would naïvely think that a school or university is a learning organisation, when not all are, even if they are all teaching organisations. A university which only hires staff who already have all the experience needed for a particular job is not a learning organisation, as actual learning organisations invest in the development of their staff, choosing them on the basis of what they could achieve and not only with reference to what they have already achieved. Thus, a learning organisation is one that facilitates learning for all of its members, and thereby continuously transforms itself and knowledge within it (Rowley, 1998). What is central to the concept of a learning organisation is both organisational learning, defined as the intentional use of learning processes to continuously transform the organisation, and the related concept of knowledge (Thomas & Allen, 2006). Whilst a teaching organisation will focus on the knowledge transformation of its customers (i.e. students), a learning organisation invests in the personal development of all those that are part of it. Even so, whilst learning organisations are founded on the learning process of individuals in the organisation, individual learning does not necessarily lead to organisational learning (Wang & Ahmed, 2003). A whole organisational strategy that applies a learning culture to include customers, suppliers and other significant stakeholders, is essential (Barlow & Jashapara, 1998).

Crowd-Funding and Agile Development

Consumers engage in virtual new product developments mainly because they consider the engagement as a rewarding experience (Marchi, Giachetti, & De Gennaro, 2011). Different types of co-creation are evolving, from the discrete participation in 'crowdsourcing' to 'extreme and mass collaboration' models that offer deeper levels of engagement and participation (Kerrigan, 2010). Crowd-funding, is a collective effort by people who network and pool their money together, usually via the Internet, in order to invest in and support efforts initiated by other people or organisations (Ordanini, Miceli, Pizzetti, & Parasuraman, 2011). Agile software development is most suited to those organisations that embrace interprofessionalism, which involve several specialist teams of individuals who contribute to the overall project whilst otherwise maintaining their independence. Contingent working is highly suited to interprofessional environments, as those individuals with targeted skillsets can be brought in when required and then allowed to continue working for other clients when not engaged.

The 1990s fashion of focus groups has been in many cases given way to 'crowd-sourcing,' which is where across the Web a gathering a mass of people for the purpose of generating new ideas or solutions, have been rewarded by the paying profits to seekers and solvers (Blight & Ainley, 2008). Out of this came crowd-funding, serving as a bottom-up model of financing used for various purposes, from software development to political campaigns (ibid). Crowd-funding markets have recently emerged as a new source of capital supporting, yet participants' behaviour in these markets is not yet well understood (Burtch, Ghose, & Wattal, 2011). It could be argued that non-profit-organizations have always sought donations resembling crowd funding, generally more acceptable for the pursuit of charitable purposes, which is more acceptable to many than those for-profit-organizations that aim to maximise profit (Metzler, 2011). One means for evaluating the success of such projects is analysing Big Data, which allows the opportunity to go beyond traditional measurements, such as geo-demographic factors, by considering behaviour data of Internet users (de Fortuny, Martens, & Provost, 2013).

Contingent Working and Inter-Professionalism

In crowd-funded projects, where income sources may be disparate, contingent working as a means to engage workers for tasks where there is finance available could be seen to be essential. There is no single and clear definition of contingent working. Some have defined contingent working as a period of self-employment, or full or part-time employment lasting less than 1 year before a change of state (Gorard, 2003), but this fails to include freelancers and people on zero-hours contracts. Others define it as a situation where a worker is brought in only as required (Davis, 2000), which is generally how the author conceptualises the practice. Some argue that contingent working is synonymous with temporary working or short-term employment (Cam, Purcell, & Tailby, 2003; Cunha, Cunha, Morgado, & Brewster, 2003), but this does not account for the fact that contingent workers can be available to a particular business on an on-going basis.

The use of contingent working has been increasing modestly but decisively (Coyle-Shapiro & Kessler, 2002). In the UK, two groups of highly skilled, unionised workers where contingent working is common, namely fixed-term workers in UK higher education institutions (HEIs) and performers in the entertainment industry (Simms & Dean, 2014). Contingent working is, however, not universal as logistics firms surround themselves with concentric circles of workers who are more or less central to their operations (Sealey, 2010). Even so, contingent working arrangements are becoming increasingly commonplace in the United States, as the number of temps, part-timers and contract workers continues to expand, while the temporary help 'industry' has experienced explosive growth rates (Peck & Theodore, 2001). Although some workers choose a contingent working status (often for family or other personal reasons), a large and growing percentage of these workers are finding contingent positions their only option as US corporations continue to restructure their operations on a global scale (Parker, 2002). Even Japanese companies, although often through to be the most paternalistic, are now turning to contingent working to reduce fixed overheads (Davis, 2000).

EXTENT AND LIMITATIONS FOR LEARNING FROM CURRENT METHODOLOGIES FOR SOFTWARE DEVELOPMENT

There are perhaps any number of software development and project management methods in existence, serving specialist markets and in some cases too generic to have any merit. This section reviews some of the methods used for the development of online communities and e-learning, in addition to more generalised models used for software design and development.

Standardised Software Development Methods

The search for an effective and standardised means for developing computer software has been met with challenges due to each person taking part in a project having different ideas and intentions. Attempts to create structured and systematic approaches to designing interactive hypermedia systems have failed to materialise (Mbakwe & Cunliffe, 2007; Mbakwe & Cunliffe, 2003). This section explores the strengths and weaknesses of two models that have been adopted by the UK Government in recent years, where during each one's peak the respective government in power has hailed it as the method that is best and above all others.

Structured Systems Analysis and Design Method (SSADM)

Structured Systems Analysis and Design Method (SSADM) is a good example of a method that is used in both the requirements and design stages of a software development project (Dawson & Dawson, 2014). SSADM is one particular implementation of project management that builds on the work of various schools of structured analysis and development methods, being very popular in Great Britain (Coleman, 2013). A limitation in SSADM, it has been argued, is that it is paper-based, meaning common problem with it is the difficulties it poses in managing the volume of documents produced (Brownbridge, 1990), but this is less relevant today with Cloud-based computing. SSADM is also considered not good at defining a consistent level of abstraction for its requirements as much information is duplicated, whilst other features are not consistently documented (Polack & Mander, 1994).

Projects in Controlled Environments Version 2 (PRINCE2)

Whilst SSADM was once the standard structured method used for computer projects in UK government departments, in the UK and Europe (Ashworth, 1988), PRINCE2 is now the project management methodology of choice by many, and is required by the UK government for all projects it commissions (Siegelaub, 2004). PRINCE2 focuses on the products to be produced by the project, not the activities to produce them in order, it is argued, to "ensure quality" (Siegelaub, 2004). While at first one might think this is helpful, in that it does not restrict people to a set way of working, it requires specific additions to the process, which people outside professional settings might not have the knowledge to define. Like SSADM, PRINCE2 heavily depends on paperwork as almost every step in PRINCE2 is documented, which it has argued makes it unsuitable to agile methods, especially extreme programming, which rely on oral communications rather than documents (Al-Zoabi, 2008).

As one can see from Figure 1 PRINCE 2 is quite simple and clear in many ways. However, even with its simplicity, there are a number of serious flaws in the PRINCE2 method for user-centred design of software. The scope of a project, as defined by PRINCE2, is limited to the development and does not involve the use of the product (Blaauboer, Sikkel, & Aydin, 2007).

Specialised Software Development Methods

A number of specialist models have been designed for the development of interactive hypermedia and multimedia interfaces (Bishop, 2004; Bishop, 2005; Bishop, 2007b; de Souza & Preece, 2004; Fogg, 2002; Mbakwe & Cunliffe, 2003; WRONG, 2009). This section will explore a number of these, namely

Figure 1. PRINCE 2

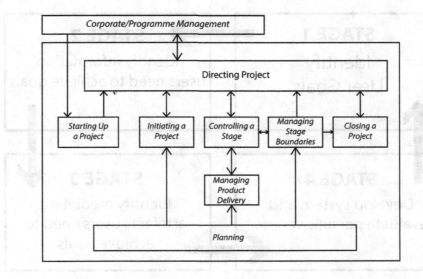

the Five Factor Online Community Development Model (WRONG, 2009), the Mediating Artefacts for Persuasive E-Learning Model (Bishop, 2005), The Star Lifecycle (Bishop, 2007b), and the PASS Approach (Bishop, 2004).

Five-Factor Online Community Development Model (OCD5)

The Five Factor Online Community Development Model (OCD5), presented in Figure 2, was designed to make it easier for online community developers to consider the most important factors in building online communities (WRONG, 2009). It aimed to bring into one model the factors discussed by various online community experts (Figallo, 1998; Kim, 2000; Powazek, 2002; Young & Levine, 2000).

Figure 2. The Five Factor Online Community Development Model (OCD5)

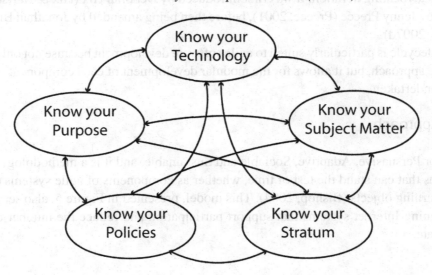

Figure 3. The Mediating Artefacts for Persuasive E-Learning (MAPEL) Model

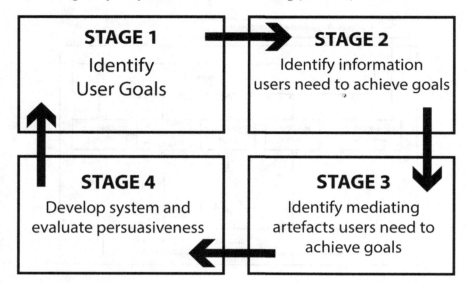

Mediating Artefacts for Persuasive E-Learning Systems (MAPEL)

Figure 3 depicts the Mediating Artefacts for Persuasive E-Learning (MAPEL) model (Bishop, 2005). This four stage framework was first presented at the 2005 International Conference on Internet Technologies and Applications (Bishop, 2005). Its main purpose was to help develop systems that made use of electronic environments to link the 'external environment' of a user to their 'internal environment' in such a way that it increase their flow and made the system more persuasive.

The Star Lifecycle

The Star Lifecycle, shown in Figure 4, was created in its current form following years of change as an iterative model advocating iteration. It was first introduced by Deborah Hix (Hix & Hartson, 1993), and then modified by Jenny Preece (Preece, 2001), before then being amended by Jonathan Bishop (Bishop, 2007b; Bishop, 2007d).

This Star Lifecycle is particularly suited to agile software development because not only is it based on a rapid iterative approach, but it allows for the modular development of each component of the software project being undertaken.

The PASS Approach

PASS stands for Persuasive, Adaptive, Sociable and Sustainable, and it is a methodology for designing Internet systems that can stand the test of time, whether as components of agile systems or as platform independent learning objects (Bishop, 2004). This model, presented in Figure 5, also serves as a useful guide for designing Internet systems that support participation and reduce the number of lurkers that do not participate.

Figure 4. The Star Lifecycle

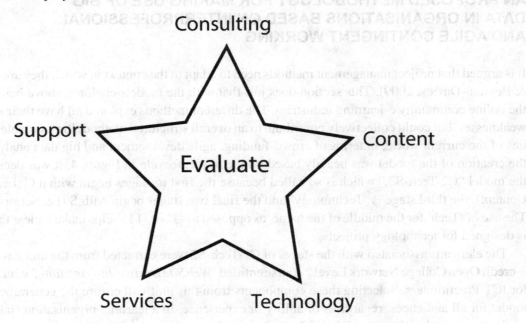

Figure 5. The PASS Approach to Cooperative Design

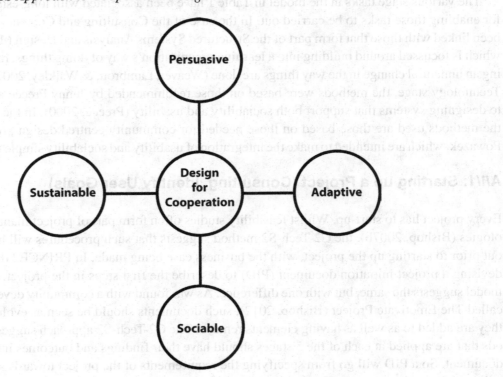

AN PROPOSED METHODOLOGY FOR MAKING USE OF BIG DATA IN ORGANISATIONS BASED ON INTERPROFESSIONAL AND AGILE CONTINGENT WORKING

It is argued that project management methods need to adapt to the context in which they are used (Berger & Beynon-Davies, 2009). This section does just that with the models explored above being adapted to the online community e-learning industries. The different methods explored all have their strengths and weaknesses, but could collectively contribute to an overall structured methodology suitable for the realities of the current world, in terms of crowd-funding, agile development and big data analysis. Because the creation of the model was heavily based on the Star Lifecycle in Figure 4, it was decided to name the model "C2-Tech-S2," which is so called because the first to stages begin with a C (i.e. Consulting, Content), the third stage is 'Technology' and the final two stages begin with S (i.e. Services, Support). The use of 'Tech' for the middle of the name, as opposed to 'T' or 'T1' helps make it clear that the model is designed for technology projects.

The elements associated with the stages of C2-Tech-S2 were extracted from the unit description for a 3-credit Open College Network Level 2 course entitled '*Web Site Design: Intermediate*,' which is designed for ICT Practitioners. Selecting these components from this unit will ensure the generalizability of the model for all audiences, regardless of ability or experience. In a learning organisation staff are chosen on the basis of what they could do, and not simply what they can do. Founding a software development methodology around first principles can ensure that C2-Tech-S2's adoption in any organisation is set up for staff development as opposed to one set-up to take on those who have left a teaching organisation as if it were a production line. The detail of the C2-Tech-S2 is in Table 1.

The various stage tasks in the model in Table 1 have been associated with long-established methods for enabling those tasks to be carried out. In the case of the Consulting and Content stages, these have been linked with those that form part of the Structured Systems Analysis and Design Method (SSADM), which is focussed around building into a learning organisation's way of doing things, rather than expecting an unnatural change in the way things are done (Weaver, Lambrou, & Walkley, 2002). In terms of the Technology stage, the methods were based on those recommended by Jenny Preece as being essential to designing systems that support both sociability and usability (Preece, 2000). In the case of Services, the methods used are those based on those needed for community-centred design proposed by Derek Powazek, which are intended to make the integration of usability and sociability simple (Powazek, 2002).

A/I/1: Starting up a Project (Consulting, Identify User Goals)

Every project has to start-up. Whilst feasibility studies often form part of project management methodologies (Bishop, 2007b), the C2-Tech-S2 method suggests that such procedures will have been carried out prior to starting up the project, with the business case being made. In PRINCE2 this stage involves devising a project initiation document (PID) to describe the first steps in the project. The C2-Tech-S2 model suggests the same, but with one difference. As was found with a community development activity called The Emotivate Project (Bishop, 2012), such documents should be seen as evolutionary – where they are added to as well as having elements remove. The C2-Tech-S2 approach suggests that the methods that are applied at each of the 5 stages should have their findings and outcomes integrated into this document. So a PID will go from specifying the requirements of the project towards setting out how it will be delivered, through the Project Delivery Document. Whilst PRINCE 2 has lots of separate docu-

Table 1. C2-Tech-S2 - A proposed model for managing projects in learning organisations

Star Lifecycle Iteration (OCD5 Stage)	Stage Aim (MAPEL Stage)	Stage Tasks (Task Methods)
A. Consulting (OCD5.3 Know your Stratum)	**I. Identify User Goals** (MAPEL Stage 1)	**1. Starting up a project** 1.1. Discuss the suitability of given systems in terms of style, ease of use and the end user (User Experience Analysis) 1.2 Produce a design concept in terms of customer, purpose and target audience (Scenario Based Design) 1.3. Prepare flow diagrams showing navigation through system (Requirements Analysis)
B. Content (OCD5.2. Know your subject matter)	**II. Identify Information Users need to Achieve Goals** (MAPEL Stage 2)	**2. Initiating a project** 2.1 Collect a range of source materials (e.g. text, graphics, forms, processes) that can be used and modified in various contexts (Business Activity Modelling) 2.2 Create index of source material identifying copyright status and other meta data of each, indicating relevance to requirements, and ensuring recognition of user participation (Current Environment Analysis). 2.3 Select the most appropriate materials, considering file size, customs and practice, and save files in appropriate format to maintain user interest (Entity Behaviour Modelling) 2.4 Store files in a preparation folder for easy access in a range of contexts (Requirements Cataloguing).
C. Technology (OCD5.1. Know your technology)	**III. Identify Mediating Artifacts Users need to Achieve Goals** (MAPEL Stage 3)	**3. Managing product development** 3.1 Create a simple system that can accommodate different users (User Task Analysis and Prototyping) 3.2 Create hyperlinks as mediating artefacts to avoid dead links (Third-Party Resource Refinement and Tuning) 3.3 Create text and image based mediating artefacts to enhance participation (User Scenario Testing). 3.4 Create persuasive links for e-mail and other applications (Social Planning and Modelling).
D. Services (OCD5.4. Know your policies)	**IV. Develop System** (MAPEL Stage 4)	**4. Managing product delivery** 4.1 Create a homepage or menu screen and other nodes compliant with standards (Two-Tree Modelling). 4.2 Create and format system nodes to ensure compliance with policies and law (Connected-Dots Modelling). 4.3 Create tables and format cells, columns and rows that take account of accessibility and multi-platform standards (Nuts and Bolts Audit). 4.4 Set text colour, font styles and heading size and size, location, borders of images, to accommodate those with disabilities and other needs (Design Matters Audit).
E. Support (OCD5. Know your purpose)	**V. Evaluate Persuasiveness** (MAPEL Stage 4)	**5. Closing a project** 5.1 View results in preview environment and run testing sequences (Inspection/ Walkthrough). 5.2 Collect feedback, from at least three users, in terms of suitability for purpose, ease of use and style (User Focus Groups and Interviews). 5.3 Test out system in real world, showing regard for effect on body posture, potential eyestrain and positioning of user hardware (Direct Observation).

ments, it is envisaged that with C2-Tech-S2, these will be integrated into the PID/PDD as the project progresses. This has happened in other projects, which has been found to be effective (Bishop, 2012).

As can be seen in Table 2, it is envisaged that an important part of this stage is assessing suitability of given systems in terms of style, ease of use and the end user, based on what is termed as a User Experience Analysis. One type of user experience analysis that can be very effective is competitive analysis. Competitive analysis involves the analysis of existing sites that provided by similar organizations with

Table 2. Methods used for starting up a project

Method	Description
User Experience Analysis	User Experience Analysis can take many forms and take variable lengths of time, but all those techniques used aim to assess the most suitable approaches to ensuring effective use of the envisaged system by users.
Scenario Based Design	Scenario Based Design focuses on the goals and plans of the user as opposed to the tasks they may or may not carry out.
Requirements Analysis	Requirements Analysis is the means for identifying and documenting user requirements in a way that transfers what users want into a form that is programmable.

similar business goals, which serve to identify perceived strengths and weaknesses and an informal group derived from desirable properties (Cunliffe, 2000).

As can also been seen from Table 2, also deemed important at this stage is the requirement to produce a design concept in terms of customer, purpose and target audience, based on Scenario Based Design. Scenario Based Design methods are an addition to task analysis, which involved focusing on the goals and plans of the user as opposed to the tasks they may or may not carry out. It allows the developers of systems to get a significant understanding of what the user wants to experience in their use of the system (Bishop, 2007b).

Finally, it is considered important during this stage to prepare flow diagrams showing navigation through system, based on using Requirements Analysis.

B/II/2: Initiating a Project (Content, Know Your Subject Matter)

With the project started up and initial specifications of the intended system in place, the next stage to the documentation is to specify the exact requirements of the users intended to benefit from the project and the functions the system needed in order to achieve it. This is the first step in transforming the Project Initiation Document into a Project Delivery Document.

As can be seen from Table 3, Business Activity Modelling is the process of describing business activities, business events and business rules, in order to allow the system being developed to enhance and develop the existing means of doing things rather than replace them (Weaver et al., 2002). Business activity modelling is often based on conceptual models for collaborative systems, with the main concepts being activity, role, participant, and artefact (Hawryszkiewycz, 2008). Examples of such approaches

Table 3. Methods used in SSADM for facilitating the effective initiation of a project and content design

Method	Description
Business Activity Modelling	A method for assessing the scope of the project and confirm this scope is realistic with requires to what is state-of-the art and required by clients and users.
Current Environment Analysis	A means for describing all aspects of a current system (manual and computerised), together with a definition of its shortfalls and problems
Entity Behaviour Modelling	The analysis of models and their effects on entities, such as the effect each system event can have on other elements of the system.
Requirements Cataloguing	A method for cataloguing all user requirements (function and non-functional), including details of measures of success, final solutions and priority.

include ecological cognition (Bishop, 2007a; Bishop, 2007c), distributed cognition (Hutchins, 1995) and activity theory (Engeström & Miettinen, 1999; Kuutti, 1996).

Current Environment Analysis, a can been seen from Table 2, is a means for describing all aspects of a current system (manual and computerised), together with a definition of its shortfalls and problems (Weaver et al., 2002). Looking at Table 2 again, Entity Behaviour Modelling, formerly called Entity-Event Modelling, is for the analysis of models and their effects on entities (Weaver et al., 2002). Entity Behaviour Modelling anticipates each system event that can affect an entity's occurrences and provides a view of allowable sequencing of these events (Weaver et al., 2002). This can be helped through the use of scenarios to identify what features users are likely to want (Bishop, 2005; Carroll, 2000; Preece, 2001).

Requirements Cataloguing, as shown in Table 2, is the assembling of all user requirements, whether functional or non-functional, including details of measures of success, final solutions and priority (Weaver et al., 2002).

C/III/3 Managing Product Development (Technology, Identify Mediating Artifacts Users Need to Achieve Goals)

This stage involves selecting technology, designing, implementing and testing prototypes and refining and testing usability, sociability and learning (Bishop, 2007b). This stage adds significant detail to the Project Delivery document so that it is clearly to see the extent and limitations of the previous two stages and for such difficulties to be ironed out.

In terms of User Task Analysis and Prototyping shown in Table 4, the goals and requirements of the users of the intended virtual community are mapped with the features of possible software and the overall conceptual design is determined (Bishop, 2007b). This stage can involve many small iterations of design-and-test or in larger projects, and when designing the system, should involve developers consulting design guidelines to determine the most effective means of meeting the goals of users (Bishop, 2007b; Preece, 2001).

Table 4 shows the requirements of Social Planning and Modelling (Preece, 2001, p.222). This stage builds on the task analysis to determine how the registration for a website should work, in order to determine how many barriers to entry there needs to be in order to ensure only the most appropriate users participate (Powazek, 2002). It also considers whether a moderator is needed in order to manage user behaviour (Bishop, 2014a; Preece, 2001; Salmon, 2003), order whether users have such strong social ties

Table 4. Methods recommended by Jenny Preece for managing product delivery and user-centred design

Method	Description
User Task Analysis and Prototyping	Assessing what the core features that users will need from the day the system is launched and how they might want these represented.
Social Planning and Modelling	Builds on previous stage to determine how the registration for a website should work, such as how many barriers to entry there needs to be in order to ensure only the most appropriate users participate
Third-Party Resource Refinement and Tuning	Testing that third-party resources are active and suitable for use, whether remotely or within the system
User Scenario Testing	Expressing what a user wants for a system then involving them in testing it to see if they get what they want.

there will be little disruption, known as the Figallo effect (Bishop, 2011a; Figallo, 1998). This part also considers which links are needed to be create the opportunity for users to be aware of policies or other information, such as making a frequently asked questions link accessible (Preece, 2001) or providing notification, such as to distract a user's attention (Bishop, 2011b).

As can be seen from Table 4, Third-Party Resource Refinement and Tuning is essential for testing that third-party and other resources are active and suitable for the new system (Preece, 2001, p.356). This method can, among other uses, determine where best to place links to third-party websites or other services, use fonts and highlighting to indicate the use of the resource, and statements or other indicators to explain whether it is accessible through the system or externally.

User Scenario Testing, as can be seen from Table 4, is a method for expressing in written form what a particular user is looking to getting out of a system and then test it to see that it provides what they want (Carroll, 1996; Carroll, 2000; Preece, 2001, p.224).

D/IV/4: Managing Product Delivery (Services, Develop System)

This stage of the project, which mostly occurs after a significant amount of technology prototyping and development, aims to bring this together with user interface design processes so that the system, however technologically constructed within its core, is easily usable by those who are its intended user group. Table 5 shows the methods proposed for determining whether a system meets the requirements of this stage.

Table 5. Methods recommended by Derek Powazek for managing the delivery of effective of a system

Method	Description
Two-Tree Audit	This method allowed for the connection of content with community so that they are not separate but inter-connected.
Connected-Dots Modelling	This methods allows formatting of a system so that content is connected and easily accessible for all.
Nuts and Bolts Audit	This method provides for the effective analysis of a system to test it is designed for its audience, flexibility, experience, simplicity, readability, beauty.
Design Matters Modelling	This method ensures that colour choice, shares and patterns, photos and illustrations, and attention to detail are considered in the design/redesign process.

Figure 6. A badly designed online community with content (left) not integrated with community (right)

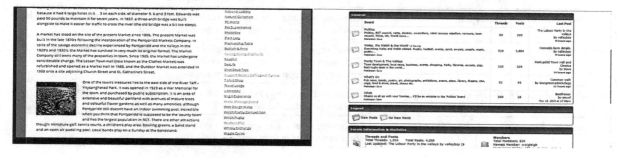

Figure 7. A well designed online community with content (left) integrated with community (right)

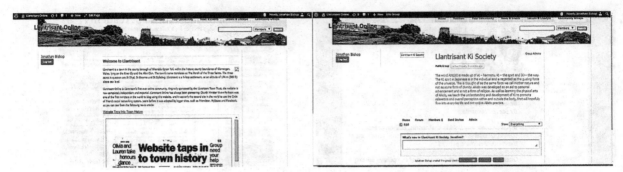

A Two-Tree Audit is an approach for enabling the connection of content with community so that they are not separate but inter-connected (Powazek, 2002). The approach suggests that user-generated content, often called social media, which is produce by a websites users, should be as closely as possible tied to the more permanent information for the website.

Figure 6 shows a website that fails to carry out two-tree modelling. The website, Pontytown.co.uk is notorious for the Internet trolling that occurs via it, including of a racist nature (Bishop, 2013), and the design does nothing to achieve that. If this website had gone through two-tree modelling, then the clear difference in the design of the information and discussion sections could be avoided, promoting a cohesion between the positive aspects of the site in terms of the locality, with the forum where there are less than savoury characters.

Figure 7 on the other hand shows a well-designed system, where context and discussion are integrated. Llantrisant Online has a history section, like Pontytown, but unlike that site it has the information on the locality in the same design and style as the forum. The web address for Pontypridd's history on Ponty-town is www.pontytown.co.uk/history, whereas the forum is hosted on pontypriddtown.proboards.com. In the case of Llantrisant Online, the information on the town's history is hosted www.llantrisant.info/history-of-llantrisant/ and the forums are at www.llantrisant.info/llantrisant-clubs-and-societies/ and this is a clear example of how two-trees modelling can be effectively done so that not only the webpage design is the same, but the permalink structure is similar also.

Connected-Dots Modelling is an approach for allowing the formatting of a system so that content is connected and easily accessible for all, avoiding the two-tree problem (Powazek, 2002). As can be seen from Figure 8 there are good examples and bad examples that can be used to show effective Connected-Dots Modelling. Both websites shown relate to Internet trolling, but it is the one on the right that is a model example. This one not only has an article about trolling, but easily allows users to comment on the article within the page, compared to the one on the left where one needs to click the 'Board' link at the top of the page to go to the message boards section. The one on the right of Figure 8 also uses tags, enabling users to find other articles related to the content they are interested in.

Nuts and Bolts Audit is a method for enabling the effective analysis of a system to test it is designed for its audience, flexibility, experience, simplicity, readability, beauty (Powazek, 2002). Figure 9 shows a website that would fail a Nuts and Bolts Audit (left) and one that would pass it (right). In terms of the one on the left, by a self-proclaimed Internet expert, the purpose of the site is unclear other than boasting about the clients the person works for. The one on the right on the other hand makes it clear that the person is a researcher and available to hire to respond to calls for papers. These call-outs are

Figure 8. A website without connected-dots modelling (left) and one with (right)

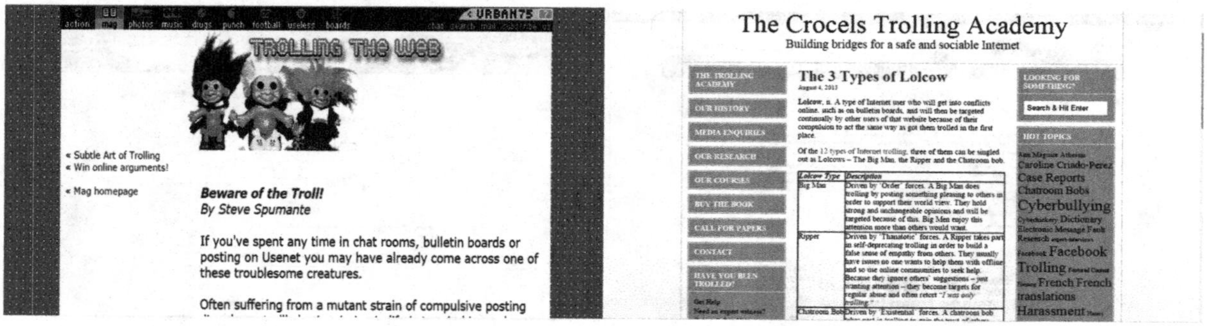

easily readable, and there is additional information below the navigation, whereas the one on the left is a splash-page, meaning the user has to go to another page to find out the person's expertise. In terms of beauty, the one on the right is bright and appealing and welcoming, whereas the one on the left could be considered boring and indeed menacing. The one on the left may have more simplicity, but it lacks the core information the one on the right has, such as a mini-biography, ability to search, and ease of accessing navigation.

Design Matters Modelling is a method for ensuring that colour choice, shares and patterns, photos and illustrations, and attention to detail are considered in the design/redesign process (Powazek, 2002). To be effective the audit must consider multi-platform issues and the specific needs of the users most likely to benefit from the system. There is a never ending supply of books setting out design guidelines for Internet applications, some based on established principles that can be used in the pervasive multi-platform market place that exists today (Nielsen, 2000), and others based on archaic coding and design methods, not suited to HTML5 and other emerging technologies (Slocombe, 2001). In conducting a Design Matters Audit, judgement will need to be exercised in terms of selecting the most appropriate design factors, considering user requirements from the outset.

As can be seen from Figure 10, there is an example of a website that is not optimised so that it can work effectively on a mobile phone (left) and an example of one that does (right). The left image shows a website for a self-published author on an iPhone using mobile Internet. The image that is designed for the top of the website is too big to be loaded and the lack of textual content – due to it being a splash page – makes the purpose of the site unclear. As can be seen in the one on the right, for a researcher and

Figure 9. A badly designed homepage (left) and a well-designed homepage (right)

Figure 10. A website that does not work properly on a mobile phone (left) and one that does (right)

multimedia professional, the advertisements for the website have been resized from the 468x60 size to still be viewable on the mobile phone, and the most relevant parts of the website – the main menu and body text – are easily viewable, even on the small screen.

E/V/5: Closing a Project (Support, Evaluate Persuasiveness)

One of the errors often made in a software development project is not considering the final, and often on-going area of support. The launching of a product onto the market is not the final step in the commercialisation process, but the beginning of its commercial realisation and social acceptance. There are a number of common methods used to transition a product onto the market and to ensure its continued growth. As can be seen in Table 6 there are a number of standard methods that can be used at the support stage to ensure the product's constant evolution (Cunliffe, 2000).

On this basis, this stage amends the Project Delivery Document (PDD), for the final section to resemble a project initiation document, in terms of a commitment to continually evolve the system. The methods shown in Table 6 therefore should be regularly carried out so that the PDD as a whole can be amended to reflect the changes in the design of the software after its release, making it a detailed specification document that can always be referred to, including for best practice in future projects, making it highly suited to a learning organisation.

Direct Observation, as shown in Table 6, involved users being asked to use the system and then metrics are collected on their use, either in the background or via a researcher coding the video record-

Table 6. Methods recommended by Daniel Cunliffe for enabling the closure of a project and ongoing support

Method	Description
Direct Observation	Users are asked to use the system and then metrics are collected on their use, either in the background or via a researcher coding the video recordings or similar recorded observations.
Inspection/Walkthrough	Users are invited to use the system and give critical feedback, either through being explained the features or independently using the system and providing information during that process
User Focus Groups, Interviews and Feedback	Users are asked in groups or individually to provide their feedback on their use of the system. This may be through feedback forms on the website, group-based discussions, or one-to-one conferencing.

Figure 11. A website suited to a 2000s audience (left) and a 2010s audience (right)

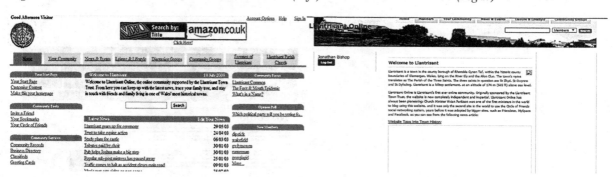

ings or similar recorded observations. Direct observation is argued to be the most feasible and efficient approach to evaluate the usability of web-based systems, not only because of the limitations of the other methods but also for its own strengths (Benbunan-Fich, 2001). Direct observation is ideally a method which uses real users and real tasks— real usability problems can be identified with only a small number of test users (Cunliffe, Kritou, & Tudhope, 2001). The method is reusable and can be used to test initial concepts, prototypes and completed systems (Cunliffe et al., 2001), making it ideally suited to the approach in this methodology for amending the design document on an on-going and iterative basis. As direct observation is a relatively quick and inexpensive approach (Armstrong, Brewer, & Steinberg, 2002), it is capable for use in identifying the critical flaws in a design on an ongoing basis as the once final system starts to no longer meet the aims of its user-base.

The next two items in Table 6, Inspection/Walkthrough, will be contextualised with the example of Llantrisant Online, which can be seen Figure 11. It can be seen that the version on the left from the 2000s is very different from the one on the right from the 2010s. The Inspection/Walkthrough approach is where users are invited to use the system and give critical feedback, either through being explained the features or independently using the system and providing information during that process. As can be seen in Figure 12 an inspection/walkthrough can be helpful at determining a user's 'theory of mind' – that is the worldview they have that affects the way they use the system as it is. In this case, from the 2000s very of the website, the user is looking to send a greeting card to another user. This shows some complexity in the system, which today might be replaced with a 'share' feature rather than an email based system, as the share feature is known to improve social proof among users (Bishop, 2014b).

(1) Clicking on the 'sign-in' option. (2) Entering my username and password, clicking on 'sign-in'. (3) I'm going to send my partner a card, clicking on 'Your Community' looking for 'Greetings Cards'. (4) Clicking on the link, Clicking on 'South Wales'. (5) I think I'll pick this one. (6) Comment B3.6 I'm typing in his name, typing in his username. (7) Erm, what shall I say... (8) Changing the colour, to pink. (8) Clicking on 'Preview' (9) Clicking on 'Send' (10) It's sent (11) Clicking on 'Sign Out.' (11) On top of the page it says 'see you soon'!

Table 6 also shows that User Focus Groups, Interviews and Feedback is where users are asked in groups or individually to provide their feedback on their use of the system, which may be through feedback forms on the website, group-based discussions, or one-to-one conferencing. Focus groups can be useful following more structured approaches such as questionnaires, which allow that feedback to be

Figure 12. Example of a walkthrough for 'Llantrisant Online'

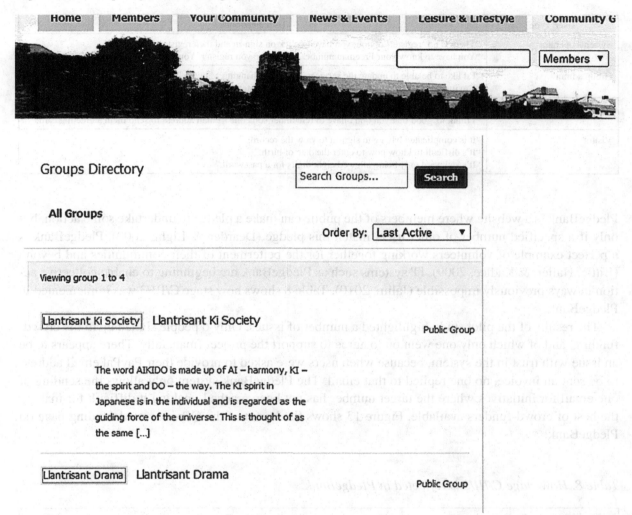

explored in more depth (Cunliffe, Morris, & Prys, 2013; Morris, Cunliffe, & Prys, 2012). Focus groups are therefore an ideal means to continue the evolution of a system after its initial launch, in order to ensure it continues to meet the needs of users. Table 7 shows some of the example feedback generated in relation to Llantrisant Online.

A PILOT STUDY FOR ASSESSING THE POTENTIAL OF A LEARNING ORGANISATION APPROACH TO PROJECT MANAGEMENT

This pilot study sought to test the third stage – managing project delivery – on a system that had already been through the earlier phases, including a user experience analysis of those who subscribe to the QMETHOD discussion list. A crowd-funding platform was identified, namely PledgeBank, on which persuasive text could be presented based on the principles of ecological cognition (Bishop, 2007c).

Table 7. Examples of user feedback from Llantrisant Online

User Type	User Feedback
Systems operator	"There is no 'register' option; you have to click on sign-in and then register." "You have to know your Freeman number at the time you register. You should be able to look it up."
Group admin	"I'd like to be able to update the services. They are changing May 5th." "I'm impressed with the site, I'm not very computer literate and it's quite easy to access things."
Member	"I think the site's nice. It's got personal things on there. It's friendly." "I think its good that you don't have to remember someone's email address to send them a greeting card."
Visitor	"It is complicated having to sign-in to view the records." "It's difficult to know how to enter the date of birth." "It's awkward only being allowed eight digits for a password."

PledgeBank is a website where members of the public can make a pledge to undertake some action, but only if a specified number of other users match this pledge (Dearden & Light, 2009). PledgeBank is a perfect example of volunteers working together for the betterment of their communities and beyond (Bittle, Haller, & Kadlec, 2009). IT systems such as PledgeBank are beginning to enable collective action in ways previously impossible (Jalim, 2010). Table 8 shows how stage C/III/3 was implemented in PledgeBank.

The results of the pilot study highlighted a number of issues. Only 6 people signed up to the crowd-funding, and of which only one went on to agree to support the project financially. There appears to be an issue with trust in the system, because when users were asked to provide their PayPal email address to be sent an invoice, no one replied to that email. The PledgeBank system only allows the sending of one email for initiatives where the target number has not been reached, making it difficult for making the best of crowd-funders available. Figure 13 shows the layout of the QPress crowd-funding page on PledgeBank.

Table 8. How stage C/III/3 is reflected in PledgeBank

Process	Examples
3.1 Create a simple system that can accommodate different users (User Task Analysis and Prototyping)	The PledgeBank webpage greeted users with the following introduction: "WordPress plug-in developers iFlair.com have been commissioned to develop a WordPress plug-in called QPress. This application will enable data to be collected on the Q-methodology approach using the WordPress Content Management System and then outputted to SPSS and PCQ. If people sign this pledge then it will be extended to include PQMethod and those who pledge will get a share of the profits."
3.2 Create hyperlinks as mediating artefacts to avoid dead links (Third-Party Resource Testing)	The PledgeBank website should the link "— Jonathan Bishop FBCS CITP, Q-method fanatic (contact)" so people who wanted more information could contact the proposer. The webpage also had the link, "Anything wrong with this pledge? Tell us!" in order for users to report any problems.
3.3 Create text and image based mediating artefacts to enhance participation (User Scenario Testing).	"Deadline to sign up by: 6th September 2011" "Sign up now" "(we only use this to tell you when the pledge is completed and to let the pledge creator get in touch)," "People searching for your name on the Internet might be able to find your signature."
3.4 Create persuasive links for e-mail and other applications (Social Planning and Modelling).	"Print out customised flyers," "Promote on your site or blog," "Create a local version of this pledge." "Or text 'pledge QPress' to 60022 (in the UK only)"

Figure 13. The page layout of PledgeBank for the QPress crowd-funding

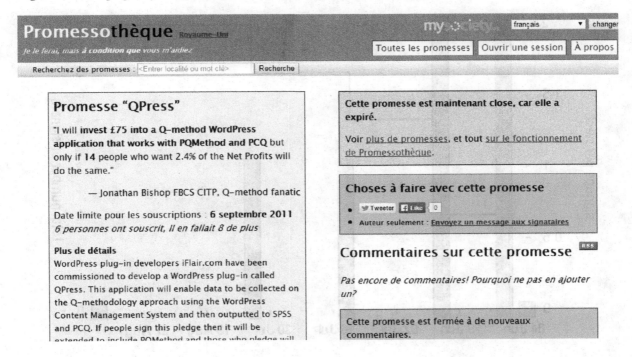

If one were to apply the criteria for the 'Support' stage of C2-Tech-S2, it is possible to see there are a number of limitations with PledgeBank as a way to build a buzz around a product. In terms of a Two-Tree Audit, PledgeBank fails this because there is no way to embed detailed information or discussion in with the page seeking funding. Whilst in passes the Connected-Dots modelling in terms of ease of access of information (like that in Table 8), there is still little way to integrate core information about the site or build community. In terms of the Nuts and Bolts Audit PledgeBank is quite successful. The webpage for the crowd-funding makes it clear who it is aimed at and makes it simple to understand how they can participate. Many aspects of the page are customisable and flexible and the design is not overly complicated. An issue with the platform is that it is not designed to produce lasting communities, especially as organisers are only allowed to email funders once. This therefore makes it impossible to redesign the website to increase participation. Other aspects of the Design Matters Modelling make PledgeBank effective, such as that the design is simple, yet offers the complexity needed to provide information. The conclusion might be that PledgeBank is not best suited to crowd-funding projects where one expects money to be handed over at the end, but would be more suited to project where the aim is to raise awareness of an issue, rather than actually recruiting others. It is thus the case that for the C2-Tech-S2 model to be successful, all aspects of it need to be applied to the development of a system at the point of development, because as shown with PledgeBank whilst the technology might be appropriate if it does not take account of other factors, in this case 'support,' then the solution developed or used might not be appropriate to the intended aim, such as to increase participation.

Whilst there was not the Big Data produced that would be needed to effectively evaluate the success of the project, there were a number of figures available on the PledgeBank platform. As can be seen from Figure 14 there was a significant trend between the start date of 3 June 2011 and the end date of

Figure 14. Graph showing sign-up rate of sponoring QPress on PledgeBank

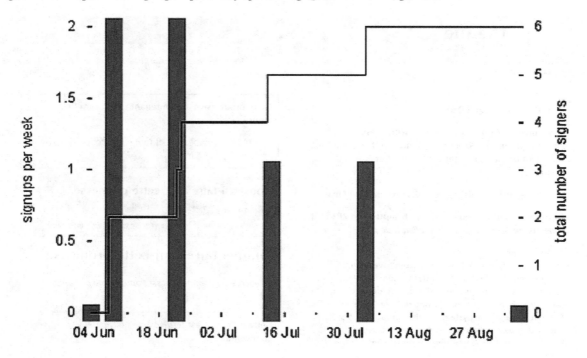

6 September 2011. It can be seen a clear peak of 2 pledges per week within the first two weeks of June when the crowd-funding being advertised, dropping to 1 per week for the weeks in the middle of July, before dropping to none between August and September. With additional data in the larger scale study after this pilot study it might be possible to say whether the sign-up rates for crowd-funded projects match that for other sales, such as the sales of DVDs (Cockrill & Goode, 2010).

IMPLICATIONS AND FUTURE RESEARCH DIRECTIONS

The C2-Tech-S2 approach defined in this chapter is based on a number of well-established project management methodologies. Its purpose is to allow people from non-typical backgrounds, such as those with certain special educational needs, or otherwise those without an advanced education, to be able to take part in software projects without the technical knowledge needed in more complex methodologies. However, C2-Tech-S2 has not been tested in an environment in which people without a technical background are taking part, meaning further research is needed to test its efficacy for created an inclusive workplace within a learning organisation.

DISCUSSION

This chapter has explored the design and construction of a software project management method that is fit for use in a learning organisation where people are of mixed ability and experience. A number of existing methods were explored, both specialist and generalist and a new methodology developed. The new methodology was based on a unit from the Open College Network, used for people at entry level to web design. This allowed the model to go back to basic and ensure it was open to people of all abilities, so there was both simplicity for those who needed it, and also the opportunity for complexity for those who take on a greater role in the design and development of the product. The methodology, named C2-Tech-S2, after the 5-stage Star Lifecycle it in part derived from, was tested in part with a website called PledgeBank. The purpose of this website is to bring together people who wanted to collaborate on a particular initiative, in the case the development of a Q-Methodology plug-in for WordPress called QPress. The outcome of this pilot study showed that it is not possible to complete only one stage of the C2-Tech-S2 model, as to have an effective model all aspects of this methodology need to be implemented. A significant advantage of C2-Tech-S2 is that it can integrate with the PRINCE2 methodology, but in such a way that the specific tasks required in software development projects are part of it, rather than it simply being a generalise model for any project, software or otherwise. This chapter has clearly shown there is a lot of potential in C2-Tech-S2 for learning organisation, where people of all abilities can take part.

REFERENCES

Al-Zoabi, Z. (2008). *Introducing discipline to XP: Applying PRINCE2 on XP projects*. Paper presented at the 3rd International Conference on Information and Communication Technologies: From Theory to Applications (ICTTA 2008), Damascus, Syria. doi:10.1109/ICTTA.2008.4530347

Armstrong, S. D., Brewer, W. C., & Steinberg, R. K. (2002). Usability testing. In S. G. Charlton & T. G. O'Brien (Eds.), *Handbook of human factors testing and evaluation* (pp. 403–432). Arlington, VA: Office of Naval Research.

Ashworth, C. M. (1988). Structured systems analysis and design method (SSADM). *Information and Software Technology, 30*(3), 153–163. doi:10.1016/0950-5849(88)90062-6

Barlow, J., & Jashapara, A. (1998). Organisational learning and inter-firm "partnering" in the UK construction industry. *The Learning Organization, 5*(2), 86–98. doi:10.1108/09696479810212051

Benbunan-Fich, R. (2001). Using protocol analysis to evaluate the usability of a commercial web site. *Information & Management, 39*(2), 151–163. doi:10.1016/S0378-7206(01)00085-4

Berger, H. (2007). Agile development in a bureaucratic arena—A case study experience. *International Journal of Information Management, 27*(6), 386–396. doi:10.1016/j.ijinfomgt.2007.08.009

Berger, H., & Beynon-Davies, P. (2009). The utility of rapid application development in large-scale, complex projects. *Information Systems Journal, 19*(6), 549–570. doi:10.1111/j.1365-2575.2009.00329.x

Bishop, J. (2004). The potential of persuasive technology for educating heterogeneous user groups. (Unpublished MSc). University of Glamorgan, Pontypridd.

Bishop, J. (2005). *The role of mediating artifacts in the design of persuasive e-learning systems*. Paper presented at the 1st International Conference on Internet Technologies and Applications (ITA'05), Wrexham, UK.

Bishop, J. (2007a). Ecological cognition: A new dynamic for human-computer interaction. In B. Wallace, A. Ross, J. Davies & T. Anderson (Eds.), The mind, the body and the world: Psychology after cognitivism (pp. 327-345). Exeter, UK: Imprint Academic.

Bishop, J. (2007b). *Evaluation-centred design of E-learning communities: A case study and review.* Paper presented at the 2nd International Conference on Internet Technologies and Applications (ITA'07), Wrexham, UK.

Bishop, J. (2007c). Increasing participation in online communities: A framework for human–computer interaction. *Computers in Human Behavior, 23*(4), 1881–1893. doi:10.1016/j.chb.2005.11.004

Bishop, J. (2007d). *An investigation into how the european union affects the development and provision of e-learning services. Unpublished LLM.* Pontypridd, UK: University of Glamorgan.

Bishop, J. (2011a). All's WELL that ends WELL: A comparative analysis of the constitutional and administrative frameworks of cyberspace and the United Kingdom. In A. Dudley-Sponaugle & J. Braman (Eds.), *Investigating cyber law and cyber ethics: Issues, impacts and practices.* Hershey, PA: IGI Global.

Bishop, J. (2011b). *The equatrics of intergenerational knowledge transformation in techno-cultures: Towards a model for enhancing information management in virtual worlds. (Unpublished MScEcon).* Aberystwyth, UK: Aberystwyth University.

Bishop, J. (2012). Lessons from the emotive project for increasing take-up of big society and responsible capitalism initiatives. In P. M. Pumilia-Gnarini, E. Favaron, E. Pacetti, J. Bishop, & L. Guerra (Eds.), *Didactic strategies and technologies for education: Incorporating advancements* (pp. 208–217). Hershey, PA: IGI Global. doi:10.4018/978-1-4666-2122-0.ch019

Bishop, J. (2013). Increasing capital revenue in social networking communities: Building social and economic relationships through avatars and characters. In J. Bishop (Ed.), *Examining the concepts, issues, and implications of internet trolling* (pp. 44–61). Hershey, PA: IGI Global. doi:10.4018/978-1-4666-2803-8.ch005

Bishop, J. (2014a). Getting to know your users for effective e-moderation. *Multimedia Information & Technology, 40*(2), 18–36.

Bishop, J. (2014b). My click is my bond: The role of contracts, social proof, and gamification for sysops to reduce pseudo-activism and internet trolling. In J. Bishop (Ed.), *Gamification for human factors integration: Social, educational, and psychological issues* (pp. 1–6). Hershey, PA: IGI Global. doi:10.4018/978-1-4666-5071-8.ch001

Bittle, S., Haller, C., & Kadlec, A. (2009). *Promising practices in online engagement No. 3.* New York, NY: Center for Advances in Public Engagement.

Blaauboer, F., Sikkel, K., & Aydin, M. N. (2007). *Deciding to adopt requirements traceability in practice.* Paper presented at the 9th International Conference on Advanced Information Systems Engineering (CAiSE'07), Trondheim. doi:10.1007/978-3-540-72988-4_21

Blight, L. K., & Ainley, D. G. (2008). Southern ocean not so pristine. *Science, 321*(5895), 1443. doi:10.1126/science.321.5895.1443b PMID:18787149

Brownbridge, D. (1990). *Using Z to develop a CASE toolset*. Paper presented at the Z User Workshop, Oxford, UK. doi:10.1007/978-1-4471-3877-8_9

Burtch, G., Ghose, A., & Wattal, S. (2011). *An empirical examination of the antecedents of contribution patterns in crowdfunded markets*. Academic Press.

Cam, S., Purcell, J., & Tailby, S. (2003). Contingent employment in the UK. In O. Bergström & D. W. Storri (Eds.), *Contingent employment in europe and the united states* (pp. 52–78). Cheltenham, UK: Edward Elgar Publishing. doi:10.4337/9781781008126.00010

Carroll, J. M. (1996). Becoming social: Expanding scenario-based approaches in HCI. *Behaviour & Information Technology*, *15*(4), 266–275. doi:10.1080/014492996120184

Carroll, J. M. (2000). Five reasons for scenario-based design. *Interacting with Computers*, *13*(1), 43–60. doi:10.1016/S0953-5438(00)00023-0

Cockrill, A., & Goode, M. M. H. (2010). Perceived price fairness and price decay in the DVD market. *Journal of Product and Brand Management*, *19*(5), 367–374. doi:10.1108/10610421011068603

Coleman, J. P. (2013). Data flow sequences: A revision of data flow diagrams for modelling applications using XML. *International Journal of Advanced Computer Science & Applications*, *4*(5).

Coyle-Shapiro, J. A., & Kessler, I. (2002). Contingent and Non-Contingent working in local government: Contrasting psychological contracts. *Public Administration*, *80*(1), 77–101. doi:10.1111/1467-9299.00295

Cunha, R., Cunha, M., Morgado, A., & Brewster, C. (2003). Market forces, strategic management, HRM practices and organizational performance, A model based in a european sample. *Management Research*, *1*(1), 79–91. doi:10.1108/15365430380000519

Cunliffe, D. (2000). Developing usable web sites–a review and model. *Internet Research*, *10*(4), 295–308. doi:10.1108/10662240010342577

Cunliffe, D., Kritou, E., & Tudhope, D. (2001). Usability evaluation for museum web sites. *Museum Management and Curatorship*, *19*(3), 229–252. doi:10.1080/09647770100201903

Cunliffe, D., Morris, D., & Prys, C. (2013). Young bilinguals' language behaviour in social networking sites: The use of welsh on facebook. *Journal of Computer-Mediated Communication*, *18*(3), 339–361. doi:10.1111/jcc4.12010

Davis, C. (2000). Maintaining a balance? In A. Scammell (Ed.), *I in the sky: Visions of the information future* (pp. 18–29). London: Routledge.

Dawson, C., & Dawson, R. (2014). Software development process models: A technique for evaluation and Decision-Making. *Knowledge and Process Management*, *21*(1), 42–53. doi:10.1002/kpm.1419

de Fortuny, E. J., Martens, D., & Provost, F. (2013). Predictive modeling with big data: Is bigger really better? *Big Data*, de Souza, C. S., & Preece, J. (2004). A framework for analyzing and understanding online communities. *Interacting with Computers*, *16*(3), 579–610.

Dearden, A., & Light, A. (2009). *Designing for e-social action an application taxonomy*. Sheffield, UK: Communication & Computing Research Centre.

Engeström, Y., & Miettinen, R. (1999). *Perspectives on activity theory*. Cambridge, UK: Cambridge University Press. doi:10.1017/CBO9780511812774

Figallo, C. (1998). *Hosting web communities: Building relationships, increasing customer loyalty, and maintaining a competitive edge*. New York, NY: John Wiley & Sons, Inc.

Fogg, B. J. (2002). *Persuasive technology: Using computers to change what we think and do*. San Francisco, CA: Morgan Kaufmann.

Gibb, A. A. (1997). Small firms' training and competitiveness. building upon the small business as a learning organisation. *International Small Business Journal, 15*(3), 13–29. doi:10.1177/0266242697153001

Gorard, S. (2003). Patterns of work-based learning. *Journal of Vocational Education and Training, 55*(1), 47–64. doi:10.1080/13636820300200218

Hawryszkiewycz, I. (2008). Supporting complex adaptive processes with lightweight platforms. In L. M. Camarinha-Matos & W. Picard (Eds.), *Pervasive collaborative networks* (pp. 381–388). Wien, Austria: Springer. doi:10.1007/978-0-387-84837-2_39

Hix, D., & Hartson, H. R. (1993). *Developing user interfaces: Ensuring usability through product & process*. New York, NY: John Wiley & Sons, Inc.

Hutchins, E. (1995). Cognition in the wild. MIT Press.

Jalim, S. (2010). Green IT and collective action. In T. Tomlinson (Ed.), *Information technology for environmental sustainability* (pp. 147–170). Cambridge, MA: MIT Press.

Kerrigan, F., & Graham, G. (2010). Interaction of regional news-media production and consumption through the social space. *Journal of Marketing Management, 26*(3), 302–320. doi:10.1080/02672570903566334

Kim, A. J. (2000). *Community building on the web: Secret strategies for successful online communities*. Berkeley, CA: Peachpit Press.

Kuutti, K. (1996). Activity theory as a potential framework for human-computer interaction research. In Context and consciousness: Activity theory and human-computer interaction (pp. 17-44). Academic Press.

Marchi, G., Giachetti, C., & De Gennaro, P. (2011). Extending lead-user theory to online brand communities: The case of the community Ducati. *Technovation*.

Mbakwe, C., & Cunliffe, D. (2003). Conceptualising the process of hypermedia seduction. In *Proceedings of the 1st International Meeting of Science and Technology Design: Senses and Sensibility – Linking Tradition to Innovation through Design*. Lisbon, Portugal: Academic Press.

Mbakwe, C., & Cunliffe, D. (2007). Hypermedia seduction: Further exploration of the process of "seductive" online user interaction. In B. Ganor & K. von Knop (Eds.), *Hypermedia seduction for terrorist recruiting* (p. 207). New York, NY: Ios Pr Inc.

Metzler, T. (2011). *Venture financing by crowdfunding*. Munich: GRIN Verlag.

Morris, D., Cunliffe, D., & Prys, C. (2012). Social networks and minority languages speakers: The use of social networking sites among young people. *Sociolinguistic Studies, 6*(1), 1–20. doi:10.1558/sols.v6.i1.1

Nielsen, J. (2000). *Designing web usability*. New York, NY: New Riders.

Ordanini, A., Miceli, L., Pizzetti, M., & Parasuraman, A. (2011). Crowd-funding: Transforming customers into investors through innovative service platforms. *Journal of Service Management, 22*(4), 443–470. doi:10.1108/09564231111155079

Parker, R. E. (2002). The global economy and changes in the nature of contingent work. In *Labor and Capital in the Age of Globalization: The Labor Process and the Changing Nature of Work in the Global Economy* (pp. 107-123). Academic Press.

Peck, J., & Theodore, N. (2001). Contingent Chicago: Restructuring the spaces of temporary labor. *International Journal of Urban and Regional Research, 25*(3), 471–496. doi:10.1111/1468-2427.00325

Polack, F., & Mander, K. C. (1994). *Software quality assurance using the SAZ method*. Paper presented at the Z User Workshop, Cambridge, UK. doi:10.1007/978-1-4471-3452-7_13

Powazek, D. M. (2002). *Design for community: The art of connecting real people in virtual places*. Upper Saddle River, NJ: New Riders.

Preece, J. (2000). *Online communities: Designing usability, supporting sociability*. Chichester, UK: John Wiley & Sons.

Preece, J. (2001). *Designing usability, supporting sociability: Questions participants ask about online communities*. Paper presented at the Human-Computer Interaction: INTERACT'01: IFIP TC. 13 International Conference on Human-Comupter Interaction, Tokyo, Japan.

Rowley, J. (1998). Creating a learning organisation in higher education. *Industrial and Commercial Training, 30*(1), 16–19. doi:10.1108/00197859810197708

Salmon, G. (2003). E-moderating: The key to teaching & learning online. London: Taylor & Frances Books Ltd.

Sealey, R. (2010). Logistics workers and global logistics: The heavy lifters of globalisation. *Work Organisation, Labour & Globalisation, 4*(2), 25–38.

Siegelaub, J. M. (2004). *How PRINCE2 can complement PMBOK and your PMP*. Paper presented at the PMI Global Congress, Anaheim, CA.

Simms, M., & Dean, D. (2014). Mobilising contingent workers: An analysis of two successful cases. *Economic and Industrial Democracy*.

Slocombe, M. (2001). Max hits: Building successful websites (1st ed.). Hove, UK: Rotovision.

Thomas, K., & Allen, S. (2006). The learning organisation: A meta-analysis of themes in literature. *The Learning Organization, 13*(2), 123–139. doi:10.1108/09696470610645467

Wang, C. L., & Ahmed, P. K. (2003). Organisational learning: A critical review. *The Learning Organization, 10*(1), 8–17. doi:10.1108/09696470310457469

Weaver, P. L., Lambrou, N., & Walkley, M. (2002). *Practical business systems development using SSADM: A complete tutorial guide*. London: Pearson Education.

WRONG. R. (2009). *Increasing membership in online communities: The five principles of managing virtual club economies.* Paper presented at the 3rd International Conference on Internet Technologies and Applications (ITA'09), Wrexham, UK.

Young, M. L., & Levine, J. R. (2000). *Poor richard's building online communities: Create a web community for your business, club, association, or family.* Top Floor Pub.

KEY TERMS AND DEFINITIONS

Agile Development: A development approach where many embodiments of an invention are built with the intention of them forming part of a wider system in the long-run, for which the nature of may not be known at the time the individual embodiments are made.

Contingent Working: An approach to employment where people are engaged for a specific task at a specific time in a project's progression, and are not engaged when their skills are not required. Contingent workers usually work for a number of different clients.

Crowd-Funding: A means by which funds can be raised to pay for the programming of a software application or other venture where the funders are often potential users of the system.

Interprofessionalism: Essential to contingent working, a set-up where a number of different professionals work together maximising their individual ability in a collaborative way.

Knowledge Transformation: The process by which learning is gained through the internalisation of external representations into higher order thinking.

Learning Organisation: An organisation focussed around individual development where people are chosen for what they can be and not what they already are. Contrasts with a teaching organisation that focusses on imparting information rather than supporting knowledge transformation.

Software Project Management: An approach, usually structured, that allows for a software product to be developed for a client or specific user group.

Chapter 7
Motivation behind Agile Software Development over Traditional Development

Karun Madan
SD College, India

ABSTRACT

Out of the many revolutions in software development methodologies over the past years, no new methodology withstands completely in one way or the other. The failure rate of projects is still very high in spite of so much of revolutionary methodologies come in existence. Unsuccessful projects not only mean the incomplete projects even after deadline or outdated projects but there may be several other scenarios like project did not meet up the real requirements or lack of ability to deal with the changing requirements etc. In this kind of circumstances, projects were never successfully utilized, and another high percentage of projects again required massive rework to be utilizable. Factors like changing requirements and late testing and integration are few of the main causes of this high percentage of failure. This paper reveals how agile development is a way out to the issues linked with traditional software development. Agile development primarily focuses on the rapid delivery of enterprise worth in the form of working software.

INTRODUCTION

Over the years, traditional software development proved to result in huge failure percentage in one or the other way. Most of the projects entirely fail, or may be of no use due to several reasons. Generally software are developed in waterfall-style methodology and this methodology is proved to be one of the prime contributing factor for almost all types of failures. Failures may be total failures or mostly software does not meet the actual needs in spite of the fact that they met on-paper specifications. So they are never successfully utilized. Even if one wants to re-tailor them, it requires extensive amount of rework to make them usable. Most of the time, re-tailoring decision goes wrong as compare to making a fresh start.

In contrast to traditional software development, agile development has shown promising results in the past few years. The Manifesto for Agile Software Development was agreed and signed by experienced

DOI: 10.4018/978-1-4666-8510-9.ch007

and recognized software development "gurus", inventors and practitioners (Cusumano et. al., 2003). This manifesto declares the main values of agile software development (Murauskaite et. al., 2008).

Agile software development is based on the methodology in which at first attempt, working software is given to the client. Client takes it as complete software and gives feedback to the team. This feedback may be some shortcomings or some new features or some change requirements. The new features were those which were put into notice at the time of requirements specifications or some change requirements. In Agile software development, development team takes these change requirements in a positive way even at late stages of development. In contrast to this, in traditional software development, team can only present documents at this stage as first attempt to test or run software would be at last stage. Actual working software is far more useful than just offering documents to product owners in the meetings.

Agile software development is termed as lightweight development methods as an answer to heavy-weight waterfall-based methodology. In Agile software development requirements need not be fully gathered at the beginning stages of the software development, rather continuous customer involvement is vital. Customer should be called in each and every meeting along with development team. As a result, customer satisfaction increases a lot by rapid delivery of useful working software. This rapid delivery increases customer's interest in development process. This results in daily cooperation between business clients and developer team.

AGILE PRINCIPLES

The Agile Manifesto is based on 12 principles (Beck et. al., 2001):

1. Customer satisfaction is the prime priority by means of rapid and continuous delivery of useful workable software.
2. Welcome changing requirements throughout the development process, even late in development to oblige customer's competitive arena
3. Working software is delivered frequently not only at the end, so weekly releases are preferred over releases after months of wait
4. Close collaboration among the business people and developers on the daily basis
5. Projects must be built around motivated individuals, Provide them the environment and support, more importantly show trust in them.
6. Face-to-face discussion is the excellent form of conveying information among the teammates, so try to assemble them together under one roof frequently
7. Working deployable software is the key measure of progress as compare to less effective documentation
8. Sustainable development must be supported, all the team members of agile software development ought to maintain a constant pace
9. Continuous attention to the technical brilliance and good design boosts the effect of agile software development.
10. Simplicity- the art of make the most of the quantity of work not done is necessary.
11. Self-organizing teams results in best architectures, requirements, and designs for the project.
12. Regular adaptation to ever changing situations, then modify its behavior accordingly at regular intervals.

COMPONENTS OF AGILE SOFTWARE DEVELOPMENT

Agile software development team is quite different from the traditional software development team in a number of ways. The decision making is not under the hands of single boss. The Agile software development methodology encourages the concept of team empowerment. As privileges and rights, are not given to a single person but to a whole team. the components includes the Agile software development team, artifacts of agile methodology and the proceedings of agile team.

1. Agile Software Development Team

a. Customer

As compared to other methodologies, in Agile software development, the role of customer is far more important. Being the product's prime stakeholder, he is involved from the very first day till the project is over. He joins each and every day to day meeting of every iteration along with the other members of development team and managers etc. product owner can come himself or even some public relation officer or some kind of representative can join the project team on the product owner's behalf. Product Owner is the person, who pass on the whole mission and vision of the product in hand to the development team. This is a big setback for a project team, when customer shows lack of interest to participate in the project or even thinks it a waste of time to involve with the development process with the team. You may have delivered software that just doesn't meet return on investment (ROI). You may have delivered software that is frustrating to use (Wells D., 2009). While facing this alarming scenario, try to restore the relationship as early as possible. Team has to give assurance to customer that his valuable time is an asset for the team, during each iteration. When one thinks about adopting an Agile development process, we are thinking about n no. of iterations and continuous testing. But even before all this, the very first thing you must think to take up Agile process is to set up a very good relationship with your project owner or his representative taking as domain expert. This is the very first step towards agile development process.

b. The Development Team

In the past, the term developer was used interchangeably with the term programmer. Nowadays developer doesn't mean merely programmers but anyone, who take part in achieving the goal of delivering incremental software. All the units of development team works in collaboration of each other. The intra-department communication is encouraged all the time during development process. All the members from different units or departments contribute towards a common goal i.e. to deliver the incremental software per sprint as per the plan.

c. Manager

In Agile software development, focus is on making the whole team empowered rather than the single boss. One cannot compare manager of an Agile software development with the traditional managers. Here in this context, manager means more of a facilitator, who makes sure that the team stick on the predefined rules, practices, vision and mission. The solitary objective of manager is to put all his efforts to facilitate the team perform at the peak level. Manager may conduct training session, arrange meetings and helping teammates to groom their skills.

2. Events and Proceedings of Agile Team

a. The Iteration

Iteration is the main specialty of the Agile software development process. It is actually a time period during which precise amount of productive work has to be completed by the Agile software development team. This work is not at all in the form of mere documentation but a real workable product that is deployed at the site. This workable product after deployment is made ready for the evaluation and assessment now. Sprints/iterations are generally 3-4 weeks long but can be planned short as just only one week long.

b. Iteration Planning

Iteration planning or Sprint Planning team meetings are arranged to settle on which product backlog matter and features will be delivered in the upcoming sprint and how the work will be achieved is also the area of planning. This sprint planning is the next step to the previous review of the product and getting feedback of the previous sprint.

c. Daily Short Meetings

The Daily short meeting is a type of casual informal meeting which is actually formal and a short exchange of ideas meeting of 10-20 minutes long, in which each Agile software development team member swiftly describe progress since his last short meeting and describe one's work planned for the next task before the next meeting. Team members can also discuss any hindrance that may prove to be bottleneck in the progress of his next milestone. In simple words, this is not a long term planning but rather a short term planning for the day. Whether the goals (set at the beginning of the day) were achieved, is realized at the end of the day. All the members attend the meeting in stand-up position in order to keep the meeting short. If it has been found that the day's planned work was not done at the end of the day, the same matter is put forward in the next morning's short meeting.

d. Post Iteration Assessment

In post iteration assessment, agile development team exhibit and demonstrate the product to put on the work concluded during the current iteration. The Product Owner or its representative verify the work against predefined approval criteria and on the basis of this verification, product owner can either accepts or rejects the work of Agile development team. The stakeholders give feedback, may be comment or opinion to make sure that the next delivered incremental product of subsequent sprint must meet the true needs of the business. This post iteration assessment has been scheduled after the end of every iteration. This is the sort of weekly or monthly homework checking and is the must to have yardstick for the Agile software development product. This post iteration assessment is given such an importance by the Agile software development team because the basic planning, requirements and landmark for the next iteration or next increment can be set only if the review of previous sprint is done right. Real outcome of the sprint review is the correct and appropriate planning for the subsequent iteration.

e. Demonstration of Working Product

Other than the daily scrum meetings, there is even more important meeting at the end of each sprint. In this conversation, agile development team uncovers the missing features as well as to find out what they did well or what didn't go well. The strategy of the team is prepared to deal with what didn't go well and how the team can improve the shortcomings in the upcoming Sprint. This meeting is attended by all the components of the agile software development i.e. the development team, manager and the product owner or his nominated representative. This can be seen as a real opportunity for the Agile software development team to focus on its performance, identify the weaknesses and most importantly for making strategy to overcome the bottleneck. If not done properly, or by taking this opportunity lightly, there is strong probability for the agile software development team to carry forward the mistakes to the next level of sprint. This is just like prolonging the repair work for the later stages and "stitch in time saves nine" is a well known fact. By avoiding rectify the loopholes in early stages and persevering a lot of work for later stages, means team putting pressure on itself or making the work tough for itself.

3. Artifacts of Agile Software Development

Artifacts play a vital role in agile software development methodology just like in traditional software development. Following are some important artifacts to be used in agile software development:

a. Global Product Documentation

The word global itself describes the significance of this artifact. This artifact meant for the overall final product not for any single iteration. The Global Product Documentation can be assumed as a to-do list consisting of work items, each of which contributes to generate a final deliverable product with business worth. The Global Product Documentation is the single most important artifact that sketches each and every requirement for the system. The efforts put on the making of Global Product Documentation, is much more than any other artifact of Agile development. Because the area and scope to be covered, in this artifact is much more than any other artifact. As Solitary Iteration Documentation has to deal with only the single sprint and global product Documentation is expected to cover whole project or in other words, need to cover all the sprints. So the Agile software development team i.e. the development team, manager and the product owner need to give many sitting while fabricating this artifact. Other artifacts revolves around this artifact directly or indirectly. So the efforts put on by the Agile software development team on this global product documentation, will defiantly be realized in all the artifacts as well. A weakly fabricated, global product artifact may give birth to other weak artifacts, which increases the likelihood that the project may go in wrong direction.

b. Solitary Iteration Documentation

The Solitary Iteration Documentation is the specific documentation meant for each particular sprint. Global Product Documentation is common for all the sprints and similar for the overall final product.

In complete contrast to this, solitary Iteration documentation is unique for each sprint. Solitary Iteration Documentation includes the items taken from the software backlog which have to be completed in a single sprint. Opposite to the Global product documentation, this Solitary Iteration Documentation can be taken as a to-do list for a single sprint.

c. Augmentation List

An Augmentation is the summation of all the pending product backlog stuff as well as the new additions that have been incorporated since the last product released by the Agile software development. Product Owner in formal talk with the development team and the manager, make a decision on when an increment is released in. It is up to the Agile development team to take up the responsibility to ensure that everything that is incorporated in an augmentation list, what is all set to be released. All the future references related to the increments can easily be made through these augmentation lists. So the correctness and completeness of the document is itself a task to be carefully carried out. Along with the Solitary Iteration Documentation, this augmentation artifact is referenced more frequently than the other artifacts.

ADVANTAGES OF AGILE DEVELOPMENT OVER TRADITIONAL DEVELOPMENT

The tactic put up by agile software development is the answer to the crisis resulted directly or indirectly due to traditional software development. Agile software development keeps a focus on just the rapid delivery of owner's money worth by postponing go to greater details till next few iterations. Due to this vision and its related benefits, Agile software development teams can accomplish the task of considerably reducing the overall risk involved with traditional software development.

Agile development team actually picks up the pace of delivering of final product through a course of continuous planning based on the feedback from previous iterations. After getting feedback from preceding iterations, at the start of next iteration, Agile software development team calls fresh scrum meeting to elucidate the plan for the sprint in progress. There may be daily meetings of Agile software development team. These scrum meetings cannot be attended only by the development team and manager but also by the project owner. As this is the inevitable requirement of Agile development process to make the product owner or his representative the most active member of the team. As a result of this kind of iterative planning and feedback, one can easily adapt to changing needs throughout the process as continuously desired business needs. Refer to figure 1 to see how changing requirements are effortlessly accepted in agile software development. By delivering operational, tested and deployable product on an incremental basis, agile method of development delivers flexible, early return on investment and adaptable type of product a lot earlier by reducing project risk considerably.

The main problem with traditional software development was the too late delivery of the product, as product has to go through so many phases i.e. all waterfall model phases. Due to this late delivery, many a times product become outdated. Outdated products are taken into account as unsuccessful projects, just like the incomplete projects even after deadline. In traditional software development, most of the time, even after project completion during deadline, project does not meet up the real requirements or sometimes there is product's lack of ability to deal with the changing requirements. In these cases, projects cannot be utilized properly or at all, and another high percentage of projects again required massive

Figure 1. Changed requirements are effortlessly accepted in agile software development even at the later stages

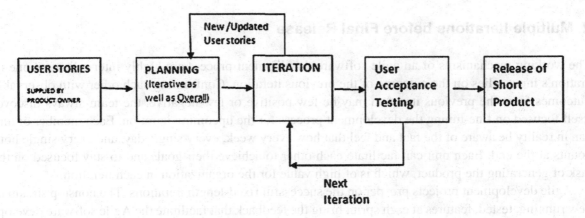

rework to be utilizable. This re-tailoring was again not tolerable. So in this context, the risk mitigation in Agile software development process is a real asset.

CHARACTERISTICS WHICH MAKES AGILE DEVELOPMENT A SUCCESS

The secret behind the success rate of Agile software development over the traditional software development is not a magical wend. Success of Agile software development is a mixed blend of many of its unique characteristics, that makes it a excellent choice over other development methodologies.

1. Working Software: Measure of Progress

In traditional software development, the measure of progress may be line of code, no. of modules covered till now, size of the team etc. But in Agile software development, the measure of progress is the workable, tested and releasable software product. Working characteristics act as the basis for facilitating and improving the teamwork as there is a lot of concreteness as far as the outcome of every release is concerned. This workable software assist to a great deal in improving product owner's feedback as the customer is not at all dependent now on mere documentation at the early stages. Not only the above features but also the overall project visibility have great effects of the tested workable software product. In starting sprints of a new project, the Agile software development team may not bring many features. Just within few subsequent sprints, the project is generally put on the track by the development team. As the system development process goes on, the product design, structure and system priorities are all constantly assessed. At every stage along the way to achieve the overall goal, the agile software development team gets the latest input from the stakeholder's side. Iteration by iteration, all the members of agile team can see whether or not the product is on the track and meet the requirements. Time after time measuring success with actual workable and tested software gives an agile development project a very unique feeling than traditional projects. After actual exposure with the workable product, the managers, development team and even the stakeholders, all turn into more focused, more energetic, more optimistic and on the top of their confidence level.

2. Multiple Iterations before Final Release

The working mechanisms of an agile software development process are highly inter-reliant as one iteration's input relies on the outcome of the previous iteration. Confronting each other with observable outcomes from the previous iteration may be few positive or few negative, the team always discover itself focused on fine-tuning the development process for the upcoming iteration. Each member or unit can in reality be aware of the fact and feel that how every week, every single day, and every single hour counts at the end. Each unit can facilitate each other to achieve their goals and to stay focused on the task of generating the product, which is of high value for the organization in each iteration.

Agile development projects prosper on the successful fixed-length iterations. The nonstop stream of new running, tested, features at each sprint bring the feedback that facilitate the Agile software development team to keep an eye on the project, so that project cannot go off the track. Just from the features and characteristics from the time-bound iterations, one can infer meaningful feedback like "How much work did the team do last month contrast to what we planned for future iteration? Team's predicted target can only be based practically on the past iteration. In the same way development teams compare the work done in previous iteration with the work of the older iterations. In this way one can get the practical idea that how many features team should concentrate on during the iteration in progress based on the deadline.

Every day the agile development team plans, execute and achieve milestones while the software product is being designed, coded, tested in all respects and integrated for stakeholder's acceptance. In every iteration the team is planning hard, testing is done in all respects and delivering working software to the user. Each and every release, the team is planning, testing properly and deploying software into production unit. With the intention to coordinate and successfully deliver such a vastly adaptive and fruitful productive product, team communication and co-ordination is very much critical right through the whole agile development process. The result of the each sprint is totally working, tested thoroughly tiny software with prioritized features.

A release is a result of several iterations, each of the iteration is just like a micro-project of its own type. Characteristics, flaws, enhancement feature requests and other entities are structured in a approximately prioritized manner, and finally allocated to a particular release. Within a single release, these entities are then allocated to the sprint based on its estimated priority.

3. Comparative Estimation

Estimates play a key role in every kind of planning. Estimates may be in the form of days like some task may take 5-7 days. Some time, estimation may be in the form of story points like 5,6,10 story points. Estimation may be in the form of days, or hours or story points. In traditional software development, most of the time, our estimation goes wrong. Often, this discrepancy cannot come to picture at the early stages of the software development process. This finally gives rise to a situation where team has to re think about its planning and specially schedule.

But in case of agile software development process, just as per the nature of agile software development process, we get improved and improved as we go along. Agile development team can redefine its estimation from time to time as per the need. This characteristic not only save significant time as well as the effort by planning with the fresh estimates for the future work but also rescue the team from budget imbalance due to vague estimates and scheduling.

The correct estimation can result in providing better planning. If a characteristic go beyond an decided maximum estimate, then it is better that the feature should be broken down further into several relatively smaller features. These relatively smaller features generated as a result of this planning eventually need to be released within a single iteration.

4. Nonstop Endless Planning

At the onset of project launch, the development team does just need to perform enough planning for the overall project development, instead the Agile software development team just need to get going with the initial iteration planning only. Agile software development planning is based much on historical data not on speculations of traditional development.

In fact iterating is the key to constant planning. One can take each iteration as a mini-project that demands just-enough of its own planning. At the onset of iteration, the Agile development team selects a set of features to incorporate for this release, and recognizes each technical task to be done for each feature. Task estimation for the features selected is a critical agile skill. The planning in Agile software development is not so easy as it seem to be.

There is one important aspect, where agile software development has an edge over traditional development. In traditional software development like waterfall projects, there is very low percentage of software products, which one can consider so called successful. These so called successful waterfall projects just tend to deliver what was originally demanded in the requirements document at the very beginning, not what the product owner discover they actually needed as the project.

In this regard, agile software development is far more successful due to its iterative approach and its constant planning. This constant planning, gives scope for any kind of changed requirement at any stage of the project, even at the last stage to accommodate the ever changing business needs. The simple reason behind this is the constant planning till the project terminates.

5. Release Level Planning vs. Iteration Level Planning

Planning at different levels in agile software development is an important factor for its success over traditional development. Constant planning is of real value if it occurs on at least two levels. The first level is release level and the second is the iteration level.

1. **Release Level Planning:** In this planning, teams identify the overall features of the entire project and also prioritize the features, so that these features can be split into various iterations.
2. **Iteration Level Planning:** As the name suggest, this planning is of lower level. Here planning needs to be done just for particular iterations. If some features are too large to be released within a single iteration, then team has to split the feature down further. The remaining part of the feature can be put into the next iteration.

Once the features are prioritized and planned for an iteration, they will be broken down into discrete technical tasks, so that the tasks can be assigned to the members or units of the agile team.

AGILE SOFTWARE DEVELOPMENT METHODOLOGIES

There are several agile software development methodologies. The most widely used methodologies among them are XP and Scrum methodology. Both these methodologies have basic approach common i.e. the iterative approach, as both belong to the same family of agile software development. The diverse characteristics of both the methodologies are as follows.

1. Extreme Programming

The abbreviation of extreme programming is XP. XP is a "lightweight" development method that is tolerant of changes in requirements (Pressman, R. S.,2005). It gives more attention to the actual development rather than managerial aspects of software project development. There is no constraint on the organizations to fully adapt the methodology of XP or partially by implementing only some part of the methodology. It means extreme programming provides flexibility.

a. Unique Features of Extreme Programming Development

Customers write user stories to explain the necessity of the software. User stories facilitate the development team to calculate approximately of the time and resources needed to create the release. A customer or its nominated representative is part of the extreme programming team, so a product owner can append points and give directions for the requirements as the product is being built. Extreme programming projects always starts merely with just preliminary planning phase, succeeded by several iterations, each of these iterations finish off with user acceptance testing. When the team realizes that the product has adequate features to satisfy product owner's business needs, the development team cease iteration and releases the software.

At the early stages, the extreme programming team split up the development tasks into further iterations. The release plan defines each and every iteration plan, which guides the development for that iteration. In the last part of each iteration, acceptance tests are performed against the user written stories. If discrepancies found in the testing phase of this iteration, then these discrepancies will be rectified in the next iteration as a new task in the subsequent iteration. Iterative user acceptance testing can bring about release of the software product. In some situations, all the user stories planned at the early stages, have not been implemented yet but product owner feels that enough user stories have been implemented, then the extreme programming team can make a decision to terminate the project before all of the earlier planned user stories have been delivered.

b. Extreme Programming Notions

- **Joint Programming:** A unique characteristics of extreme programming is that all code for a product delivery is done by two persons working together at a single PC. Extreme programming recommends that two programmers coding together will convince user stories at the similar rate as the two programmers coding alone, although with a great deal of higher quality. So extreme programming encourage this practice a lot.
- **Project Rate:** It means a measure of how much development work is done on the project during a time span. This important metric guides the rest of release planning and schedule planning.

- **Daily Integration:** At least once a day, extreme programming development teams must integrate changes into the development baseline.
- **Unique Format of User Story:** extreme programming specifies a unique format of the user stories. An user story illustrate problems to be solved by the product under fabrication. These stories must be given by the customer and should be about few sentences long. Since user stories are not so long and illustrative, extreme programming team will only work if the product owner representative is readily accessible to review and give consent the user story implementations. This is one of the prime challenges to the extreme programming methodology as well as one of its utmost strengths. These user stories do not specify any solution or use any technical language.

2. Scrum

Scrum software development methodology turn up from the rapid prototyping community as prototype community seriously needed to have a development methodology that would encourage an environment in which the requirements were not only partial at the beginning, but also could change quickly and continuously during development process. In contrast to extreme programming, Scrum development methodology includes both managerial and development processes. In scrum software development, the core activity is to issue a release.

a. Perspective of Scrum Methodology

As soon as the scrum team completes the preliminary project high-level designs and planning, it splits the whole development process into a series of small iterations also termed as sprints. Each sprint intended to implement a predetermined number of backlog items. Before each iteration, the scrum team members find out the backlog items to be implemented for the sprint. Towards the end of the sprint, the scrum team reviews the sprint to articulate the exposure gained and check progress. There is a backlog list of work to be done, at the middle of each Scrum project,. This backlog is written during the planning phase of a delivery and also defines the scope of the release in detail.

During each sprint, the whole scrum team has a daily meeting called a scrum. In this meeting the progress from the day before is discussed. Anyone can discuss any kind of hurdles or obstacle, unit is facing. This is the right platform to discuss the obstacle and to get it rectified, as each member of the team is there for face to face communication. Also, each member of the team describes the assigned work to be done that day as per his role. To keep these kind of meetings short, these meeting are arranged as stand-up meetings but under the one roof.

There may be the case, when a lot of backlog is still left and a lot of the backlog is already implemented, and the product owner believes that the release is worth deployable into production site, then the team shut down the development. Next task for the team now is to performs integration testing, training modules and documentation as essential for the release of the product.

b. Scrum Process

During development process, the scrum team find out the changes necessary to realize a backlog item. The scrum team then write down the code, tests and changes are marked in artifacts. Then the team generates the executable necessary to illustrate the changes. Later in the review, the scrum team reveal the new features, append the backlog items. The Scrum development process focuses on managing iteration. Before each iteration begins, the scrum team plans the sprint, recognize the backlog items and most importantly allocating teams to these.

After the completion of each sprint, the entire scrum development team i.e. manager, product owner and the developer team exhibits progress from the sprint and also re-examine the backlog progress. The entire team then re-examines and reviews the left over backlog. The team then append, erase or repriotizes the entities as required to justify new information gathered during the sprint.

As both the methodologies i.e scrum as well as extreme programming, have their unique ways and features to achive the team's targets. Some organizations like to have a mixed blend of both the methodologies, to exploit the positives from both the scrum methodology and the extreme programming. This has not been done often but this trend spreads with time.

c. Scrum Concepts

- **Outstanding List:** This list is modified every day, reflects the work remaining within the sprint. This outstanding list is used to *'kill two birds with one stone'*. This list is used to both track the progress of the sprint and to resolve what items must be erased from the backlog of the sprint and postponed to the upcoming sprint.
- **Global Backlog List:** Global backlog list is the complete list of requirements including all types of errors, features augmentation requests and operational improvements, that are not in the product release at present.
- **Solitary Sprint Backlog List:** Solitary sprint backlog is the list of all kinds of backlog items allocated to a sprint, but not yet finished. In general, no solitary sprint backlog item should take much time to complete i.e. two or three days. The solitary sprint backlog help out the team to foresee the level of effort needed to complete a sprint.

OBSTACLES IN AGILE SOFTWARE DEVELOPMENT

1. Misperceptions about Importance of Training

The time span of single iteration is so small that generally teams make misperception in mind that there is no scope of formal prolonged rules and principals in Agile software development. Teams assume that there is sufficient amount of time to implement rules, principals and exposure in traditional software development. But in Agile software development there is no scope for all these things due to short span of individual iterations of 1-2 weeks long.

2. Design Phase Missing

In case of traditional software development, a lot of time is invested in design phase. In contrast to this, in Agile software development, main focus of the team is on making the working software in the first iteration as early as possible. Iteration may be of month long or may be of 1-2 weeks. Meetings are held on daily basis. Plans and milestones are made and achieved on daily basis. So in these short deadlines, it is not at all possible to make formal design like in traditional software development. The omitted design phase give rise to many side effects, which Agile software development team has to sustain with. It is just like constructing a building without any draft or blueprint.

3. Daily Scrum Technical Discussions

One of the indispensable elements of the Agile software development is the daily scrum. In this, all the members of the team has to attend, no matter the member is from development team, manager or the product owner. In this conversation, it is quite common to discuss the technical aspects of the project with each other. Among this gathering, the product owner or its representative is the one, who is not from technical background. In the technical discussion, few members cannot actively or productively participate and that's why in reality is not the finest use of the whole team's time. In this situation, it is far more sensible to make sub-teams for some particular daily scrum. In this way, non technical members of the team remain assured that they called in scrum meetings with purpose. Making sub-teams out of the full fledged team on the basis of their potential and area of interest is not that much easy. If during the Scrum the team starts diving into problem-solving, it should be tabled until a sub-team can discuss immediately after the Daily Scrum completes (Cohn M., 2014).

4. Reluctant to Switch to New Methodology

People often reluctant, to adopt changes. Although this may not be the problem with technical people like development team but for the authorities, who have to sponsor the project and to provide financial support as well as resources to the team, is not so easy. So often non technical sponsors show little interest in adopting Agile software development over traditional software development.

5. Changes Are Welcome Inter-Iterations but Not Intra-Iteration

Scrum certainly provides provision to change product backlog priorities mid-project however this needs to occur between sprints and not during them." (Goldstein I., 2011). If some sprint is in progress and team of Agile software development is working on it and meanwhile some new facts come into existence related to the sprint, then it is not advisable to enforce these new facts into the sprint in progress. If the new facts inhibit the user from being fabricated in the current sprint, then it should be carry forward into the subsequent sprint. If there is an issue which arises which requires additions to a sprint, here recommendation is to perform an abnormal sprint termination (Goldstein I., 2011). Well, in this situation of prolonging the user story for the next sprint scheduling, that user story should be prioritized in contrast to all the planned user stories for the new sprint. Instead, if that user story was forcefully imposed in-between that sprint, then not only one could harm that sprint in progress, but also the effect could be seen in the subsequent sprints.

6. Misjudgment about Preparation

This is a regular mistake of teams not much familiar with the Agile development process. Teams over try to gain complete understanding of all the user stories and try mistakenly to get the unnecessary knowledge about the problem domain. In this process, they go deep into the domain, which is not necessary as far as the current sprint is concerned. The information gained at this point may not needed in this sprint. As this information acquired should be applied to the next iteration.

7. Team Members Overburdened

If Agile software development team members have several projects/tasks, it will be easier said than done for anyone to facilitate complete the iteration. "While having information developers working on multiple scrum teams is not ideal, it can be done with some proper planning and judicious evaluation of which meetings you should attend." (Fox, A., 2014)

8. Trying to Undertake Over and Above in a Single Iteration

A common misconception is Agile allows continuous change, however a Sprint backlog is an agreement of what work can be completed during the Sprint (Waters K., 2007). Additionally having too much Work-In-Progress(WIP) can result in inefficiencies due "to avoid the penalties of wasted time, effort and resources." (George C., 2014).

This is not an exceptional situation, but rather it is quite common that a team try to undertake excessive work in a single iteration due to one reason or the other. When you slip your schedule you acknowledge and trying to catch up only puts you further behind long term (Wells D., 2009). "An important point to reiterate here is that it's the team that selects how much work they can do in the coming sprint. The product owner does not get to say, 'We have four sprints left so you need to do one-fourth of everything I need.' We can hope the team does that much (or more), but it's up to the team to determine how much they can do in the sprint." (Cohn M., 2014). Being ahead of schedule does occasionally happen. Keep your pace steady. Some slack time is nice (Wells D., 2009).There is not a single factor responsible for this excessive work in one iteration but may be several factors. It may be possible that Agile software development team being forced into taking such a decision of doing additional work. Perhaps the manager wanted to compensate the slow speed of starting iterations or may be the product owner wanted to add new user stories in the subsequent editions of iterations. If this is the case of product owner's willingness to add new user stories in the following iterations, then egoistically product owner wanted to add without presenting it as a new user story. Finally this action prove to be harmful for Agile software development.

CONCLUSION AND FUTURE WORK

Nowadays, in most cases product owners or customers are not considered to be the component of development team owing to various factors. Agile software development firstly pulls right this illusion by taking customer/product owner as part of development squad and let the customer direct the project day by day. Any development team can't gain knowledge in weeks what product owner has learned over the years. In projects where client side, bear in mind a waste of time to take part in the project, greater the chances of software not to meet the actual needs.

Agile software development ensures that changes or even late changes must not become the bottleneck but become routine change campaigns by taking feedback from incremental release of the working software. The features left in one iteration can fit in the next iteration. Iterative set up is all about making a plan, construct some software, release it, take feedback and again make plan based on what you experienced. Before the next iteration, the development team, managerial team and the product owners again sit together for the shortcoming and missing features along with the planning of next iterations as well. The most exciting feature of Agile software development is that the prime measure of progress is actually the working software.

A lot of work has to be done in Agile software development as not much work has been done yet on risk factors and risk analysis in Agile software development. Another important aspect to be work in future is to accomplish reusability in Agile Software Development.

REFERENCES

Beck, K., Beedle, M., Van Bennekum, A., Cockburn, A., Cunningham, W., Fowler, M., . . . Thomas, D. (2001). *Principles behind the agile manifesto*. Retrieved December 22, 2014 from www.agilemanifesto. org/principles.html

Cohn, M. (n.d.a). *Daily Scrum Meeting*. Retrieved December 21, 2014, from http://mountaingoatsoftware.com/agile/scrum/daily-scrum

Cohn, M. (n.d.b). *Sprint Planning Meeting*. Retrieved December 21, 2014, from http://mountaingoatsoftware.com/agile/scrum/sprint-planning-meeting

Cusumano, M., MacCormack, A., Kemerer, C. F., & Crandall, W. (2003). A global survey of software development practices. *eBusiness@ MIT, 178*, 1-17.

Fox, A. (n.d.). *Working on Multiple Agile Teams*. Retrieved December 20, 2014, from http://techwhirl. com/working-multiple-agile-teams/

George, C. (n.d.). *Why Limiting Your Work-in-Progress Matters*. Retrieved December 20, 2014, from http://leankit.com/blog/2014/03/limiting-work-in-progress/

Goldstein, I. (2011). *Sprint issues – When sprints turn into crawls*. Retrieved December 18, 2014, from http://axisagile.com.au/blog/planning-and-metrics/sprint-issues-when-sprints-turn-into-crawls/

Murauskaite, A., & Adomauskas, V. (2008). *Bottlenecks in Agile Software Development using Theory of Constraints (TOC) Principles* (Doctoral dissertation, Master's Thesis, Gothenburg, Sweden). (Report No. 2008:014)

Pressman, R. S. (2005). *Software engineering: a practitioner's approach*. New York, NY: McGraw-Hill.

Waters, K. (2007). *Sprint Planning (Tasks)*. Retrieved December 20, 2014, from http://www.allaboutagile. com/how-to-implement-scrum-in-10-easy-steps-step-4-sprint-planning-tasks/

Wells, D. (2009). *Agile Software Development: A gentle introduction*. Retrieved December 20, 2014, from http://agile-process.org

KEY TERMS AND DEFINITIONS

Agile Software Development: A methodology which focuses on the rapid delivery of working software and then on the basis of feedback loop working team can plan its next improved iterative working software.

Extreme Programming: It is a method that is tolerant of changes in requirements and provides flexibility.

Iteration: It is a short period activity or actually a time period during which precise amount of productive work has to be completed as a real workable product that can be deployed.

Product Owner: Client side, which requires the software to automate the functioning of the organization.

Scrum: Scrum is a software development methodology encourage an environment in which the requirements were not only partial at the beginning, but also could change quickly and continuously during development process. This methodology includes both managerial and development processes.

Traditional Software Development: A software development methodology, in which first workable interface is presented to the client only after the requirement, design, coding, testing and deployment stages.

User Story: A user story illustrates problems to be solved by the product under fabrication. These stories must be given by the customer.

Waterfall-Model: Most common model which follows the Traditional Software Development methodology.

Chapter 8
Agile Enablers and Adoption Scenario in Industry Context

Vinay Kukreja
Chitkara University, India

Amitoj Singh
Chitkara University, India

ABSTRACT

In the globalization of fast changing business and technology environment, it becomes very important to respond quickly to changing user requirements. Traditional methodologies are not appropriate for the projects where user requirements are not fixed. Agile methodologies have been developed to cope up with user changing requirements and emphasize more on working software and customer collaboration. Agile is an umbrella term and it is used for many software development methodologies which shares common characteristics. This chapter mainly focuses on the working methodology of agile development and the usage areas of industry where agile development is implemented. Agile software development is difficult in distributed environment as the team members are at distributed locations. This chapter discusses agile industry applicability enablers which are useful for agile software development in distributed environment.

INTRODUCTION

The globalization that started in the last decade of the twentieth century has great impact on the development of various sectors of society and industry. Globalization not affected the social, cultural, behavioral, political and economic aspects of present society and industry but also the engineering and technology fields. It has affected the software industry sector immensely. Before globalization, there were sophisticated traditional software development methods, approaches, tools and techniques which made software development a time consuming and costly affair. The globalization of software development has an evolutionary impact on the industry. It has reshaped and reinvented the traditional software development methods, approaches, tools and techniques. Now days, customer priorities and requirements are changing in the projects at any time and at any stage, which really never suits to the traditional soft-

DOI: 10.4018/978-1-4666-8510-9.ch008

ware development approaches, processes and methodologies. A set of new generation of processes and agile methodologies has been appeared in the picture. Due to simple rules, principles and light weight processes, the agile methodologies are the first choice for many software industries (Akbar et al., 2011). The objective of this chapter is to explore the usage areas of agile development and the key enablers for the agile applicability in distributed environment.

AGILE METHODOLOGY DEFINITION

Agile methodology is a "sunshade term for various iterative and incremental well-defined software development methodologies". Agile software development is a collection of software methods in which response to changing requirements; priority of requirements, adaptive planning, iterative and evolutionary development, early delivery of product, continuous improvements in product development is done through self organizing teams and cross functional teams, the teams can be co-located as well as distributed.

Now the question arises is that what do you understand by term "AGILE"?

In Dictionary agile means "nimble, quick, supple, limber, flexible, and lithe".

According to Alistair Cockburn, "Agile suggests being valuable and maneuverable. An agile process is weightless and capable. The weightlessness is a mean of staying maneuverable. The capability is a matter of staying in the race." (Rüping, A., 2003).

According to Barry Boehm, "Agile methods are an outcome of quick prototyping and rapid development experience as well as the resurrection of a philosophy that programming is a craft rather than an industrial process." (Abrahamsson, P. 2008).

The various popular agile methodologies are Extreme Programming (XP), Scrum, Crystal, Pair-programming and Lean development. Let's try to understand these models in detail and how they have impacted the industry? But before that we have to understand agile manifesto and agile principles.

AGILE MANIFESTO PURPOSE

The purpose of agile manifesto according to (Beck et al., 2001) is "We are uncovering better ways of developing software by doing it and helping others to do it. We value

- Individuals and interactions over processes and tools.
- Working software over comprehensive documentation.
- Customer collaboration over contract negotiation.
- Responding to change over following a plan."

That is, while there is value in the items on the right, we value the items on the left more.

Above manifesto purpose statement have a number of important aspects to consider. First, the word "uncovering" was selected to assure the people that all the Alliance members don't have all the answers. Second the word "by doing it" was selected to indicate that alliance members actually practice these methods in their own work. Third, alliance members group is about helping, not telling. The alliance members want to help others with agile methods, and to further their own knowledge by learning from those whom they try to help.

AGILE MANIFESTO PRINCIPLES

The agile methods are principle-based, rather than rule-based (Larman, C. 2004).The co-located teams as well as distributed teams do not have any already explained rules regarding their responsibilities, roles and relationship, the teams and managers are guided by these principles (Beck et al., 2001):-

1. *Our highest priority is to satisfy the customer through early and continuous delivery of valuable software.* Generally, customers do not care about documents, architectural documents and UML diagrams. Customers care only whether you are delivering a working product at the end of each development cycle or not. This principle devotes more efforts on "CUSTOMER VALUE".

2. *Welcome changing requirements, even late in development. Agile processes harness change for the customer's competitive advantage.* While developing software, everyone knows that customer's feedback is important. Result of feedback is change. Traditional approaches resist changing but agile processes strap up changes for customer advantage. Agile advocates understand that facilitating change is more effective than preventing it.

3. *Deliver working software frequently, from a couple of weeks to a couple of months, with a preference to the shorter time scale.* Agile processes must use incremental or iterative style of software development, with multiple deliveries to reduce development time where each delivery has some functionality. Bear in mind that "deliver is not same as release".

4. *Business people and developers must work together daily through the project.* In the above statement, more stress is given to the word "daily". It means business people must actively interact with developer for the software project so that the project is according to the business people needs.

5. *Build projects around motivated individuals. Give them the environment and support they need, and trust them to get the job done.* Project success or failure depends upon the people who will be implementing the processes, tools and techniques. Managers must trust the developer's staff so that they can take decisions in a development situation because they are the best judgers of the solution of the problematic situation.

6. *The most efficient and effective method of conveying information to and within a development team is face to face conversation.* Tacit knowledge a team has gained from doing a task is made available to other teams doing similar work in another part of the organization. Tacit knowledge cannot be transferred from people's heads onto paper. The issue is not the "documentation" but is "understanding". Basically, agile methodologies are a mixture of documentation and face-to-face communication required to elicit understanding (Dixon, N.M. 2000).

7. *Working software is the primary measure of progress.* The question is what is the measure for progress in the project? Only working software is the primary parameter for measuring the progress of project. By this way, customers and developer's can know how many requirements are completed.

8. *Agile processes promote sustainable development.* Agile development mainly depends upon the people who are inventive and observant, and can maintain their inventiveness and alertness for the full length of a software development project. Sustainable development means finding a working space that the team can carry on over time and remain vigorous, energetic.

9. *Continuous attention to technical excellence and good design enhances agility.* Agile processes give emphasis to quality of design. It is an important factor to sustain agility. Agile processes presume and promote the amendments of requirements while the code is written.

10. *Simplicity- the art of maximizing the amount of work not done – is essential.* Any software development can be done by a number of methods. In an agile project, it is very important to use simple approaches for software development because they are easier to change. It is very easy to add something in a simple process rather than to add something in a complicated process. Simple rules, encouraging creativity, clear purpose and solid principles can help in better outcomes rather than complex and rigid regulations, says Dee Hock, former CEO of visa international.

11. *The best architectures, requirements and designs emerge from self-organizing teams.* he self organizing teams in which communication between members is very high and the process rules are few can lead to emergent properties. According to (Larman, C., et al. 2003), the self organizing teams work together on iterative and evolutionary methods for agile software development, it results in best architectures of the system.

12. *At regular intervals, the team reflects on how to become more effective, then tunes and adjustments its behavior accordingly.* Agile methodologies consist of many models for software development. It is not like that you pick any agile model and follow profusely for software development. You may start with one of these models, but at later stage agile teams recognize that it is not the right model for that situation, they can refine it and continuously improve its practices for completion of project.

WHY INDUSTRY HAS MOVED FROM TRADITIONAL APPROACHES TO AGILE APPROACHES

Below given table 1 shows the numbers of reasons for the industry to switch from traditional time consuming software development approaches to agile software development approaches.

WORKING OF AGILE METHODOLOGY

The most important role in agile software development is that how it works? The diagrammatically representation of agile methodologies is shown in figure 1 and its explanation is given below:-

1) Initial Project Study and Meetings of Product Owner, Scrum Master, and Stakeholders

In the functioning of agile methodology, firstly initially project study will be made. Then, meetings of product owner, scrum master and stakeholders will be arranged so that they all have idea about overall features and structure of the project. After this, user will tell its requirements in the form of user stories and if the user wants some changes in the requirements of the project, this will also mostly be stated in the form of user stories. Now the question arises is that what do you understand by user stories? User stories are the system software requirements which are preferred by customer for the project. Usually, user stories are short, clear and consist of several sentences. User stories help the development team to understand the customer requirements in a quick way. User stories reduce the efforts of development team not to craft large number of documents and not to maintain large number of documents which are

Table 1. Difference between Agile and Traditional Approaches

	Traditional Approaches	**Agile Approaches**
Driven Towards	Rules	Principles
Centric towards	Process	People
Testing	Testing is done at the end of the project.	Testing is performed throughout the project, test driven development and pair programming helps in reduction of the errors.
Follow Agility software development	No	Yes
Method usage	Sequential and formal method	Iterative and enhancement method
Communication and Meetings within team and between team members and customers.	Low	High
Level of Documentation	High	Low
Working Software	Given at end and normal release of software is from 1 year to 2 years	Given in small iterations and normal release is around 6 months to 9 months
Most Suitable	When requirements are fully identifiable and unsurprising	When requirements are not fully identifiable, not certain and unsurprising
Communication way between team members	Formal	Informal
Customer's role	Vital	Very critical
Project Cycle	Based on tasks	Based on product features
Management Style	Authoritative	Collaborative
Examples	Waterfall model, Spiral Model etc.	Extreme programming, Scrum etc.

(Pathak, K., and Saha, A., 2013, Nerur, S, et al., 2005, Nerur, S., and Balijepally, V., 2007, Aoyama, M., 1997).

required in traditional approaches of software development for elicitation of requirements. User stories swing focus from written documents to verbal communication. User stories are not scenarios as well as not use cases (Cohn, M. 2004). Now the question arises that what are the requirements for user stories and what are the different ways of getting the user stories from the user by different ways?

2) User Stories and Analysis

a) Requirements for the User Story (Grinys, A. 2012)

The most important point in the development is requirements gathering. Have a good user stories can revolutionize how the user requirements are well tested and delivered? According to Bill Wake a user story must carry the following attributes INVEST:-

I: Independent

User stories must be self-reliant i.e one user story must be independent of the other user story point. If there are dependencies between user stories, this makes difficulty in planning, prioritization and estimation.

N: Negotiable

Figure 1. Working of Agile Methodology

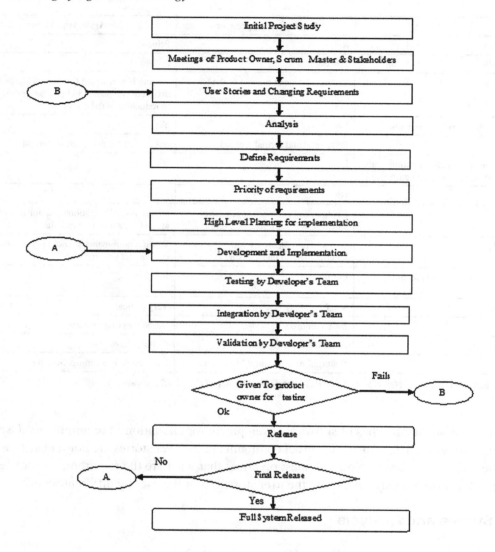

According to Bill Wake, a good user story always captures the most important features rather than the details. A user story can always be changeable and rewriteable.

V: Valuable

User stories always contain value to the customer. The team must bring actual project related value to the customer by implementing various user story points.

E: Estimable

A user story must be properly estimated. It helps in good planning and proper prioritization of sprints. If a user story cannot be estimated, it can never be a part of planning and sprint.

S: Small

User story must have small number of story points. A story point is the evaluation unit of user story. User story can have 1 to 16 story points and these must be completed within 1-2 weeks.

T: Testable

Every story point in the user story must be testable. We cannot develop what we cannot test. So, for test driven development, the user story must provide necessary information to make it possible.

b) Techniques for Fishing the User Stories Are (Cohn, M. 2004)

1. User interviews
2. Questionnaires
3. Observation
4. Story Writing Workshops.

After describing the user stories, the analyst of the team do the analysis and estimation of user stories so that relevant user stories can be helpful into define customer requirements (Georgsson, A. 2011). When customer requirements are defined, then these requirements are prioritize. Prioritize of requirements mean which candidate requirements of a software product should be included in a certain release. Prioritization is done to minimize the risk in the software development product by implementing the high risk requirements firstly. The projects producing large complex software systems can have hundreds or even thousands of requirements. It is not unusual that the customer organization have valid reasons for acquiring each of these requirements in their project. Such projects must have to prioritize the requirements.

c) Prioritize the Requirements on the Following Basis (Firesmith, D., 2004)

1. **Difference in Importance:** All requirements in the project are not equally important. High risk requirements are most important. Stakeholders, product owner and scrum master play a vital role in prioritizing the requirements.
2. **Limited Project Resources:** All requirements to be implemented in one release is not possible due to budget, staff and schedule. The systems are generally implemented in iterative, enhancement cycle in which requirements are incrementally developed and implemented.
3. **Long Schedule:** As the project implementation is a long process so it is advisable to prioritize the requirements so that developers must know which requirements should be implemented in which release.

Some authors (Sommerville et. al, 1997) recommended another way of prioritizing the requirements. According to them, prioritizing requirements means categorizing raw potential requirements from the stand point of importance into-

1. **Essential Requirements:** Actual requirements that must be included in the project.

2. **Useful Requirements:** These requirements will lessen the project effectiveness if these are left out.

3. **Desirable Requirements:** These requirements are most desirable to certain stake- holders.

d) Proper Prioritize Requirements Provide Following Benefits to the Project (Firesmith, D., 2004)

1. **Amend Schedule:** When using an iterative, enhancement development cycle in the project, it enables the scrum master, project manager and product owner to modify the project schedule according to available limited resources and fixed deadlines.

2. **Customer Satisfaction Enhancement:** Prioritization of requirements enhances the customer level of satisfaction because customer requirements most essential requirements are implemented first and delivered first.

3. **Less Risk of Abandonment of Project:** The project rejection chances are very less as the project is implemented in iterations. Suppose, the project is cancelled still there will not be total loss as lots of vital functionality has been implemented.

4. **Concentrating All System Requirements:** Prioritizing of requirements keeps the stakeholders to concentrate on all system requirements and not just on their own requirements.

5. **Estimate Cost-Benefit Analysis:** Prioritization of requirements helps the project managers, stakeholders to do cost-benefit analysis. It helps them to know for completion of which requirement how much project resources and staff is required? And how useful is this requirement for the project?

e) Challenges and Risks in Prioritization of Requirements (Firesmith, D., 2004)

1. **Mandatory Nature of Requirements:** All requirements are mandatory in a project. In the project, it is very difficult to differentiate which requirements lead to mandatory (most important) and less important for the completion of project.

2. **Very Large Number of Requirements:** The complex software project consists of hundreds or thousands of requirements. Now, it becomes very difficult to prioritize such large number of requirements. This is why requirements are often grouped into a small number of categories. After requirements grouping, the techniques for determine the prioritization of all requirements are used. These techniques are pair-wise comparisons or Quality Function deployment (QFD).

3. **Resources Limitation:** Due to the limitation of resources and staff, it is not possible to prioritize or put all the system requirements in single iteration.

4. **Quality Requirements:** As most of the costs are spent on architectural design, development and maintenance but quality requirements like consistency, portability, availability, safety, usability and security are not specified at all. This leads to no prioritization of quality requirements.

5. **Goal Requirements:** It is very difficult in the project to prioritize the requirements such that it leads to the business goal.

6. **Compatibility Between Stakeholders and Developers:** Stakeholders can properly judge the priority of requirements whereas developers can judge the cost and schedule of stakeholders' requirements in a proper way. Here, the challenge is that proper communication between stakeholders' and developers' is required consistently.

7. **Poor Prioritization:** If the requirements are not properly prioritized, then it can leads to huge financial losses and even to project failure.

f) Prioritization Dimensions (Firesmith, D., 2004)

Various customer requirements can be prioritized along with dissimilar and correlated dimensions. And these dimensions vary according to different stakeholders. The requirements can be prioritized on the following dimensions:-

1. **Business Importance:** Some requirements are very critical to the business and some are not as vital for the business. So, requirements are prioritized on the basis of its business value.
2. **Personal Inclination:** Different stakeholders like users, customers, maintainers, designers, architects, operators and testers will prefer some requirements over others. This can be due to the cost and schedule associated with the project. So, prioritization of requirements can be based on stakeholders' inclination.
3. **Damage Prevention:** This is just opposite of business importance. In this requirements are prioritize on the basis of their damage which can be done to assets of company if they are not completed.
4. **Risk Evaluation:** Each requirement is evaluated and its associated risks with that particular requirement. The requirement which have highest risk is prioritized more than the requirement which have lower risk.
5. **Cost Factor:** The implementation of different requirements have different development life cycles. Here, costs play a major role for the prioritization of requirements. Shortage of costs can be overriding factor for prioritization of requirements.
6. **Changing Nature of Requirements:** Some requirements are stable and some requirements are subject to change during development and implementation. Stable requirements generally have more priority than the changing nature requirements.
7. **Legal Mandate:** Requirements may be given privileged if requirements are mandated by law, rule, and guidelines by government or industry standard.

3) High Level Planning, Implementation, and Testing

When prioritizations of requirements are completed, some high level planning is done to achieve these requirements. Then, implementation and development is done by developers' team. After implementation and development is complete for an iteration then testing, integration and validation is done by developers' team. After all these steps, the working project is given to product owner for further testing, if it passes from product owner then whole process is carried out for next iteration. If the working project is not passed from the product owner then whole process is repeated for the same iteration.

AGILE ADOPTION IN THE INDUSTRY

According to the Version One Seventh Annual "State of Agile Development" survey, 84% of the respondents told that their organizations are practicing agile development up from 80% in 2011. Respondents also told about the personnel in the organization which are knowledgeable about agile. The below given

Table 2. Survey table showing knowledgeable persons hierarchy regarding agile

Percentage	Personnel	Most Knowledgeable		
43%	Scrum Master	Most		
14%	Dev Manager/Director/VP	Less		
14%	Project Manager			
11%	Developer			
6%	Product Manager			
2%	QA			
2%	Executive			
2%	Business Analyst			
1%	Product Owner			
5%	Others			

table 2 shows the hierarchy of least knowledgeable persons to the most knowledgeable persons regarding agile.

The most popular agile methodology used is Scrum or Scrum variants. The most important technique employed in agile is Daily Standup and Iteration Planning. Many respondents have also told about the leading causes of failure of agile development, the prominent cause of failure is Organization policy or culture at odd with agile core values. Some of the agile tools used are Task boards, Kanban boards, Agile project management tools etc. (VersionOne,2012).

AGILE USAGE IN INDUSTRY

1) Agile Usage in Automotive Industry

According to Gunasekaran (1998, 1999a), agile manufacturing is ''the potential to fight and flourish in a complex and competitive environment of nonstop and unpredicted change by reacting rapidly and efficiently to changing markets scenarios which is driven by user-designed products and services. Automotive companies are more paying attention towards agile manufacturing systems as it leads to equipment reusability and equipment cost reductions over time. Automotive manufacturing systems prefer more to flexible manufacturing systems. Agile manufacturing systems promote flexible manufacturing systems. The automotive industry is currently looking for agile systems because they need the elasticity of flexible systems, but also want lower equipment costs and their reusability. In industry applications, agile and flexible systems both use CNC machines and have short parallel lines for systems. This results in higher system reliabilities as compared to longer serial lines of dedicated systems (Elkins, D. A. et al., 2004). Agile manufacturing systems allow fast introduction of products models with minimal time and cost.

Various models like decision tree model, spreadsheet model are studied to know the importance of system agility. These helps to know that agile manufacturing systems are just like flexible manufacturing systems with more advantages like cost reduction, time saving and equipments reuse.

2) Lean or Agile Usage in Supply Management in the Textile and Clothing Industry

According to Harland (1997), supply chain management can be used to portray a number of concepts – manufacturing processes; purchasing management; supply management related with purchasing; the overall chain sequence; and finally a total firm network. Supply chain generally refers to the sale of goods from the initial production process to the end customer. Textile and clothing industry has some market characteristics like short product life cycle, high product variety, low predictability and high levels of price competition. The companies in these sectors do not hold even small stock of quantities as the profit margins are less. The companies in this sector have to produce products quickly and with low cost to meet the market demands to sustain in the competition. So, textile and clothing companies prefer agile, lean and leagility (combination of both) for production as it leads to shorter product life cycle, more products in less time and less investment costs which increases the profit margins (Bruce, M., Daly, L., and Towers, N. 2004). Textile and clothing supply chain management is highly miscellaneous and heterogeneous. The lean and agile provides a solution to the supply chain management of textile and clothing industry applications.

3) Agile Approach Usage in Mobile Applications

Mobile applications development in recent years is very difficult task. But, the symbian operating systems and java technologies like android has opened up the opportunities for developing application software like games for the mobile terminals. Still, mobile application development is a challenging task due to its specific demands and technical constraints. The distinctive, specific requirements and constraints related with mobile systems have brought new challenges to software development. As mobile development demands extensive improvements to traditional systems development methodologies in order to accomplish the unique and specific needs of this field. For doing extensive improvements in mobile development, investigation of challenges for developing software for mobile systems is done. By examine the different challenges of mobile development, agile methodologies are appropriate methods for the development of such systems (Rahimian, V., and Ramsin, R. 2008); based on this assumption, an agile based approached is developed i.e (Mobile-D application) for developing mobile applications (Abrahamsson, P., et al., 2004, October).

4) Agile Approach Usage in Robot Development

Mechatronic systems are very complex to develop and use whether it is developed or used for single component or overall full system. This complexity of developing mechartonic and robot systems arise the need of new software concept and usage of such systems. A new agile robot development concept is introduced which is flexible, simple adaptive, rapid and pragmatic. The agile robot development is successful because of the functional view of a net of communicating blocks which is required for developing complex robotic systems (Hirzinger, G., and Bauml, B. 2006, October).

5) Agile in FDA regulated environment

Over the last few years, agile has been adopted in many mission critical industries where high degree of reliability and safety is required such as aerospace and defense. But, the medical industry has been slow to adopt the agile methodology for software development. The reasons can be:-

1.   FDA follows waterfall model for software development.
2.   Medical devices need to be reliable, effective and safe.

All the above reasons are based on the misconception (Pathfinder, 2013), let's deal with the issues one at a time.

a) The FDA and Agile

FDA does not prescribe waterfall model as their standard for development of software for medical devices. It is a misconception that waterfall model is the standard of FDA. Instead FDA says that "The waterfall model effectiveness is limited, for complex and uncertain devices an engineering model is required". In order to give clarity whether the agile practices can be used for medical device software development? The AAMI medical device software committee created the agile task force which gives AAMI TIR45. AAMI TRI45 investigates all the parameters which are associated with the agile development. This gives clarity and direction that agile methodologies can be aligned for the software development of medical devices and these are aligned with the regulatory requirements.

b) Agile and Deliverable on Reliable, Safe, and Effective

There is not a single software known that provides 100% safety. Basically, medical device software promotes three principles which are required for safely use of medical software. These basic principles includes:-

1.   Risk Management.
2.   Priority of quality in agile practices.

Agile approach follows above principles thoroughly than the waterfall model (Pathfinder, 2013).

i. Risk Management in Agile Practices

Risk can be introduced in any stage of software development. When risk is found, it should be resolved with an immediate action, so that the project will not lead to a project failure. So, risk management should be integrated with agile practices at each level of the software development life cycle. Now the question arises is that, how risk management can be integrated with agile practices? Risk investigation, risk estimation and risk control should be done at each iteration or sprint when agile practices are in use. By performing risk management at each level of software development, risk identification as well as risk prioritization can be done early. By introducing risk management early in the process, it helps in discovering, eliminating or lessening the risks which are associated with the project, it also saves time as well as cost when the risks are identified early.

ii. Priority of Quality in Agile Practices

Quality maintenance is one of the main objectives of agile methodologies and practices. The traditional development teams (like waterfall development teams) do not stress much on quality attribute as compared to agile teams. The traditional development teams spent 30% to50% of their time on finding the defects and correcting them, while agile teams find the defects as early as possible as correct them with the corrective action. Agile teams find the defects when the defects are easy to find and cheap to correct. The agile methodology and practices support agile teams in reducing risk, improving quality and overall productivity. The agile methodologies and practices include:-

- Feedback Loops
- User Stories
- Unit Testing
- Test Driven development
- Agile Model Driven Development
- **Feedback Loops:** Feedback loops are used in the process. Feedback loops tells whether the results of running process are allowed to influence the future working of the process itself or not. These are the core factors for iterative and evolutionary development. Some scrum practices provide feedback loops over longer times are:
  - Sprints
  - Daily Scrum Meetings.

A key role behind feedback loops is facilitating a speedy increase in the future potential of the process.

- **User Stories:** User stories are written by users to help the release of the software and its iteration planning. User stories act as placeholders for future. User stories are not use cases as well as scenarios. User stories mainly focus on customer requirements rather than documentation. User stories are also known as gathering stories. The common metaphors used for requirements are "eliciting requirements", "capturing requirements" and gathering requirements. All these metaphors which are used for requirements are wrong. The correct metaphor is "Trawling for requirements". Trawling for requirements aspects mean gathering requirements needs the skill, requirements can be gathered with different sized, requirements can be change, mature and even die at any stage of development (Cohn 2004). There are various techniques for trawling requirements. These are:
  - Questionnaire
  - User Interviews
  - Observation
  - Story-writing workshops.

User stories help the designer and developer to focus on the user goals. This increases the quality of the software as well as less overheads.

- **Unit Testing:** Unit testing is done by the developers/testers in the laboratory to check that whether the program meets the requirements which are set in the design specifications. It also means testing the smallest separate module in the system. Unit testing strengthen the quality of the software as well as product. Unit testing when used in agile methods or practices improves the functionality of the system which indirectly contributes to the quality (Runeson, P. 2006).

- **Test Driven Development:** Test driven development creates the software in very small sprints with minimal upfront design. In test driven development, the automated tests are written prior to the development of the code which is to be developed in small, rapid iterations. Test driven development is a programming technique that guides the developer to write new code if the automated test fails. Then, the new code is again tested against the automated test cases. This whole process is repeated again and again till the software passes all the automated test cases and the quality of the software has not been achieved (Janzen and Saiedian 2005). Test driven development reduces the defect density in the project. Test driven development is more oriented towards detecting defects and improving the overall quality of the software product.

- **Agile Model Driven Development:** As the name suggests, above is the agile version of model driven development. Agile model driven development is an agile, model driven and evolutionary incremental process. In model driven development, the extensive models are created much before the source code is written but in agile model driven development, agile models are created which are just good enough that drive for overall development efforts of the project. In AMDD, firstly high level requirements are identified then iteration modeling, model storming and test driven development are done in iteration 1 and this whole process is repeated from iteration modeling to TDD development till the whole software is developed. AMDD also improves the quality of the software (http://www.agilemodeling.com/essays/amdd.htm).

MAIN SUCCESS ATTRIBUTES FOR THE AGILE DEVELOPMENT

The success of a agile development mainly depends upon the following attributes (Chow and Cao, 2008).). These are:

1. **Good Quality Product:** The product which is to be delivered at the end of development cycle should be error free and always deliver a good working product.
2. **Less Expenditure and Effort:** The product which is to be delivered must be developed within estimated efforts and cost.
3. **Timeliness:** Agile methodologies always promote to deliver the working product to the customer within time.
4. **Meet Customer Requirements:** Agile development stresses on developing the product in iterations so that one by one all the customer requirements are fulfilled.

MOTIVATIONAL REASONS FOR ADOPTING AGILE METHODOLOGY

1. **Ability to Adapt Quickly to Change:** Agile methodologies welcome changes at any stage of development. The one of the agile methodology principle is that customer can change the requirements at any stage of development.

2.   **Market Pressure to Have Short/Small Releases of Software:** The markets are changing rapidly, so agile methodologies are suitable for such type of scenarios as agile methodologies believes in releases of working software in 1 or 2 week iterations. Agile methodologies like Scrum, XP have 1 or 2 week iterations between releases of working software.

3.   **Promotes Risk Management:** Risk investigation, risk estimation and risk monitoring should be done at each iteration or sprint in agile methodologies. Agile methodologies promote risk management. Risk management is integrated with agile methodologies.

4.   **Ability to Get Quick Feedback from the Users:** Short time between releases of working software allows developers to gather quick feedback from users and customers. After getting the feedback from the users, the developers do the changes according to the customer or user requirements.

5.   **Proper Scheduling:** Agile methodology main motto is to have customer satisfaction. So, one of the factor for customer satisfaction is to have timely releases of the software.

6.   **Ability to Give High Quality Software which Is Bug Free:** Agile methodologies uses unit testing, integration testing and test driven development and feedback loops help in achieving bug free product of high quality at the end of development cycle (Rao et al., 2011).

BARRIERS TO THE AGILE ADOPTION IN THE INDUSTRY

1.   **Planning Documentation:** As agile motto is to do less documentation, when software product is developed and its various versions are characterized then it becomes difficult in agile to be sure what to document and what not to document?

2.   **Lack of Up-Front Planning:** Agile practices focus on welcome requirement changes at any stage which makes difficult to do up-front planning (McHugh, M. et al., 2012).

3.   **Risk Management:** As in agile more focus is on working software rather than documentation. Changes are welcomed and expected at any stage in agile software development, so chances of risks in managing the software are more as compared to traditional approaches where focus is on documentation and requirements are frozen.

4.   **Lack of Experience using Agile:** Overall many of the industries are using traditional approaches for software development, these industries do not have the exposure for agile development. So, these industries and their employees resist going for agile development.

5.   **Management Opposed to Change:** Management thinks that more costs, more risks and more botheration is there in agile development as compared to traditional way of developing software. Some more specific type of employees and activities will be required for managing agile like scrum master and daily scrum meetings etc. These leads to more costs and more time.

6.   **Level of Training Required:** Agile development requires special tasks and trained employees. So, it requires extensive training by employees to handle agile tasks (Singh, A et al., 2012).

7.   **Mindset for Traditional Waterfall Model:** Organizations are working in waterfall model from last many years and they are showing reluctance to the adoption of agile methodologies like:- Scrum, XP etc. (Benjamin J. 2011).

8.   **Cultural Issues:** Organizations when adopting agile values, practices and principles require a major cultural change for managers, e.g. shared team responsibility and self-organization (Singh, A et al., 2010).

9. **Time Lag:** It is very difficult to cope up or share responsibility between employees when teams are distributed located and the teams working hours or timing are different i.e one employee is in India and other employee is in USA, then it is matter of concern in the organization, how these employees will share knowledge and cope up with each other to complete the tasks.

10. **Knowledge Sharing:** When the teams are distributed, then it becomes very difficult for the team members to share their knowledge or share their work correctly and timely (Singh, A et al., 2012), when knowledge sharing between team members is done that results in a project success.

AGILE INDUSTRY APPLICABILITY ENABLERS IN DISTRIBUTED ENVIRONMENT

In the globalization period of business, the agile software development plays a key role when agile development teams are distributed. When teams are distributed then it becomes very important to identify the key enablers for applicability of agile in distributed environment. By doing a lot of literature, the various enablers have been identified for applicability of agile in distributed environment. These are:

1. **Planning and Scheduling:** In agile software development, planning and scheduling are the two most important enablers. Planning and Scheduling includes the activities like Upfront Modeling and Designing (Berczuk 2007), Progress monitoring in every iteration (Miranda and Bourque 2010), planning of the small releases of working software (Cottmeyer 2008), project duration (Avision et al., 1995), small iteration cycles (Cannizzo et al., 2008), short feedback cycles (Ågerfalk et al., 2008), how many and what type of domain experts required in the project (Sharp and Ryan 2011) and most important activity behind planning and scheduling is management support (Cockburn and Highsmith 2001).

2. **Communication and Collaboration:** Agile methodologies put a lot of emphasis on communication and collaboration (Singh, A. et al., 2012) between team members when team members are co-located or distributed. In agile methodologies, a lot of stress is also put on customer assimilation. For building good communication and collaborative culture, stand up meetings are held of very short duration. Agile practices are seen to develop team relations by reducing social restrictions. Some of the social barriers are unwillingness of team members to waste their time, lack of enthusiasm to interrupt others and aversion to expose or discuss problems. There are many ways in which agile practices increases communication and collaboration in the team surroundings despite these barriers – by increasing investment and involvement in the collective effort, and by supporting frequent and informal face-to-face interaction.

3. **Risk Management and Employees Nurturing:** Risk management is an integral part of traditional development approaches. The shift from traditional development approaches to agile development approach has put a lot of new challenges in the field of risk management. In modern era of globalization, risk mitigation becomes an important part of end product. Risk management in agile approaches must start from the beginning phases of the project and must be there till the whole development cycle. The challenges while dealing with risk management in agile environment are:
    a. The goal of each sprint in agile environment is to release working software, so there is hardly any time and resources for doing risk analysis and its evaluation.

b. Less amount of training is given to employees about the risk management.

c. Risk communication is a problem.

d. Sprints Definition of done lacks risk aspects. Risk management must include following activities:

    i. **Risk Planning:** Risk planning is done before the project starts. In risk planning, a checklist is made for high-level risks and also adequate training/nurturing is given to team members so that they can deal with risks.

    ii. **Risk Identification:** Risk identification is done before the implementation of the feature. In this activity, risks are identified and risks are categorized into high level risks or low level risks.

    iii. **Risk Assessment:** This activity is done after the identification of the risk. In this activity, assess the impact and probability of the identified risk.

    iv. **Risk Response:** This activity is done during the implementation of the feature. Various responses are collected and the best response is collected to deal with the risk.

    v. **Risk Acceptance:** This activity is done during the sprint review. In this activity, it will be made sure that all the risks are accepted by the risk owner and the product owner.

    vi. **Risk Monitoring:** In this activity, monitoring and re-evaluation of larger risks is done (which is found earlier) between few sprints so that project is not a failure (Ylimannela, V., 2011).

4. **Documentation:** Agile software development supports only need based documentation (Nisar et al., 2004, Whitworth et al., 2007). One of the main principles of agile practices and methodologies to have less documentation as compared to traditional practices and methodologies and agile methodology prefers working software over documentation.

5. **Tools:** In agile methodology, tools are the enabler for the applicability of agile in distributed environment. Tools enabler includes synchronous and asynchronous communication tools (Ågerfalk 2008), integrated and continuous development tool (Avision et al., 1995) and status tracking and reporting tools (Braithwaite et al., 2005). Tools enabler helps in proper and timely communication and knowledge sharing between team members when teams are distributed. This enabler also helps in keep an eye of the status of the project too.

6. **Adaptability-Flexibility-Commitment:** This enabler believes in self-motivated, self-directed and self-organized teams (Ågerfalk et al. 2008) i.e teams should be highly cohesive. Team members should be inculcated and aware about models, technology and tools, practices and frameworks (Drummond et al., 2008). Team members should be adaptable to the work culture (Nerur et al., 2005) and have cultural alertness (Braithwaite et al., 2005). Overall, team members should emphasize constant commitment (Cockburn et al., 2001) on all aspects of the project. There should be strong bonding of trust between team members in distributed as well as co-located environment.

7. **Financial and Time Aspects:** This enabler is related with increase in the productivity (Doherty 2011), minimizing the cost expenditures (Shrivastava et al., 2010) and makes the product timely according to the market scenario (Schubert 2011). This enabler is the most suitable enabler for agile development in this fast globalization business world.

CONCLUSION

This chapter mainly concentrates on software development, which is very important now days for all the facets of the modern world. The tools and technology are changing quickly and best development practices, methodologies and methods are constantly being created. *"Walking on water and developing software from a specification are easy if both are frozen"* (Edward V. Berard). A lot of efforts have been put in for the success of software development in the quickly changing requirements scenarios but still project managers have not find the suitable model or method. Still software development results in projects failure, delays and discards. The software which is developed with traditional approaches may need expensive on-going maintenance and corrective service releases. Agile software development has brought new insights in the software development. Agile methodologies develop the software in short iteration and releases the working software in the hand of customers within few weeks. Agile methodologies are principle based. Agile methodologies manifesto supports twelve principles which must be followed while development of the software. Agile software development success attributes are timeliness, customer collaboration, less cost and efforts and end product must cover all customer requirements. Agile methodologies now days used in all the types of industry like automotive, textile and clothing, mobile applications, manufacturing, robot development and medical devices software. Still there are lot of motivational reasons and barriers for adoption of agile methodologies in industry. As long as the agile project picks a high-caliber committed team, practices agile principles and agile software engineering techniques and executes an accurate agile-style delivery strategy, the project could be likely to be great success. Agile software development has proven their importance in software industry but still there are lot of factors which need to be improved like knowledge sharing, requirement elicitation, communication and collaboration between team members and cultural issues in distributed and co-located environment. These factors are important for the management when they embark on adopting agile methods in their software development projects.

REFERENCES

Abrahamsson, P. (2008). *Agile processes in software engineering and eXtreme programming*. Germany: Springer. doi:10.1007/978-3-540-68255-4

Abrahamsson, P., Hanhineva, A., Hulkko, H., Ihme, T., Jäälinoja, J., Korkala, M., . . . Salo, O. (2004). Mobile-D: An Agile Approach for Mobile Application Development. In *Proceedings of the 19th Annual ACM Conference on ObjectOriented Programming, Systems, Languages, and Applications, OOPSLA'04*. Vancouver, Canada: ACM.

Ågerfalk, P. J. B. F., Holmström Olsson, H., and Ó Conchúir, E. (2008). Benefits of Global Software Development: The Known and Unknown. Lecture Notes in Computer Science, 5007, 1-9.

Akbar, R., Hassan, M. F., Abdullah, A., Safdar, S., & Qureshi, M. A. (2011). Directions and Advancements in Global Software Development: A summarized review of GSD and agile methods. *Research Journal of Information Technology*, *3*(2), 69–80. doi:10.3923/rjit.2011.69.80

Aoyama, M. (1997, August). Agile software process model. In *Proceedings of the 21st IEEE International Computer Software and Applications Conference COMPSAC '97* (pp. 454-459). IEEE.

Avison, D., & Fitzgerald, G. (1995). *Information systems development: methodologies, techniques and tools*. London, UK: McGraw-Hill Publishing.

Balter, B. (2011). Towards a more agile government: The case for rebooting federal IT procurement. *Public Contract Law Journal, 41*(1), 149–171.

Beck, K., Beedle, M., Van Bennekum, A., Cockburn, A., Cunningham, W., Fowler, M., . . . Thomas, D. (2001). Manifesto for agile software development. *Agile Alliance*. Available online: www.agilemanifesto.org

Berczuk, S. (2007, August). Back to basics: The role of agile principles in success with an distributed scrum team. In *Proceedings of the AGILE 2007*. Washington, DC: IEEE Computer Society. doi:10.1109/AGILE.2007.17

Boehm, B. (2002). Get ready for agile methods, with care. *IEEE Computer, 35*(1), 64–69. doi:10.1109/2.976920

Boehm, B., and Turner, R. (2005). Management challenges to implementing agile processes in traditional development organizations. *IEEE Software, 22*(5), 30-39.

Braithwaite, K., and Joyce, T. (2005). XP expanded: Distributed extreme programming. In *Proceedings of 6th International Conference on Extreme programming and agile processes in software engineering (LNCS)*, (vol. 3556, pp. 1524– 1526). Springer.

Bruce, M., Daly, L., & Towers, N. (2004). Lean or agile: A solution for supply chain management in the textiles and clothing industry? *International Journal of Operations and Production Management, 24*(2), 151–170. doi:10.1108/01443570410514867

Cannizzo, F., Marcionetti, G., & Moser, P. (2008, August). Evolution of the tools and practices of a large distributed agile team. In *Proceedings of the Agile 2008 Conference, IEEE Computers and Society*. IEEE.

Chow, T., & Cao, D. B. (2008). A survey study of critical success factors in agile software projects. *Journal of Systems and Software, 81*(6), 961–971. doi:10.1016/j.jss.2007.08.020

Cockburn, A., & Highsmith, J. (2001). Agile software development: The people factor. *Computer, 34*(11), 131–133. doi:10.1109/2.963450

Cohn, M. (2004). *User stories applied: For agile software development*. Addison-Wesley Professional.

Cottmeyer, M. (2008, August). The good and bad of Agile offshore development. In *Proceedings Agile 2008* (pp. 362–367). Academic Press.

Dixon, N. M. (2000). *Common knowledge: How companies thrive by sharing what they know*. Boston: Harvard Business Press.

Doherty, M. J. (2011). *Examining Project Manager Insights of Agile and Traditional Success Factors for Information Technology Projects: A Q-Methodology Study*. (PhD Dissertation). Marian University.

Drummond, B., and Unson, J. F. (2008, August). Yahoo! Distributed Agile: Notes from the world over. In *Proceedings of the Conference on Agile 2008*. IEEE Computer Society. doi:10.1109/Agile.2008.21

Elkins, D. A., Huang, N., & Alden, J. M. (2004). Agile manufacturing systems in the automotive industry. *International Journal of Production Economics*, *91*(3), 201–214. doi:10.1016/j.ijpe.2003.07.006

Firesmith, D. (2004). Prioritizing Requirements. *Journal of Object Technology*, *3*(8), 35–48. doi:10.5381/jot.2004.3.8.c4

Georgsson, A. (2011). *Introducing story points and user stories to perform estimations in a software development organisation. A case study at Swedbank IT*. (Unpublished master's thesis). Umeå University, Umeå, Sweden.

Grinys, A. (2012). *Agile Project Estimation*. Retrieved from http://skemman.is/stream/get/1946/11973/30239/4/AG_MSthesis.pdf

Gunasekaran, A. (1998). Agile manufacturing: Enablers and an implementation framework. *International Journal of Production Research*, *36*(5), 1223–1247. doi:10.1080/002075498193291

Gunasekaran, A. (1999). Editorial: Design and implementation of agile manufacturing systems. *International Journal of Production Economics*, *62*(1-2), 1–6. doi:10.1016/S0925-5273(98)00216-3

Harland, C. M. (1997). Supply chain operational performance roles. *Integrated Management Systems*, *8*(2), 6–14.

Hirzinger, G., and Bauml, B. (2006, October). Agile robot development (aRD): A pragmatic approach to robotic software. In *Proceedings of IEEE/RSJ International Conference on Intelligent Robots and Systems* (pp. 3741–3748). IEEE.

Janzen, D., & Saiedian, H. (2005). Test-driven development: Concepts, taxonomy, and future direction. *Computer*, *38*(9), 43–50. doi:10.1109/MC.2005.314

Larman, C. (2004). *Agile and iterative development: a manager's guide*. Boston: Addison-Wesley Professional.

Larman, C., & Basili, V. R. (2003). Iterative and incremental development: A brief history. *IEEE Computer*, *36*(6), 47–56. doi:10.1109/MC.2003.1204375

McHugh, M., McCaffery, F., & Casey, V. (2012). Barriers to adopting agile practices when developing medical device software. In *Software Process Improvement and Capability Determination* (pp. 141–147). Springer Berlin Heidelberg. doi:10.1007/978-3-642-30439-2_13

Miranda, E., & Bourque, P. (2010). Agile monitoring using the line of balance. *Journal of Systems and Software*, *83*(7), 1205–1215. doi:10.1016/j.jss.2010.01.043

Nerur, S., & Balijepally, V. (2007). Theoretical reflections on agile development methodologies. *Communications of the ACM*, *50*(3), 79–83. doi:10.1145/1226736.1226739

Nerur, S., Mahapatra, R., & Mangalaraj, G. (2005). Challenges of migrating to agile methodologies. *Communications of the ACM*, *48*(5), 72–78. doi:10.1145/1060710.1060712

Nisar, M. F., and Hameed, T. (2004, December). Agile methods handling offshore software development issues. In *Proceedings of INMIC 2004, 8th International Multitopic Conference*. INMIC.

Pathak, K., & Saha, A. (2013). Review of Agile Software Development Methodologies. *International Journal of Advanced Research in Computer Science and Software Engineering, 3*(2), 270–276.

Pathfinder. (2013). *Agile in an FDA Regulated Environment.* Retrieved from http://himss.files.cms-plus.com/FileDownloads/2013-1101%20Agile%20in%20FDA%20Environment%20Pathfinder%20White%20Paper_1387316073933_4.pdf

Rahimian, V., and Ramsin, R. (2008). Designing an agile methodology for mobile software development: a hybrid method engineering approach. In *Proceedings of International Conference on Research Challenges in Information Science (RCIS).* Academic Press. doi:10.1109/RCIS.2008.4632123

Rao, K. N., Naidu, G. K., and Chakka, P. (2011). A study of the agile software development methods, applicability and implications in industry. *International Journal of Software Engineering and its Applications, 5*(2), 35-45.

Runeson, P. (2006). A survey of unit testing practices. *Software, IEEE, 23*(4), 22–29. doi:10.1109/MS.2006.91

Rüping, A. (2003). *Agile documentation: a pattern guide to producing lightweight documents for software projects.* New York: John Wiley and Sons.

Schubert, L. (2011). *The Keys To Distributed and Agile Application Development.* White Paper. CollabNet Inc. Retrieved from http://visit.collab.net/rs/collabnet/images/keys_to_distributed_agile_app_dev_in_cloud.pdf

Sharp, J. H., & Ryan, S. D. (2011). Best Practices for Configuring Globally Distributed Agile Teams. *Journal of Information Technology Management, 22*(4), 56.

Shrivastava, S. V., & Date, H. (2010). A Framework for Risk Management in Globally Distributed Agile Software Development (Agile GSD). *Interscience Management Review, 2*(1), 32–41.

Singh, A., & Singh, K. (2010). Agile Adoption – Crossing the Chasm. In *Proceedings of the International Conference on Applied Computer Science.* ACS.

Singh, A., Singh, K., and Sharma, N. (2012). Managing Knowledge in Agile Software Development. In *IJCA Proceedings on International Conference on Recent Advances and Future Trends in Information Technology* (iRAFIT 2012), (vol. 9, pp. 33-37). IJCA.

Singh, A., Singh, K., & Sharma, N. (2014). Agile knowledge management: A survey of Indian perceptions. *Innovations in Systems and Software Engineering, 10*(4), 297–315. doi:10.1007/s11334-014-0237-z

Sommerville, I., & Sawyer, P. (1997). *Requirements engineering: A good practice guide.* John Wiley and Sons, Inc.

Thakur, S., & Kaur, A. (2013). Role of Agile Methodology in Software Development. *International Journal of Computer Science and Mobile Computing, 2*(10), 86–90.

VersionOne. (2012). *7ᵗʰ Annual State of Agile Development Survey.* Retrieved from http://www.versionone.com/pdf/7th-Annual-State-of-Agile-Development-Survey.pdf

Whitworth, E., and Biddle, R. (2007, August). The social nature of agile teams. In *Proceedings of Agile Conference (AGILE)* (pp. 26-36). Academic Press.

Ylimannela, V. (2011). *A Model for Risk Management in Agile Software Development. Communications of Cloud Software*. Tampere: Tampere University of Technology.

KEY TERMS AND DEFINITIONS

Agile Adoption: It means how you use agile practices in the organization so that software quality can be improved.

Agile Distributed Environment: In agile software development, the team members are not co-located at one place. So, how they use to communicate, share their knowledge at distributed locations.

Agile Enablers: These are the parameters which promotes agile software development.

Agile Software Development: It is an umbrella term for various software development methodologies. These are used by self organizing and distributed teams to help businesses for responding to unpredictability.

Agile Usage: Agile usage denotes the areas or fields where agile methodologies are used.

Barriers: It means what are the obstacles which come in front of agile software development.

User Stories Attributes: It means that when a user is telling its requirements, the requirements must have some parameters like Independent, Negotiable, Valuable, Estimate, Small and Testable.

Chapter 9
The MFC Cybersecurity Model Extension and Diagnostic toward a Depth Measurement:
E-Learning Systems Case Study

Neila Rjaibi
Institut Supérieur de Gestion de Tunis, Tunisia

Latifa Ben Arfa Rabai
Institut Supérieur de Gestion de Tunis, Tunisia

Ali Mili
New Jersey Institute of Technology, USA

ABSTRACT

This chapter presents a quantitative security risk management cybersecurity measure namely the Mean Failure Cost (MFC). We illustrate it to quantify the security of an e-Learning application while taking account of its respective stakeholders, security requirements, architectural components and the complete list of security threats. Moreover, in the mean time, security requirements are considered as appropriate mechanisms for preventing, detecting and recovering security attacks, for this reason an extension of the MFC measure is presented in order to detect the most critical security requirements to support the quantitative decision-making. Our focus is widespread to offer a diagnostic of the non secure system's problems and a depth insight interpretation about critical requirements, critical threats and critical components. This extension is beneficial and opens a wide range of possibilities for further economics based analysis. Also this chapter highlights the security measures for controlling e-Learning security problems regarding the most critical security requirements.

DOI: 10.4018/978-1-4666-8510-9.ch009

INTRODUCTION

The purpose of this chapter is to examine one among the current knowledge in the field of systems and software engineering. We address particularly the issue of the system's safety and cybersesecurity and more specifically the quantification and measure of security risk in a financial value for all the systems' stakeholders, this is the concept of risk to the security risk management approach.

This chapter focuses in general on the advancements in the engineering of systems, in particular in the software security engineering in the design or development phase of current e- systems.

In today's Internet age, E-systems are widespread and considered essential in our modern society. These systems require the sharing and the distribution of information. E-systems are vulnerable; serious security threats include software attacks (viruses, worms, macros, denial of service), espionage, acts of theft (illegal equipment or information) and intellectual property (piracy, copyright, infringement) (MohdAlwi & Fan, 2010).

Security is a current issue that needed to be addressed to ensure a safer running of systems and a higher quality. It is important to assess and to measure the security risk and its potential impact (Aissa et al., 2010 a; Aissa et al., 2012; Aissa et al., 2010 b). Research has been conducted in this perspective to improve security management approaches and models which are quantitative or qualitative. These strategies are useful to highlight the power of the security management.

Quantitative security management models are considered as a hard task in practice in order to measure the potential security risk impact caused by the attacks. But they are more useful in estimative values analyze and interpretation to provide a good plan for risk mitigation (Abercrombie et al., 2008; Mili & Sheldon, 2009).

Cybersecurity is emerging as a major concern for organizations including management systems, communication systems, critical infrastructure control, medical platforms and e-services. E-learning systems are complex given their openness, necessity, heterogeneity and widespread scope. In such systems, the danger is multiplied, and the security issue becomes an important challenge. It is of our interest to focus on the security of E-learning platforms to study their integrity, confidentiality and availability. In fact, having a stable platform without technical problems leads to a high-quality learning processes (Rjaibi & Rabai, 2011; Sun et al., 2008; Rjaibi & Rabai, 2012), competition, adequate cash, profitability and a good commercial image.

To the best of our knowledge and according to the literature review we note ignorance in addressing security topic of e-learning systems and a lack in quantitative security management models (Nickolova & Nickolov, 2007; MohdAlwi & Fan, 2010). In addition, in-depth security interpretations are also not discussed.

Our goal is to study a cybersecurity measure for the E-learning network and to schedule a deep insight and diagnostic of the critical threats, the critical architectural components and the critical security requirements. Also it is a challenging tasks, it is useful to scout about the main cybersecurity diagnostics.

This chapter highlights the definition and computation of a recent and rigourous cybersecurity measure namely the Mean Failure Cost (MFC), it computes for each stakeholder of the given system his loss of operation ($/H). This quantitative model is a cascade of linear models to quantify security threats in term of loss that results from system vulnerabilities (Aissa et al., 2010; Aissa et al., 2012; Aissa et al., 2009).

The MFC is independent from the system but depends on system users. It can be applied to manage and quantify security threats of all e-System like e-Commerce, e-Learning, e-Government and other such services.

This chapter focalizes on the quantification of security threats of a given e-system in general and for e-learning system in particular using an economic measure abridged by MFC (Mean Failure Cost). Our contribution in this chapter can be generalized to other practical E-systems because according to Mohd Alwi and Fan (2010) an E-learning systems share similar characteristics with other e-services. These are the accessibility of service via the Internet, the consumption of services by a person via the Internet and the payment of a service by the consumer. Therefore, management security approaches to quantify security in E-learning are common with other E-services.

Given the strengths of the MFC cybersecurity measure in quantifying security with a financial risk measure we propose to study the way of quantifying security within e-learning platforms. The overall objectives of this chapter are:

- First, we focus on presenting security aspects of current and standard e-Learning applications, and analyze its respective stakeholders, security requirements, architectural components and common potential threats. This first step is the definition of a quantitative security risk management attributes. Moreover, the strength is in the refinement of the catalog of security threats and the presentation of its classification versus the security requirement.

- Second, we illustrate the MFC cybersecurity measure to quantify security of an e-Learning application while taking account of the complete list of security threats, we focuses on improvements in the catalogue of threats and its respective empirical data. This second step is the computation of the MFC values.

- In the mean time, security requirements are considered as appropriate mechanisms for preventing, detecting and recovering security attacks, for this reason an extension of the MFC measure is presented in order to detect the most critical security requirements to support quantitative decision-making. Our focus is to enrich the MFC measure in order to develop a comprehensive science of cybersecurity and to get more safe and effective systems.

- Our focus is widespread to offer a diagnostic of possible problems of the non secure systems and a depth insight interpretation about critical requirements, critical threats and critical components regarding the cybersystem. This extension is beneficial and opens a wide range of possibilities for further economics based analysis.

- Then basing on the classification of threats by security requirements, we optimize the reading and interpretation in depth of the MFC and offer a complete diagnosis and a roadmap of the system such as the critical security requirement presentation, the critical architectural components and the critical threats.

- Also this chapter highlights the security measures and guidelines for controlling e-Learning security policies regarding the most critical security requirements.

- Finally, we present a comprehensive survey of known relationships among security requirements and security measures and the possible associated security mechanisms

The theoretical aspects, the practical case study and the deep of interpretation developed in this chapter offer strengths guidelines in the science and knowledge of cybersecurity in our modern society and for all context and e-systems.

BACKGROUND: DEFINITION OF THE E-LEARNING SYSTEM'S ATTRIBUTES

In this section, we go on to define the e-learning system's attributes namely the system's stakeholders and the related security requirements then the refinement of the catalog of security threats and the decomposition of the architectural components of current and standard e-learning platforms and applications.

E-Learning Basic Architectural Components

Much e-learning architecture including different components has been introduced. It is based on the architecture standard diagram presented by Selvi et al. (2008), which considers six basic and common architectural components.

- The browser
- The Web server
- The Application server
- The Database server
- The Firewall server
- The Mail server.

The List of Stakeholders

An E-learning system is a complex system, it incorporates different stakeholders, and it may be related to the entire system or to sub application of the related system. The two primary system's stakeholders are the student and the teacher. They are the engine and the maestro of the leaning situation. The third stakeholder is the technician. The fourth stakeholder is the system administrator.

- The system administrator
- The teacher
- The student
- The technician.

List of Security Requirements

We can classify the following basic security requirements of the E-learning systems into six aspects; confidentiality, integrity, availability, non-repudiation, authentication and privacy (Kumar & Dutta, 2011; Stapié et al., 2008; Naaji & Herman, 2011; Luminita, 2011).

- Authentication
- Confidentiality
- Integrity
- Availability
- Non-repudiation
- Privacy.

Table 1. E-learning security threats

References	Authentication Attacks		Availability Attacks	Confidentiality Attacks			Integrity Attacks					
	1	2	1	1	2	3	1	2	3	4	5	6
(Kumar and Dutta, 2011)	*	*	*	*	*	*	*	*	*	*	*	*
(Stapié et al., 2008)	*	*	*	*	*	*	*	*	*	*	*	*
(Naaji and Herman, 2011)			*									
(Luminita, 2011)	*	*										

The List of Security Threats

In this section, we present the complete list of threats and their classification by security requirements as presented in Table 1.

Stapié et al. (2008) summarizes E-learning systems security threats as follows:

- **Authentication attacks:**
  - Broken authentication and session management.
  - Insecure communication.
- **Availability attacks:**
  - Denial of service.
- **Confidentiality attacks:**
  - Insecure cryptographic storage.
  - Insecure direct object reference.
  - Information leakage and improper error handling.
- **Integrity attacks:**
  - Buffer overflow.
  - Cross Site Request Forgery.
  - Cross Site Scripting.
  - Failure to restrict URL access.
  - Injection flaws.
  - Malicious file execution.

According to the literature (Kumar & Dutta, 2011; Stapié et al., 2008; Naaji & Herman, 2011; Luminita, 2011), we recognize the detail of possible security threats:

- **Authentication:** Authentication is the process of confirming that something or someone is really who they claim to be. It is the verification of the identity of someone. It occurs when the attacker steals password and identity of legitimate end-user. In the case of authentication broke, they are the opportunity of availability, confidentiality or integrity attacks. There are two dangerous authentication attacks:
  - **Broken Authentication and Session Management (BroA):** Authentication and session management include all aspects of handling user authentication and managing active ses-

sions. This attack occurs when the account credential management functions (e.g. remember my password, forgot my password, change my password, etc.) and session tokens are not properly protected. An attacker can intercept and steal the authenticated session of a legitimate user (Kumar & Dutta, 2011; Stapié et al., 2008).

- **Insecure Communication (InsC):** This vulnerability occurs when we transmit sensitive information (e.g. session tokens) without proper encryption. The attacker can impersonate a user and have access to unprotected conversations. Communication is under attack during the information transmission phase without encryption, so the attacker can easily intercept the credentials of a user and have access to these conversations (Kumar & Dutta, 2011; Stapié et al., 2008).

- **Availability:** The web application should be available, so the main purpose of availability attacks is to make e-learning services and data unavailable to authorized end-users: Denial of service (DoS) attack is considered among the most popular form of availability attack.
  - **Denial of Service (Dos):** This attack is the abuse of the finite bandwidth and connectivity resources of an LMS system. In a denial-of-service attack, an attacker attempts to prevent legitimate users from accessing information or services in the platform (Stapié et al., 2008).
    - There are two types of DoS attack: logic and flooding attacks. Logic attacks (e.g. ping) exploit existing LMS flaws to crash remote server or significantly decrease its performance. Flooding attacks overloads LMS with a high number of requests to disable legitimate users from accessing e-learning resources (Stapié et al., 2008).

- **Confidentiality Attacks:** It is the divulgation of confidential data, hence cryptography is considered as the solution. This is the kind of passive attacks; it allows unauthorized access to confidential resources and data. The main intention of attacker is not data modification but data access and dissemination (such as user name, password). We recognize the most frequently confidentiality flaws are:
  - **Insecure Cryptographic Storage (CrypS):** Sensitive information does not have appropriate encryption because LMS systems rarely use cryptographic functions properly to protect data. Insecure cryptographic storage occurs when an application does not securely encrypt its sensitive data when it is stored into a database (Stapié et al., 2008).
  - **Insecure Direct Object Reference (DOR):** This vulnerability occurs when LMS uses object references (files, database records and primary keys) directly in web interfaces contained either by URL or form parameters without authorization checks being implemented. The attacker abuses with direct object references to access other objects without authorization (Kumar & Dutta, 2011).
  - **Information Leakage and Improper Error Handling (InfL):** It refers to unintentional disclosure of sensitive data and unneeded information through error messages. LMS can leak sensitive information about its logic, configuration and other internal details of the organization of the application (e.g. SQL syntax, source code, etc.). This information can be used to plan an attack. Broken authentication and session management, weak session tokens and weak passwords allow an attacker to assume other user's identities (Kumar & Dutta, 2011).

- **Integrity Attacks:** This group refers to attacks that attempt to create, modify and delete e-learning data. Today's most critical integrity authentication vulnerabilities are:
  - **Buffer Overflow (Buff):** This attack happens when an LMS component (e.g. libraries, drivers, server components) attempts to store data in an available buffer without validating its

size. This occurs with the insertion of larger values than expected (e.g. 800 characters in a limited length field). Attackers can inject attack code or use code which is already in the LMS address space (Stapié et al., 2008).

- ○ **Cross Site Request Forgery (CSRF):** Known as XSRF, CSRF, and Cross Site Reference Forgery. This vulnerability is dangerous because it can potentially perform an action unauthorized in the platform with the rights of a legitimate user access and consent. The attacker embeds malicious HTML or JavaScript code into an email or website, then if a user is logged into the site, the attacker tricks his browser into making a request to one of URLs site. Request comes with the user's cookies. So the server will perform it as if it is the original (Stapié et al., 2008).

- ○ **Cross Site Scripting (CSS):** Cross-Site Scripting or Malicious code injection (abbreviated XSS or CSS) attacks are attacks targeting websites that dynamically display user content without checking and encoding the information entered by users. The attacker injects a malicious script and executes it in victim's browser in order to gather user data. It forces a website to display HTML code or scripts entered by users. The code injected in the web page can be used to display a form to fool the user and get him/her to enter authentication information. Also, it can redirect the user to a web page controlled by the hacker and possibly featuring the same graphical interface (Luminita, 2011). Protection: By configuring their browsers to prevent the execution of script languages to design non-vulnerable websites. We should verify the format of data entered by users; Encode displayed user data by replacing special characters with their HTML equivalents.

- ○ **Failure to Restrict URL Access (FURL):** Some resources of the system are limited to a small subset of privileged users. This weakness allows an attacker to recover, if only by guessing, the URL address and perform unauthorized operations (Kumar & Dutta, 2011).

- ○ **Injection Flaws (InjecF):** Using the input data from the client, the attacker can insert or "inject" SQL query to the application. Then the attacker can read sensitive data, modify and execute administration operations on the database (such as shutdown the DBMS) (Luminita, 2011).

- ○ **Malicious File Execution (MFile):** This attack occurs when the system cannot control the execution of uploaded files. The malicious code is uploaded via the upload function such as homework (Kumar & Dutta, 2011).

THE MFC CYBERSECURITY MEASURE TO QUANTIFY SECURITY: E-LEARNING SYSTEMS CASE STUDY

The MFC measure of cybersecurity takes into account complex system specifications, and considers variations by stakeholders, security requirements, architectural components, and threats.

The mathematical infrastructure of the MFC is defined as (Aissa et al., 2010 a; Aissa et al., 2012; Aissa et al., 2010 b):

$$MFC = ST \circ DP \circ IM \circ PT \tag{1}$$

Table 2. The Stakes matrix (ST)

Requirements Stakeholders	Confidentiality	Integrity	Availability	Non-Repudiation	Authentication	Privacy
Administrator	40	30	60	10	10	50
Teacher	20	20	60	20	30	40
Student	0	5	5	0	5	0
Technician	10	7	15	5	5	15

where the Stake matrix (ST), the Dependability matrix (DP) and the Impact matrix (IM) are three matrixes and PT is the vector of probability:

The Stakes Matrix (ST)

The related systems' stakeholders enter the data of the stake matrix with respect to security requirements; they specified a premium on each relevant clause (Rabai et al., 2012) as presented in Table 2.

Each row in this matrix is filled by relevant stakeholders who have internal or external usage for the platform, each cell expressed in monetary terms and represents the loss incurred and/or premium placed on requirement. To fill ST Matrix we did a survey for the Virtual University of Tunis (UVT). We rely on an online survey for data collection available at (Rjaibi, 2013).

ST (H$_i$, R$_j$): Is the stake that stakeholders H$_i$ has in meeting requirement R$_j$.

The Dependency Matrix (DP)

Each row in this matrix is filled by System Architects; each cell represents the probability of failure with respect to a requirement given that a component has failed as presented in Table 3.

DP (R$_j$, C$_k$): The probability that the system fails to meet requirement R$_j$ if component C$_k$ is compromised. To fill this matrix we have used values from (Aissa, 2013).

Table 3. The Dependency matrix with hypotheses (DP)

Components Requirements	Browser	Web Server	Application Server	DB Server	Firewall Server	Mail Server	No Failure
Confidentiality	0.075	0.123	0.123	0.186	0.37	0.123	0.0
Integrity	0.09	0.152	0.152	0.0	0.454	0.152	0.0
Availability	0.333	0.111	0.111	0.0	0.333	0.111	0.0
Non-repudiation	0.09	0.152	0.152	0.0	0.454	0.152	0.0
Authentication	0.075	0.123	0.123	0.186	0.37	0.123	0.0
Privacy	0.075	0.123	0.123	0.186	0.37	0.123	0.0

Table 4. The Impact matrix (IM)

Threats Components	BroA	InsC	DoS	CryptS	DOR	InfL	Buff	CSRF	CSS	FURL	InjecF	MFile	No Threats
Browser	0.477	0.119	0.006	0.000	0.000	0.000	0.000	0.000	0.000	0.397	0.000	0.000	0.000
Web server	0.273	0.137	0.001	0.000	0.000	0.000	0.342	0.007	0.014	0.227	0.000	0.000	0.000
Application server	0.271	0.135	0.007	0.000	0.000	0.000	0.338	0.007	0.000	0.225	0.014	0.003	0.000
DB server	0.187	0.094	0.005	0.155	0.155	0.155	0.234	0.005	0.000	0.000	0.009	0.002	0.000
Firewall server	0.143	0.143	0.714	0.000	0.000	0.000	0.000	0.000	0.000	0.000	0.000	0.000	0.000
Mail server	0.375	0.187	0.009	0.028	0.028	0.028	0.000	0.009	0.000	0.312	0.019	0.005	0.000
No Failure	0.523	0.813	0.286	0.845	0.845	0.845	0.658	0.991	0.986	0.603	0.981	0.995	1.000

The Impact Matrix (IM)

Each row in this matrix is filled by the verification and validation team; each cell represents probability of compromising a component given that a threat has materialized, it dependent on the target of each threat, likelihood of success of the threat. To fill this matrix we have used the values from (Aissa, 2013) as presented in Table 4.

$IM(C_k, T_h)$: The probability that Component C_k is compromised if Threat T_h has materialized.

The Threat Vector (PT)

Each row in this vector is filled by a security team member; each cell of Table 5 represents the probability of realization of each threat, it is dependent on perpetrator models, empirical data, known vulnerabilities, known counter-measures, etc.

$PT(T_i)$: The probability that threat T_i materialized for a unit of operation time (one hour of operation).

The empirical data of the DP, IM matrix and PT vector are determined from previous empirical investigation in (Aissa, 2013) and updated from a combination of collected empirical data and survey from antivirus reports like Kaspersky (Kaspersky Security Bulletin 2013 The overall statistics for 2013), AVG (avg threat report 2013), etc. (Rjaibi et al., 2012, Rjaibi et al., 2013)

The data collection took 1 research year to construct. The used empirical data base for quantifying security threats is available at (Rjaibi & Aissa, 2013).

Using this data, we compute the vector of the mean failure costs using the MFC formula presented in Table 6.

Table 6 presents the MFC for each stakeholder, therefore the system administrator stands to lose 0.617 $/ hour if the system is threatened, the teacher loses about 0.590 $/ hour. For a student and a technician it can appear insignificant but for a failure to long-term they are significant.

Nevertheless, in the science of cybersecurity it is very important to find the critical security requirements, which open a wide range of interpretation in depth, of a given non secure system. Our focus is on measuring the Mean Failure Cost for critical security requirements which will be discussed in the next section throughout an extension of MFC formula.

Table 5. The Vector of probability (PT)

Threats	Probability
Broken authentication and session management (BroA)	$4.20 \ 10^{-3}$
Insecure communication (InsC)	$3.00 \ 10^{-3}$
Denial of service (Dos)	$3.08 \ 10^{-3}$
Insecure cryptographic storage (CrypS)	$7.00 \ 10^{-4}$
Insecure direct object reference (DOR)	$7.00 \ 10^{-4}$
Information leakage and improper error handling (InfL)	$7.00 \ 10^{-4}$
Buffer overflow (Buff)	$1.00 \ 10^{-4}$
Cross Site Request Forgery (CSRF)	$4.20 \ 10^{-4}$
Cross Site Scripting (CSS)	$1.80 \ 10^{-4}$
Failure to restrict URL access (FURL)	$9.80 \ 10^{-3}$
Injection flaws (InjecF)	$2.17 \ 10^{-3}$
Malicious file execution (MFile)	$5.04 \ 10^{-4}$
No Threats	$974.44 \ 10^{-3}$

MFC EXTENSION: COMPUTING CRITICAL SECURITY REQUIREMENTS

Results of security threats analysis may also be useful in a practical plan to provide us with pertinent information in order to implement a secure environment. In the science of cybersecurity except the assessment of the risk, other challenges are required, especially in a complex system we need the knowledge of the critical security requirements in quantitative way. Hence, we propose in this section an expansion of the MFC formula to underline the estimation of the critical security requirements.

Nowadays, security requirements become an important issue in information systems, it improves the quality of software process and products. Security requirements are considered as the level of protection necessary for equipments, data, information and applications to meet security policy.

Measuring in a structured way the critical security requirements regarding the complexity of a given architecture system is beneficial to make more effective system in the development phase and in earlier phases. A well-defined security process is advantageous and a well-defined security requirements plan is recommended.

In addition, our extension of the MFC formula to measure the critical security requirements is beneficial to a better security management, assessment and control of the non-secure system. These theoretical and practical improvements lead to the enrichment of the MFC application, to provide more

Table 6. The Mean Failure Cost for e-learning Systems with hypotheses

Stakeholders	Mean Failure Cost \$ /Hour
System administrator	0.617
Teacher	0.590
Student	0.047
Technician	0.173

comprehensive science of cybersecurity and their related metrics, especially to interpret in the deep and to get more safe and effective systems. Besides, the quantification of security threats and their impact throughout a financial measure open a wide range of further interpretations.

The MFC Formula Extension: The Approach

The MFC vector is the mean failure cost of system / stakeholder during a unit of operating time. The values of MFC do not distinguish between the low and the high cost of security requirement for the global system. In this section we introduce a new extension of the MFC formula to define which requirement is more critical.

To build a new extension of the MFC formula, we proceed as follows:

- Instead of defining the ST matrix for all security requirements, we create a vector ST' which evaluates each requirement cost for every stakeholder.
- Instead of computing DP matrix which represents the component failure probabilities if a requirement fails, we compute the transpose vector DP' which computes the components failure probabilities for every requirement.
- Finally, we compute the sum of the failure costs for every security requirement. Most costly requirements are considered as critical.

The MFC Formula Extension: Computing the Critical Security Requirements

In the stake matrix ST, we have introduced the costs that can be lost by the stakeholders. The stakes depend on the stakeholders and the security requirements. The MFC vector is the mean failure cost of system during a unit of operating time those values don't distinguish between the low and the high cost of security requirements. In this section we will use a simple extension of the MFC formula to define which requirement is more critical than the others. We consider a system S, we let H_1, H_2,..., H_K be stakeholders of system and R one of the security requirements of system. Let MFCR be the random variable that represents the mean failure cost of the requirement R. We let PR the probability that the system fail to meet the requirement R.

We quantify this random variable in term of financial loss per unit of operation time. If we suppose that we have k stakeholders the stake matrix can be presented as a vector as shown in table 7.

We consider the architecture of system S and let C_1, C_2,...C_h be the components. Using the same principle of dependency matrix and under the constraint that we have one requirement R, the stake matrix can be presented as a linear vector as shown in Table 8.

Taking the same impact matrix IM and the threat vector PT, the mean failure cost of the requirement R can be written as:

$$MFCR = \left(\sum_{i=1}^{k} MFC_i \right) \tag{2}$$

Applying the above formula, we can define the MFC for each security requirement and which requirement is more critical than the others.

Table 7. The Stake vector (ST')

ST'		R
Stakeholders	H_1	Stake that stakeholders H_i has in meeting requirement R
	...H_i...	
	Hm	

Table 8. The dependency vector (DP')

DP'	Components		
	C_1	...C_k...	C_{h+1}
R		Prob of failing requirement R. once component C_k has failed	

The Mean Failure Cost \$/hour calculated in Table 9 is realistic and for a failure to long-term it will be very significant. Therefore, if the system is threatened and the system fails to meet the security requirement availability stakeholder of the system stand to lose 538 10-3 \$/ hour as an estimative value. In this case, a variety of security measures can be established regarding to the most critical security requirement in order to reduce the failure cost.

As it's appearing in table 9 the availability is the most important security requirement in this system. This leads us to look for some solutions in order to attenuate the security risk related to this requirement by introducing the needed countermeasures.

When we talk about availability, the most known concerned attack is the denial-of-service (DoS) attack, an attacker attempts to prevent legitimate users from accessing information or services in the platform.

Depth of Interpretation: The Most Critical Threats Diagnostics

After identifying the critical requirements throughout the extension of the MFC formula and its related computing, it is interesting to identify their most critical threats to offer the suitable countermeasures

Table 9. MFCR Vector for Security Requirements

Security Requirements	Mean Failure Cost \$/Hour
Confidentiality	185 10-3
Integrity	186 10-3
Availability	538 10-3
Non-repudiation	105 10-3
Authentication	131 10-3
Privacy	277 10-3

in order to reduce the impact of each threat. This is possible by using the classification of the security requirements versus threats, then it is more important to investigate the most critical threats and to schedule a good risk mitigation plan.

In our practical case, given the classification of security requirements versus threats presented in section of the refined list of security threats, an availability requirement covers one security threat which is the Denial of Service. DoS happens when the attacker tries to lock the server using a high-speed connection, it jams the network card, or blocks the legit traffic (Tugui et al., 2008).

There are two types of DoS attacks:

- **Logic Attacks** (e.g. ping) exploit existing LMS flaws to crash (the remote server or significantly weaken its performance.
- **Flooding Attacks** overloads LMS with a high number of requests to disable legitimate users from accessing e-learning resources (Stapié et al., 2008).

The DoS problem is considered as a generic one and a complex security threat as it is difficult to prevent and very difficult to trace. Some solutions can be suggested by router vendors to add new traffic shaping and filtering. In addition, according to the MFC metric and especially the IM matrix we consider that the architectural components: the application server, the firewall server and the database server need these precious practical instruments of security.

In addition, we need to highlight the necessity of securing the system in the development phase, the availability of the E-learning system is required to be considered as the most critical requirements.

This idea of highlighting in quantitative way the critical security requirements forms a special adding to develop a comprehensive science of cyber security in general and a rigorous quantitative security risk management in particular. Extension of the MFC and especially its depth interpretation can be expanded to be applied to each critical security requirements of the given system. This diagnostic leads to a more secure system and in our case to learn safely.

Security Measures Regarding the Critical Security Requirement

According to the MFC values for security requirements presented in Table 9, we recognize that availability is considered as the most critical security requirement, we stand to lose 0.538 $/hour when the system is threatened.

In the mean time, security measures needed to be highlighted and enhanced (Rjaibi et al., 2013b). They represent the generic and independent forms of security controls. In addition, they represent what the system should do to provide a secure environment. They describe security in a behavioral sense. In this context, there are many types of security measures for each category of security requirements. Table 10, describes the associated security measures and their related security mechanisms for the critical security requirement which is availability (Christian, 2010):

The chapter concludes with an outlook to ongoing research efforts related to security risk analysis regarding fundamental security requirements.

Table 10. Security measures regarding the critical security requirement

The Most Critical Security Requirement	Associated Security Measures	Associated Security Mechanisms
Availability	System recovery	Backup and restoration Configuration management Connection service agreement Disaster recovery Off-site storage Redundancy
	Physical protection	Access cards Alarms Equipment tagging Locks Offsite storage Secured rooms Security personnel
	Attack detection	Administrative privileges Alarms Incident response Intrusion detection systems Logging and auditing Malware detection Reference monitor

SECURITY MEASURES REGARDING FUNDAMENTAL SECURITY REQUIREMENTS

Some of the most fundamental security measures are described and a survey of known relationships among security requirements and measures as well as common mechanisms is presented. This information is useful in the design of decisions to requirements (Christian, 2010).

- **Confidentially:**
  - Access control.
  - Physical protection.
  - Security policy.
- **Integrity:**
  - Access control.
  - Non repudiation.
  - Physical protection.
  - Attack detection.
- **Availability:**
  - System recovery.
  - Physical protection.
  - Attack detection.
- **Accountability:**
  - Non repudiation.
  - Attack detection.
- **Conformance:**

- ○ Access control.
- ○ Physical protection.
- ○ Attack detection.
  1. **Access Control:** is a one of the most important and fundamental security measure; it means the access to a resource that is restricted to those who are authorized. Access control makes use of three subsidiary measures to provide secure access to system resources: identification, authentication, and authorization of actors
  2. **Physical Protection:** is a Security measure; it means the protection from physical threats such as theft, tampering, or destruction of equipment, including defenses against accidents and disasters. Physical protection includes a wide variety of defenses against accidents, disasters, and intruders.
  3. **Security Policy:** is a Security measure; is a set of rules or practices that a system must enforce. It specifies how a system should handle its assets in a secure manner.
  4. **Non Repudiation:** is a Security measure; is the monitoring of events and recording of relevant information to disprove an actor's false denial of involvement in an incident.
  5. **Attack Detection:** is a Security measure; is the active or passive monitoring of behaviors and conditions for evidence of an attack.
  6. **System Recovery:** Security measure; services that minimize the effects of a security failure by restoring the system to a secure state during or after an attack or accident.

SECURITY MEASURES AND ASSOCIATED SECURITY MECHANISMS

Security requirements (quality sub-factors) are broken down into security measures, which define general behaviors that support quality sub-factors. Requirements are then mapped to security measures and their associated security mechanisms of protection and prevention as presented in (Christian, 2010).

- **Access control:**
  - ○ Biometrics
  - ○ Certificates
  - ○ Multilevel security
  - ○ Passwords and keys
  - ○ Reference monitor
  - ○ Registration
  - ○ Time limits
  - ○ User permissions
  - ○ VPN
- **Security policy:**
  - ○ Administrative privileges
  - ○ Malware detection
  - ○ Multilevel security
  - ○ Reference monitor
  - ○ Secure channels
  - ○ Security session

- ○ Single access point
- ○ Time limits
- ○ User permissions
- ○ VPN
- **Non repudiation:**
  - ○ Administrative privileges
  - ○ Logging and auditing
  - ○ Reference monitor
- **Physical protection:**
  - ○ Access cards
  - ○ Alarms
  - ○ Equipments tagging
  - ○ Locks
  - ○ Offsite storage
  - ○ Secured rooms
  - ○ Security personal
- **System recovery:**
  - ○ Backup and restoration
  - ○ Configuration management
  - ○ Connection service agreement
  - ○ Disaster recovery
  - ○ Off-site storage
  - ○ Redundancy
- **Attack detection:**
  - ○ Administrative privileges
  - ○ Alarms
  - ○ Incident response
  - ○ Intrusion detection systems
  - ○ Logging and auditing
  - ○ Malware detection
  - ○ Reference monitor
- **Boundary protection:**
  - ○ DMZ
  - ○ Firewalls
  - ○ Proxies
  - ○ Single access point.

We present a comprehensive survey of known relationships among security requirements and security measures and the possible associated security mechanisms. It helps to achieve better decisions to requirements and a reuse of security requirements with a common definition and understanding of the related security concepts.

CONCLUSION

As distributed systems, e-learning systems epitomize the security concerns that such systems raise, including:

- The privacy of student and teacher personal records,
- The confidentiality (protection from exposure) and integrity (protection from alteration) of student performance records and transcripts,
- The authentication and access rights to course materials, grade records, etc.

Also, these systems offer a relatively uniform architecture, and a common set of system stakeholders (students, teachers, administrators, technician, etc.). As such, these systems are prime candidates for the Mean Failure Cost as a measure of cyber security,

This chapter highlights first the definition of current and standard e-learning attributes namely the stakeholders and the related security requirements and the decomposition of the architectural components. Moreover, the strength is in the refinement of the catalog of security threats and the presentation of its classification versus the security requirement list. Second it presents the computation of the MFC cyber security measure based on a survey done for the first matrix and various collected empirical investigation.

In addition, we have extended the MFC model in order to offer a depth interpretation about critical requirements, critical threats and critical components regarding the cyber system. This extension is beneficial and opens a wide range of possibilities for further economics based analysis. Therefore, the extended MFC model provides the security specialist with valuable quantitative resources for rational decision making.

On the practical side, our future plans are to explore such opportunities for mobile learning and other systems. On the theoretical side, we plan to provide an expansion of the MFC model, to refine it and explore more opportunities for security related decision-making for example for privacy. About privacy, it is the non-disclosure of information for each user. Security guidelines in the development phase are required to protect the privacy of student and teacher personal records, the protection of their personal information when using E-learning services is primordial.

REFERENCES

Abercrombie, R. K., Sheldon, F. T., & Mili, A. (2008, December). Synopsis of evaluating security controls based on key performance indicators and stakeholder mission value. In *Proceedings of High Assurance Systems Engineering Symposium, 2008. HASE 2008. 11th IEEE* (pp. 479-482). IEEE. doi:10.1109/HASE.2008.61

Aissa, A. B. (2013, Winter). *Vers une mesure économétrique de la sécurité des systèmes informatiques* (Unpublished doctoral dissertation). Faculty of Sciences of Tunis.

Aissa, A. B., Abercrombie, R. K., Sheldon, F. T., & Mili, A. (2009). Quantifying security threats and their impacts, In *Proceedings of 5th Annual Cyber Security and Information Intelligence Research Workshop* (CSIIRW-2009). ACM.

Aissa, A. B., Abercrombie, R. K., Sheldon, F. T., & Mili, A. (2010). Quantifying Security Threats and Their Potential Impacts: A Case Study. *Innovations in Systems and Software Engineering, 6*(4), 269–281. doi:10.1007/s11334-010-0123-2

Aissa, A. B., Abercrombie, R. K., Sheldon, F. T., & Mili, A. (2012). Defining and computing a value based cyber-security measure. *Information Systems and e-Business Management, 10*(4), 433-453.

Aissa, A. B. A., Mili, A., Abercrombie, R. K., & Sheldon, F. T. (2010). Modeling stakeholder/value dependency through mean failure cost. In *Proceedings of 6th Annual Cyber Security and Information Intelligence Research Workshop* (CSIIRW-2010). ACM.

Christian. (2010). *Security Requirements Reusability and the SQUARE Methodology* (cmu/sei-2010-tn-027). Carnegie Mellon University, the Software Engineering Institute.

Kumar, S., & Dutta, K. (2011). Investigation on Security in Lms Moodle. *International Journal of Information Technology and Knowledge Management, 4*(1), 233–238.

Luminita, D. C. (2011). Information security in E-learning Platforms. *Procedia Social and Behavioral Sciences, Elsevier, 15*, 2689–2693. doi:10.1016/j.sbspro.2011.04.171

Mili, A., & Sheldon, F. T. (2009). Challenging the Mean Time to Failure: Measuring Dependability as a Mean Failure Cost. In *Proceedings of 42nd Hawaii International Conference on System Sciences (HICSS-42)*. Waikoloa, HI: IEEE.

MohdAlwi, N. H., & Fan, I. S. (2010). e-Learning and information security management. *International Journal of Digit Society, 1*(2), 148-156.

Naaji, A., & Herman, C. (2011). Implementation of an e-learning system: Optimization and security Aspects. In *Proceedings of the 15th WSEAS International Conference on Computers, Part of the 15th WSEAS CSCC Multiconference*. WSEAS.

Nickolova, M., & Nickolov, E. (2007). Threat model for user security in e-learning systems. *International Journal Information Technologies and Knowledge, 1*, 341–347.

Rabai, L. B. A., Rjaibi, N., & Aissa, A. B. (2012). Quantifying Security Threats for E-learning Systems. In *Proceedings of IEEE International Conference on Education & E-Learning Innovations- Infrastructural Development in Education* (ICEELI 2012). IEEE. doi:10.1109/ICEELI.2012.6360592

Rjaibi, N. (2013). *Questionnaire MFC*. Retrieved Jan, 2013, from https://docs.google.com/forms/d/1N PT64kSdJhXaWDeBhXft5WQiPYZNHutW5WL2CpU7Fmw/edit?usp=sharing

Rjaibi, N., & Aissa, A. B. (2013). *The empirical data base for quantifying security threats.* Retrieved Jan, 2013, from https://docs.google.com/file/d/0B0Z2laATxEo7Tlk2TGd4elJjNFk/edit

Rjaibi, N., & Rabai, L. B. A. (2011). Toward A New Model For Assessing Quality Teaching Processes In E-learning. In *Proceedings of 3rd International Conference on Computer Supported Education, CSEDU'2011* (Vol. 2, pp. 468-472). SciTePress.

Rjaibi, N., & Rabai, L. B. A. (2012). Modeling The Assessment of Quality Online Course: An empirical Investigation of Key Factors Affecting Learner's Satisfaction. *IEEE Technology and Engineering Education, 7*(1), 6-13.

Rjaibi, N., Rabai, L. B. A., & Aissa, A. B. (2013). A basic security requirements taxonomy to quantify security threats: an e-learning application. In *Proceedings of The Third International Conference on Digital Information Processing and Communications* (ICDIPC2013), Session: Information security, Islamic Azad University (IAU),Dubai, United Arab Emirates (UAE). SDIWC. Retrieved from http://www.sdiwc.net/conferences/2013/Dubai/

Rjaibi, N., Rabai, L. B. A., Aissa, A. B., & Louadi, M. (2012). Cyber Security Measurement in Depth for E-learning Systems. *International Journal of Advanced Research in Computer Science and Software Engineering, 2*(11), 107-120.

Rjaibi, N., Rabai, L. B. A., Aissa, A. B., & Mili, A. (2013). Mean failure Cost as a Measurable Value and Evidence of Cybersecurity: E-learning Case Study. *International Journal of Secure Software Engineering, 4*(3), 64-81. doi:10.4018/jsse.2013070104

Selvi, R. T., Balasubramanian, N. V., & Manohar, G. T. (2008). Framework and Architectural Style Metrics for Component Based Software Engineering. In *Proceedings of the International MultiConference of Engineers and Computer Scientists* (vol. 1, pp. 19-21). Hong Kong: Academic Press.

Stapié, Z., Orehovacki, T., & Danié, M. (2008). Determination of optimal security settings for LMS Moodle. In *Proceedings of 31st MIPRO International Convention on Information Systems Security.* MIPRO.

Sun, P. C., Ray, J. T., Finger, G., Chen, Y. Y., & Yeh, D. (2008). What drives a successful e-learning? an empirical investigation of the critical factors influencing learner satisfaction. *Computers and Education, Elsevier, 50*(4), 1183–1202. doi:10.1016/j.compedu.2006.11.007

Tugui, O., Funar, S., & Cofari, A. (2008). Trends of Integrating the E-Learning Platform in the Graduate Agronomic Educational System in Romania. *Bulletin of the University of Agricultural Sciences & Veterinary, 65*(2), 621–626.

KEY TERMS AND DEFINITIONS

Dependency Matrix (DP): Is filled by the system architect (i.e., cybersecurity operations and system administrators) according to how each component contributes to meet each requirement.

Impact Matrix (IM): Is filled by analysts according to how each component is affected by each threat.

Mean Failure Cost: Is a recent value based measure of cyber-security, it computes for each stakeholder of the given system his or her loss of operation (\$/H). it is a cascade of linear models to quantify security threat in term of loss that results from system vulnerabilities.

Risk: Is the product of the probability that a particular threat will occur and the expected loss.

Security Risk Analysis Process: Is used to assess security threats and their potential impact in order to anticipate attacks, to weaken their impact and to propose some countermeasures.

Security Risk Management: Is the determination of the worthiest attack and the ignored one, it is the one way to focus on the serious attacks to better manage the budget and find the best way to use it.

Stakes Matrix (ST): Is filled by stakeholders according to the stakes they have in satisfying individual requirements.

Threat Vector: Is emergences probabilities (PV) represents the probability of emergence of the various threats. It is done empirically, by simulating and/or operating the system for some length of time and estimating the number of threats that have emerged during that time.

Threat: Is a category of object, person or other entities that present a danger. Like spam, Trojan horse and fishing.

Chapter 10
Applicability of Lehman Laws on Open Source Evolution

Nisha Ratti
Rayat Institute of Engg. and Information Technology, India

Parminder Kaur
Guru Nanak Dev University, India

ABSTRACT

Software evolution is the essential characteristic of the real world software as the user requirements changes software needs to change otherwise it becomes less useful. In order to be used for longer time period, software needs to evolve. The software evolution can be a result of software maintenance. In this chapter, a study has been conducted on 10 versions of GLE (Graphics Layout Engine) and FGS (Flight Gear Simulator) evolved over the period of eight years. An effort is made to find the applicability of Lehman Laws on different releases of two softwares developed in C++ using Object Oriented metrics. The laws of continuous change, growth and complexity are found applicable according to data collected.

BACKGROUND

Open Source Software

The fundamental idea behind open source is making the source code available to public, so that any user can use it or modify it and redistribute it in the improved form. Open source help the users to interact with and learn from other users. There is no particular way to run an open source project. Some are democratic in nature and they welcome volunteers to contribute in all activities. In some projects, all the users work for one company, do all the development work and share the bugs and thereby think of the solution together. In some other projects, developers do not make any community at all, just share a web page. On that particular web page, they just share the development, let the other people download. And many a times, they send the response by emails. There are some wrong conceptions regarding Open Source Software Development (OSSD). Some people say that open source software development is a new software development paradigm. In fact, this paradigm is working since the age of ARPAnet and

DOI: 10.4018/978-1-4666-8510-9.ch010

UNIX. Another misconception regarding OSSD is that it is not done by professionals. But truth is that professional programmers are hired and paid huge remuneration to do the software development using this paradigm. Some people still believe that OSSD produce the low quality software. In fact, developers do the quality assurance during the development itself.

Open Source Software Development Process

In open source software development process, a number of groups of developers are formed. Every group has their own leaders. OSSD follow very less formalized method for development. Only a little number of projects has any explicit process for development. Overhead related to the introduction and enforcement of the formal method are the main reasons for not having any particular process model. Email is the prime means of communication among the developers. So the log of messages is maintained which in turn help in design decisions (Boldyreff, 2003).

W. Scaachi (Scaacchi, 2001) has given five type of development processes for open source software development:

1. Requirements analysis and specification
2. Coordinated version control, system build, and staged incremental release
3. Maintenance as evolutionary redevelopment, refinement, and redistribution
4. Project management
5. Software technology transfer.

Open Source Software Development Models

There are several basic differences between Open Source Software Development (OSSD) and traditional methods. The system development life cycle (SDLC) of traditional methods have generic phases into which all project activities can be organized such as planning, analysis, design, implementation and support (Satzinger et al, 2004). Also, open source life cycle for OSSD paradigm demonstrates several common attributes like parallel development and peer review, prompt feedback to user and developer contributions, highly talented developers, parallel debugging, user involvement, and rapid release times.

Vixie (1999) holds that an open source project can include all the elements of a traditional SDLC. Classic OSS projects such as BSD, BIND and SendMail are evidence that open source projects utilize standard software engineering processes of analysis, design, implementation and support. Mockus et al (2000) describe a life cycle that combines a decision-making framework with task-related project phases. The model comprises six phases like roles and responsibilities, identifying work to be done, assigning and performing development work, pre-release testing, inspections, and managing releases. Jorgensen (2001) provides a more detailed description of specific product related activities that support the OSSD process. The model (figure. 1) explains the life cycle for changes that occurred within the FreeBSD project (Kaur, 2011)

Jorgensen's model is widely accepted (Feller et al, 2001; FLOSS Project Report, 2002) as a framework for the OSSD process, on both macro (project) and micro (component or code segment) levels. However, flaws remain. When applied to an OSS project, the model does not adequately explain where or how the processes of planning, analysis and design take place (Kaur, 2011).

Figure 1. Jorgensen life-cycle, 2001

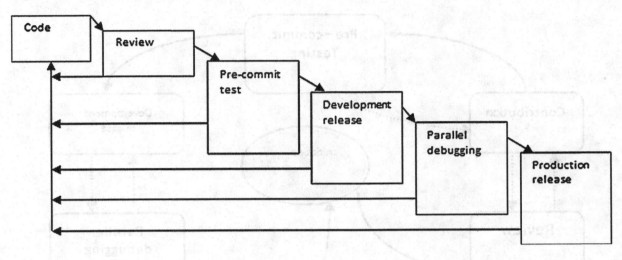

Schweik and Semenov (2003) propose an OSSD project life cycle comprising three phases: *project initiation, going 'open', and project growth, stability or decline.* Each phase is characterized by a distinct set of activities.Wynn (2004) proposes a similar open source life cycle but introduces a *maturity phase* in which a project reaches critical mass in terms of the numbers of users and developers it can support due to administrative constraints and the size of the project itself. Roets, Minnaar, *et al.* (2007) expands Jorgensen life-cycle model and incorporates aspects of previous models, particularly that of Schweik and Semenov (2003). In addition, this model attempts to encapsulate the phases of the traditional SDLC (figure 2). This model facilitates OSS development in terms of improved programming skills, availability of expertise and model code as well as software cost reduction (Kaur, 2011).

Comparison of Traditional Life-Cycle with OSSD Life-Cycle

Figure 3 compares different phases of traditional software development life-cycle with OSSD life-cycle mentioned in Figure 2.

Initiation phase of OSSD life –cycle combines three phases i.e. planning phase, analysis phase and design phase of traditional software development life-cycle. As it is suggested that it may be more important to get design right prior to actual programming so that all developers are working towards a clearly defined common purpose. Implementation phase combines the different aspects like review, contribution, pre-commit test and release of production. As multiple users as well as skilled personnel are involved in OSSD, parallel debugging and different versions of one piece of code can be grouped together with support phase of traditional software development life-cycle.

SOFTWARE EVOLUTION

Software evolution reflects *a process of progressive change in the attributes of the evolving entity or that of one or more of its constituent elements.* Specifically, software evolution is related to how software

Figure 2. Roets, Minnaar, et al. life-cycle model of OSSD projects, 2007

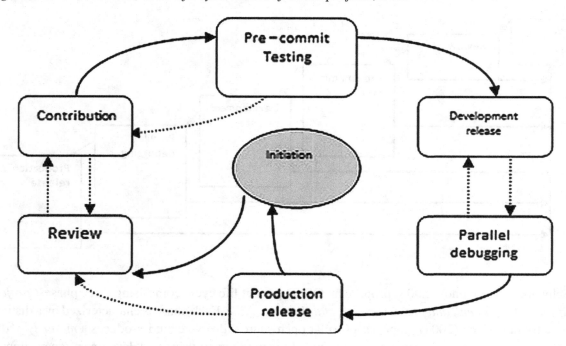

Figure 3. Comparison of Traditional Life-Cycle with OSSD Life-Cycle

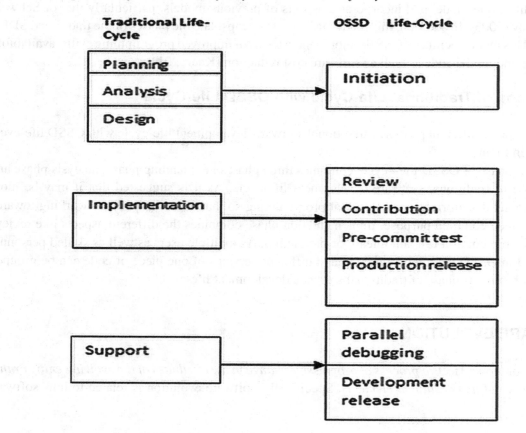

systems evolve over time. Such systems are evolved after repeated modifications and results in increasing complexity Software is not prone to wear and tear but still it may become useless if not revised in response to ever changing user requirements. Software needs to evolve in order to be used for longer period. Lehman has done extensive research on evolution of large and long lived software. Lehman's laws of software evolution, based on the empirical study, indicate that continuous change and growth is required for keeping the software long-lived. The laws also suggest that over the period, due to changes and growth, software system becomes complex and it becomes more and more difficult to add new functionalities to it. (Kaur, 2014)

Software Evolution vs. Maintenance

Software maintenance is defined in IEEE standard 1219 (Erdil, 2003) as the modification of the software product after the delivery to correct the faults, to improve the performance or other attributes, or to adapt the product to different modified environment. Software maintenance is different from the maintenance of physical goods because it normally leads to a changed or improved software system. Physical goods maintenance seeks to restore the item or entity as close as possible to factory condition. Software doesn't wear out but it degrades through suboptimal quick fixes and through an increasing number of unfulfilled requirements. Nontrivial software isn't free from defects: some maintenance is always required as long as the software is in use. Software evolution is also different from the evolution of physical goods. It's mainly concerned with changes in a software system over versions or releases of the same system, while physical goods tend to evolve over generations of products, that is, there's little or no evolution of a specific physical product (Mens, 2010).

Swanson (Leintz, 1980) has categorized software maintenance into three categories: corrective, adaptive, and perfective.

- **Corrective Maintenance:** Refers to the changes that fix bugs in the code base.
- **Adaptive Maintenance:** Is changes that allow a system to run within a new technical infrastructure.
- **Perfective Maintenance:** Are any other enhancements intended to make the system better, such as adding new features, boosting performance, or improving system documentation.

According to this categorization, corrective and adaptive maintenance tasks do not alter the outward semantics of the system, while perfective maintenance includes a wide variety of possible changes to the system. Some later taxonomy adds a fourth category: Preventive maintenance is changes made to ease future maintenance and evolution of the system, such as reorganizing internal dependencies to improve cohesion and coupling. While the terms evolution and maintenance are often used interchangeably with respect to software, there are important semantic differences between them. Firstly, Evolution subsumes the idea of essential change that maintenance simply does not connote. Maintenance suggests preservation and fixing, whereas evolution suggests new designs evolving from old ones. Second, maintenance is usually considered to be a set of planned activities; one performs maintenance on a system. Evolution, on the other hand, concerns whatever happens to a system over time; in addition to the planned activities, unplanned phenomena often manifest themselves also.

In response to the change in the environment or user requirement the software continues to evolve after the release of first version. The software evolution is the necessity of real world software. In order to be used for longer time period, there is a need to evolve with time otherwise it will become less useful. Software evolution was first addressed by MM Lehman in 1974 (Lehman, 1974), while studying the software process within IBM. Lehman demonstrated that the software continues to evolve over time. Due to changes in the growth of software, it becomes complex. It has been more than three decades, since the Lehman laws were proposed but there are very few empirical studies to support their applicability.

The work proposed here is based on the analysis of two open source case studies i.e. GLE and FGS both developed in object oriented language, C++. Different releases have been examined to find the applicability of Lehman laws of evolution on object oriented software. It is based on the computation of object oriented metrics proposed by (Chidamber, 1994).

Lehman Laws

Belady and Lehman (Belady, 1976) studied 20 releases of the OS/360 operating system software, and observed the dynamic behavior of this system. Belady et al. (Lehman, 1978), (Belady, 1976) described three fundamental laws of software evolution:

1. **Law of Continuing Change:** *A system that is under use undergoes continuous changes until it is judged more cost effective to freeze and recreate it.* Software development starts with the minimum set of assumptions or requirements. But as the development expands, the requirement also increases, thereby increasing the raise of opportunities. Another reason of expecting the change is the changes occurring in the real world which in turn affect the application areas and the domain of the system. Following are the practical problems while implementing the change in the required domain:

   a. Broad, well formatted documentation should be maintained as that all the changes can be tracked.

   b. Regular subsequent review is required. In order to do that all the changes made, implicit, explicit assumptions made and adopted should be recorded.

   c. As the changes are made, it is required that complexity should be controlled if not reduced.

   d. The requirement analysis should be made regularly so as to investigate the clash with old existing requirements.

   e. As the number of changes increases, complexity and fault rate increases more than linearly. Consequently, further releases will focus on fixing these faults. So after doing this analysis, user can put a limit on the change rate.

   f. Analyzing the number of projects, it has been observed that disproportionate number of changes in a release may have opposite effect on the quality, growth and freedom of action for successive releases.

   g. It is advisable that all the releases of the system should not be focusing on the all the issues of the system. Rather, choice should be made in alternate manner among the releases which focus on fault fixing and which focus on the implementation of the new development made.

   h. Change validation should be done necessarily.

2. **Law of Increasing Entropy/Complexity:** *The entropy of a system (the complexity) increases with time, unless specific work is done to maintain or reduce it.* The simple reason behind the growing complexity is continuous changes made with the evolution process. As the number of elements

increases, so their connections and interactions too. As the growth in the development and design increases, so as the user support and expenses incurred, which in turn result in the decline of product quality. Following interpretations are to be considered regarding complexity:

a. System complexity has many aspects. They include but are not limited to:
    i.   Application and functional complexity – including that of the operational domain
    ii. Specification and requirements complexity
    iii. Architectural complexity
    iv. Design and implementation complexity
    v.   Structural complexity at many levels (subsystems, modules, objects, calling, sequences, object usage, code, documentation, etc.)

b. The benefits of System complexity control have very long term impact. Its impact may decide about the survival or the replacement, whatever required.

c. Growth of complexity should be measured along with the evolution and maintenance of the system. It will decide when anti regressive activity as above should be initiated to reverse adverse trends.

d. If the level is reduced or even abandoned so as to free resources for *progressive* activity such as system enhancement and extension, system complexity and future effort/cost are likely to increase, productivity, evolution rates, stakeholder dissatisfaction and system quality to decline.

e. The fraction of total activity that should, on average be devoted to anti-regressive work is likely to vary as a function of factors such as organizational, project, process, and application area and so on.

f. Approaches should be made for the optimization of anti-regressive activities.

3. **Law of Statistically Smooth Growth/Self-Regulation**: *Global E-type system evolution processes are self-regulating.* Growth trend measures of global system attributes may appear to be stochastic locally in time and space, but statistically they are cyclically self-regulating with well-defined long-range trends. The conclusion that feedback is a major source of the behavior described by the third law. Some of the feedback based mechanisms are progress monitoring and control, checks, balances and control on resource usage. These mechanisms are used by third law so that software should be self-regulating. In some complex systems, it is hard to identify the sources of the feedback forces. Important process and product behavioral characteristics are probably determined to a significant degree by feedback mechanisms not themselves consciously controlled by management or otherwise. To identify the feedback mechanisms and controls that play a role in self-stabilization and to exploit them in future planning, management and process improvement the following steps should be helpful:

a. Applying measurement and modelling techniques such as determine typical patterns, trends, rates and rates of change of a number of projects within the organization.

b. There is a need to set up the limits for process rates such as growth, faults, changes over the entire system, units changed, units added, units removed and so on. These baselines have to be counted per release or per unit time. Results generated over the time and over the releases are required to be compared so as to draw the conclusions. Incremental values, that of people working with the system in various capacities, person days in categories such as specification, design, implementation, testing, integration, customer support and costs related to these activities. Another set of measures related to quality factors is to be considered.

c. Data is collected from the new releases added and with the passage of time. It can be used to improve the models and revalidate the models, thereafter doing the testing part.

d. As per the FEAST/1 project, while planning for a new release, the first step is to determine which of the three possible scenarios exits. Let m be the mean of the incremental growth m_i of the system in going from release i to release $i+1$ and s the standard deviation of the incremental growth both over a series of some five or so releases or time intervals. The scenarios may, for example, be differentiated by an indicator $m+2s$ that identifies a release plan as *safe*, *risky* or *unsafe* according to the conditions listed below. The rules are here expressed in release based units. For observations based on incremental growth per standard real time unit, analogous safe limits are likely to exist. They are likely to be a function of the interval between observations.

    i. Those studies suggest that a *safe* level for planned release content m_i is that it be less than or equal to m. If the condition is fulfilled growth at the desired rate may proceed safely.

    ii. The desired release content is greater than m but less than $m+2s$. The release is *risky*. It could succeed in terms of achieved functional scope but serious delivery delays, quality or other problems could arise. If pursued, it would be wise to plan for a follow-on clean-up release. Even if not planned, a zero growth release may to be required. Note that $m+2s$ has long been identified as an alarm limit, for example, in statistical process monitoring/control [Boxg].

    iii. The desired release content is close to or greater than $m+2s$. A release with incremental growth of this magnitude is *unsafe*. It is likely to cause major problems and instability over one or more subsequent releases. At best, it is likely to require to be followed by a major clean up release which concentrates on fault fixing, documentation updating and *anti-regressive* work such as restructuring, the elimination of *dead code* and other anti-regressive work.

e. Number of items on the "to be done" list for a release in planning would, if implemented in one release, lead to incremental growth in excess of the levels indicated above. Such a strategy would be appropriate whenever the size and/or complexity of the required addition is large. In that event, several alternatives may be considered. They include spreading the work over two or more releases, the *delivery* to users of the new functionality over two or more releases with mechanisms in place to return to older version if necessary, support group reinforcement, preceding the release with one or more clean up releases or preparing for a fast follow on release to rectify problems that are likely to appear. In either of the last two instances provision must be made for additional user support.

In a later paper, (Lehman, 1978) adds two additional laws:

4. **Conservation of Organizational Stability:** *Unless feedback mechanisms are appropriately adjusted, average effective global activity rate in an evolving E-type system tends to remain constant over product lifetime.* The average effective global activity rate in an evolving system is invariant over the product lifetime. According to Lehman, the observations on which this law is based date back to the late seventies. Further data gathered in FEAST/1 neither supports nor negates it. Insight into the underlying process mechanisms and related phenomena supported the interpreta-

tion encapsulated in the law. Subsequent observations suggested, for example, that the average activity rate measured by the *change rate*, is *stationary* but with changes of the mean and variance at one or more points during the observed life time of the released-based systems. The influence of feedback on the process has been apparent since the early 70s but the full extent was not fully appreciated until recently. If further observations yield similar results and when more understanding is achieved, refinement of the law may be indicated. Aspects of the law relating to the role of feedback stabilization and its implications are discussed below. Management implications are not considered further here except in so far that they are reflected in the rules (Lehman, 1985).

5. **Conservation of Familiarity:** *The average incremental growth remains invariant as the system evolves.* In general, the incremental growth and long term growth rate of E-type systems tend to decline. The reason behind the declining growth and growth rate may be due to the reduction in the demand for correction and change as the system ages. Another reason could be system maintenance over a series of releases. Resources are split among fixing, enhancement and extension. As the system ages, fixes too increase. If investment in system maintenance remains constant, a drop in resources available for system growth and, hence, a declining growth rate is implied as system complexity increases. Equally the budget allocation may be declining because it has, for example, been decided that it is no longer in the organization's interest to expand the system or because it is believed that increasing maintenance productivity, as personnel experience and system familiarity increases, permits the reduction of maintenance funding. A related aspect of that investigation is the relationship between incremental growth which tends to reflect the addition of new functionality, and modification of existing software elements to reflect changes in the application, the domain or other parts of the system.

   a. The sixth law was introduced in the footnote (Belady, 1976).

6. **Continuing Growth:** *The functional capability of E-type systems must be continually increased to maintain user satisfaction over the system lifetime. Functional content of a program must be continually increased to maintain user satisfaction over its lifetime.*

   a. This law must be distinguished from the first law which asserts 'Continuing Change'. The need for change reflects a need to *adapt* the system as the outside world, the domain being covered and the application and/or activity being supported or pursued change. Such exogenous changes are likely to invalidate assumptions made during system definition, development, validation, installation and application or render them unsatisfactory. The software reflecting such assumptions must then be adapted to restore their validity.

The sixth law reflects the fact that all software, being finite, limits the functionality and other characteristics of the system to a finite selection from a potentially unbounded set. The domain of operation is also potentially unbounded, but the system can only be designed and validated, explicitly or implicitly, for satisfactory operation in some finite part of it. Sooner or later, excluded features, facilities and domain areas become bottlenecks or irritants in use. They need to be included to fill the gap. The system needs to be evolved to satisfactorily support new situations and circumstances that is new requirements.

Though they have different causes and represent, in many ways, different circumstances, the steps to be taken to take cognizance of the sixth law do not, in principle, differ radically from those listed for the first. There are, however, differences due to the fact that the former is, mainly, concerned with functional and behavioral change whereas the latter leads, in general, directly to additions to the existing system and to its growth. In practice, it may be difficult or inappropriate to associate a given change with either law. Nevertheless, since the two are due to different phenomena they also are likely to lead different, though overlapping, and recommendations. This report, however, does not distinguish between the rules implied by one, the other or both. In general, the cleaner the architecture and structure of the system to be evolved the more likely is it that addition may be cleanly added with firewalls to control the exchange of information between old and new parts of the system. There must, however, be some penetration from the additions to the existing system. This will, in particular, be so when one considers the continued evolution of systems that were not, in the first instance, designed or structured for dynamic growth by the addition of new *components*. Sadly, the same remarks, limitations and consequent precautions, apply when one is dealing with systems that are component based or that make widespread use of COTS [13, 29]. They too will evolve. A sound architectural and structural base and application of the rules in this report will reduce the effort that will inevitably be required when such systems are extended. The comments of this paragraph may be taken as an additional rule.

Seventh and eighth law was published in (Belady, 1976)

7. **Declining Quality:** *The quality of E-type systems will appear to be declining unless they are rigorously adapted, as required, to take into account changes in the operational environment. E-type programs will be perceived as of declining quality unless rigorously maintained and adapted to a changing operational environment.* This law follows directly from the first and sixth laws. Functionality as well as behavioral detail must be changed and extended. To achieve this, new blocks of code are attached, new interactions and interfaces are created on top of one another. If such changes are not made, embedded assumptions become falsified, mismatch with the operational domains increases. Additions will tend to be increasingly remote from the established architecture, function and structure. All in all the complexity of the system in terms of the interactions between its parts, and the potential for such interaction, all increase. Performance is likely to decline and the faults potential will increase as embedded assumptions are inadvertently violated and the potential for undesired interactions created. From the point of view of performance, behavior and evolution, adaptation and growth effort increase. Growing complexity, mismatch with operational domains, declining performance, increasing numbers of faults, increasing difficulty of adaptation and growth, all lead to a decline in stakeholder satisfaction. Each represents a factor in declining system quality. In summary we observe that the underlying cause of the seventh law, the decline of software quality with age, appears to relate, primarily, to a growth in complexity associated with ageing. It follows that in addition to undertaking activity from time to time to reduce complexity, practices in architecture, design and implementation that reduce complexity or limit its growth should be pursued, i.e.:

   a. Design changes and additions to the system in accordance with established principles such as information hiding, structured programming, elimination of pointers and GOTOs, and so on, to limit unwanted interactions between code sections and control those that are essential.

   b. Devote some portion of evolution resources to complexity reduction of all sorts, restructuring, and the removal of "dead" system elements and so on. Though primarily *anti-regressive*, without immediate revenue benefit, this will help ensure future changeability,

   c. Train personnel to seek to capture and record assumptions, whether explicit or implicit, at all stages of the process in standard form and in a structure that will facilitate their being reviewed.

   d. Verify the validity of assumptions with users and/or other stakeholders.

e. Assess the impact if the assumptions were to be invalid, for example what changes would need to be made to correct for the invalid assumption?

f. Review relevant portions of the assumption set at all stages of the evolution process to avoid design or implementation action that invalidates even one of them. Methods and tools to capture, store, retrieve and review them and their realization must be developed.

g. Monitor appropriate system attributes to predict the need for cleanup, restructuring or replacement of parts or the whole.

8. **Feedback System:** *E-type evolution processes are multi-level, multi- loop, multi-agent feedback systems.* E-type Programming Processes constitute Multi-loop, Multi-level Feedback systems and must be treated as such to be successfully modified or improved. This is the key law and underlies the behavior encapsulated by the other seven. It is hoped to develop a formal theory that covers and describes the observed phenomenology and the relationships between the laws [34].

The behavior of feedback systems is not and cannot, in general, be described *directly* in terms of the aggregate behavior of its forward path activities and mechanisms. Feedback constrains the ways that process constituents interact with one another and will modify their individual, local, and collective, global, behavior. According to the eighth law the software process is such a system. This observation must, therefore, be expected to apply. Thus, the contribution of any activity to the global process6 may be quite different from that suggested by its open loop characteristics. If the feedback nature of the software process is not taken into account when predicting its behavior, unexpected, even counter-intuitive, results must be expected both locally and globally. For sound software process planning, management and improvement the feedback nature of the process must be mastered.

The positive and negative feedback loops and control mechanisms of the global E-type process involve activities in the many domains, organizational, marketing, business, usage and so on, within which the process is embedded and evolution is pursued. It develops a dynamics that drives and constrains it. Many of the characteristics of this dynamics are rooted in and will be inherited from its history in wider, global, domains. As a result there are significant limitations that management can exert on control of the process. The basic message of the eighth law is, in fact, that in the long term managers are not absolutely free to adopt any action considered appropriate from some specific business or other point of view. Reasonable decision can, generally, be locally implemented. The long-term, global, consequences that follow, may not be what was intended or anticipated.

Lehman also elaborates on the meaning of these laws in the context of real systems and presents empirical data on a number of releases of a general-purpose batch operating system. He showed how the empirical data supports the five laws of software evolution and describes how examining the software releases can be used to predict and plan the next release. He also demonstrates how initial estimates were likely to be optimistic until corrected using the historical data available describes software evolution as "the dynamic behavior of programming systems as they are maintained and enhanced over their life time". Summary of Lehman Laws of Evolution with the year of introduction is given in Table 1.

OPEN SOURCE SOFTWARE EVOLUTION AND LEHMAN LAWS

Lehman's well known eight laws of software evolution address the fundamental concepts underlying the dynamics of software evolution. Free software complies exceptionally well with Lehman's laws,

Table 1. Summary of Lehman Laws for software evolution

No.	Name	Year	Description of Law
I	Continuing Change	1974	E-Type systems must continually be changed in order to be used for longer time period else it will become progressively less useful
II	Increasing Complexity	1974	As E-Type system evolves its complexity increases unless sufficient efforts are applied to maintain or reduce the complexity.
III	Self- Regulation	1974	E-type system evolution process is self-regulating with distribution of product and process measures close to normal.
IV	Conservation of Organizational Stability	1980	The average effective global activity rate in an evolving E-type system is invariant over product lifetime.
V	Conservation of Familiarity	1980	As an E-type system evolves all associated with it, the average incremental growth remains invariant as the system evolves.
VI	Continuing Growth	1991	As an E-Type system evolves its functionality and size is increased in order to fulfill the customer needs.
VII	Declining Quality	1996	The quality of E-type systems will appear to be declining unless they are rigorously maintained and adapted to operational environment changes.
VIII	Feedback System	1996	E-type evolution processes constitute multi-level, multi- loop, multi- agent feedback systems and must be treated as such to achieve significant improvement over any reasonable base.

(Lehman, 1997)

although both the laws and the free software development process emerged independently: free software is continuously changed (law I), complexity increases noticeably (law II), and the self-regulation of the evolution process is obvious (law III). Many researchers have performed empirical studies to validate the Lehman laws on open source softwares by analyzing their different releases over their evolution period. Johari *et. al.* (Johari, 2011) in their research paper has analyzed different versions of two open source software i.e. Jhotdraw and Rhino released through evolution process, by applying package level, class level and method level metrics, the main objective of the study was to examine the applicability of Lehman laws. Some laws have a direct relevance to computed metrics whereas for some of laws they did not find the direct relevance to software metrics used. They observed that the reflection of some laws namely law 1, law 2,and law 6 was easily determined but the relatedness of law 3, law 4 and law 5 to open source software system are hard to determine and will require more empirical studies with the relevant data. Chris J Arges evaluate the Lehman laws for an open source software projects; Linux Kernel. Godfrey *et.al.* (Godfrey, 2000) studied the Linux kernel evolution. Chris has given the view that Linux kernel showed a super-linear growth rate in lines of code and that the fourth Lehman's law did not apply. The fourth Lehman law states that development is constant and independent of the resources devoted to it. Then he has given the view that if open source E-type software violates Lehman's fourth law and compares its results with Godfrey and Tu's study. The Linux kernel showed super-linear growth as well as some other open source projects. However, many open source projects exhibited just linear growth and supported Lehman's fourth law.

Metrics Used

This contains the brief description of metrics used to compute data required for study. A number of object oriented metrics (CBO, WMC, RFC, DIT, NOC, and LCOM) are proposed by Chidamber et al. (Chidamber, 1994).

1. **WMC:** Weighted Methods per Class. The WMC metrics is the sum of the complexities of its methods.

    Consider a class Ci with methods M_1 --------M_n that are defined in the class, let C_1----- C_n be complexity of methods then

$$WMC = \sum_{i=1}^{n} Ci$$

2. **DIT:** Depth of Inheritance Tree. DIT is used for a class involving multiple inheritances. The DIT will be maximum length from the node to the root of the tree.
3. **NOC:** Number of Children. Number of immediate subclasses subordinated to a class in class hierarchy.
4. **CBO:** Coupling Between Objects. CBO classes is the count of number of classes coupled .Two classes are coupled when the methods declared in one class are used by methods of other class.
5. **RFC:** Response for Class. RFC metrics measured the number of methods being invoked in response to the message received by an object of that class.
6. **LCOM:** Lack of Cohesion of Methods. Number of methods in a class that are disjoint with respect to the member of class being accessed by them.
7. **LOC:** Lines of Code. LOC includes lines of source code except commented and blank lines.
8. **NOM:** Number of Methods. NOM for class defines the number of methods defined in the class.
9. **NOV:** Number of variables. NOV is the number of variables used in source code.
10. **NOF:** Number of Functions. NOF is the count of the number of functions in the source code.

INTRODUCTION TO CASE STUDIES

This section introduces two open source software's under consideration namely GLE and FGS, developed in C++. The revisions details and source code is available online (SourceForge), (Flight Gear Simulator), (Fight Gear Simulator, 1996) (Graphics Layout Engine, 2012).

Case Study 1: Graphics Layout Engine (GLE)

GLE is a graphics scripting language designed for creating publication quality graphs, plots, diagrams, figures and slides. GLE relies on LaTeX for text output. Its output formats include EPS, PS, PDF, JPEG, and PNG. It is developed in C++ language. The source code is available on SourceForge (SourceForge).

Since registration on source forge on 11-9-2000, 23 releases are available till date. Out of the 23 releases, we have considered latest 10 releases from 25-12-2007 to 14-03-12. The details of releases of Graphics Layout Engine are given in Table 2.

Case Study 2: Flight Gear Simulator (FGS)

The goal of the Flight Gear project is to create a sophisticated and open flight simulator framework for use in research or academic environments, pilot training, as an industry engineering tool, for DIY-ers to pursue their favorite interesting flight simulation idea, and last but certainly not least as a fun, realistic, and challenging desktop flight simulator. It is developed in C++ language and is and open source. Source code of 20 releases is available online (Flight Gear Simulator). 10 latest releases of the software are observed. Table 3 gives the revision details of the Flight Gear simulator.

METHODOLOGY USED FOR DATA COLLECTION

Since software used, are open source, the source code required for study is available online. Various tools are used accordingly to compute different metrics .the revision details of Graphics Layout Engine are available on (Graphics Layout Engine, 2012) and Fight Gear Simulator are available on (Fight Gear Simulator, 1996).

OBSERVATIONS AND ANALYSIS OF SOFTWARE EVOLUTION

In this section the evolution of two software is observed to find the applicability of Lehman laws on the bases of computed data.

Table 2. Revision Details of GLE

Version (GLE)	Release Date	LOC	No. of Functions	No. of Variables	No. of Classes
4.1.0	25/12/2007	88115	4725	12078	366
4.1.1	5/1/2008	88155	4722	12076	366
4.1.0	9/2/2009	88770	4724	12076	366
4.2.0	20/4/2009	95293	5477	13409	414
4.2.1	5/9/2009	94524	9472	24570	495
4.2.2	6/10/2010	94749	5510	13493	417
4.2.3	23/10/2010	96943	5739	13938	435
4.2.4	1/1/2012	100812	6074	14630	482
4.2.4b	14/1/2012	100851	6076	14635	482
4.2.4c	14/3/2012	100741	6079	14635	492

Table 3. Revision Details of FGS

Version (FGS)	Release Date	LOC	No. of Functions	No. of Variables	No. of Classes
0.9.9	18/11/2005	70112	3291	9344	182
1.0.0	15/12/2007	80326	3705	10632	216
1.9.0	20/12/2008	85413	3395	10974	207
1.9.1	26/1/2009	85413	3418	10974	207
2.0.0	17/2/2010	88000	3420	11375	213
2.4.0	16/8/2011	91883	3681	11896	217
2.6.0	17/2/2012	99060	3879	12896	242
2.8.0	16/8/2012	99043	4137	14102	258
2.10.0	18/2/2013	103771	5436	21402	494
2.12.0	16/9/2013	108772	5919	23734	550

1. **Law 1: Continuing Change:** Law of continuing change states that in order to use the software for longer period, it should change continuously according to the needs of user and environment. The change can be due to some bug fixing activity or the change can be due to addition of new function or class to the software. In case of GLE and FGS, the size and functionalities are changed in each successive release of the software. In FGS the number of functions and classes are increased in each successive release except in release 1.9.1 as it was a bug fix release. In GLE, the number of functions and number of classes are changed in each successive release .The law of continuing change is reflected by both the software.

2. **Law 6: Continuing Growth:** Law of continuous growth states that the software should grows continuously in order to satisfy the requirements of user. The growth of the software can be measured in terms of its size and functionality. LOC of each version is computed to analyze the growth in terms of size and computed number of classes and number of functions to observe the growth in terms of functionality.

   a. **Size Metrics:** The LOC growth for GLE and FGS is showed in Figure 4&5. The growth of lines of code is the measure of lines in source code. LOC curve for FGS showed the increase in LOC in each release except in 2.8.0 (Figure 5), few lines were removed may be in response to the bug fix activity. LOC graph GLE showed the increase in lines of code. In release 4.2.0 (Figure 4), the increase was sharp, which further decreases in next version. But in later versions, it again shows the increase in LOC. So the law of continuing growth is reflected in terms of size metrics

   b. **Function Metrics:** The growth of the software in terms of functionality can be measured in terms of number of classes and number of functions. Functionality of software can be increased by addition of class or functions Figures 6 and 7 shows the number of classes for different releases of GLE and FGS and Figures 8 and 9 represent the number functions in different releases of GLE and FGS. In case of the FGS, the number of classes and functions are increased in each successive release of a software. In case of GLE, the number of classes and functions are increased in linear fashion from version 4.1.0 to 4.1.2. In version 4.2.0, the number of functions and classes are increased sharply but in next version these are decreased. The later versions showed the increase in the number of classes and number of functions.

3. **Law 2: Increasing Complexity:** Law of increasing complexity states that as the software grows, its complexity increases unless certain measures are taken to keep the complexity under check. Complexity may arise due to changes or addition of functions. The object oriented metrics is used for object oriented software to determine the complexity, CBO, RFC, WMC, DIT, LOCH metrics are used to determine the complexity of GLE and FGS, represented in Table 4&5 .WMC for GLE and FGS is shown by Figures 10 and 11. The FGS shows the increase in WMC in first 8 versions but in later two versions it shows the decrease, this can be due to some bug fixing activity .In case of GLE the WMC showed the increasing trend in first in 4 versions but in 5th version it increased sharply, which were decreased in next successive version. In later versions, the WMC are increased, again in version 4.2.4b, the WMC are decreased, due to bug fix activity.

The RFC and CBO are represented by Figures 12 and 14. For FGS, the RFC and CBO curve has shown the average increasing trend of complexity. The CBO and RFC for GLE is shown by Figures 13 and 15, has shown the increase earlier releases before 4.2.1 after that it shows the downfall in release 4.2.2., but in later releases the RFC and CBO count in seen to be increased. DIT and NOC for FGS (Figures 16 and 18) and GLE (Figures 17 and 19) are increased in successive releases of FGS and GLE, which showed the increase in complexity. LOCH (Figures 22 and 23) for the successive releases of FGS and GLE are increased in the mid bit showed the downfall in later releases which indicates the increase in complexity. Mc cabe complexity (Figures 22 and 23) for both the software is increased in each successive release. From above interpretations the law of increasing complexity is reflected by FGS and GLE.

Figure 4. Growth curve of LOC for GLE

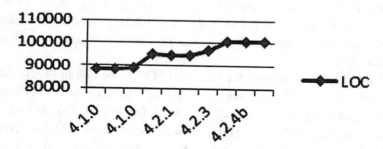

Figure 5. Growth curve of LOC for FGS

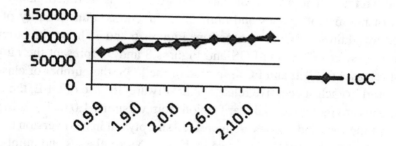

Figure 6. Growth curve of number of classes for GLE

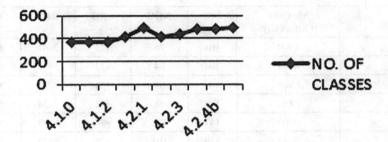

Figure 7. Growth curve of number of classes for FGS

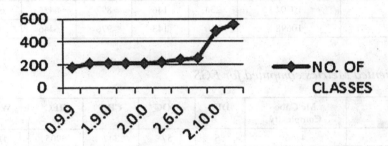

Figure 8. Growth curve of number of functions for GLE

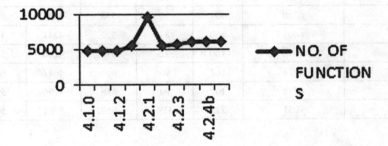

Figure 9. Growth curve of number of functions for FGS

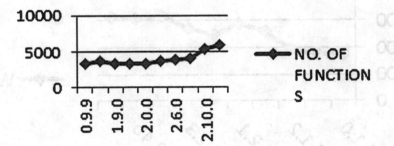

Table 4. Object Oriented Metrics computed for GLE

Version (GLE)	Mc Cabe Complexity	DIT	NOC	CBO	RFC	WM	LOCH
4.1.0	8900	104	76	423	3461	3547	18128
4.1.1	8898	104	64	433	3487	3493	17997
4.1.0	8908	104	80	424	3716	3902	18197
4.2.0	10061	148	98	482	5138	5145	28598
4.2.1	9905	147	102	990	6189	5835	32648
4.2.2	9942	149	102	575	4777	4943	27524
4.2.3	10187	178	114	724	5419	5494	24518
4.2.4	10692	224	146	886	6385	6369	30921
4.2.4b	10702	234	146	897	6431	6120	30656
4.2.4c	10698	210	143	976	6446	6326	29894

Table 5. Object Oriented Metrics computed for FGS

Version (FGS)	Mc Cabe Complexity	DIT	NOC	CBO	RFC	WMC	LOCH
0.9.9	4766	86	57	347	3905	4139	44121
1.0.0	5532	113	75	433	4295	5162	45751
1.9.0	6000	120	82	545	4298	5245	39941
1.9.1	6000	120	73	558	4233	5258	40489
2.0.0	6240	131	90	558	4243	5746	41868
2.4.0	6401	150	87	522	4241	5873	43023
2.6.0	6692	160	92	572	4246	5982	41652
2.8.0	6774	162	90	569	4647	6004	44878
2.10.0	6718	162	90	688	4796	5948	41843
2.12.0	7051	213	119	689	5381	5782	40269

Figure 10. Growth curve for the average weighted methods for different releases of GLE

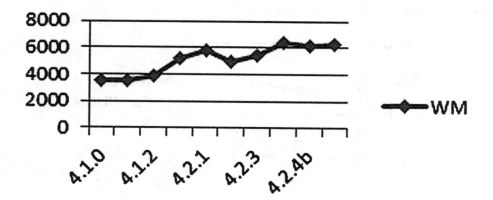

Figure 11. Growth curve for the average weighted methods for different releases of FGS

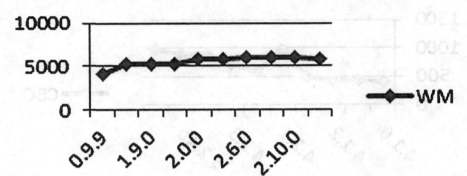

4. **Law 7: Declining Quality:** Law of declining quality, states that the software system evolving will decline with time unless it is rigorously maintained. The law is similar to the law2 increasing complexity. As the complexity of the software increases, its quality is decreased. Open source developers are free from any restrictions and pressures; they work according to their own interest which results in the declining quality of open source software. The decline of the quality of GLE and FGS is reflected by law 2.

5. **Law 8: Feedback System:** The law of feedback system states that the evolution of the software is multi-level, multi agent and multi - loop feedback system. The existence of feedback system in case of open source software is reflected as the feature request and bugs are reported by the user community. In case of open source multi agent and multi loop system, it is difficult to determine.

6. **Law 4: Conservation of Organizational Stability:** Law of conservation of organizational stability states that the average global rate of activity on evolving software is invariant over the product life i.e. over the product lifetime, the amount of work that goes into evolution, is fixed. But the measure of the work done in case of open source system is extremely difficult to determine as in overall development of software includes the community efforts and community size increases in case of open source systems.

7. **Law 5: Conservation of Organizational Familiarity:** Law of conservation of organizational familiarity, states that familiarity with the evolving software is conserved. The average incremental growth rate should be constant as the software evolves i.e. to properly evolve the software, the team should do it in fixed increments or there will be risk of losing the understanding of the software. By observing the revision details of Flight Gear Simulator, it is found that the changes to the number of classes or functions were few thereby the familiarity is maintained .In GLE, there is sharp change in release 2.1.0 (Figure 23) which were decreased in next successive version and later versions shows the regular change and increase in size.

8. **Law 3: Self-Regulation:** Law of self-regulation, states that the evolution process is self-regulating leading to steady process. There is the balance between what is desired to change and what is actually achieved. The growth curve of Flight Gear Simulator shows the regular change and increase in size but in GLE there is sharp change in release 2.1.0 (Figure 23) but in later shows the regular change and increase in size.

Figure 12. Growth curve for average coupling of objects of all classes for different releases of GLE

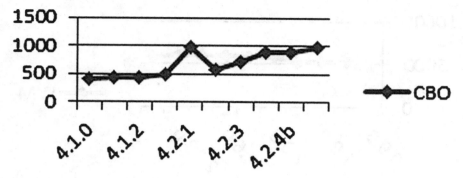

Figure 13. Growth curve for average coupling of objects of all classes for different releases of FGS

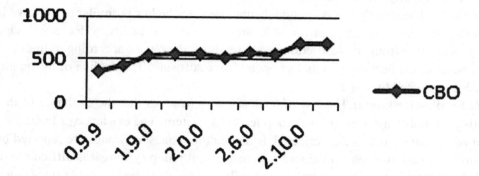

Figure 14. Growth curve for the response for all the classes for different releases of GLE.

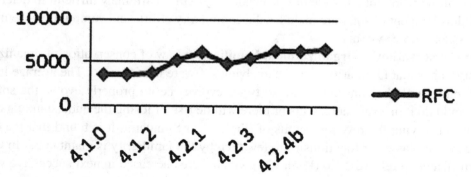

RELATED WORKS

The study carried out in this paper is closely related to some prior studies carried out by various researchers, includes Johari et al (Johari, 2011) find the applicability of Lehman laws on two open source softwares by considering 12 releases of Jhot and 16 releases of Rhino. Chris .J.Arges (Chris) evaluates Lehman laws on Linux kernel by studying 810 versions of Linux kernel over the period on 14 years. Godfrey et al. (Godfrey, 2000) examined the 96 version of Linux kernel to find applicability of laws.

Figure 15. Growth curve for the response for all the classes for different releases of FGS

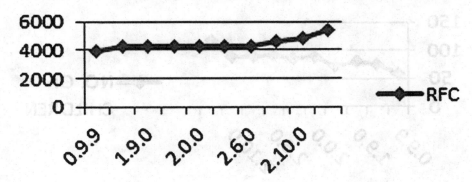

Figure 16. Growth curve for total depth of inheritance tree for all classes for different releases of FGS.

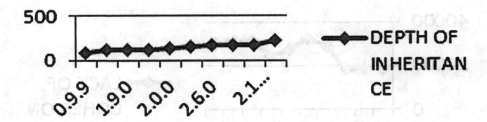

Figure 17. Growth curve for total depth of inheritance tree for all classes for different releases of GLE.

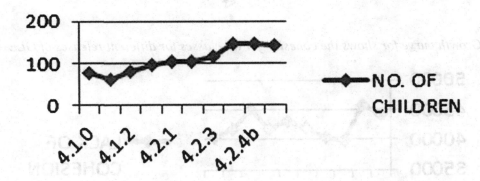

Figure 18. Growth curve for total number of direct descendent for all classes for different releases of GLE.

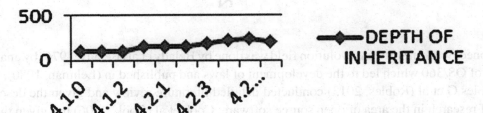

Figure 19. Growth curve for total number of direct descendent for all classes for different releases of FGS

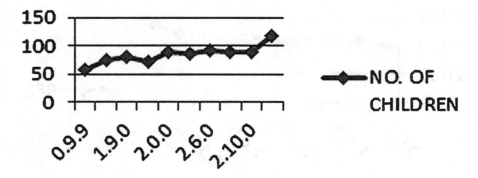

Figure 20. Growth curve for shows the cohesion for all classes for different releases of GLE

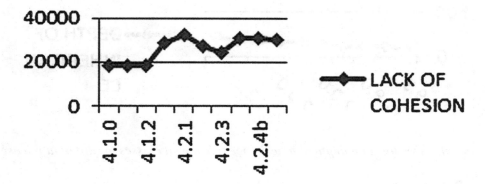

Figure 21. Growth curve for shows the cohesion for all classes for different releases of GLE

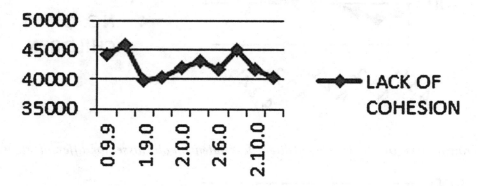

The pioneer work in software evolution field was done by Belady et al (Belady, 1976) by analyzing the 20 release of OS/360 which led to the development of laws and published in (Lehman, 1980), (Lehman, 1980). Robles.G et al (Robles, 2013) conducted detailed literature review and given the description of the state of research in the area of open source software. Cook et al (Cook, 2006) has given the detailed explanation of SPE classification.

Figure 22. Growth of Mc cabe Cyclomatic complexity for GLE.

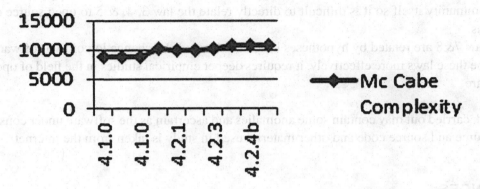

Figure 23. Growth of Mc cabe Cyclomatic complexity for FGS

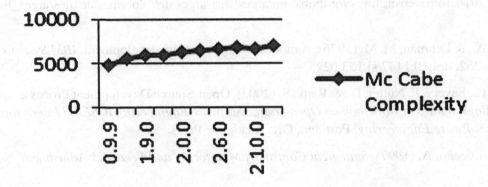

FUTURE RESEARCH DIRECTIONS

The future works can involve the other concepts of object oriented platforms such as code reuse in case open source software. The work may proceed in the direction how Lehman laws can be applied to component based software. The applicability of law 3, 4, 5 to the open source software is still pending to be done. So research may proceed in that direction.

CONCLUSION

The wok described above is based on the study of different releases of two open source software by using different metrics to find the applicability of Lehman laws on the open source software. It is observed that:

- The law 1, 2 & 6 can be determined directly using different metrics, these laws are reflected to have direct relevance with the open source evolution.
- But law 3, 4 & 5 are difficult to determine in case of open source software as the community size grows in case of open source software, no single person or organization is held responsible for

the evolution process, the request for change is from the community and the request is fulfilled by the community itself so it is difficult to directly relate the law 3, 4, & 5 to open source evolution process.

- And law 7&8 are related by hypotheses based on the study of change log of two software. To determine these laws more effectively, it requires deeper empirical studies in the field of open source software.

The work carried out may contain some anomalies and ascertain as the software under consideration are open source and source code and other material used in study is taken from the internet.

REFERENCES

Arges, C. J. (n.d.). *Linux and Lehman- Literature Review of Open Source Evolution Analysis*. Retrieved August 10, 2014 from website https://github.com/arges/chrisarges.net/blob/master/files/arges_linux_evolution.pdf

Belady, L. A., & Lehman, M. M. (1976). A model of large program development. *IBM Systems Journal, 15*(3), 225–252. doi:10.1147/sj.153.0225

Boldyreff, C., Lavery, J., Nutter, D., & Rank, S. (2003). Open-Source Development Processes and Tools. In *Proceedings of the 3rd Workshop on Open Source Software Engineering ICSE'03 International Conference on Software Engineering*. Portland, OR: Academic Press.

Box, G., & Luceño, A. (1997). *Statistical Control by Monitoring and Feedback Adjustment*. New York: Wiley.

Chidamber, S. R., & Kemerer, C. F. (1994). A metrics suite for object oriented design. *IEEE Transactions on Software Engineering, 20*(6), 476–493. doi:10.1109/32.295895

Cook, S., Harrison, R., Lehman, M. M., & Wernick, P. (2006). Evolution in software systems: Foundations of the SPE classification scheme. *Journal of Software Maintenance and Evolution: Research and Practice, 18*(1), 1–35. doi:10.1002/smr.314

Erdil, K., Finn, E., Keating, K., Meattle, J., Park, S., & Yoon, D. (2003). *Software Maintenance As Part of the Software Life Cycle*. Comp180: Software Engineering Project.

Flight Gear source code available (Parent Directory). (n.d.). Retrieved February 15, 2014 from FGS website http://fgfs.physra.net/ftp/Source

FlightGear Flight Simulator. (1996). *Flight Gear Revision details*. Retrieved February 20, 2014 from website: http://www.flightgear.org

GLE Source Code. (n.d.). Retrieved March 13, 2014 from SourceForge website: http://sourceforge.net/projects/glx/files/gle3.3h%20(old%20version)/source%20code/

Godfrey, M. W., & Tu, Q. (2000). Evolution in open source software: A case study. In *Proceedings of IEEE International Conference on Software Maintenance (ICSM'00)*. IEEE Computer Society Press.

Graphics Layout Engine. (2012). *GLE revision details*. Retrieved March12, 2014 from GLE website, http://www.gle-graphics.org

Johari, K., & Kaur, A., (2011). Effect of software evolution on software metrics: An open source case study. *ACM SIGSOFT Software Engineering Notes, 36*(5), 1-8. DOI: 10.1145/2020976.2020987

Kaur, P., & Singh, H. (2011). Measurement of Processes in Open Source Software Development. In *Proc. Trends in Information Management* (vol. 7). Academic Press.

Kaur, T., Ratti, N., & Kaur, P. (2014). A Review of Lehman's Laws in Open Source Software Systems. *International Journal of Computer Science and Communication Engineering, 3*(2).

Lehman, M. M. (1974). Programs, Cities, Students, Limits to Growth? Inaugural Lecture, May 1974. Imp. Col of Sc. Tech. Inaug. Lect. Ser., 9, 211 - 229.

Lehman, M. M. (1978). Laws of Program Evolution - Rules and Tools for Programming Management. In *Proc. Infotech State of the Art Conf., Why Software Projects Fail*. Academic Press.

Lehman, M. M. (1980). On Understanding Laws, Evolution and Conservation in the Large Program Life Cycle. *Journal of Systems and Software, 1*(3), 213–221.

Lehman, M. M. (1980). Programs, life cycles and the laws of software evolution. *Proceedings of the IEEE, 68*(9), 1060–1076. doi:10.1109/PROC.1980.11805

Lehman, M. M., & Belady, L. A. (Eds.). (1985). *Program Evolution. Processes of Software Change*. San Diego, CA: Academic Press Professional, Inc.

Lehman, M. M., Ramil, J., Wernick, P., Perry, D., & Turski, W. (1997), Metrics and laws of software evolution - the nineties view. In *Proceedings of the Fourth Intl Software Metrics Symposium*. Portland, OR: Academic Press. doi:10.1109/METRIC.1997.637156

Lientz, B. P., & Swanson, E. B. (1980). *Software Maintenance Management, A Study Of The Maintenance Of Computer Application Software In 487 Data Processing Organizations*. Reading, MA: Addison-Wesley.

Mens, T., Guehénéuc, Y. G., Ramil, J. F., & D'Hondt, M. (2010, July-August). Guest Editors' Introduction: Software Evolution. *IEEE Software, 27*(4), 22–25. doi:10.1109/MS.2010.100

Robles, G., Amor, J., Barahona, G. J., & Herrariz, I. (2013). The evolution of the laws of software evolution. A discussion based on a systematic literature review. *ACM Computing Surveys, 1*(1).

Roets, R., Minnaar, M., & Wright, K. (2007). Towards Successful Systems Development Projects in Developing Countries. In *Proceedings of the 9th International Conference on Social Implications of Computers in Developing Countries*. São Paulo, Brazil: Academic Press.

Scacchi, W. (2001). Software Development Practices in Open Software Development Communities: A Comparative Case Study. In *Proceedings of the First Workshop on Open Source Software Engineering*. Toronto, Canada: Academic Press.

Vixie, P. (1999). Software Engineering. In M. Stone, S. Ockman, & C. Dibona (Eds.), *Open sources: Voices from the open source revolution*. Sebastopol, CA: O'Reilly & Associates.

KEY TERMS AND DEFINITIONS

Lehman Laws of Evolution: M.M. Lehman has given the concept of software evolution. He has given the eight laws of evolution. These laws of evolution generally apply to all the traditionally developed software. And now work is going on that whether they apply to open source software or component based software also.

Object-Oriented Metrics: Metrics are the units of measurement. Metrics help to identify and quantify the improvements and the estimations of the software product.

Open Source Evolution: It refers to the modifications done by different users, i.e. how new processes are added or how modifications are performed in order to enhance the functionality of the available source code.

Open Source Software: Open source software are the software that are not proprietary. The source code is free of cost available for public and can be modified also.

Software Complexity: Software complexity is the quantitative measure. It lowers down the risk of introducing the defects in the software. Software maintenance cost can be lowered down by measuring the complexity.

Software Evolution: Software evolution is required to overcome the problem of software ageing. The major concern in software industry is to evolving existing software rather than development of new software. Software must evolve otherwise they become less useful.

Software Maintenance: Software maintenance is the amendments done to the software after the software is delivered. It is done to improve the performance, make the additions and to make the changes according to the changing requirements.

Software Quality: Software functional quality reflects how well it complies with or conforms to a given design, based on functional requirements or specifications. Software structural quality refers to how it meets non-functional requirements that support the delivery of the functional requirements, such as robustness or maintainability, the degree to which the software was produced correctly.

Chapter 11
Decreasing Service Coupling to Increase Enterprise Agility

Jose Carlos Martins Delgado
University of Lisbon, Portugal

ABSTRACT

The agility with which an Enterprise Information Systems (EIS) can be changed is of primordial importance in today's fast paced, competitive market. This depends on the changeability of the EIS software resources, which in turn is heavily influenced by the coupling between the services implemented by these resources. This chapter presents a solution to the coupling problem based on the concepts of structural compliance and conformance, in which compatibility between interacting services does not rely on a shared schema. Instead, it checks resources component by component, recursively, until primitive elements are reached. However, coupling is not a single-faceted issue and involves several aspects and slants. To help in understanding and systematizing them, the chapter proposes a multidimensional framework that caters for EIS lifecycle stages, concreteness (with various levels of abstraction), interoperability (based on structural compliance and conformance), and concerns (to deal with non-functional aspects such as security, reliability and quality of service).

INTRODUCTION

Enterprise agility can be defined as the capacity of an enterprise to adapt (reactively and/or proactively) to changes in its environment in a timely and cost efficient manner (Ganguly, Nilchiani, & Farr, 2009). Agile software development methods (Dingsøyr, Nerur, Balijepally, & Moe, 2012) seek to improve productivity in the development of Enterprise Information Systems (EIS) by trying to provide a better match between human abilities (such as creativity and programming) and problem solving constraints, such as complexity and team management.

A complex, potentially distributed software system, such as an Enterprise Information Systems (EIS), typically involves many interacting *resources* (modules, subsystems) with many decisions to take and

DOI: 10.4018/978-1-4666-8510-9.ch011

many tradeoffs to endure, not only in each resource but also in the ways in which the various resources interact. In this chapter, "resource" is a generic designation that can refer to a simple module, an EIS subsystem, a complete EIS or even a set of EIS (in a multi-enterprise collaboration).

Ideally, resources should be completely decoupled, with no constraints on one another and completely independent lifecycles. This would allow separate development of each resource and elimination of agile programming inefficiencies due to interactions between the specifications of resources, which usually cause iterations and changes in their requirements.

However, resources do need to interact and to cooperate, to collectively fulfill the intended goals of the application. Therefore, a fundamental tenet of agile programming is to reduce resource coupling as much as possible without hindering the interaction capabilities necessary to support the required resource interoperability. Decoupling also translates into a higher:

- Changeability (a change in a resource is less likely to have a significant impact on other resources);
- Adaptability (less constraints require less effort to adapt to changes in other resources);
- Reusability (a resource with less requirements and constraints has an increased applicability range);
- Reliability (a smaller set of requirements simplifies the task of finding an alternative in case of failure).

Although decoupling may be deemed a fairly obvious goal, tuning it to the right degree in practice is not an easy task.

To start with, an EIS should be as independent as possible from technological solutions, but the fact is that existing architectural models, such as SOA (Service Oriented Architecture) (Erl, 2008) and REST (Representational State Transfer) (Fielding, 2000), impose much more constraints and coupling than those actually required by the specifications of the systems under programming.

SOA is good at modeling enterprise systems but involves rather complex and static software specifications and entails sharing schemas between consumer and provider, which is a heavy form of service coupling. Performing a change in an interaction between Web Services (the typical SOA instantiation) is not trivial. RESTful APIs (Application Programming Interfaces) are much simpler, justifying the increasing popularity of REST (Pautasso, Zimmermann & Leymann, 2008), but is rather low level and not the best match for general-purpose, state-oriented enterprise applications. It also hides a high level of coupling, since it requires that both interacting resources share the same media type specification.

In addition, coupling is not a monolithic issue and needs to be detailed in its various slants. The main goal of this chapter is to systematize the aspects pertinent to interoperability and coupling and how they can contribute to enterprise agility, taking a service-oriented perspective (each resource is modeled by the service its implements) and a coupling minimization approach (how should resources interact to minimize coupling). The topics discussed can be equally applied at intra-application and inter-application levels (interacting resources compiled and linked together or distributed, respectively), although the emphasis is on distributed resources, in which reducing coupling is more critical, since resources can be changed independently at any time.

The chapter is organized as follows. The Background section describes some of the existing technologies and frameworks relevant to the context of this chapter, followed by a discussion on the meaning of enterprise agility and on the coupling problem. To understand it better, and how it relates to the interoperability problem, a multidimensional framework is outlined, presenting several levels of abstraction of interoperability. Next, the concepts of structural compliance and conformance are presented, as the main solution to both the interoperability and coupling problems. A simple example is provided. The chapter ends by comparing this approach with existing ones, outlining future directions of research, and drawing the main conclusions of this work.

BACKGROUND

The main topics tackled by this chapter are *interoperability* (how can resources meaningfully exchange information) and *coupling* (how changes in one resource affect the others with which this resource interacts). The two are intrinsically intertwined.

Historically, interoperability has been the main goal in Web-based distributed systems, whereas coupling has been one of the top concerns in software engineering, when developing an application, along with other metrics such as cohesion (Saxena & Kumar, 2012).

This dichotomy can be easily understood. Software development methods emphasize changeability and agility, which means structuring the resources within an application so that a change somewhere affects as little as possible the remaining resources and can be implemented in a very short time. Interoperability within an application is the easy part. Type names and inheritance are shared and there is usually a single programming language.

Distributed systems are completely different. Interoperability is hard, since interacting applications are developed, compiled, and linked independently. Most likely, this means different type names, inheritance hierarchies, programming languages, execution platforms and data formats. In this context, coupling has been treated as a side issue, a best-effort endeavor after achieving interoperability.

The two main technological solutions for distributed interoperability, Web Services (Papazoglou, 2008) and RESTful APIs (Webber, Parastatidis & Robinson, 2010), are based on data description languages, such as XML and JSON. Although they have been able to connect independent and heterogeneous systems, supporting enterprise integration, they are not brilliant solutions from the point of view of coupling.

XML-based interoperability, essential for Web Services, assumes that both interacting resources share the same schema, namely in WSDL documents and other data schemas. XML Schema (Wyke & Watt, 2002) and other schema languages are complex enough to award additional coupling concerns. This means that changing something in a schema affects all resources that use it, both service providers and consumers, entailing a significant coupling and reducing agility.

Services based on RESTful APIs follow the REST architectural style, developed by Fielding (2000), who claims that this reduces coupling because the consumer does not depend on the provider's specification since all it needs to do is to traverse the structured data representation of the server's resources, by following its links (URIs). If a resource changes at the server, it changes the data structured returned, but as long as the data types are the same the consumer will still be able to traverse it without modification. However, as this chapter shows in section "The REST approach", this decoupling is limited to protocol and data syntax. The interacting resources still depend on the shared knowledge about the data types, not to mention higher-level semantics and behavior.

To understand coupling, interoperability must be understood first, which requires a framework to systematize the various aspects of interoperability. Several interoperability frameworks have been proposed, some following a layered approach, with just one dimension, and others organizing the interoperability aspects in several dimensions.

The layered frameworks essentially follow the approach of the venerable OSI Reference Model (ISO/IEC, 1994), in which higher-level layers build on concepts of lower-level layers. For example, the C4IF framework, proposed by Peristeras & Tarabanis (2006), is based on four layers: Connection (basic use of a channel), Communication (data formats), Consolidation (meaning through semantics) and Collaboration (through compatible processes). Other frameworks, with differences in the layer organization but with a similar approach, include LCIM (Wang, Tolk & Wang, 2009), the European Interoperability Framework (EIF, 2010), and the frameworks proposed by Lewis, Morris, Simanta & Wrage (2008) and Monfelt, Pilemalm, Hallberg & Yngström (2011).

The multidimensional frameworks, usually applied at enterprise level, recognize that a single set of layers is not enough and add other dimensions, to cater for other aspects of interoperability, including lifecycle and non-functional concerns. Examples include SOSI (Morris *et al*, 2004), the ATHENA Interoperability Framework (Berre *et al*, 2007), the Framework for Enterprise Interoperability (FEI) defined by the CEN EN/ISO 11354-1 standard (ISO, 2011), and an interoperability framework conceived for ultra large scale systems, proposed by Ostadzadeh & Fereidoon (2011).

These frameworks and technologies emphasize interoperability and treat coupling as a second-class problem. Other approaches, such as the Enterprise Service Bus (ESB) (Chappell, 2004) and Event-based Programming (Faison, 2006), try to provide an additional emphasis on coupling, but not with as good results as it may seem, since interacting resources are essentially decoupled temporally, which does not improve data or behavior dependencies. ESBs also provide adapters and transformers, but these are no more than a centralization of interoperability solutions.

The existence of several types of coupling has been recognized by Page-Jones (1992), who coined the term *connascence* to relate resources in which a change in one implies a change in the other to maintain correctness of the application. He identified coupling at the levels of name, type, value, position (in a list or sequence), algorithm, and meaning. Timing coupling has also been included (Page-Jones, 1995).

Many metrics have been proposed to assess software quality, namely maintainability for object-oriented and service-based computing, based essentially on structural features.

Babu & Darsi (2013) present an extensive set of metrics for service coupling, cohesion and complexity. Other authors focus on dynamic, rather than static, coupling. Geetika & Singh (2014) present a survey of metrics for assessing coupling during program execution. Although centered on object-oriented programming, many of these metrics can also apply to distributed services.

There are also approaches trying to combine structural coupling with other levels of coupling, such as semantics. The work presented by Alenezi & Magel (2014) is an example. Hock-Koon & Oussalah (2010) had already presented a study on coupling metrics at the semantic, syntactic, and physical levels. Bavota *et al* (2013) performed a study on the perception by software developers about coupling at the structural, syntactic, semantic and logical (co-changing relationships) levels.

Other approaches establish principles and guidelines on how to organize the resources of an application so that it exhibits a low coupling and high maintainability, therefore promoting agility.

SOLID is an acronym referring to five principles enunciated by Martin (2003) for good object-oriented software design and low coupling, which can be extrapolated to service-based design:

- Single responsibility (a resource must have only one reason to change);
- Open-closed (resources must be open for extension but closed for modification);
- Liskov substitution (a resource must be replaceable by another with the same capabilities);

- Interface segregation (a resource's interface must be small and cohesive instead of all-encompassing. Compose resources instead of enriching an interface);
- Dependency-inversion (resources must depend on higher-level abstractions, not on lower-level resource components).

Normalized Systems Theory (Mannaert, Verelst, & Ven, 2011; De Bruyn, Van Nuffel, Verelst & Mannaert, 2012) applies concepts of system stability theory to software engineering. The basic tenet is that a software system should be stable with respect to a set of possible changes, and that a bound set of change requests should not require an unbounded set of changes in resources. There is a set of primitive resource types, which must be used as the building blocks for more complex systems, and a limited set of possible changes. In addition, the theory includes a set of theorems that must hold in order to ensure stability (limiting coupling and change propagation effects), dealing with:

- Separation of concerns (similar to the SOLID's single responsibility principle);
- Data and action version transparency (admitting new versions as long as previous ones are not affected);
- Separation of states (isolating atomic workflows by maintaining state between them).

This theory limits coupling by ensuring software stability.

ENTERPRISE AGILITY

The Enterprise Information System (EIS) is the core of any modern enterprise. It is hard enough to conceive, design, implement, and operate it, with a complexity stemming from a myriad of resources that perform specific tasks and must interact and cooperate in a seamless, effective, and efficient way to achieve the goals set out by the enterprise's strategy. However, no enterprise can thrive alone and must be part of a larger system, the value chain built from many independent but also cooperating enterprises, each with its own EIS. Therefore, the design of an EIS must also contemplate collaboration with others, in a structurally recursive scenario, in which a complex resource is composed of simpler resources. This section deals essentially with EIS, but it is also applicable, with the necessary adaptations, to less complex resources.

To make matters worse, EIS are constantly changing. As Heraclitus, an ancient Greek philosopher (Heraclitus & Patrick, 2013), once wrote, "The only thing that is constant is change". Complex systems like an EIS start being changed while they are still being conceived. Therefore, an EIS must be designed for both interoperability (to be able to interact with other EIS) and changeability (to accommodate inevitable changes as effortlessly as possible), throughout its lifecycle.

The drivers for changes in an EIS are mostly external, stemming from competition, suppliers and customers, which define the market environment in which the enterprise operates (the environment of smaller resources is formed by other resources in the same EIS). The agile enterprise needs to react quickly to market changes or, better still, anticipate the necessary changes in a proactive way. The EIS needs to be designed with this goal in mind.

Figure 1 depicts the lifecycle of an EIS, emphasizing changeability, centered on customers but suffering the influence of both suppliers and competition. The left part concerns governance, with innovation

Figure 1. The lifecycle of an EIS (or any other resource)

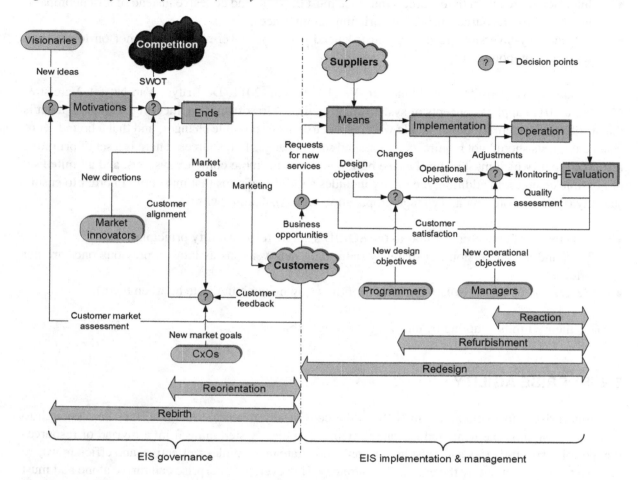

and competition differentiation as workhorses to gain customer preference, and the right part tackles implementation and management, geared towards customer satisfaction.

Although Figure 1 describes the case of a typical EIS, the same lifecycle structure applies to smaller resources, in which suppliers and customers refer to other resources (as service providers and consumers, respectively) and other actors correspond to roles in the software development method.

This customer-centric lifecycle is inspired by the Business Motivation Model (Malik, 2009) and contemplates three main concepts, which embody three of the main questions about system development that were popularized by the Zachman framework (O'Rourke, Fishman & Selkow, 2003):

- **Motivations:** Emphasize the reasons behind the architectural decisions taken (*why* the EIS is this way), in accordance with the specification of the problem that the EIS is designed to solve (innovative ideas for services that will appeal to customers, by being cheaper, better or easier to use than those available on the market);

- **Ends:** Express the desires, expectations, goals, and objectives of the stakeholders for which the EIS is relevant (*what* is the EIS trying to achieve, namely with respect to competition and market share);
- **Means:** Describe the mechanisms and actions used to fulfill those expectations (*how* can the EIS do it). A well-designed EIS, in an agile enterprise, should be able to create new services to satisfy (or drive) customer demand, exploiting business opportunities.

The subsequent stages in the lifecycle follow the typical organization adopted by classical development methods, such as the Rational Unified Process (Kruchten, 2004), adapted to take into account the dynamic features of an agile enterprise:

- **Implementation:** Implements the mechanisms defined in the Means stage and includes tasks such as development, testing, deployment, configuration, and setup;
- **Operation:** Corresponds to executing the EIS, inserting it in the market environment and dealing with customers and suppliers;
- **Evaluation:** Monitors the EIS and measures indicators and metrics to assess how well the EIS meets the expectations stemming from the motivations.

This model is maximalist, open, and non-prescriptive, in the sense that any EIS (or a resource component thereof) should go through all the stages, at least conceptually, but the level of emphasis and detail in every stage does not have to be always identical. The higher the level of the resource, the more important the motivations and goals will be, but it must also go all the way down to operations if it is meant to work. Lower-level resources will emphasize development and operation, but must also have underlying motivations and goals to achieve.

Each stage in Figure 1 is associated with an improvement loop, which assumes that indicators are defined so that expectations for that stage can be assessed. If the difference between the desired and measured indicators is greater than some acceptable measure, the loop should be iterated to decide which changes need to be implemented in order to reduce that difference. The following loops are considered, in rightmost to leftmost order:

- **Reaction:** All changes involve state only, so the cost and time to detect (monitoring) and to produce a change (of state) are usually very small. The changes are very frequent and occur as a reaction to events or to foreseeable trends, in adaptive systems. This is the loop more amenable to automation. However, and not considering self-changing systems (hard to build, particularly in complex systems), every possible change must have been included in the design;
- **Refurbishment:** The changes stem only from bugs, evolution of support libraries or performance enhancements. The specifications of the EIS are not modified, i.e., no changes are made at the leftward stages. Nevertheless, this corresponds to a new version of the EIS;
- **Redesign:** The EIS needs to be changed in a way that has not been included in the current design. A new version with new specifications needs to be produced and deployed, which may not be completely compatible with the previous one and may imply changing other resources as well. This entails changing the Means stage and propagating the changes to the subsequent stages;

- **Reorientation:** A reorientation is a profound reorganization of the EIS, as result of changes in the expectations provided by the EIS. This is usually driven by external factors, such as evolution of competitors or customers, but can also be demanded by an internal restructuring to increase competitiveness;
- **Rebirth:** The motivations for the EIS can also suffer significant changes, driven by factors such as stiff competition, technology evolution, merges/acquisitions, or even replacing the person fulfilling the CEO role. This implies changes that are so profound that, in practice, it has to be rethought and redesigned almost from scratch. This loop can also correspond to a diversification of business areas, making it necessary to build a new EIS (or a relevant fraction of its component resources).

Figure 1 also indicates the typical actors involved in the change/no change decision taken at the decision points (the circles with a question mark). The market innovators range from entrepreneurs, in small enterprises, to a full-fledged team driven by the CEO in large enterprises (including the various chief-level officers, or CxOs). Visionaries are hard to come by and do not always exist as such (innovators are more common and frequently take on this role). Customers, although not part of the actors designing the EIS, have an active role in it since indirectly drive decisions. Programmers and managers take care of implementation and operation, respectively.

Typically, a change is decided upon when an actor realizes that the benefit value of changing (BoC) is higher than the cost value of the implementation of that change (CoC). Agile enterprises need low change costs (Ganguly, Nilchiani & Farr, 2009), so that changes can be frequent, either reactively (to market changes) or proactively (anticipating market trends).

Since the EIS is not synchronized with its environment (namely, customers and suppliers), it tends to progressively diverge from it as time goes by (the EIS unalignment and the need for change grow). To realign the EIS, more and more changes will be needed and the CoC will grow, as illustrated by Figure 2.

If the BoC grows faster than the CoC, as in the case of Figure 2a, then the change becomes cost effective and should be made (at time T_c, when the BoC equals CoC). If the change is made too early (at T_{c-}), the cost will outweigh the benefit. If the change is made late by waiting too long and (at T_{c+}), some benefits will be lost.

Figure 2. Change benefits versus cost of changes: (a) Light EIS (b) Complex EIS

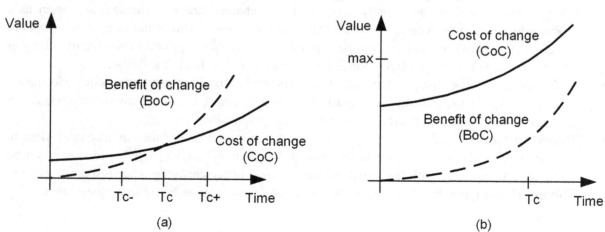

If, however, the EIS is complex and resorts to diversification (spawning a new version, or an adapter) instead of agility to cope with changing requirements, the CoC is higher and may never be lower than the corresponding BoC, as illustrated by Figure 2b. In this case, the time to change (T_c) is determined more by the need to limit the CoC than by its cost-benefit effectiveness. Having a light EIS, including only what is currently needed so that it becomes reasonably easy to change, is preferable to a complex, very encompassing one, which takes a long time and effort to change.

Note that T_c is just the time at which the change is deemed necessary and, ideally, required to be complete and in operation. However, the change will take some time to implement and deploy. Suppose that the change starts to be implemented at T_s and is deployed at T_d. This leads to several cases, described in Table 1.

Although proactiveness is a desirable feature, the fact is that guessing the future is still an art and many things can happen between T_s and T_c. In the most unfavorable case, the change made can be completely wrong, given the latest events, and lead to losses compared to doing no change at all. Therefore, in most cases a fast reactive behavior is the best approach.

In that case, the *change delay* (T_d-T_c) will determine how fast the EIS is able to realign and accommodate a change in requirements. If its average value is small compared to the MTBC (Mean Time Between Changes), the system can be classified as very agile or even real-time.

Agility, as a desirable property, is generally associated with quick response to a changing environment (Fricke & Schulz, 2005; Patten, Whitworth, Fjermestad & Mahinda, 2005), although it has also been defined in terms of low change cost (Ganguly, Nilchiani & Farr, 2009) and proactiveness (Putnik & Sluga, 2007). However, it is preferable to separate the several factors that characterize a change, with the following definitions (taken as average values) related to EIS changes:

- **Agility:** An indication of the change delay in relation to the rate at which changes are needed ((T_d-T_c)/MTBC);
- **Dynamicity:** An indication of the implementation time of a change in relation to the rate at which changes are needed ((T_d-T_s) /MTBC);
- **Proactiveness:** An indication of the proportion of the proactive part of the change in its implementation time, or how early the need for change is decided compared to the time required to implement the change ((T_c-T_s)/(T_d-T_s)). Applicable only when $T_s \leq T_c$;
- **Reactiveness:** An indication of the time required to implement the change in relation to the change delay ((T_d-T_s)/(T_d-T_c)). Applicable only when $T_c \leq T_s$;
- **Efficiency:** An indication of the average ratio between the benefit value of a change and the corresponding implementation cost (BoC/CoC).

Table 1. Types of change: from reactiveness to proactiveness

Timings	Type of Change	Description
$T_c \leq T_s < T_d$	Reactive	Completely reactive change, since its implementation starts only after realizing that it should be in place
$T_s < T_c < T_d$	Mixed	Change with a proactive and a reactive part. It starts before T_c, but some time afterwards is still needed to complete the change
$T_s < T_d \leq T_c$	Proactive	Completely proactive change, since its implementation starts and finishes even before it is needed. There is no much point in having T_d much before T_c
$T_s < T_d = T_c$	Just in time	The ideal case: change is complete precisely when it is needed

Agility should not depend on implementation cost or proactiveness, because it is a necessity caused essentially by external factors, such as competition or technology advances. However, what the market perceives is only whether a given enterprise responds fast enough or slowly to an evolving environment. The cost of that responsiveness, or how much in advance the enterprise has to anticipate the need for change, is an internal matter of that enterprise. Sometimes, it is preferable to pay more for a faster solution and be less efficient in implementing a change, just to beat the competition and gain the competitive edge of being first on the market. If time pressure is not high, optimization can focus on the implementation cost, rather than on the change delay.

It is also important to acknowledge that these indicators can be measured in each of the loops of Figure 1 but all need to be considered, according to the theory of constraints (Stein, 2003). If, for example, an enterprise is very agile in innovation and market perception (reorientation loop) but sluggish in implementing and deploying changes (refurbishment loop), the overall agility will be hampered by this slower loop.

THE COUPLING PROBLEM

The need for changes is seldom localized. The fact is that enterprises need to collaborate and their EIS (and their component resources) must be designed to interoperate. Changing a collaboration partner, even if not changing anything else, most likely means changing objectives, processes, data formats, and so on. This applies not only to a chain value of EIS but also to any set of resources that interact, both within an EIS and between EIS.

This means that a specific change somewhere may very well entail the need for many other changes throughout the system, to avoid breaking the required functionality. The impact of a change in the rest of the system is an indication of how much the resource in which that change occurred is coupled to that system.

In general, the resource interaction problem revolves around two conflicting goals:

- **Interoperability:** A resource needs to interact to accomplish collaboration. This necessarily entails some form of mutual knowledge and understanding, but it creates dependencies on other resources that may hamper evolution (a new iteration in the lifecycle – Figure 1);
- **Decoupling:** A resource needs to be independent of the other ones so that it can evolve freely and dynamically, without constraints. Unfortunately, independent resources do not understand each other and are not able to interact.

Therefore, the fundamental problem of resource interaction is to provide the *maximum decoupling* possible while ensuring the *minimum interoperability* requirements. In other words, the main goal is to ensure that each resource knows just enough to be able to interoperate but no more than that, to avoid unnecessary dependencies and constraints. This is an instance of the *Principle of Least Knowledge* (Palm, Anderson & Lieberherr, 2003) and minimizes the impact of a change in the rest of the system.

Enterprises are complex systems and suffer exactly from this problem, with the additional concern that agility is a critical requirement for the survival of even the largest enterprises. These are in fact quite vulnerable, because their complex architecture has typically woven a large web of dependencies.

Current integration technologies, such as Web Services (Papazoglou, 2008) and RESTful APIs (Webber, Parastatidis & Robinson, 2010) do not necessarily comply with the principle of least knowledge. In fact, both require resources that interact to share the type (schema) of the data exchanged, even if only a fraction of the data values is actually used. A change in that schema, even if these resources actually do not use the part of the schema that has changed, entails a change in these resources, because the resource that receives the data must be prepared to deal with all the values of that schema. This issue is further discussed in section "Reducing coupling with compliance and conformance".

Resources can be distributed and interact by sending messages, in the roles of consumer (sends requests and eventually expects responses) and provider (expects requests and eventually sends responses). A resource can act as either consumer or provider, or even both, in complex interactions.

Figure 3 depicts the scenario of a resource immersed in its environment. It acts as provider for a set of resources (its consumers), from which it receives requests, and as a consumer of a set of resources (its providers), to which it sends requests.

Coupling between this resource and others expresses not only how much it depends on (is affected by changes in) its providers but also how much its consumers depend on (are affected by changes in) it.

Dependency on a resource can be assessed by the fraction of its features that another resource is constrained about. A feature can be a function, a variable, a type, and so on. Two coupling metrics can thus be defined, from the point of view of a given resource:

- C_F (*forward coupling*), which expresses how much a resource is dependent on its providers, defined as:

$$C_F = \frac{\sum_{i \in P} \dfrac{Up_i}{Tp_i \cdot N_i}}{|P|} \tag{1}$$

where:

Figure 3. Coupling between a resource and its consumers and providers

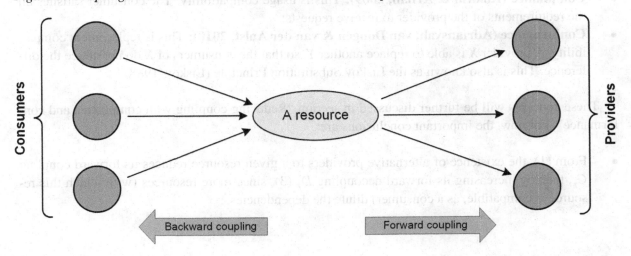

P - Set of providers that this resource uses, with $|P|$ as its cardinality

Up_i - Number of features that this resource uses in provider i

Tp_i - Total number of features that provider i has

N_i - Number of providers with which this resource is compatible as a consumer, in all uses of features of provider i by this resource

- ∘ C_B (*backward coupling*), which expresses how much impact a resource has on its consumers, defined as:

$$C_B = \frac{\sum_{i \in C} \dfrac{Uc_i}{Tc \cdot M}}{|C|} \qquad (2)$$

where:

C - Set of consumers that use this resource as provider, with $|C|$ as its cardinality

Uc_i - Number of features of this resource that consumer i uses

Tc - Total number of features that this resource has

M - Number of known resources that are compatible with this resource and can replace it, as a provider

These coupling metrics yield values between 0 (completely unrelated and independent) and 1 (completely dependent, constrained by all features). Decoupling metrics can also be defined, as the complement to 1 of each coupling metric:

- D_F (*forward decoupling*): $D_F = 1 - C_F$ (3)
- D_B (*backward decoupling*): $D_B = 1 - C_B$ (4)

Defining coupling this way is based upon two very important concepts:

- **Compliance (Kokash & Arbab, 2009):** This is usage compatibility: The consumer satisfies all the requirements of the provider to receive requests;
- **Conformance (Adriansyah, van Dongen & van der Aalst, 2010):** This is replacement compatibility. A provider X is able to replace another Y, so that the consumers of X do not notice the difference. This is also known as the Liskov Substitution Principle (Liskov, 1988).

These concepts will be further discussed in section "Reducing coupling with compliance and conformance". For now, the important conclusions are:

- From (1), the existence of alternative providers to a given resource reduces its forward coupling C_F, thereby increasing its forward decoupling D_F (3), since more resources (with which this resource is compatible, as a consumer) dilute the dependencies.

- From (2), having alternatives to a resource, in its role as a provider, reduces the system dependency on it, thereby reducing the impact that resource may have on its potential consumers. Backward coupling C_B decreases and backward decoupling D_B (4) increases;
- From both (1) and (2), the smaller the fraction of features used, the smaller coupling is.

A very interesting thought is that alternative resources as providers can be found not only by designing and building them on purpose but also by reducing the fraction of features needed for compatibility to the minimum required by the interaction sought between resources, according to the overall EIS (or set of EIS) choreography or orchestration. This is a consequence of the fact that the lower the number of constraints, the higher the probability of finding resources that satisfy them.

This means that both factors on which coupling depends (the fraction of features used and the number of provider alternatives available) work in the same direction, and the first reinforces the second. Therefore, reducing coupling means reducing the fraction of features used, or the knowledge of one resource about another.

Technologies, such as Web Services (Papazoglou, 2008) and RESTful APIs (Webber, Parastatidis & Robinson, 2010) are poor solutions in terms of coupling, since Web Services rely on sharing a schema (a WSDL document) and RESTful APIs require data types to have been previously agreed. These technologies solve the distributed interoperability problem, but not the coupling problem.

But how can coupling be reduced? Several authors researching the coupling problem try to separate several coupling cases in syntactical terms, with separate metrics for functions, arguments, types, and so on (Babu & Darsi, 2013; Geetika & Singh, 2014). Others try to add semantics (Hock-Koon & Oussalah, 2010; Alenezi & Magel, 2014), but mainly in terms of data types and their composition. Having a set of metrics instead of just one, without an underlying rationale, can make the problem harder instead of helping to solve it.

The fact is that resources can interact in many slants, both functional and non-functional. A framework is needed to separate the various aspects and dimensions of resource coupling. This is the goal of the following section.

A MULTIDIMENSIONAL COUPLING FRAMEWORK

Before analyzing coupling between resources, one resource needs to be understood first, namely the various aspects involved in its design.

The Dimensions of a Resource

The starting point of the design of any resource is its lifecycle. Figure 1 shows how this can be organized, but is nothing more than a very high-level model and with not enough separation of concerns to allow us to understand what is really involved in the design of that resource, in its several slants and dimensions. More than a mere lifecycle, a pipeline from a conceptual to an operational level, a multidimensional framework is needed, in which independent dimensions can be analyzed separately.

Actually, the lifecycle is just one dimension (or axis) of our framework, which includes the following dimensions (or axes), depicted in Figure 4:

Figure 4. The axes of the coupling framework, with the front plane detailed.

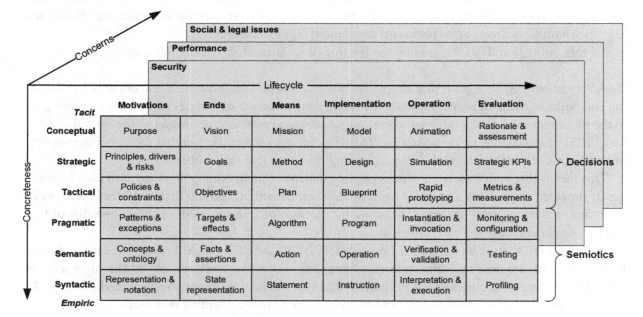

- **Lifecycle:** This axis is discretized into the six stages of Figure 1;
- **Concreteness:** Each stage in the lifecycle can be viewed at a very high and abstract level, or at a very detailed and concrete level. This axis has been discretized into six levels: *Conceptual, Strategic, Tactical, Pragmatic, Semantic,* and *Syntactic.* Stages of the lifecycle and their level of concreteness are orthogonal concepts. The Implementation stage can be considered at a conceptual level (just ideas on how to do it) as well as the Motivations stage at a very concrete level (justification for the lowest level actions);
- **Concerns:** The focus words (*what, how, where, who, when, why*) in the Zachman framework (O'Rourke, Fishman & Selkow, 2003) are generic but do not address the entire focus range. Other questions are pertinent, such as *whence* (where from), *whither* (where to), *how much* (quantitative assessment), and *how well* (qualitative assessment). It is important to be able to express the dynamics of the resource, its quality (how good it is, quantitatively and qualitatively), and other concerns (performance, standards, security, reliability, and so on), both functional and non-functional. This axis is discretized as needed, according to the number of concerns considered. Therefore, this framework is open-ended.

The front plane in Figure 4 is formed by the Lifecycle and Concreteness axes. Each cell, resulting from crossing the values of both axes, represents one lifecycle stage at a given level of concreteness. Each row is a refinement of the level above it, by including decisions that turn some abstract aspects into concrete ones. Each concern, functional or non-functional, represents a new plane, along the Concerns axis. Some concerns have been illustrated, with details omitted in subsequent planes for simplicity.

The levels in the Concreteness axis are organized in two categories:

- **Decisions** taken, which define, structure and refine the characteristics of the resource, at three levels:
  - **Conceptual:** The top view of the resource, including only global ideas;
  - **Strategic:** Details these ideas by taking usually long lasting decisions;
  - **Tactical:** Refines these decisions into shorter-term decisions;
- **Semiotics (Chandler, 2007):** The study of the relationship between signs (manifestations of concepts) and their interpretation (pragmatics), meaning (semantics), and representation (syntax). In this chapter, these designations correspond to the following levels:
  - **Pragmatic:** Expresses the outcome of using the resource, most likely producing some effects, which will depend on the context in which the resource is used;
  - **Semantic:** Specifies the meaning of the resource, using an ontology to describe the underlying concepts;
  - **Syntactic:** Deals with the representation of the resource, using some appropriate notation or programming language.

All the concreteness levels express a range between two opposite thresholds, also represented in Figure 4:

- **Tacit:** This is the highest level, above which concepts are too complex or too difficult to describe. It encompasses the tacit knowledge and know-how (Oguz & Sengün, 2011) of the designers of the resource, expressing their insight and implicit expectations and assumptions about the problem domain;
- **Empiric:** The lowest level, below which details are not relevant anymore. The resource designers just settle for something that already exists and is known to work, such as a standard or a software library.

The Interoperability Dimension

The 24765 standard (ISO/IEC/IEEE, 2010) provides one of the most cited definitions of interoperability: "*The ability of two or more systems or components to exchange information and to use the information that has been exchanged*". This means that interoperability involves more than mere communication. Interacting resources must be able to understand and use the information they receive.

This standard actually provides three definitions, stemming from previous and now superseded standards. The other definition relevant to this chapter is: "*The capability to communicate, execute programs, and transfer data among various functional units in a manner that requires the user to have little or no knowledge of the unique characteristics of those units*". Here the emphasis is on decoupling, meaning that interacting resources need not be designed for a full match, as long as some of their features support the interaction, and can evolve independently, as long as these features are not changed. This leads to the concept of partial interoperability, expressing that a resource can access only a fraction of the features of another (ranging from none to the full set). This is precisely what the goal of reducing resource coupling requires.

However, these definitions are very encompassing and do not adequately express aspects such as:

- The asymmetric nature of interoperability, expressed in the differences between the consumer and provider roles;
- The motivations and intentions behind interoperability;
- The minimum requirements (both functional and non-functional) to impose on interacting resources to make interoperability possible;
- How interoperability actually works to produce meaningful results.

As Figure 4 shows, the ability to meaningfully interact involves higher levels (upper levels in the Concreteness dimension) and lifecycle stages to the left of Operation. If the Concerns dimension is taken into account, things get even more complex. For example, an interaction may fail due to excessive response times (making timeouts expire), even if the design is functionally correct, or lack of an access privilege.

Interoperability and coupling between two resources, consumer and provider, can occur at any level and aspect of the resources, but always under the compliance and conformance concepts introduced in section "The coupling problem". Since Figure 4 details several dimensions of each resource, it can be used to add the dimension of interoperability, yielding the full multidimensional framework, depicted in Figure 5. Compliance and conformance describe the two directions in the interoperability axis, which has been discretized into several values, described in Table 2.

The basic idea is that a resource X should be able to interact with another Y only if each cell of the three-dimensional space (stemming from Figure 4) of resource X satisfies the requirements of the corresponding cell in the three-dimensional space of resource Y. This is valid even in the design stages, before Operation. For example, the motivations of X to send a message should fit the motivations of Y to receive it and to honor its purpose.

In practice, most of these interactions between corresponding cells are dealt with *tacitly*, not explicitly. In particular, stages to the left of Operation are usually tackled at the documentation level only. However, they are very relevant, because what happens in the design stages allows us to understand the true capabilities and limitations of interoperability solutions and technologies, as well as the coupling involved. Nevertheless, the Operation stage is the most visible, in terms of interoperability and coupling.

As any complex issue, interoperability can be considered at various levels of abstraction. Table 2 establishes a linearized classification of interoperability levels.

The interoperability categories in this table (first column) should be interpreted as follows:

- **Symbiotic:** Expresses the purpose and intent of two interacting resources to engage in a mutually beneficial agreement. Enterprise engineering is usually the topmost level in resource interaction complexity, since it goes up to the human level, with governance and strategy heavily involved. Therefore, it maps mainly onto the symbiotic category, although the same principles apply (in a more rudimentary fashion) to simpler subsystems. This can entail:
  - A tight coordination under a common governance (if the resources are controlled by the same entity);
  - A joint-venture agreement (if the two resources are substantially aligned);
  - A collaboration involving a partnership agreement (if some goals are shared);
  - A mere value chain cooperation (an outsourcing contract).
- **Pragmatic:** The effect of an interaction between a consumer and a provider is the outcome of a contract, which is implemented by a choreography that coordinates processes, which in turn implement workflow behavior by orchestrating service invocations. Languages such as Business

Figure 5. Complete framework, with interoperability axis

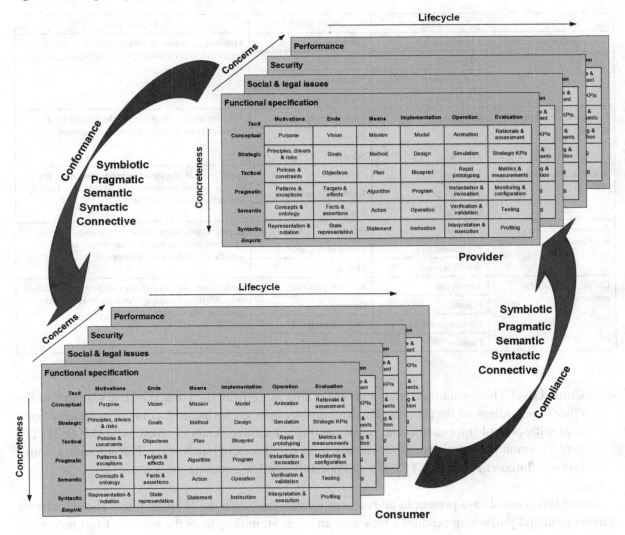

Process Execution Language (BPEL) (Juric & Pant, 2008) support the implementation of processes and Web Services Choreography Description Language (WS-CDL) is an example of a language that allows choreographies to be specified;

- **Semantic:** Both interacting resources must be able to understand the meaning of the content of the messages exchanged, both requests and responses. This implies interoperability in rules, knowledge, and ontologies, so that meaning is not lost when transferring a message from the context of the sender to that of the receiver. Semantic languages and specifications, such as OWL and RDF, map onto this category;
- **Syntactic:** Deals mainly with form, rather than content. Each message has a structure, composed of data (primitive resources) according to some structural definition (its schema). Data need to be serialized to be sent over the network as messages, using representations such as XML or JSON;

Table 2. Discretization of the interoperability axis

Category	Level	Main Artifact	Description
Symbiotic (purpose and intent)	Coordination	Governance	Motivations to have the interaction, with varying levels of mutual knowledge of governance, strategy and goals
	Alignment	Joint-venture	
	Collaboration	Partnership	
	Cooperation	Outsourcing	
Pragmatic (reaction and effects)	Contract	Choreography	Management of the effects of the interaction at the levels of choreography, process and service
	Workflow	Process	
	Interface	Service	
Semantic (meaning of content)	Inference	Rule base	Interpretation of a message in context, at the levels of rule, known resource components and relations, and definition of concepts
	Knowledge	Knowledge base	
	Ontology	Concept	
Syntactic (notation of representation)	Structure	Schema	Representation of resource components, in terms of composition, primitive components and their serialization format in messages
	Predefined type	Primitive resource	
	Serialization	Message format	
Connective (transfer protocol)	Messaging	Message protocol	Lower level formats and network protocols involved in transferring a message from the context of the sender to that of the receiver
	Routing	Gateway	
	Communication	Network protocol	
	Physics	Media protocol	

- **Connective:** The main objective is to transfer a message from the context of one resource to the other's, regardless of its content. This usually involves enclosing that content in another message with control information and implementing a message protocol (such as SOAP or HTTP) over a communications network, according to its own protocol (such as the Transmission Control Protocol/Internet Protocol – TCP/IP) and possibly involving routing gateways.

These levels are always present in all resource interactions, even the simplest ones. There is always a motivation and purpose in sending a message, an effect stemming from the reaction to its reception, a meaning expressed by the message, and a format used to send it over a network under some protocol.

However, what happens in practice is that some of these layers are catered for *tacitly* or *empirically*:

- The Connective category is usually dealt with empirically, by assuming some protocol, such as HTTP or SOAP;
- Syntactic is the most used category, because it is the simplest and most familiar, with interfaces that deal mainly with syntax or primitive semantics, with data description languages such as XML and JSON;
- The Semantic category, given the increasing relevance of the Semantic Web (Shadbolt, Hall & Berners-Lee, 2006), is beginning to be explicitly addressed with semantic annotations and languages, based either on XML or JSON, but is still largely subject to tacit assumptions, for example regarding XML's namespaces or JSON's predefined media types;

- The Pragmatic category is usually considered at the documentation level only, with many tacit assumptions, or implemented by software but without formal specification. Choreography specifications and verification tools are seldom used;
- The Symbiotic category is considered explicitly only with very complex resources (such as EIS) and in the conceptual stages of the lifecycle, again just at the documentation level. In most cases, it is simply assumed that, if a resource exposes a service, it can be invoked regardless of motivations, purpose, or any other high-level concerns.

Note that the pragmatic, semantic, and syntactic levels in the Concreteness and Interoperability axes do not refer to the same aspects. In Concreteness, these levels describe each resource on its own, with its behavior, meaning, and programming representation. In Interoperability, these levels describe the compatibility of the interaction of resources, namely the request and response messages, the protocol they use, the format in which they are sent, how they are interpreted, and the effects they produce.

Another important aspect is non-functional interoperability. It is not just a question of invoking the right operation with the right parameters. Adequate service levels, context awareness, security, and other non-functional issues must be considered when resources interact, otherwise interoperability will be less effective or not possible at all. The levels of Table 2 must be considered for each plane in Figure 4.

Finally, all these interoperability categories constitute an expression of resource coupling. On the one hand, two uncoupled resources (with no interactions between them) can evolve freely and independently, which favors adaptability, changeability and even reliability (if one fails, there is no impact on the other). On the other hand, resources need to interact to cooperate towards common or complementary goals, which implies that some degree of previously agreed mutual knowledge is indispensable. The more they share with the other, the more integrated they are and the easier interoperability becomes, but the greater coupling gets.

The interoperability levels expressed by Table 2 provide a classification that allows us to understand better the coupling details, namely at what levels they occur and what is involved in each level, instead of having just a blurry notion of dependency. In this respect, it constitutes a tool to analyze and to compare different coupling models and technologies.

Simpler models can be achieved by relaxing some coupling constraints along each of the axes. This means considering them tacitly or empirically, instead of explicitly. For example:

- **Concerns:** Not all concerns are identically relevant. Security may require fulfilling every detail, but other concerns may have fuzzier rules, such as social and cultural issues, or vary dynamically, such as quality of service (in a best effort approach) or financial conditions (with dynamic optimizations);
- **Lifecycle:** The columns Implementation and Evaluation are less relevant to coupling than the others, since different implementations can support the same operational specifications, and each interacting resource can be evaluated separately;
- **Concreteness:** In Figure 5, lowering the Tacit threshold and raising the Empiric threshold in some planes, the levels of concreteness at which interoperability and coupling is considered for each concern can be adjusted. The most common case in programming is to deal explicitly with the syntactic level, with some incursions into higher levels in some columns (mostly Means and Implementation). Nevertheless, integration at higher levels and at lower levels can use different technologies, by using APIs that raise the empiric level and hide the details of different implementations.

Exercising the Framework

A method will be needed to exercise this framework, to navigate from the top-left cell in Figure 4 (conceptual motivations, or purpose) and symbiotic interoperability category in Figure 5 to the bottom-right cell in Figure 4 (operation at the syntactic level, or interpretation & execution) and connective interoperability category in Figure 5, eventually looping back for lifecycle evolution.

The path taken determines the method to use, which should resort to agile best practices. This methodology is outside the scope of this chapter and constitutes future work.

REDUCING COUPLING WITH COMPLIANCE AND CONFORMANCE

Most resources are made interoperable by design, i.e., conceived and implemented to work together, in a consumer-provider relationship. Web Services are a typical interoperability solution, in which case:

- Schemas are shared between interacting services, establishing coupling for all the possible documents satisfying each schema, even if they are not actually used;
- Searching for an interoperable service is done by schema matching with *similarity* algorithms (Jeong, Lee, Cho & Lee, 2008) and ontology matching and mapping (Euzenat & Shvaiko, 2007). This does not ensure interoperability and manual adaptations are usually unavoidable.

The interoperability concept, as defined in this chapter, introduces a different perspective, stronger than similarity but weaker than commonality (the result of sharing the same schemas and ontologies). The trick is to allow partial (instead of full) interoperability, by considering only the intersection between what the consumer needs and what the provider offers. If the latter subsumes the former, the degree of interoperability required by the consumer is feasible, regardless of whether the provider supports additional features or not. When this is true, the consumer is said to be *compatible* with the provider or, more precisely, that a resource X is compatible with a resource Y regarding a consumer-provider relationship.

The main advantages of this are:

- Coupling is limited to the resources that actually contain the used features and not to all possible resources that satisfy the schema;
- A consumer is more likely to find suitable providers based on a smaller set of features, rather than on a full schema;
- A provider will be able to serve a broader base of consumers, since it will impose fewer restrictions on them.

All these factors contribute to reduce coupling, as shown in section "The coupling problem". In this respect, two resource relationships are of relevance:

- **Consumer-Provider:** Compatibility between a consumer and a provider is known as *compliance* (Kokash & Arbab, 2009). The consumer must satisfy (*comply with*) the requirements established by the provider to accept requests sent to it, without which these cannot be validated, understood, and executed. It is important to note that any consumer that complies with a given provider can use it, independently of having been designed for interaction with it or not. The consumer and provider need not share the same schema. The consumer's schema needs only to be compliant with the provider's schema in the features that it actually uses. Since distributed resources have independent lifecycles, they cannot freely share names, and schema compliance must be tested structurally, feature by feature, between messages sent by the consumer and the interface offered by the provider;

- **Provider-Provider:** The issue is to ascertain whether a provider Y, serving a consumer X, can be replaced by another provider Z such that the consumer-provider relationship enjoyed by X is not impaired. In other words, the issue is whether Z is replacement compatible with Y. Replacement compatibility between two providers is known as *conformance* (Kim & Shen, 2007; Adriansyah, van Dongen & van der Aalst, 2010). The provider must fulfill the expectations of the consumer regarding the effects of a request (including eventual responses), therefore being able to take the form of (*to conform to*) whatever the consumer expects it to be. Note that a provider may be conformant to another with respect to one consumer but not with respect to another consumer. It all depends on the set of features used by the consumer. The reasons for replacing a provider with another may be varied, such as switching to an alternative in case of failure or lack of capacity of Y, evolution of Y (in which case Z would be the new version of Y), or simply a management decision. The important aspect to note is that, again, Z does not need to support all the features of Y, but just those that X actually uses (partial compatibility).

Compliance and conformance are not symmetric relationships (e.g., if X complies with Y, Y does not necessarily comply with X).

Figure 6 illustrates compliance and conformance, as well as its effects on reducing coupling, either by limiting dependency to the required features, either by increasing the set of possible alternative providers or consumers.

Figure 6. Resource compatibility, by use and replacement

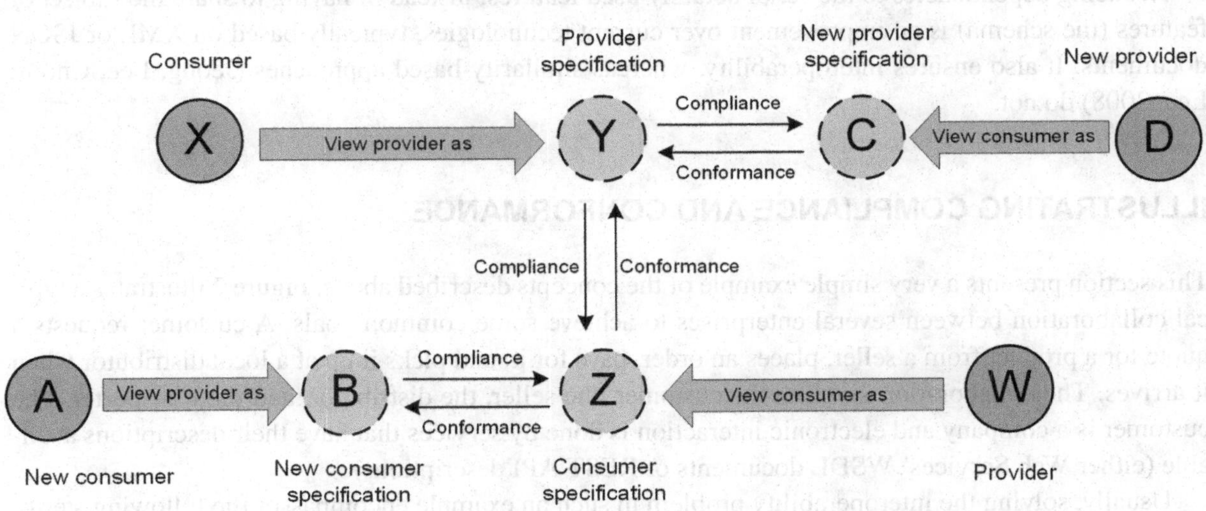

245

A resource X, in the role of consumer, has been designed to interact with a resource, in the role of provider, with a specification Y, which represents the set of features that X requires as its provider. Nothing prevents the actual provider from having additional features, as long as it includes this set.

Now consider a resource W, in the role of provider, which has been designed to expect a consumer Z, which represents the set of features that W expects that the actual consumer will access. Nothing prevents the consumer from accessing less features, as long as they are included in this set.

X and W were not designed to interoperate, since what one expects is not what the other is. They have been developed independently, or at least do not constitute a full match of features (in other words, do not share the same schema). However, interoperability is still possible, as long as:

- Y complies with Z. This means that the set of features that Y represents is a subset of the set of features that Z represents. X cannot access a feature that W does not expect to be accessed;
- Z conforms to Y. This means that the set of features that Z represents is a superset of the set of features that Y represents.

Although it seems that these two items assert the same thing, it is not the case when optional features exist, such as optional arguments to functions or optional fields in an XML document. For compliance, the consumer needs to specify only the mandatory features (minimum set), whereas for conformance all features (mandatory and optional) must be supported by the provider (maximum set).

Now consider adding a new consumer A to provider W, or simply replacing X. A does not have to bear any relationship to X, the previous consumer. It may even use a completely different set of features of W (represented as specification B) as long as B complies with Z and Z conforms to B. This also applies if A is a changed version of X.

A similar reasoning can be made if X now uses a new provider, D, with the set of requirements on consumers represented by specification C. Again, interoperability is still possible as long as Y complies with C and C conforms to Y. Apart from this, D and W need not bear any relationship. This also applies if D is a changed version of W.

Reducing dependencies to the set of actually used features, instead of having to share the full set of features (the schema) is an improvement over current technologies, typically based on XML or JSON documents. It also ensures interoperability, whereas similarity-based approaches (Jeong, Lee, Cho & Lee, 2008) do not.

ILLUSTRATING COMPLIANCE AND CONFORMANCE

This section presents a very simple example of the concepts described above. Figure 7 illustrates a typical collaboration between several enterprises to achieve some common goals. A customer requests a quote for a product from a seller, places an order, pays for it, and picks it up at a local distributor when it arrives. The collaboration involves the customer, the seller, the distributor, and the transporter. The customer is a company and electronic interaction is done by services that have their descriptions available (either Web Services' WSDL documents or REST API descriptions).

Usually, solving the interoperability problem in such an example encompasses the following steps:

Figure 7. A simple example of enterprise collaboration

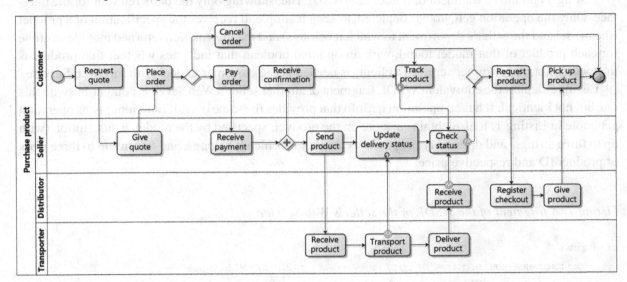

- The customer searches for a seller supplying the product(s) needed;
- The customer downloads the seller's API (in either SOA or REST) and develops a client matched for it, as well as the necessary adapter(s) to enable its EIS to deal with this client;
- If semantic information is available, the customer may use it to improve the programmatic treatment of interoperability;
- Same thing for the interface with the distributor;
- The highest levels of interoperability (Table 2) are dealt with manually, through documentation;
- If the seller or the distributor change something in the functionality of their interfaces, the client program at the customer needs to be changed accordingly, to reflect the new schemas. This is the consequence of coupling resulting from sharing interface specifications.

This is a classical view of interoperability in enterprise integration, in which the schema of the data exchanged is the centerpiece and EIS are made interoperable for the full variability range of that schema, even if the interaction actually exercises only a fraction of that variability. This leads to unnecessary coupling.

The framework described in this chapter proposes a minimalist vision, reducing interoperability to the minimum coupling needed and, at the same time, widening the range of partners with which interoperability can be established.

To illustrate this, consider the interoperability needed between the customer and the seller, in Figure 7. For the customer, this involves not only finding a suitable seller but also avoiding lock-in with that seller, by allowing the seller to be replaced by another with a compatible interface.

Current technologies, such as Web Services, RESTful APIs and the tools that deal with them, have not been conceived with compliance and conformance in mind, but an example can give an idea of how that can be done. Consider the seller as a Web Service offering several operations, including getQuote, which allows the customer to implement its RequestQuote activity in Figure 7.

Listing 1 contains a fragment of the seller's WSDL file, showing only the parts relevant for the interface. Only the operation getQuote is depicted, to keep it simple. It receives the specification of a product (the model and the seller's department to which it belongs) and the information returned includes a quote for each product of that model found, with an optional boolean that indicates whether that product is in stock or not. A consumer service (a client) is needed at the customer to deal with this Web Service.

Listing 2 depicts the equivalent WSDL fragment of another seller's Web Service, compatible with this one but not identical. It has an operation getInfo that provides the same overall functionality as operation getQuote in Listing 1. It also obtains a quote on the product, specified by the model, a description (with up to three strings) and optionally the product category to which it belongs, and returns up to three pairs of product ID and respective price.

Listing 1. A fragment of the WSDL of the seller's Web Service

```
<types>
    <xs:schema xmlns:xs="http://www.w3.org/2001/XMLSchema"
            targetNamespace="http://example.com/schema/seller1"
            xmlns="http://example.com/schema/seller1"
            elementFormDefault="qualified">
        <xs:element name="product" type="Product"/>
        <xs:element name="prodInfo" type="ProdInfo"/>
        <xs:complexType name="Product">
            <xs:sequence>
                <xs:element name="model" type="xs:string"/>
                <xs:element name="department" type="xs:string"/>
            </xs:sequence>
        </xs:complexType>
        <xs:complexType name="ProdInfo">
            <xs:sequence minOccurs="0" maxOccurs="unbounded">
                <xs:element name="ID" type="xs:string"/>
                <xs:element name="cost" type="xs:decimal"/>
                <xs:element name="inStock" type="xs:boolean" minOccurs="0"/>
            </xs:sequence>
        </xs:complexType>
    </xs:schema>
</types>
<interface name="Seller_1">
    <operation name="getQuote" pattern="http://www.w3.org/ns/wsdl/in-out">
        <input messageLabel="In" element="seller1:product"/>
        <output messageLabel="Out" element="seller1:prodInfo"/>
    </operation>
</interface>
```

Listing 2. A fragment of the WSDL of another seller's Web Service

```
<types>
    <xs:schema xmlns:xs="http://www.w3.org/2001/XMLSchema"
            targetNamespace="http://example.com/schema/seller1"
            xmlns="http://example.com/schema/seller2"
            elementFormDefault="qualified">
        <xs:element name="productSpec" type="ProductSpec"/>
        <xs:element name="productInfo" type="ProductInfo"/>
        <xs:complexType name="ProductSpec">
            <xs:sequence>
                <xs:element name="model" type="xs:string"/>
                <xs:element name="description" type="xs:string"
                        minOccurs="0" maxOccurs="2"/>
                <xs:element name="category" type="xs:string"
                        minOccurs="0" maxOccurs="1"/>
            </xs:sequence>
        </xs:complexType>
        <xs:complexType name="ProductInfo">
            <xs:sequence minOccurs="0" maxOccurs="3">
                <xs:element name="productID" type="xs:string"/>
                <xs:element name="price" type="xs:decimal"/>
            </xs:sequence>
        </xs:complexType>
    </xs:schema>
</types>
<interface name="Seller_2">
    <operation name="getInfo" pattern="http://www.w3.org/ns/wsdl/in-out">
        <input messageLabel="In" element="seller2:productSpec"/>
        <output messageLabel="Out" element="seller2:productInfo"/>
    </operation>
</interface>
```

These two WSDL fragments correspond to two different schemas and the usual way to invoke the respective services would be to generate two different clients, one for each service. However, by looking at both the WSDL fragments, the following assertions can be drawn:

- The In element of the getInfo operation in Listing 2, of type ProductSpec, conforms to the In element of the operation getQuote in Listing 1, of type Product, as long as there is an ontological mapping between getInfo and category in Listing 2 and getQuote and department, respectively, in Listing 1. In other words, the getInfo operation in Listing 2 is equipped to handle all the possible In values supplied to the getQuote operation in Listing 1;

- The Out element of the getInfo operation in Listing 2, of type ProductInfo, complies with the Out element of the getQuote operation in Listing 1, of type ProdInfo, as long as there is an ontological mapping between productID and price in Listing 2 and ID and cost, respectively, in Listing 1. This means that all the possible values returned by the operation in Listing 2 are included in the set of all possible values returned by the operation in Listing 1.

The conclusion is that Listing 2 can replace Listing 1 without impairing the service provided to the consumers (assuming ontological mappings). Intuitively, the operation getInfo in Listing 2 can accept more values as input and returns fewer values as output than the getQuote operation in Listing 1. Although the services provided by Listing 1 and Listing 2 are different, a client generated to invoke the service of Listing 1 can also be used, without changes, to invoke the service of Listing 2. This reasoning could be extended when considering WSDL documents with several operations. Compliance and conformance would only need to hold for actually used operations and not for the entire interface.

This reduces coupling because alternative providers can be used seamlessly and constraints are limited to those features actually used. Two conditions are essential to ensure this:

- Compliance and conformance need to be checked structurally (Delgado, 2012), in which complex types are checked recursively, component by component, until primitive (or ontologically recognized) types are reached. Corresponding components need to either have the same name in the same ontology or be mapped one to the other when reconciling ontologies. This is why different type names (such as ProductSpec and Product in this example) or belonging to different ontologies can be checked for compliance and conformance even without an ontological mapping, since this is done structurally and not by type name;
- Compliance and conformance must hold at all interoperability levels (Table 2). Typically:
  - The connective and syntactic categories are dealt with by using the same protocol (such as HTTP) and description language (such as XML and JSON);
  - The semantic category is based on semantic annotations (using languages such as RDF and OWL);
  - The pragmatic category may use BPEL or simply API documentation (implemented by general-purpose programming languages);
  - The symbiotic level is tackled either tacitly or by documentation only.

Current technologies, such as Web Services or RESTful APIs, do not use compliance and conformance. With Web Services both client (consumer) and service (provider) share the WSDL document describing the service. If this changes, both parties need to change. RESTful APIs rely on specifying previously agreed or standardized media types. If a media type is changed, both interacting parties need to be changed.

COMPARISON WITH OTHER APPROACHES

This section performs a broad and qualitative comparison between the framework presented in this chapter, as well as the techniques for reducing coupling, and other existing approaches, already mentioned in the "Background" section.

The Connascence Approach

Page-Jones (1992) recognized different types of coupling, such as name, type, value, position, algorithm, and meaning. In our approach, Table 2 also identifies different levels of interoperability where coupling can occur, but in a more systematized and complete way, from the communications level protocol up to the intentions of the interacting resources. Algorithm corresponds to pragmatics, meaning and type to semantics, position is included in the compliance and conformance checking (for unnamed resources), and name is included in semantics (ontology). It should be noted that Page-Jones' approach was meant for applications and not for distributed resources.

The SOLID Approach

The principles underlying the SOLID approach (Martin, 2003) are universal, although with some adaptations for services and distributed systems. For example, in the SOLID approach the open-closed and Liskov principles are based on inheritance and named subtyping polymorphism, respectively, since they apply to resources in the same application, with their lifecycles synchronized. In our approach, which supports distributed services, these principles are based on structural compliance and conformance. There is no inheritance and named typing across distributed resources, since that would constitute an unacceptable coupling.

Interface segregation is natural in our approach. Structural compliance and conformance limit resource interaction to the actually used features. A resource is affected by a change in another's interface only if it actually uses the changed feature.

Dependency-inversion is dealt with in a similar way in both approaches, although it becomes more flexible in our approach since the notions of abstraction and interface are not mutually bound, thanks to structural compliance and conformance.

The Normalized Systems Approach

Normalized Systems Theory (Mannaert, Verelst, & Ven, 2011) emphasizes stability as a solution for coupling, but does not tackle interoperability with identical importance. The primitive resource types proposed by Mannaert, Verelst & Ven (2012), data, action, workflow, connector, and trigger, are essentially structural building blocks, either in space (code) or in time (control flow). The same happens with the set of possible changes, which essentially deal with adding a new resource or a new feature to an existing resource.

This theory does not explicitly include notions such as ontology changes or workflow compliance and conformance. Changes to resources are considered a deletion and an addition of a new resource, with deletion subject to garbage collection. This means that they will only disappear when no other resource uses them, which constitutes a case of reversed coupling (the lifetime of the provider depends on the consumer's usage). The effects of having a potentially growing number of versions of a resource, in terms of behavior interference, coupling, interoperability, and complexity are hard to assess, particularly in a distributed service environment.

A complete solution to the coupling problem needs to consider not only structural and behavioral stability, but also interoperability at various levels (Table 2) and the other dimensions described in the framework presented in this chapter. Combining both frameworks constitutes an interesting future research work.

The SOA (Web Services) Approach

Web Services (Papazoglou, 2008) are one of the main solutions for enterprise integration today, with the main goal of achieving interoperability between distributed enterprise applications with XML-based technologies. It was a natural evolution of the object-oriented style, now in a distributed environment and with large-grained resources to integrate. Therefore, the emphasis was put in modeling applications as black boxes, by emphasizing their external functionality with an interface composed of a set of operations, application specific.

SOA, the architectural style underlying Web Services, tries to minimize the semantic gap (Ehrig, 2007) by modeling resources as close as possible to real world entities. Since each of these is different from the others, offering a specific set of functionalities, the result is a set of resources with different interfaces (services), with a different set of operations. This implies that the consumer must know the specific interface of the provider. In fact, usually the consumer and the provider share the service's description (a WSDL file), even if the consumer only uses a small fraction of the operations offered by the service.

Another limitation of SOA is that it assumes that all resources are at the same level and that exposing their services is just providing some interface and the respective endpoint. The fallacy is to assert that resource structure is unimportant. This may be true when integrating very large-grained resources, but not in many applications that include lists of resources that need to expose their services individually.

These limitations entail a toll in changeability. Changing the interface of the provider means most likely requiring changes in the consumers as well. Web Services are essentially an interoperability solution, poor on decoupling (the opposite of the Normalized Systems approach).

Modeling real world resources by services is good, since it entails a low semantic gap, but structure needs to be considered as well and service coupling should only involve the operations actually used, not the full WSDL description.

The REST Approach

Interface coupling is precisely what the REST architectural style (Fielding, 2000) tries to avoid, with a simple idea: to decompose complex resources into smaller ones (with links to other resources), until they are so primitive and/or atomic that they can all be treated in the same way, with a common interface. The initial complexity is transferred to the richness of the structure of the links between resources. The most distinguishing feature of REST is this uniform interface for all resources, with a common set of operations. This corresponds to separating the mechanism of traversing a graph (the links between resources) from the treatment of each node (resource). The expectation is that a universal link follow-up mechanism, coupled with a universal resource interface, leads to decoupling between providers and consumers, allowing providers to change what they send to the consumers because these will adapt automatically, by just navigating the structure and following the links to progress in the interaction process.

However, there is a fallacy in this reasoning. The uniform interface approach only works at the syntactic level (Table 2). There are mitigations for this problem at the semantic level, such as SA-REST (Sheth, Gomadam & Lathem, 2007), but the pragmatic and symbiotic levels (Table 2) are not catered for. The reaction of resources needs to be considered, which means that following a link cannot be done blindly. The consumer needs to know which kind of reaction the provider is going to have, to check if it matches its expectations. In the same way, traversing a structured resource implies knowing the type of that resource, otherwise the consumer may not know which link should follow next. This means only one thing: since there is no declaration of resource types, all types of resources to be used must be known in advance, either standardized or previously agreed (with custom media types). This is a relevant limitation of REST. However, what happens in practice is that many developers are more than happy to agree on simple resource structures, and a matched API to follow, than to use more complex technologies, such as Web Services.

As with Web Services, the schemas of complex data are shared, even if only a fraction of the structure of these data is used. Therefore, REST is another interoperability-oriented approach and does not really contribute to solving the coupling problem.

The Structural Services Approach

Delgado (2013) presents an architectural style, Structural Services, based on the framework described in this chapter, including compliance and conformance, which allows a resource:

- To refer to other resources by distributed references (e.g., URIs);
- To return a description of itself, under request (the equivalent of a WSDL document, to be used in compliance and conformance tests);
- To expose its own set of operations, as needed for a low semantic gap in complex resource modeling;
- To expose structure, to easily model resources that are naturally structured;
- To use structural (rather than inheritance-based) polymorphism, for increased interoperability, adaptability and changeability, without the need to have resource types necessarily shared or previously agreed, with the goal of balancing interoperability and coupling concerns.

This corresponds to use the object-oriented paradigm as a foundation, with the addition of distributed references, structural polymorphism, and self-description. It combines the behavior flexibility of SOA's service interfaces with the structural hypermedia capabilities of REST, while providing coupling minimization by using structural interoperability based on compliance and conformance.

It also needs to cater for the semantic and pragmatic levels of Table 2 (the symbiotic level is still dealt with manually, by documentation), as well as to promote performance. Instead of being based on a text-based data description language, such as XML or JSON, it uses a programming language (supporting distributed programming, compliance, and conformance), which is compiled to a binary format, used in message serialization. The service description (the equivalent of a WSDL) is obtained automatically from the program, instead of having to be developed separately. Although compliance and conformance checks are slow, a cache is used to avoid rechecking types that have already been used.

A server and an interpreter complete a universal platform, from which is possible to link to programs in other languages. Lack of space prevents us from providing additional details here, for which the reader is referred to Delgado (2013).

FUTURE RESEARCH DIRECTIONS

Compliance and conformance are basic concepts in interoperability and can be applied to all domains and levels of abstraction and complexity. Although work exists on its formal treatment in specific areas, such as choreographies (Adriansyah, van Dongen & van der Aalst, 2010), an encompassing study needs to be conducted on what is the exact meaning of compatibility (compliance and conformance) at each of the interoperability levels of Table 2. Their formal definition, across all levels, needs to be made in a systematic way, building on previous work.

The interoperability and coupling framework presented in this chapter needs to be improved and made more complete, namely in the Concerns axis, to include relevant concerns such as security and common domain-specific aspects and problems, such as those uncovered by other frameworks and those being systematized by the ENSEMBLE project (Agostinho, Jardim-Goncalves & Steiger-Garcao, 2011).

Non-functional interoperability and coupling are also important, namely in context-aware applications and in those involving SLR (Service Level Requirements) design and management. Detailing how compliance and conformance can be applied in these cases awards additional research. For example, response time conformance between a resource and another that replaces it means being able to respond with a delay that must be within the delay interval of the original resource.

The method to exercise the framework described in this chapter needs to be specified and structured in a systematic way, detailing how it fits agile programming, with a comparative case study regarding agile methods being used today.

CONCLUSION

The problems of coupling and interoperability have been tackled differently by local and distributed applications. The former emphasize coupling, since interoperability is simply based on local pointers and on a type system with shared names. The latter had to solve the interoperability problem first and coupling became an afterthought. Both SOA- and REST-based solutions depend on shared schema data description languages and as a result introduce a higher level of coupling than actually needed.

This chapter contends that both problems, interoperability and coupling, need to be dealt with in a balanced way. The fundamental problem of resource interaction is precisely satisfying the interoperability requirements of the interacting resources while reducing coupling to the minimum level possible. This way, changeability will be maximized and will significantly contribute to the agility of an enterprise when introducing the necessary changes in its EIS.

To achieve these goals, this chapter has presented a multidimensional framework to describe the interoperability and coupling aspects of resources, in an orthogonal fashion, including lifecycle, levels of concreteness, levels of interoperability, and non-functional concerns.

Sharing data types and schemas is a frequent way of introducing more coupling than needed for interoperability. To solve this issue, this chapter proposes the use of structural typing, with type compatibility based on compliance and conformance. Reducing the number of features of a resource on which another depends not only reduces the perceivable width of the interface but also increases the number of providers that are compatible with a consumer, and vice-versa. Coupling metrics have been defined, which show that these effects reinforce each other in the goal of coupling reduction.

REFERENCES

Adriansyah, A., van Dongen, B., & van der Aalst, W. (2010). Towards robust conformance checking. In M. Muehlen & J. Su (Eds.), *Business Process Management Workshops* (pp. 122–133). Berlin, Germany: Springer.

Agostinho, C., Jardim-Goncalves, R., & Steiger-Garcao, A. (2011). Using neighboring domains towards setting the foundations for Enterprise Interoperability science. In Callaos, N. et al. (Eds.) *International Symposium on Collaborative Enterprises in the Context of the 15th World-Multi-Conference on Systemic, Cybernetics and Informatics* (vol. 2, pp. 258-264). Winter Garden, FL: International Institute of Informatics and Systemics.

Alenezi, M., & Magel, K. (2014). Empirical evaluation of a new coupling metric: Combining structural and semantic coupling. *International Journal of Computers and Applications*, *36*(1). doi:10.2316/Journal.202.2014.1.202-3902

Babu, D., & Darsi, M. (2013). A Survey on Service Oriented Architecture and Metrics to Measure Coupling. *International Journal on Computer Science and Engineering*, *5*(8), 726–733.

Bavota, G. (2013). An empirical study on the developers' perception of software coupling. In *International Conference on Software Engineering* (pp. 692-701). Piscataway, NJ: IEEE Computer Society Press. doi:10.1109/ICSE.2013.6606615

Berre, A. (2007). The ATHENA Interoperability Framework. In R. Gonçalves, J. Müller, K. Mertins, & M. Zelm (Eds.), *Enterprise Interoperability II* (pp. 569–580). London, UK: Springer. doi:10.1007/978-1-84628-858-6_62

Chandler, D. (2007). *Semiotics: the basics*. New York, NY: Routledge.

Chappell, D. (2004). *Enterprise service bus*. Sebastopol, CA: O'Reilly Media, Inc.

De Bruyn, P., Van Nuffel, D., Verelst, J., & Mannaert, H. (2012). Towards Applying Normalized Systems Theory Implications to Enterprise Process Reference Models. In A. Albani, D. Aveiro, & J. Barjis (Eds.), *Advances in Enterprise Engineering VI* (pp. 31–45). Berlin, Germany: Springer. doi:10.1007/978-3-642-29903-2_3

Delgado, J. (2012). Structural interoperability as a basis for service adaptability. In G. Ortiz & J. Cubo (Eds.), *Adaptive Web Services for Modular and Reusable Software Development: Tactics and Solutions* (pp. 33–59). Hershey, PA: IGI Global.

Delgado, J. (2013). Architectural Styles for Distributed Interoperability. [IRMJ]. *Information Resources Management Journal*, *26*(4), 40–65. doi:10.4018/irmj.2013100103

Dingsøyr, T., Nerur, S., Balijepally, V., & Moe, N. (2012). A decade of agile methodologies: Towards explaining agile software development. *Journal of Systems and Software*, *85*(6), 1213–1221. doi:10.1016/j.jss.2012.02.033

Ehrig, M. (2007). Ontology alignment: bridging the semantic gap (Vol. 4). New York, NY: Springer Science+Business Media, LLC.

EIF. (2010). *European Interoperability Framework (EIF) for European Public Services, Annex 2 to the Communication from the Commission to the European Parliament, the Council, the European Economic and Social Committee and the Committee of Regions 'Towards interoperability for European public services'*. Retrieved July 21, 2014 from http://ec.europa.eu/isa/documents/isa_annex_ii_eif_en.pdf

Erl, T. (2008). *SOA: Principles of Service Design*. Upper Saddle River, NJ: Prentice Hall PTR.

Euzenat, J., & Shvaiko, P. (2007). *Ontology matching*. Berlin, Germany: Springer.

Faison, T. (2006). *Event-Based Programming*. Berkeley, CA: Apress.

Fielding, R. (2000). *Architectural Styles and the Design of Network-based Software Architectures*. (Doctoral dissertation). University of California at Irvine, CA.

Fricke, E., & Schulz, A. (2005). Design for changeability (DfC): Principles to enable changes in systems throughout their entire lifecycle. *Systems Engineering, 8*(4), 342–359. doi:10.1002/sys.20039

Ganguly, A., Nilchiani, R., & Farr, J. (2009). Evaluating agility in corporate enterprises. *International Journal of Production Economics, 118*(2), 410–423. doi:10.1016/j.ijpe.2008.12.009

Geetika, R., & Singh, P. (2014). Dynamic coupling metrics for object oriented software systems: A survey. *Software Engineering Notes, 39*(2), 1–8. doi:10.1145/2579281.2579296

Heraclitus., & Patrick, G. (Eds.). (2013). The Fragments of Heraclitus. New York, NY: Digireads.com Publishing.

Hock-Koon, A., & Oussalah, M. (2010). Defining metrics for loose coupling evaluation in service composition. In *International Conference on Services Computing* (pp. 362-369). Piscataway, NJ: IEEE Computer Society Press. doi:10.1109/SCC.2010.17

ISO. (2011). *CEN EN/ISO 11354-1, Advanced Automation Technologies and their Applications, Part 1: Framework for Enterprise Interoperability*. Geneva, Switzerland: International Standards Office.

ISO/IEC. (1994). *ISO/IEC 7498-1, Information technology – Open Systems Interconnection – Basic Reference Model: The Basic Model, 2nd edition*. Geneva, Switzerland: International Standards Office. Retrieved July 21, 2014 from http://standards.iso.org/ittf/PubliclyAvailableStandards/index.html

ISO/IEC/IEEE. (2010). *Systems and software engineering – Vocabulary. International Standard ISO/IEC/IEEE 24765:2010(E)* (1st ed., p. 186). Geneva, Switzerland: International Organization for Standardization.

Jeong, B., Lee, D., Cho, H., & Lee, J. (2008). A novel method for measuring semantic similarity for XML schema matching. *Expert Systems with Applications, 34*(3), 1651–1658. doi:10.1016/j.eswa.2007.01.025

Juric, M., & Pant, K. (2008). *Business Process Driven SOA using BPMN and BPEL: From Business Process Modeling to Orchestration and Service Oriented Architecture*. Birmingham, UK: Packt Publishing.

Kim, D., & Shen, W. (2007). An Approach to Evaluating Structural Pattern Conformance of UML Models. In *ACM Symposium on Applied Computing* (pp. 1404-1408). New York, NY: ACM Press. doi:10.1145/1244002.1244305

Kokash, N., & Arbab, F. (2009). Formal Behavioral Modeling and Compliance Analysis for Service-Oriented Systems. In F. Boer, M. Bonsangue, & E. Madelaine (Eds.), *Formal Methods for Components and Objects* (pp. 21–41). Berlin, Germany: Springer-Verlag. doi:10.1007/978-3-642-04167-9_2

Kruchten, P. (2004). *The rational unified process: an introduction*. Boston, MA: Pearson Education Inc.

Lewis, G., Morris, E., Simanta, S., & Wrage, L. (2008). Why Standards Are Not Enough To Guarantee End-to-End Interoperability. In C. Ncube, & J. Carvallo (Eds.) *Seventh International Conference on Composition-Based Software Systems* (pp. 164-173). Piscataway, NJ: IEEE Computer Society Press. doi:10.1109/ICCBSS.2008.25

Liskov, B. (1988). Keynote address-data abstraction and hierarchy. *ACM Sigplan Notices*, *23*(5), 17–34. doi:10.1145/62139.62141

Malik, N. (2009). Toward an Enterprise Business Motivation Model. *The Architecture Journal*, *19*, 10–16.

Mannaert, H., Verelst, J., & Ven, K. (2011). The transformation of requirements into software primitives: Studying evolvability based on systems theoretic stability. *Science of Computer Programming*, *76*(12), 1210–1222. doi:10.1016/j.scico.2010.11.009

Mannaert, H., Verelst, J., & Ven, K. (2012). Towards evolvable software architectures based on systems theoretic stability. *Software, Practice & Experience*, *42*(1), 89–116. doi:10.1002/spe.1051

Martin, R. (2003). *Agile software development: principles, patterns, and practices*. Upper Saddle River, NJ: Prentice Hall PTR.

Monfelt, Y., Pilemalm, S., Hallberg, J., & Yngström, L. (2011). The 14-layered framework for including social and organizational aspects in security management. *Information Management & Computer Security*, *19*(2), 124–133. doi:10.1108/09685221111143060

Morris, E., ... (2004). *System of Systems Interoperability (SOSI): final report. Report No. CMU/SEI-2004-TR-004*. Carnegie Mellon Software Engineering Institute. Retrieved July 21, 2014 from http://www.sei.cmu.edu/reports/04tr004.pdf

O'Rourke, C., Fishman, N., & Selkow, W. (2003). *Enterprise architecture using the Zachman framework*. Boston, MA: Course Technology.

Oguz, F., & Sengün, A. (2011). Mystery of the unknown: Revisiting tacit knowledge in the organizational literature. *Journal of Knowledge Management*, *15*(3), 445–461. doi:10.1108/13673271111137420

Ostadzadeh, S., & Fereidoon, S. (2011). An Architectural Framework for the Improvement of the Ultra-Large-Scale Systems Interoperability. In H. Arabnia, H. Reza, & L. Deligiannidis (Eds.) *International Conference on Software Engineering Research and Practice* (pp. 212-219). Athens, GA: CSREA Press.

Page-Jones, M. (1992). Comparing techniques by means of encapsulation and connascence. *Communications of the ACM*, *35*(9), 147–151. doi:10.1145/130994.131004

Page-Jones, M. (1995). *What every programmer should know about object-oriented design*. New York, NY: Dorset House Publishing.

Palm, J., Anderson, K., & Lieberherr, K. (2003). Investigating the relationship between violations of the law of demeter and software maintainability. *Paper presented at the Workshop on Software-Engineering Properties of Languages for Aspect Technologies.* Retrieved July 21, 2014 from http://www.daimi. au.dk/~eernst/splat03/papers/Jeffrey_Palm.pdf

Papazoglou, M. (2008). *Web services: principles and technology.* Harlow, England: Pearson Education Limited.

Patten, K., Whitworth, B., Fjermestad, J., & Mahinda, E. (2005). Leading IT flexibility: anticipation, agility and adaptability. In N. Romano (Ed.) *11th Americas Conference on Information Systems* (11–14). Red Hook, NY: Curran Associates, Inc.

Pautasso, C., Zimmermann, O., & Leymann, F. (2008). Restful web services vs. "big"' web services: making the right architectural decision. In *International conference on World Wide Web* (pp. 805-814). ACM Press.

Peristeras, V., & Tarabanis, K. (2006). The Connection, Communication, Consolidation, Collaboration Interoperability Framework (C4IF) For Information Systems Interoperability. *International Journal of Interoperability in Business Information Systems, 1*(1), 61-72.

Putnik, G., & Sluga, A. (2007). Reconfigurability of manufacturing systems for agility implementation, part I: requirements and principles. In Digital Enterprise Technology: Perspectives and Future Challenges (pp. 91-98). New York, NY: Springer Science+Business Media.

Saxena, V., & Kumar, S. (2012). Impact of Coupling and Cohesion in Object-Oriented Technology. *Journal of Software Engineering and Applications*, 5(09), 671–676. doi:10.4236/jsea.2012.59079

Shadbolt, N., Hall, W., & Berners-Lee, T. (2006). The semantic web revisited. *IEEE Intelligent Systems*, 21(3), 96–101. doi:10.1109/MIS.2006.62

Sheth, A., Gomadam, K., & Lathem, J. (2007). SA-REST: Semantically interoperable and easier-to-use services and mashups. *IEEE Internet Computing*, 11(6), 91–94. doi:10.1109/MIC.2007.133

Stein, E. (2003). *Re-Engineering the Manufacturing System: Applying the Theory of Constraints.* New York, NY: Marcel Dekker, Inc. doi:10.1201/9780203912508

Wang, W., Tolk, A., & Wang, W. (2009). The levels of conceptual interoperability model: Applying systems engineering principles to M&S. In *Spring Simulation Multiconference* (article no.: 168). San Diego, CA: Society for Computer Simulation International.

Webber, J., Parastatidis, S., & Robinson, I. (2010). *REST in Practice: Hypermedia and Systems Architecture.* Sebastopol, CA: O'Reilly Media, Inc. doi:10.1007/978-3-642-15114-9_3

Wyke, R., & Watt, A. (2002). *XML Schema Essentials.* John Wiley & Sons.

ADDITIONAL READING

Adamczyk, P., Smith, P., Johnson, R., & Hafiz, M. (2011). REST and Web services: In theory and in practice. In E. Wilde & C. Pautasso (Eds.), *REST: from research to practice* (pp. 35–57). New York, NY: Springer. doi:10.1007/978-1-4419-8303-9_2

Athanasopoulos, G., Tsalgatidou, A., & Pantazoglou, M. (2006). Interoperability among Heterogeneous Services. In *International Conference on Services Computing* (pp. 174-181). Piscataway, NJ: IEEE Computer Society Press.

Bravetti, M., & Zavattaro, G. (2007). Towards a unifying theory for choreography conformance and contract compliance. In M. Lumpe, & W. Vanderperren (Eds.) *6th International Symposium on Software Composition* (pp. 34-50). Berlin, Germany: Springer. doi:10.1007/978-3-540-77351-1_4

Bravetti, M., & Zavattaro, G. (2009). A theory of contracts for strong service compliance. *Journal of Mathematical Structures in Computer Science, 19*(3), 601–638. doi:10.1017/S0960129509007658

Castillo, P. et al.. (2013). Using SOAP and REST web services as communication protocol for distributed evolutionary computation. *International Journal of Computers & Technology, 10*(6), 1659–1677.

Chen, D. (2006). Enterprise interoperability framework. In M. Missikoff, A. De Nicola, & F. D'Antonio (Eds.) *Open Interop Workshop on Enterprise Modelling and Ontologies for Interoperability*. Berlin, Germany: Springer-Verlag.

Chen, D., Doumeingts, G., & Vernadat, F. (2008). Architectures for enterprise integration and interoperability: Past, present and future. *Computers in Industry, 59*(7), 647–659. doi:10.1016/j.compind.2007.12.016

Demchenko, Y., Makkes, M., Strijkers, R., & de Laat, C. (2012). Intercloud Architecture for interoperability and integration. In *4th International Conference on Cloud Computing Technology and Science* (pp.666-674). Piscataway, NJ: IEEE Computer Society Press. doi:10.1109/CloudCom.2012.6427607

Diaz, G., & Rodriguez, I. (2009). Automatically deriving choreography-conforming systems of services. In *IEEE International Conference on Services Computing* (pp. 9-16). Piscataway, NJ: IEEE Computer Society Press.

Dillon, T., Wu, C., & Chang, E. (2007). Reference architectural styles for service-oriented computing. In K. Li et al. (Eds.) *IFIP International Conference on Network and parallel computing* (pp. 543–555). Berlin, Germany: Springer-Verlag. doi:10.1007/978-3-540-74784-0_57

Erl, T. (2005). *Service-oriented architecture: concepts, technology and design*. Upper Saddle River, NJ: Pearson Education.

Erl, T., Balasubramanians, R., Pautasso, C., & Carlyle, B. (2011). *Soa with rest: Principles, Patterns & Constraints for Building Enterprise Solutions with REST*. Upper Saddle River, NJ: Prentice Hall PTR.

Esposito, E., & Evangelista, P. (2014). Investigating virtual enterprise models: Literature review and empirical findings. *International Journal of Production Economics, 148*, 145–157. doi:10.1016/j.ijpe.2013.10.003

Fielding, R. (2008). REST APIs must be hypertext-driven. *Roy Fielding's blog: Untangled*. Retrieved July 21, 2014 from http://roy.gbiv.com/untangled/2008/rest-apis-must-be-hypertext-driven

Fielding, R., & Taylor, R. (2002). Principled Design of the Modern Web Architecture. *ACM Transactions on Internet Technology, 2*(2), 115–150. doi:10.1145/514183.514185

Gottschalk, P., & Solli-Sæther, H. (2008). Stages of e-government interoperability. *Electronic Government. International Journal (Toronto, Ont.), 5*(3), 310–320.

Imache, R., Izza, S., & Ahmed-Nacer, M. (2012). An enterprise information system agility assessment model. *Computer science and information systems, 9*(1), 107-133.

Jardim-Goncalves, R., Agostinho, C., & Steiger-Garcao, A. (2012). A reference model for sustainable interoperability in networked enterprises: Towards the foundation of EI science base. *International Journal of Computer Integrated Manufacturing, 25*(10), 855–873. doi:10.1080/0951192X.2011.653831

Jardim-Goncalves, R., Grilo, A., Agostinho, C., Lampathaki, F., & Charalabidis, Y. (2013). Systematisation of interoperability body of knowledge: The foundation for enterprise interoperability as a science. *Enterprise Information Systems, 7*(1), 7–32. doi:10.1080/17517575.2012.684401

Jardim-Goncalves, R., Popplewell, K., & Grilo, A. (2012). Sustainable interoperability: The future of Internet based industrial enterprises. *Computers in Industry, 63*(8), 731–738. doi:10.1016/j.compind.2012.08.016

Khadka, R., ... (2011). Model-Driven Development of Service Compositions for Enterprise Interoperability. In van Sinderen, M., & Johnson, P. (Eds.), Enterprise Interoperability (pp. 177-190). Berlin, Germany: Springer-Verlag. doi:10.1007/978-3-642-19680-5_15

Läufer, K., Baumgartner, G., & Russo, V. (2000). Safe Structural Conformance for Java. [Oxford, UK: Oxford University Press.]. *The Computer Journal, 43*(6), 469–481. doi:10.1093/comjnl/43.6.469

Lewis, G. (2012). The Role of Standards in Cloud-Computing Interoperability, *Software Engineering Institute*, Paper 682. Retrieved July 21, 2014 from http://repository.cmu.edu/sei/682

Li, L., & Chou, W. (2010). Design Patterns for RESTful Communication. In *International Conference on Web Services* (pp. 512-519). Piscataway, NJ: IEEE Computer Society Press.

Loutas, N., Kamateri, E., Bosi, F., & Tarabanis, K. (2011). Cloud computing interoperability: the state of play. In C. Lambrinoudakis, P. Rizomiliotis, & T. Wlodarczyk (Eds.) *International Conference on Cloud Computing Technology and Science* (pp. 752-757). Piscataway, NJ: IEEE Computer Society Press. doi:10.1109/CloudCom.2011.116

Loutas, N., Peristeras, V., & Tarabanis, K. (2011). Towards a reference service model for the Web of Services. *Data & Knowledge Engineering, 70*(9), 753–774. doi:10.1016/j.datak.2011.05.001

Mykkänen, J., & Tuomainen, M. (2008). An evaluation and selection framework for interoperability standards. *Information and Software Technology, 50*(3), 176–197. doi:10.1016/j.infsof.2006.12.001

Pautasso, C. (2009). RESTful Web service composition with BPEL for REST. *Data & Knowledge Engineering, 68*(9), 851–866. doi:10.1016/j.datak.2009.02.016

Popplewell, K. (2011). Towards the definition of a science base for enterprise interoperability: A European perspective. *Journal of Systemics, Cybernetics, and Informatics*, 9(5), 6–11.

Uram, M., & Stephenson, B. (2005). Services are the Language and Building Blocks of an Agile Enterprise. In N. Pal & D. Pantaleo (Eds.), *The Agile Enterprise* (pp. 49–86). New York, NY: Springer. doi:10.1007/0-387-25078-6_4

KEY TERMS AND DEFINITIONS

Agility: The capacity of a system to adapt (reactively and/or proactively) to changes in its environment in a timely and cost efficient manner.

Compliance: Asymmetric property between a consumer C and a provider P (C is compliant with P) that indicates that C satisfies all the requirements of P in terms of accepting requests.

Conformance: Asymmetric property between a provider P and a consumer C (P conforms to C) that indicates that P fulfills all the expectations of C in terms of the effects caused by its requests.

Consumer: A role performed by a service A in an interaction with another B, which involves making a request to B and typically waiting for a response.

Coupling: Degree of dependency of a service on others, either as its consumers or providers, expressing the changes that this service must endure to follow changes in the services with which it interacts.

Interoperability: Asymmetric property between a consumer C and a provider P (C is compatible with P) that holds if C is compliant with P and P is conformant to C.

Interoperability Framework: Set of principles, assumptions, rules and guidelines to analyze, to structure and to classify the concepts and concerns of interoperability.

Lifecycle: Set of stages that a system goes through, starting with a motivation to build it and ending with its destruction. Different versions of a system result from iterations of these stages, in which the system loops back to an earlier stage so that changes can be made.

Provider: A role performed by a service B in an interaction with another A, which involves waiting for a request from A, honoring it and typically sending a response to A.

Chapter 12
Legacy Systems towards Aspect–Oriented Systems

Noopur Goel
VBS Purvanchal University, India

ABSTRACT

Evolution and maintainability of legacy systems is all time attention drawing subject for researchers and especially practitioners. Discovering the crosscutting concerns and separating it from core functionalities of a software system may help in evolution of the legacy systems. Aspect-oriented software development (AOSD) tries to achieve the goal. AOSD is new programming paradigm which helps to bring in modularity in the program by writing the crosscutting concerns in the form of 'aspects'. Modularity brings comprehensibility and hence maintainability of the software system. Tools and techniques, which aid in identifying the crosscutting concerns in such systems and refactoring them into aspects, are needed to apply aspect-oriented techniques to legacy systems at use in industry. This chapter aims to identify issues, problems and approaches used in the migration from legacy systems to aspect-oriented software system.

INTRODUCTION

Legacy systems in business industry are very large and complex systems. Evolution of the software systems is inherent due to many causes. A system decomposed into a well modularized system i.e. functions and classes may have some functionality that cut across that modularity. This is often referred to as tyranny of the dominant decomposition (Tarr, Ossher, Harrison, & Sutton Jr, 1999) and such functionalities are called crosscutting concerns because they are spread over many decomposition units. Examples of crosscutting concerns are logging, synchronization, exception handling, persistence, exception handling, and error management. Many crosscutting concerns are spread, either scattered or tangled, all over the code. This leads to the problem of maintenance and understandability of software systems. Identification and modularization of these crosscutting concerns are very difficult. Aspects-oriented techniques can be applied to the legacy systems in the business industry, i.e. there is a need to migrate the legacy codes into the aspect-oriented systems. Aspects represent the non-functional requirements or behaviors of the system. They are the non-functional requirements or –ilities of the system. In order to transform

DOI: 10.4018/978-1-4666-8510-9.ch012

the legacy systems to aspect-oriented systems, there is a need of tools and techniques that can help in identifying the crosscutting concerns in the systems and refactoring them into aspects. Migration of the legacy codes into the aspect-oriented systems is composed of aspect mining and aspect refactoring.

Aspect Mining is a reverse engineering process of identifying the crosscutting concerns in the given source code of the legacy system that can be potentially converted into aspects. Such concerns are referred to as 'aspects candidates'.

Aspect Refactoring is the process of converting the identified aspect candidates into real aspects in the source code.

Due to the large size of the legacy systems, complexity of the code, lack of documentation, and knowledge about the system, need for tools and techniques that can aid software engineers in locating and documenting, discovering and refactoring concerns is realized. Code duplicity in the legacy systems due to the presence of crosscutting concerns scattered and tangled throughout the system can be separated from the base code using the aspect-oriented technology, thus making the system easier to understand, maintain, and evolve.

This chapter focuses mainly on issues, drawback, approaches, tools and techniques of aspect mining and does not deal with aspect refactoring part. For over more than a decade, researchers have tried to develop tools and techniques to identify crosscutting concerns in previously developed software system, without using Aspect Oriented Programming (AOP).

In AOP, special classes called "aspects" capture crosscutting concerns. Aspects are defined by aspect declarations, which may include pointcut declarations, advice declarations, as well as declaration of those methods, which are permitted in the class declarations. The aspect is woven to produce the final system, using a special tool called weaver.

The techniques which discover crosscutting concerns, scans for either the symptoms of code duplication, code scattering, or code tangling. Code scattering means the code which implements a crosscutting concern is spread across the system. Code tangling means the code which implements some concern is mixed with code from other crosscutting concerns. The main contribution of this chapter is the presentation of state-of art of the aspect mining techniques.

The chapter is organized as follows: Section 2 presents the background of legacy systems (including concepts, issues, challenges in modernization, and various modernization techniques) and concepts of Aspect-Oriented Software Engineering paradigm. Section 3 discusses various issues involved in the evolution of legacy systems to aspect-oriented systems. In section 4, various problems and causes in aspect mining techniques are identified. Section 5 identifies and discusses various aspect mining approaches and techniques proposed by the researchers.

Figure 1. Migrating a legacy system to an aspect-oriented system

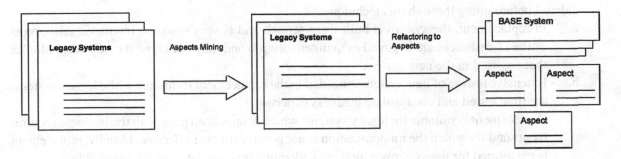

BACKGROUND

Before proceeding towards the issues and challenges, and various tools and techniques used in the migration of legacy systems towards aspect-oriented systems, we must understand the concept of legacy systems, issues/drivers and challenges in the modernization/migration of legacy systems, various modernization techniques, and Aspect-Oriented Software Engineering paradigm.

Legacy Systems

Information Technology is rapidly changing nowadays. In order to keep pace with this technology growth, evolution of software systems has become the key activity in the software industry. Organizations depend heavily on their software systems that have been developed before three decades or more and thus became legacy system. *A legacy system* is any business critical software system that significantly resists modification and their failure can have a serious impact on the business (Khadka, Batlajery, Saeidi, Jansen, & Hage, 2014). A legacy system is vital to any organization. But the constraints in using these legacy system lead to evolution of the same. The system activities can be categorized as (Comella-Dorda, Wallnau, Seacord, & Robert, 2000): maintenance, modernization and replacement. It is very challenging to determine the category of evolutionary activity which is most appropriate at different points in the software life cycle. We need to assess the legacy system and analyze the consequences of each action to make the appropriately decision.

This chapter focuses only on one phase - modernization - in the life of the system. In order to clear the concept of extent of modernisation, the other two phases in the life of the deployed system: maintenance and replacement- are described here in breif.

1. **Maintenance:** Maintenance is an incremental and iterative process in which small changes are made to the system. These changes are often bug corrections or small functional enhancements and should never involve major structural changes (Comella-Dorda *et al.*, 2000). Evolution of any software system needs the support of maintenance activity but it has certain limitations such as:
   a. The competitive advantages obtained by adopting the new technologies are limited.
   b. Increase of maintenance costs of legacy systems with respect to time.
   c. Total impact of many small changes is greater than the sum of the individual changes. Software systems tend to grow in size as efforts are rarely put to remove the unused code.
2. **Replacement:** Replacement (Comella-Dorda *et al.*, 2000, Malinova, 2010) is applicable for legacy systems which do not keep pace with business needs and for which modernization is not possible or cost effective. Generally, the systems which are undocumented, outdated or not extensible are undergone through replacement. Some risks are involved in the replacement, which must be considered before going through this technique:
   a. In replacement, the system is built from scratch and is very resource intensive. Also, most of the IT resources are engaged in maintenance job and may not know the new technologies that are used in the new system.
   b. Extensive testing of new system is needed in the replacement technique while legacy systems are time tested and encapsulate business expertise.
   c. Replacement is suitable for legacy systems which cannot keep pace with the business requirements and for which the modernization is not possible or cost effective. Usually, replacement is performed for the systems which are undocumented, outdated or not extensible.

3. **Software Modernization:** It consists of much broader changes than maintenance, but the important parts of the system are maintained. These changes may be systems restructuring, important functional enhancements, or new software attributes (Comella-Dorda *et al.*, 2000). Long term savings and a competitive advantage can be achieved by funding for innovation. So, "Legacy modernization" is an attempt to evolve legacy system, when conventional practices, such as maintenance and enhancements, can no longer achieve the desired system properties (Iyer, 2008). Software modernization is the process of evolving existing software system by replacing, redeveloping, reusing, or migrating the software components and platforms, when traditional maintenance practices can no longer achieve the desired system properties (Khadka *et al.*, 2014).

Issues in the Use of Legacy System

Followings are the issues involved in the use of legacy systems (Khadka *et al.*, 2014, Iyer, 2008):

1. **To Remain Agile to Change:** In the current scenario the business requirements are changing due to various factors e.g. intra-organizational changes, changes in law and regulations etc. The legacy systems are not flexible to support changing business requirements. Faster time-to- market is one of the drivers for legacy systems modernization.
2. **High Cost of Maintenance:** Cost of maintenance of legacy systems is very high. One of the major factors behind the modernization of legacy system is to reduce the cost maintenance cost.
3. **Lack of Knowledge/Resources:** Lack of knowledge/ resources especially scarcity of experts, unavailability of proper documentation and limited number of suppliers and venders of the legacy system leads to the modernization of legacy system. People knowing the legacy system and its technology may not be more in the organization. Suppliers may stop their products. In that case organization will have to move for another technology to keep supporting their system.
4. **Prone to Failure:** Although legacy systems are perceived as "reliable systems", they are prone to failure due to lack of experts and suppliers/venders. In comparison with other factors, "Prone to failure" is the weakest driver.

Benefits of Legacy System Modernization

Followings are the benefits of modernizing legacy system observed by the practitioners in the industry (Khadka*et al.*, 2014):

1. **Business Critical:** The legacy systems are core systems of the organization. They are very useful for the business, i.e., a system which is old and outdated and is not business critical would never get the status of legacy.
2. **Proven Technology:** Legacy systems are time tested and have been in production environment for the years. Legacies are proven technology as they are stable, always work and are quite good. Proven technology is the reason why they are still in use.
3. **Reliable Systems:** Reliable systems are reliable because they are working for years and the bugs/ technical problems are fixed over years in the past. Quality attributes like stability robustness, reliability and availability are important to this system.

4. **Performance:** Performance of legacy systems is not good in real time systems but enough okay in some cases.

Challenges in the Modernization of Legacy Systems

Some challenges faced by the practitioners during the modernization of legacy systems are as followings (Khadka *et al.*, 2014):

1. **Time Constraint to Finish Modernization:** The major challenge of modernizing legacy system is not finishing of legacy system modernization project in time. The situation mainly arises due to the lack of resources, i.e. documentation and experts. Lack of resources leads to incompletion of modernization of projects in time.

2. **Data Migration:** Data migration in the legacy system modernization project in the industry is also challenging which cannot be performed perfectly. The problem mainly arises because the legacy systems does not support modern database or does not have modern relational database model.

3. **Complex System Architecture:** The complex system architecture of the legacy system leads to non-evolvable system architecture and difficult to extract all the use cases to test which also further leads to a lot of work to compare functionalities from legacy system to a new application.

4. **Lack of Knowledge:** Different types of expertise such as database environment and operating system, middleware enterpriser services bus of architecture are needed. Another type of expert to convert the business functionality from legacy system to new system is also needed. Lack of documentation also contributes to the risk to migrate the legacy system to new one.

5. **Difficult to Extract and Prioritize Business Logic:** Lack of knowledge leads to a serious challenge to identify/extract, document and implement the business logic from the legacy system during the modernization. Prioritizing the extraction of this business logic is also equally important.

6. **Resistance from Organization:** One of the resistances is from technical staff and users of the organization. They have fear that they will not be more needed in the organization as their knowledge will become obsolete. Another resistance is from the cultural side. They think that their employees will face difficulties to adapt the new technology.

7. **Addressing Soft Factors of Modernization:** Three soft factors are people, communication and business values of the organization. The practitioners have identified these soft factors as challenges- communicating the reasons/ challenges of legacy system followed by securing funding for modernizing project from the top management and predicting return on investment by the top management.

Modernization Techniques

Depending on the required level of system understanding, modernization strategies can be classified into two different categories: "black-box" modernization and "white-box" modernization (Comella-Dorda *et al.*, 2000, Malinova, 2010).

1. Black-Box Modernization requires knowledge of the external interfaces of a legacy system. It involves the examination of input and output of a legacy system to gain the understanding of the system interfaces i.e. external behavior of the system. In black box modernization, usually, "wrap-

ping" is used. Wrapping is defined as "surrounding the legacy system with a software layer which hides the unwanted complexity of the old system and exports a modern interface". Although, it is a black box technique, the knowledge of external behavior is not sufficient for wrapping. The internals of the legacy system must also be known.

2. White-Box Modernization requires an initial reverse engineering process to gain the knowledge of internals of a legacy system. It is more complex and extensive than the black-box approach. Components of the system and their relationships are identified and the system is represented at higher level of abstraction.

   a. Reverse engineering is used in white-box modernization for program understanding. Program understanding consists of domain modeling, extracting information from code using appropriate mechanisms, and creating abstractions which help in understanding of the underlying system structure.

   b. After analyzing and understanding the code, White-box modernization requires some system or code restructuring. Software restructuring is defined as "the transformation from one representation form to another at the same relative abstraction level, while preserving the subject system's external behavior (functionality and semantics)" and is used to add some quality attribute of the system such as maintainability or performance. Program (or code) slicing is the most popular software restructuring technique.

Aspect-Oriented Software Engineering Paradigm

Generally, in large systems, a requirement may be implemented by many components and each component may implement several other requirements. In order to change a single requirement, one must have to understand and change several components. Further, a component may have code for some core functionalities but also have some code that implements various system requirements. The requirements are basically of two types: core functionalities and systems requirements. The core functionalities are known as core concerns and systems requirements are known as crosscutting concerns. Although the procedural or object-oriented programming handles the design and implementation of core concerns but cannot deal with the design and implementation of crosscutting concerns.

Aspect-Oriented Software Engineering (AOSE) is a software development approach which addresses this problem (discussed in the above paragraph) and thus brings many benefits to software engineering as- better modularization, higher productivity, software systems which are easier to reuse, maintain and evolve. AOSE introduces some new concepts like- aspects, join points, point-cut and advice- that must be understood before proceeding further.

- **Aspect:** An aspect is a new modularization unit that defines a crosscutting concern. An aspect includes the definition of a point-cut and the advice which is associated with that concern.
- **Join Point:** It is an event in the executing program where the advice associated with an aspect may be executed.
- **Join Point Model:** It is a set of events that may be referenced in a poincut.
- **Pointcut:** Pointcut is a statement that defines the join points where the associated aspect advice should be executed.
- **Advice:** A piece of code implementing a concern.
- **Weaving:** The integration of advice code at the join points by an aspect weaver is known as weaving.

Issues Involved in the Evolution of Software Systems to AOP

There are many problems with duplication of code scattered throughout in the software system due to the crosscutting concerns. This results in a less maintainable system. This problem is handled by Aspect Oriented Programming by supporting the modularization of crosscutting concerns into aspects. Modularization of software system into aspect oriented system is possible in the presence of aspects, once identified, by incremental refactoring. Following issues arise when considering this strategy (Yuen, & Robillard, 2007):

1. How to identify crosscutting concerns in a system;
2. How to determine if the concern code identified in step 1 is refactorable;
3. How to refactor crosscutting concerns into aspects, either manually or automatically.

Aspect mining addresses the first problem by identifying potential crosscutting concerns in a system using techniques such as fan-in analysis, lexical and dynamic analysis, and version history mining.

Problems and Causes in Aspect Mining Techniques

Problems Faced with Existing Aspect Mining Techniques

Followings are the problems faced with the existing aspect mining techniques (Mens, Kellens, & Krinke, 2008):

1. Poor Precision means a very low percentage of relevant aspects from the set of aspect candidates using a given technique.
2. Poor recall means low proportion of relevant aspect candidates that were identified from the set of all aspect candidates that were present in the source code.
3. Subjectivity implies that depending on the understanding of a person and definition of aspect he uses i.e., something is a candidate aspect according to one person whereas it is not an aspect candidate according to other person.
4. Scalability is derived by two factors: time-efficiency of the tool and amount of user involvement required for a given technique.
5. Empirical validation of the results found with the aspect mining techniques is very difficult.
6. Comparability of results of different techniques is difficult due to poor precision, poor recall, subjectivity, or different kinds of results.
7. Composability of different aspect mining techniques is required but is difficult.
8. Simple crosscutting concerns are not simple because of inconsistent vocabulary usage of implementing the concerns.

Root Causes of the above Mentioned Problems

Followings are the main causes of the above mentioned problems:

1. Inappropriateness of techniques used to mine for aspects,
2. Lack of a precise definition of what makes an aspect, and
3. Inadequate representation of the aspect mining results.

Aspect Mining Tools, Techniques, and Approaches

Various aspect mining tools techniques and approaches are proposed by various researchers till date. There are three main types of aspect mining approaches (Kellens, Mens, & Tonella, 2007), which may help in identifying the crosscutting concerns in a software system. These approaches may be classified as Early Aspect Discovery Techniques, Dedicated Browsers and Automated Aspect Mining Techniques.

EARLY ASPECT DISCOVERY TECHNIQUES

Early aspect mining techniques identify and manage crosscutting properties from the early software development stages (Baniassad, Clements, Araujo, Moreira, Rashid, & Tekinerdogan, 2006) of requirements and domain analysis (Baniassad & Clarke, 2004, Rashid, Sawyer, Moreira & Araújo, 2002, Tekinerdogan&Aksit, 1998) or architecture design (Bass, Klein, & Northrop, 2004). It helps not only to improve the modularity in requirements and architectural design but also the early aspects to take their position into the code as implementation aspects.

The major disadvantage of early aspect discovery techniques is that it cannot be applied to legacy systems where the requirements and architecture documents are usually outdated, obsolete or no more available. The approaches which are based on source codes are more capable.

Dedicated Browsers

The research on aspect mining has started with tools that aid a developer in manually browsing the code while looking for crosscutting concerns. These were the first aspect-mining techniques. In this technique, the programmer introduces a *seed* which may be a word, a field's name or method's name. Then, the associated tool exhibits all the places where seed is found. This technique requires an aspect seed, a location in the code from which the users start their navigation to explore other places in the code, and depends on the user's understanding of the software to be mined.

This technique is also known as *Query-Based or Explorative Search Technique*. But this technique requires that the tool user must have complete knowledge of the system, which is under analysis, as he/she has to introduce the seed. It also takes a lot of time to filter out the displayed result. Various query based aspect-mining tools are proposed by the researchers.

Examples of approaches are as follows:

Aspect Browser (Griswold, Kato, & Yuan, (1999) is the first Aspect mining approach. It uses lexical pattern matching for querying the code. Aspect Mining Tool (Hannemann & Kiczales, 2001) is the extension of lexical search from Aspect Browser with structural search for usage of types within a given piece of code.MultiVisualizerAMTex (Zhang, Gao& Jacobsen, 2002) is an extension of AMT which helps in quantifying the characterization of specific aspect. It uses type information in ranking all types based on how scattered they are throughout the code base. This ranking helps the programmer find scattered concerns. Prism (Zhang & Jacobsen, 2004)is the extension of AMTex, which supports the identification activities using lexical and type-based patterns.

JQuery (Janzen & De Volder, 2003) and Feature Exploration and Analysis Tool (FEAT) (Robillard& Murphy, 2007) are both exploration tools. Through the exploration process they help the user to identify which code is the part of a concern. FEAT is an Eclipse plug-in, based on concern graph and intends to locate, describe and analyze concerns in source code (Robillard & Murphy, 2007). A concern graph uses elements of a concern as nodes in the abstract syntax trees (AST) and their relationships. Once the starting node is found, the graph can be developed incrementally through queries. Jquery uses functional query language to accelerate the incremental process.

Automated Aspect Mining Techniques

In year 2004 and onwards, researchers focused on developing another group of approaches that aim to automatically detect aspects proposing one or more aspect candidates with as little user intervention as possible. Various approaches are used inautomated aspect mining techniques are: metrics, clustering, clone detection techniques, association rules, formal concept analysis, natural language processing, etc.

Analyzing Recurring Patterns of Execution Traces

Brew and Krinke have proposed an aspect mining technique named DynAMiT (Dynamic Aspect Mining Tool) by introducing the concept of execution relations. The kind of relation that may exist between method invocations is termed as *Execution Relation*. Four different execution relations proposed by the authors are: outside-before, outside-after, inside-first and inside-last. The proposed approach is applied both dynamically (Breu & Krinke, 2004) and statically (Krinke & Breu, 2004). In dynamic analysis, the execution relations are obtained from event traces while in static analysis, the execution relations are obtained from control flow graph. Recurring execution patterns, which show the behavioral properties of the software system, are identified and expected to be the crosscutting concerns. Breu (2004) also showed that ambiguities can be removed and results may be improved by using the hybrid approach in which the dynamic information is implemented with static type information.

Formal Concept Analysis

Concept analysis (Ganter & Wille, 1999) is a branch of lattice theory which creates *concepts* if the set of object and attributes describing those objects is given. Thus, the concepts are *maximal grouping of objects that have common attributes*. The partial order defined over a set of all concepts is organized as lattice.

Formal Concept Analysis of Execution Traces

Tonella & Ceccato (2004) proposed *Dynamo*, an aspect mining tool which uses Formal Concept Analysis (FCA), by examining execution traces for recurring execution patterns, to identify potential aspects.

Execution traces are obtained by running an instrument version of program under analysis for a set of scenarios. The relationship between execution traces and executed computational units (procedures, class methods) is subjected to concept analysis. The execution traces associated with the use cases are the *objects* of the concept analysis context, while the executed class methods are the *attributes*. In the resulting concept lattice, the concepts specific of each use case are located, when existing. These are considered as aspect candidates if the following conditions hold:

- **Scattering:** the specific attributes (methods) of the concept belong to more than one class.
- **Tangling:** different methods from the same class are specific to more than one use-case specific concept.

Formal Concept Analysis of Identifiers

Tourw´e & Mens (2004) proposed another aspect mining technique which is based on FCA. The *Delf-STof*tool analyses the source code of a system. This approach performs identifier analysis using FCA algorithm and relies on the assumption that naming conventions are the base for programmers to associate related but distant program entities i.e. methods and classes of the system. The input given to the FCA uses classes and methods in the analyzed program as the *objects* and the identifiers associated with these classes and methods as the *attributes*. Only the groups which contain at least a given number of objects that are crosscutting (i.e. involved methods and classes must belong to at least two different class hierarchies) are chosen concepts that can be used for aspect mining purposes.

From Software Repository

Breu & Zimmermann (2007) were the first to propose Version History based aspect mining approach to identify crosscutting concerns. The approach is based on the *co-change* technique of mining version archives. The idea is: Two items that are changed together in the same transaction are related to each other. Their research is based on the hypothesis that crosscutting concerns evolve within a project over time. Former approaches considered the program at a particular time. The two steped version history based mining process identifies crosscutting concerns by analyzing the location where programmers add a code to a program. In first step, Control Version System (CVS) archives for sets of methods where a call to a particular single method was added are mined. In second step, such simple crosscutting concerns are combined to complex crosscutting concerns. Formal concept analysis provides the framework for an efficient computation. Version History based aspect mining approach scales well.

Natural Language Processing on Source Code

Shepherd, Pollock, & Tourwé (2005) uses the similar technique described above, which is based on the assumption that the crosscutting concerns are often implemented by the use of naming and coding conventions. This approach determines aspect candidates by using *lexical chaining* technique of Natural Language Processing (NLP) information to get groups of related source-code entities representing a crosscutting concern. In *lexical chaining*, a group of words is given as input and semantically strongly related chains of words are output. Chaining algorithm is applied to the comments, method names, field names and class names of the system under analysis to mine the crosscutting concerns. Then, the user of this approach manually examines the resulting chains to choose the possible aspect candidates.

Detecting Unique Methods

Gybels & Kellens (2004, 2005) proposed the "Unique Methods" heuristics to mine for crosscutting concerns. "Unique Methods" is defined as "a method without a return value which implements a message implemented by no other method." Such methods with higher number of calls are identified to find the crosscutting concerns.

Clustering of Related Methods

Many researchers have used Clustering Algorithms to identify the crosscutting concerns. Clustering is defined as organizing data into clusters such that there is high intra-cluster similarity and low inter-cluster similarity. Informally, clustering is "finding natural groupings among objects".

Hierarchical Clustering of Similar Method Names

Shepherd and Pollock (2005) used agglomerative hierarchical clustering to group related methods. The objects to be clustered are the name of the methods of the system under analysis. First, each method is kept in a separate cluster, and then each cluster is merged for those methods whose distance is smaller than the specified value. The authors implemented the technique in Aspect Miner And Viewer (AMAV) tool, a viewing tool which helps users to navigate and analyze the obtained clusters.

Clustering Based on Method Invocation

He, Bai Zhang, & Hu (2005) proposed another aspect mining technique based on cluster analysis using association rules. Clustering technique is used to find the potential crosscutting concerns by finding the methods which are invoked frequently from different modules. The input given to the clustering algorithm is a set of methods along with a distance measure. The distance measure is computed on the Static Direct Invocation Relationship (SDIR) and has a value between 0 and 1, indicating that the methods which get called together are closely related and thus have approximate distance of 0 otherwise they are never called together and thus have distance of 1.

Clustering Based on Vector Space Model

Maisikeli & Mitropoulos (2010) proposed a dynamic aspect mining technique which uses neural network clustering method known as Self Organizing Map (SOM). Various software metrics like: dynamic fan-in/fan-out, information flow, method cohesion contribution, method spread etc. were computed, on a set of legacy programs, to find one that is the most suitable. Clustering is formed by giving vector space model (constructed by using these metrics) as input to the SOM. Then output obtained by SOM is manually analyzed to identify crosscutting concerns.

Moldovan & Serban (2006) proposed an aspect mining approach based on k-means and hierarchical agglomerative clustering, which finds the crosscutting concerns by seeking attributes of code scattering symptoms. In order to group the methods from the software systems (under analysis) into clusters, they used two vector space models and various clustering algorithms (hard k-means clustering, fuzzy clustering, hierarchical clustering, genetic clustering, etc.).

The approach proposed by Moldovan &Serban (2006) is improved in (Serban& Moldovan, 2006, September), by defining a new k-means based clustering algorithm in aspect mining (kAM).

Mcfadden & Mitropoulos (2012) [35] extended the work of Moldovan &Serban (2006) by using clustering algorithms based on six vector space models (two already defined by Moldovan and Serban, and four new one) to compare the outcome of each one.

Genetic Clustering Based Approach (GAM): Serban& Moldovan (2006, October) proposed a new aspect mining algorithm, the vector space model based clustering approach, which attempts to minimize the within cluster variance. GAM is a standard genetic algorithm that uses a heuristic for choosing the number of clusters, from the aspect mining perspective. They also introduced two measures ACcuracy of a Clustering based aspect mining technique (ACC) and Percentage of Analyzed MEthods for a partition (PAME) to evaluate the obtained results.

Clustering Based on Graph

Similar to (Moldovan &Serban, 2006), Serban and Moldovan (2006) proposed a new graph-based approach in aspect mining. They defined the problem of identifying the crosscutting concerns as a search problem in a graph and introduced a Graph Algorithm in Aspect Mining (GAAM) algorithm, which identifies the partition of the analyzed software system. This partition is analyzed to identify the crosscutting concerns from the system.

Clustering Based on Fan-In Analysis (CBFA)

Zhang, Guo & Chen (2008) proposed new aspect mining approach, clustering based fan-in analysis, which recommends aspect candidates in the form of method clusters, instead of single methods. Method clusters are identified using the lexical based clustering approach and a new ranking metric, cluster fan-in, is used to rank the clusters. This approach is independent of programming language. The advantage of the proposed approach is that it improves the mining coverage and reduces the cost of aspect construction during refactoring as compared to methods identifying single occurrences.

Using Meta-Model

Bernardi & Di Lucca (August, 2009) proposed an approach to identify concerns and then crosscutting concerns among them in Java systems by defining the meta-model which represent concerns as a sets of Type Fragments (portion of Type in terms of its members, properties and relationships). System source code is analyzed to identify Type Fragments implementing the Roles where each Role is associated to a concern. Using the clustering algorithm based on the combination of a structural and a lexical distance, those Roles are grouped together which contribute to implement a same semantic concern. Then each cluster of Roles and hence Type Fragments associated to them are assigned to a single more abstract concern. Then crosscutting concern is detected by observing scattering and tangling of Type Fragments within the identified concerns.

Fan-In Analysis

Marin, Van Deursen, & Moonen (2004) performed Fan-in analysis in mining candidate aspects. It searches for methods which are called from various locations and whose functionality is needed across different methods, classes, and packages. To find such methods the fan-in metric for each method is computed using static call graph. Finally, the method implementing scattered cross functionality, which largely affects the code modularity, having high fan-in value is extracted.

Clone Detection

One of the factors that affect the system modularity is code tangling due to Code clones. Code tangling affects the system maintainability and reusability of code. To improve the modularity and maintainability, (code clones are duplicates of code fragments, and are created using either exact replication, or a replication with certain modifications. Based on similarity, code clones are divided in four categories: Type 1 to type 3 are clones based on textual similarity while Type 4 is based on functional similarity. Type 1 clones are exact copies of code fragments except variations in whitespace, comments, and textual layouts. Type 2 clones have identical structure or syntax of code fragments. Besides variations in whitespace, comments, and textual layouts these clones vary in identifiers, literals and types. In Type 3 clones, code statements might have changed, removed or modified along with variations of Type 1 and Type 2 code clones. Type 4 code clones are identical in functionality but are implemented in different syntactic variants. These clones are semantically identical.

Many of these are based on the idea of detecting code duplication:

Using Program Dependency Graphs (PDG) and Abstract Syntax Tree (AST) Based Clone Detection

Shepherd *et al.* proposed the first automatic aspect mining approach based on clone detection. The approach performs on PDG to identify candidate concerns (Shepherd, Gibson, & Pollock, 2004). They base their analysis on AspectJ, especially on "before" advice. Their analysis is performed within *Ophir* (developed in Eclipse environment), a framework developed to support automatic mining analyses and manual or automatic refactoring of aspects. They used the PDG and AST representations of a program to automatically identify aspect. This tool identifies refactoring candidates without the requiring program knowledge or input from the user This method comprises of four steps: First, the automatic aspect mining is performed on a source-level PDG, followed by identifying a set of initial refactoring candidate using a control-based approach, followed by filtration of undesirable candidates, based on data dependence information. At last, in coalescing phase, identifies the similar reported candidates and coalesces the pairs into sets of similar candidates.

Using Token-Matching Based Clone Detection

It uses lexical analysis for tokenizing source code into a stream of tokens used as a basis for clone detection. Token matching (after a language dependent parse) is used by CCFinder (Kamiya, Kusumoto & Inoue, 2002) and JPlag (Prechelt, Malpohl, & Philippsen, 2002) to detect similar patterns of tokens.

Using Metrics-Based Clone Detection

Bruntink, Van Deursen, Van Engelen & Tourwe (2005) had an attempt to evaluate the accuracy and usefulness of clone detection techniques in aspect mining by using three clone detection tools: Bauhaus' ccdiml (2005), CCFinder (Kamiya *et al.* 2002), and PDG-DUP (Komondoor & Horwitz, 2001). Generally, the existing clone detection techniques produce output consisting of pair of clones, i.e., similar pair of code fragments that are clones. The authors extended the work for groups of code fragments which are all similar/clones to each other.

These techniques (Mayrand, Leblanc & Merlo, 1996) are related to hashing algorithms. The values of number of metrics are computed for each part of a program that can be further used to find similar program codes. Bruntnik (2004) extended the work of Bruntink*et al.* (2005) and identified aspect candidates by defining the clone class metrics which measure known maintainability problems such as code duplication and code scattering. Further, these clone class metrics are combined into a grading scheme designed to identify interesting clone classes for the purpose of improving maintainability using aspects.

Using AST Comparison Based Clone Detection

This technique (Baxter, Yahin, Moura, Sant'Anna, & Bier, 1998) uses parsing to represent source code into an abstract syntax tree (AST). Then, clone detection algorithm, CloneDr, uses a comparison of the AST of a program to find matching subtrees (clones).

Using Text-Based Techniques

El-Aziz, Aboutabl & Mostafa (2012) proposed a clone detection technique Differential File Comparison Algorithm (DIFF) (Hunt & McIlroy, 1976) to detect exact clones in source code files. This technique comprises of three phases: Source code normalization, Differential File Comparison, and Extracting exact clones. Being a text-based clone detection technique, firstly, white spaces and comments are removed, followed by implementation of DIFF algorithm which determines the differences of lines between two files. At last, the complement of the difference between two files is determined which results in extracting identical lines in the two source code files.

Using Random Walk Model

Based on a random walk model, the authors (Zhang & Jacobsen, 2007) proposed an aspect mining technique to mining experiences; this paper describes a random walk model to approximate how crosscutting concerns can be discovered in the absence of domain knowledge of the analyzed application. Random walk is a mathematical formulation of a trajectory which takes successive random steps. This technique is implemented on the coupling graphs extracted from the program sources. The idea of page rank algorithm is used to compute the degrees of "popularity" and "significance" for each of the program elements such as components, packages, classes, methods, on the coupling graphs. Using both types of ranks, filtering techniques are applied to generate a final list of candidates representing crosscutting concerns.

Later on, Zhang & Jacobsen (2012) performed the random walks are on concept graphs extracted from the program sources to calculate metrics of "utilization" and "aggregation" for each of the program elements. Since, complete graph structure is considered and fan-in, fan-out and transitive nature is also taken into account, many false classifications are avoided and hence improve the result. Ranking all the program elements is based on these metrics and use a threshold to produce a set of candidates that represent crosscutting concerns.

Natural Language Processing on Requirements

Mining Early Aspects from Requirements

The authors (Sampaio, Loughran, Rashid, & Rayson, 2005) proposed a new technique which uses corpus-based Natural Language Processing (NLP) techniques to effectively identify early aspects. This approach is semi automatic that enable an efficient context sensitive analysis of textual documents. It helps requirements engineer to identify aspects from requirement documents or even unstructured sources of requirements (such as interviews, natural language description of the system), and create a structured aspect-oriented model of the requirements. Besides helping in change management and traceability of requirements in a more effective manner, early identification and documentation of crosscutting concerns also improves in early identification of candidate aspects in design and implementation stages.

EA-Miner Tool Based Approach

Sampaio & Rashid (2008) used EA-Miner tool based approach, which is an automated support for identifying model abstractions and structure abstractions into various models, after the initial investigation of which NLP techniques could be used to help with Aspect-Oriented Requirement Engineering (AORE) automation (Sampaio *et al.*, 2005). The mining tool interacts needs the documents and passes it to the natural language processor WMATRIX (uses corpus based NLP approach) which can produce analyses that helps to identify concerns and viewpoints using natural language processing techniques. The aim of authors for EA-Miner is to offer a framework (tool + guidelines) that can be used with any AORE approach. The activities of EA-Miner consist of:

1. Eliciting Requirements from Stakeholders and Documenting,
2. Identification of Requirements Model Concepts,
3. Structuring the Requirements Specification, and
4. Validating Requirements and Resolving Conflicts.

Using Information Retrieval Technique

Zhu *et al.* (2013) proposed to identify the composite crosscutting concerns. Composite crosscutting concerns (CC) consist of CC seeds and relative program elements which makes the composite CC very difficult. First they adopted the link analysis technique to generate CC seeds. Then a coupling graph, showing the relationship between CC seeds is constructed. They used *community detection technique* to generate group of CC seeds as constraints for semi supervised learning. They proposed the semi-supervised clustering (an information retrieval technique) approach, constrained authority-shift clustering, to identify composite CC.

The authors Huang, Lu, & Yang (2010, August) used link analysis of information retrieval technique to design the computational model with two state model followed by ranking approach for the selection of CC candidates. The proposed a new algorithm is based on the link analysis of information retrieval technology and describes two-state model and ranking model to discover the "scatter" and "centralization" states of each node in concern graph for aspect mining. The approach is based on the assumption that concern graphs extracted from programs can show the programmers' purpose more consistently than the information from Control Version System (CVS). For mining crosscutting concerns, two kinds of software elements: implementation elements and integration elements are needed. Implementation elements performs concrete jobs such as string operations and memory operations while integration elements play role of organizing sub-operations such as function *main*. Implementation elements are called by other elements while integration elements call the elements which often finish part of the whole job.

Aspect Mining Based on Association Rules

Vidal, Abait, Marcos, Casas, & Díaz Pace (2009) proposed a semi automated approach which helps developer to discover the aspect candidates using proper aspect mining technique and then refactors them to transform into aspect-oriented system. The approach uses the method's associations from the systems execution traces obtained using dynamic analysis. It gives information about the behavior of the system to identify scattering symptoms. This approach is based on association rules which need two inputs: execution traces and execution relations. The execution trace is a sequence of method invocations during the execution of the program, and the execution relations registers the invocations from one method to another. Execution traces and execution relations are obtained by running the program under given scenarios.

Aspect Mining Based on Method Call Tree

The authors (Qu, & Liu, 2007, April) proposed an automated static aspect mining approach, which is based on the method call tree. Method call traces are generated with the help of method call tree. These traces are investigated for recurring method patterns on different constraints, such as, the requirement that the patterns exist in always the same composition and in different calling contexts in the method call trace.

Software Repository Mining

Software Repository Mining deals with extracting implicit information from software repositories, e.g. version control systems (VCS) such as CVS and Subversion. Mining VCS helps to uncover those relations which cannot be present in the source code. Mining VCS helps the user to show logical coupling: "implicit and evolutionary dependencies between the artifacts of a software system which, although potentially not structurally related, evolve together and are therefore linked to each other from an evolutionary point of view". This co-change information provides a new perspective on finding crosscutting concerns in software system, using data mining techniques.

Using Frequent Itemset Mining

The authors (Mulder & Zaidman, 2010) proposed the *Frequent Itemset Mining* (FIM) technique, to mine for items that are frequently changed together, which traces out specific relations in a database. They developed a tool-chain which mines version history at two levels of granularity: considering the names of the files which have been changed in each transaction (file--level) or mining at the finer-grained level of methods (method-level).

Using Historical Code Changes

Adams, Jiang & Hassan (2010) proposed a history-based concern mining technique named COMMIT ("COncern Mining using Mutual Information over Time") which addresses three key shortcomings in the concern mining process. First, to overcome the inability to merge seeds with variations, statistical clustering mechanism is applied to small and large variations in the instances of a concern. Second, to overcome the tendency to ignore important facets of seeds e.g., state of seeds (variables and types) and preprocessor entities (macros), COMMIT incorporates dependencies on behavior, state and preprocessor entities to point out different facets of seeds. Third, Commit considers the relation between each collaborating concerns separately. COMMIT analyses the source code history to statistically cluster functions, variables, types and macros which have been changed together intentionally.

Analyzing Line- Co-Change

The authors (Canfora, Cerulo, & Di Penta, 2006) proposed line co-changes as a technique for identifying the crosscutting concerns. This technique is performed on versioning system such as CVS with the aim of identification of source code lines which have been changed together in a commit transaction. They also showed that the performance is effectively improved when used with clone detection instead of using other approaches.

By Analysis of Type Hierarchies

The authors (Bernardi& Di Lucca, October2009) described that the ConAn Tool supports to analyzethe type hierarchies present in the object-oriented systems that helps in identifying the class members which are scattered and tangled across each class hierarchy, and in identifying Type Fragments which represents the portion of a Type in terms of its members and relationship, implementing static crosscutting concerns. The structural information of Type Fragments consisting of each concern and the crosscutting relationships among these concerns help to reengineer towards aspects.

Data Mining By Analysis of Coding Patterns

In order to identify candidate aspects, the authors (Ishio, Miyake & Inoue, 2008) have proposed a sequential data mining approach by identifying coding patterns in Java programs. Coding patterns are frequent sequence of method calls and control statements to implement a specific behavior. They applied *Prefix scan algorithm* to the sequence database, obtained from the translation of Java source code with respect to the defined set of rules.

Using Similar Interaction Concept

Nguyen, Nguyen, Nguyen & Nguyen (2011) proposed a new approach to identify those cluster of code units called *concern peers* which possibly share some crosscutting concerns, rank and recommend them for creating and updating aspects. These concern peers are identified depending on their similar interactions (similar calling relations in similar contexts, either internally or externally). These recommendations are applicable to both the aspectization of non-aspect-oriented programs (to create aspects) and for evolution of aspect-oriented programs (to update aspects).

Using Dataflow Abstraction

Trifu (2008) proposed a novel semi-automatic *data-oriented abstraction* of a concern approach to identify concerns. The proposed approach starts from a set of variables and uses static dataflow information to determine the concern skeleton. The approach aims to improve software understanding.

Model-Driven Plan-Based Approach

Nora & Ghoul (2006) proposed an automatic approach to aspect mining which perceives the code as a set of concerns inter-related by different kinds of relationship. The concern miner analyzes the source code (program model) and verifies if the program model implements models of concerns. The program dependence model is transformed to a more abstract model by using the concern library. The transformation of the concrete concerns in a program to the concern-oriented model is treated as model transformation. The concern library provides the concern descriptions in terms of *plans*. The plan refers to a unit of knowledge required to identify a crosscutting concern.

Using Idiom Driven Approach

The authors (Marin, van Deursen, Moonen, & van der Rijst, 2009) proposed a systematic approach for migration of crosscutting concerns existing in object-oriented system to aspect-oriented system, which consists of four steps: mining, exploration, documentation and refactoring of crosscutting concerns. The aspect candidates are identified using idiom-driven approach. Classification and decomposition of crosscutting concerns is the basis of crosscutting concern Sorts. Sort describes an implementation idiom and relation of crosscutting concerns. The mining strategy utilizes sort-specific idioms, which are in a specific sort, to define search-goals.

Combining Recurring Execution Relations Analysis and Fan-In Analysis

Dongjin, Xiang, & Yunlei (2014) proposed a new comprehensive approach based on the combination of the analysis of recurring execution relations and fan-in analysis. Four types of execution relations for neighboring methods (exit-entry, entry-exit, entry-entry and exit-exit) are identified by analyzing the execution traces. Then, method's left crosscutting degrees are measures which ensures that the candidate aspect recurs in a similar running context, whereas the measure of right crosscutting degrees shows how many times the candidate crosscuts different methods. The candidate aspects are obtained with methods having higher fan-in value along with the universal entry or exit of them in same running context.

CONCLUSION

Mining techniques for crosscutting concerns are very important for software maintenance, reverse engineering, reengineering and even for re-documentation (Marin, Deursen, & Moonen, 2007). Since, legacy systems are very large in size, having very complex architecture (code clones are spread all over the system) and involve several kinds of crosscutting concerns, e.g. patterns architectural styles, business rules and non-functional properties, mining the aspects from these systems are very difficult.

This chapter presents a survey of issues in the transformation of legacy systems to aspect oriented systems, problems faced with the existing techniques and causes of these problems and various approaches used in aspect mining to identify potential aspects. Presentation of various tools and techniques in this chapter reflects that the mining techniques are applied on the requirements, source codes and repositories to identify the crosscutting concerns. It is also revealed from the literature that the full automation (i.e. without requiring any input from the user) of aspect mining techniques is a very tedious process. The tools are limited as sorting out the real aspects from the aspect candidates is a manual task. This attempt may help the researchers and practitioners to clarify various concepts used in the migration of legacy system towards aspect-orientated system.

REFERENCES

Adams, B., Jiang, Z. M., & Hassan, A. E. (2010). Identifying crosscutting concerns using historical code changes. In *Proceedings of the 32ⁿᵈ ACM/IEEE International Conference on Software Engineering* (vol. 1, pp. 305-314). ACM/IEEE. doi:10.1145/1806799.1806846

Ajila, S. A., Gakhar, A. S., & Lung, C. H. (2013). Aspectualization of code clones—an algorithmic approach. *Information Systems Frontiers, 16*(5), 835–851. doi:10.1007/s10796-013-9428-7

Baniassad, E., & Clarke, S. (2004). Theme: An approach for aspect-oriented analysis and design. In *Proceedings of the 26ᵗʰ International Conference on Software Engineering* (pp. 158-167). Academic Press. doi:10.1109/ICSE.2004.1317438

Baniassad, E., Clements, P. C., Araujo, J., Moreira, A., Rashid, A., & Tekinerdogan, B. (2006). Discovering early aspects. *IEEE Software, 23*(1), 61–70. doi:10.1109/MS.2006.8

Bass, L., Klein, M., & Northrop, L. (2004). Identifying aspects using architectural reasoning. In *Proceedings of the Workshop on Early Aspects: Aspect-Oriented Requirements Engineering and Architecture Design* (pp. 51-57). Academic Press.

Baxter, I. D., Yahin, A., Moura, L., Sant'Anna, M., & Bier, L. (1998). Clone detection using abstract syntax trees. In *Proceedings of the International Conference on Software Maintenance* (pp. 368-377). Academic Press. doi:10.1109/ICSM.1998.738528

Bernardi, M. L., & Di Lucca, G. A. (2009). A role-based crosscutting concerns mining approach to evolve java systems towards AOP. In *Proceedings of the Joint International and Annual ERCIM Workshops on Principles of Software Evolution (IWPSE) and software evolution (Evol) workshops* (pp. 63-72). ERCIM. doi:10.1145/1595808.1595822

Bernardi, M. L., & Di Lucca, G. A. (2009). ConAn: A tool for the identification of crosscutting concerns in object oriented systems based on type hierarchy analysis. In *Proceedings of the 16ᵗʰ Working Conference on Reverse Engineering* (pp. 319-320). Academic Press. doi:10.1109/WCRE.2009.38

Bisbal, J., Lawless, D., Wu, B., Grimson, J., Wade, V., Richardson, R., & O'Sullivan, D. (1997) An overview of legacy information system migration. In *Proceedings of the Asia Pacific Software Engineering Conference and International Computer Science Conference* (pp. 529-530). Academic Press. doi:10.1109/APSEC.1997.640219

Breu, S. (2004). Towards hybrid aspect mining: Static extensions to dynamic aspect mining. In *Proceedings of the 1ˢᵗ Workshop on Aspect Reverse Engineering*. Academic Press.

Breu, S., & Krinke, J. (2004). Aspect mining using event traces. In *Proceedings of the 19ᵗʰ International Conference on Automated Software Engineering* (pp. 310-315). Academic Press.

Breu, S., & Zimmermann, T. (2006). Mining aspects from version history. In *Proceedings of the 21st IEEE/ACM International Conference on Automated Software Engineering* (pp. 221-230). IEEE/ACM. doi:10.1109/ASE.2006.50

Breu, S., Zimmermann, T., & Lindig, C. (2006). Mining eclipse for crosscutting concerns. In *Proceedings of the 2006 International Workshop on Mining Software Repositories* (pp. 94-97). Academic Press. doi:10.1145/1137983.1138006

Bruntink, M. (2004). Aspect mining using clone class metrics. In *Proceedings of the 1st Workshop on Aspect Reverse Engineering*. Academic Press.

Bruntink, M., Van Deursen, A., Van Engelen, R., & Tourwe, T. (2005). On the use of clone detection for identifying crosscutting concern code. *IEEE Transactions on Software Engineering, 31*(10), 804–818. doi:10.1109/TSE.2005.114

Canfora, G., Cerulo, L., & Di Penta, M. (2006). On the use of line co-change for identifying crosscutting concern code. In *Proceedings of the 22nd IEEE International Conference on Software Maintenance* (pp. 213-222). IEEE. doi:10.1109/ICSM.2006.43

Comella-Dorda, S., Wallnau, K., Seacord, R. C., & Robert, J. (2000). *A survey of legacy system modernization approaches, (No. CMU/SEI-2000-TN-003)*. Carnegie-Mellon University Pittsburgh Pa Software Engineering Institute.

D'Ambros, M., & Lanza, M. (2006). Reverse engineering with logical coupling. In *Proceedings of the 13th Working Conference on Reverse Engineering*. Washington, DC: IEEE Computer Society.

Dongjin, Y. U., Xiang, S. U., & Yunlei, M. U. (2014). Towards the Identification of Crosscutting Concerns: A Comprehensive Dynamic Approach Based on Execution Relations. *IEICE Transactions on Information and Systems, 97*(5), 1235–1243.

El-Aziz, R. M. A., Aboutabl, A. E., & Mostafa, M. S. (2012). Clone Detection Using DIFF Algorithm for Aspect Mining. *International Journal of Advanced Computer Science & Applications, 3*(8), 137–140.

Ganter, B., & Wille, R. (1999). *Formal concept analysis: Mathematical foundations*. Berlin: Springer-Verlag Berlin Heidelberg. doi:10.1007/978-3-642-59830-2

Griswold, W. G., Kato, Y., & Yuan, J. J. (1999). *Aspect Browser: Tool support for managing dispersed aspects*. In *First Workshop on Multi-Dimensional Separation of Concerns in Object-Oriented Systems*.

Gybels, K., & Kellens, A. (2004). An experiment in using inductive logic programming to uncover pointcuts. *European Interactive Workshop on Aspects in Software*.

Gybels, K., & Kellens, A. (2005). *Experiences with identifying aspects in smalltalk using 'unique methods'*. In *Workshop on Linking Aspect Technology and Evolution*.

Hannemann, J., & Kiczales, G. (2001). Overcoming the prevalent decomposition in legacy code. In *Proceedings of Workshop on Advanced Separations of Concerns, 23rd International Conference on Software Engineering (ICSE)*. Toronto, Canada: Academic Press.

He, L., Bai, H., Zhang, J., & Hu, C. (2005). AMUCA algorithm for aspect mining. In *Proceedings of the 17th International Conference on Software Engineering and Knowledge Engineering* (SEKE, 2005), (pp. 520-524). SEKE.

Huang, J., Lu, Y., & Yang, J. (2010). Aspect mining using link analysis. In *Proceedings of the 5ᵗʰ International Conference on Frontier of Computer Science and Technology* (pp. 312-317). Academic Press.

Hunt, J. W., & McIlroy, M. D. (1976). *An algorithm for differential file comparison.* Computing Science Technical Report 41. Bell Laboratories.

Ishio, T., Miyake, T., & Inoue, K. (2008). Mining coding patterns to detect crosscutting concerns in java programs. In *Proceedings of the 15th Working Conference on Reverse Engineering* (pp. 123-132). IEEE. doi:10.1109/WCRE.2008.28

Iyer, V. N. (2008). *Legacy Modernization- Modernize and Scale. View point.* Infosys.

Janzen, D., & De Volder, K. (2003). Navigating and querying code without getting lost. In *Proceedings of the 2nd International Conference on Aspect-Oriented Software Development* (pp. 178-187). ACM. doi:10.1145/643603.643622

Kamiya, T., Kusumoto, S., & Inoue, K. (2002). CCFinder: A multilinguistic token-based code clone detection system for large scale source code. *IEEE Transactions on Software Engineering, 28*(7), 654–670. doi:10.1109/TSE.2002.1019480

Kellens, A., Mens, K., & Tonella, P. (2007). A survey of automated code-level aspect mining techniques. In A. Rashid & M. Akshit (Eds.), Transactions on Aspect-Oriented Software Development IV (LNCS), (vol. 4640, pp. 143–162). Berlin: Springer-Verlag. doi:10.1007/978-3-540-77042-8_6

Khadka, R., Batlajery, B. V., Saeidi, A., Jansen, S., & Hage, J. (2014). How do professionals perceive legacy systems and software modernization? In *Proceedings of the 36ᵗʰ International Conference on Software Engineering* (pp. 36-47). ACM New York. doi:10.1145/2568225.2568318

Komondoor, R., & Horwitz, S. (2001). Using slicing to identify duplication in source code. Static Analysis. In *Proceeding of the 8th International Symposium on Static Analysis SAS '01* (pp. 40-56). London, UK: Springer-Verlag.

Krinke, J., & Breu, S. (2004). *Control-flow-graph-based aspect mining.* 1st *Workshop on Aspect Reverse Engineering.*

Maisikeli, S. G., & Mitropoulos, F. J. (2010). Aspect mining using self-organizing maps with method level dynamic software metrics as input vectors. In *Proceedings of the 2nd International Conference on Software Technology and Engineering* (*Vol. 1*, pp. V1-212 - V1-217). IEEE. doi:10.1109/ICSTE.2010.5608880

Malinova, A. (2010). *Approaches and techniques for legacy software modernization.* Plovdiv: Bulgaria Scientific Works.

Marin, M., Deursen, A. V., & Moonen, L. (2007). Identifying crosscutting concerns using fan-in analysis. *ACM Transactions on Software Engineering and Methodology, 17*(1), 3. doi:10.1145/1314493.1314496

Marin, M., Van Deursen, A., & Moonen, L. (2004). Identifying aspects using fan-in analysis. In *Proceedings of the 11th Working Conference on Reverse Engineering* (pp. 132-141). IEEE. doi:10.1109/WCRE.2004.23

Marin, M., van Deursen, A., Moonen, L., & van der Rijst, R. (2009). An integrated crosscutting concern migration strategy and its semi-automated application to JHotDraw. *Automated Software Engineering, 16*(2), 323–356. doi:10.1007/s10515-009-0051-2

Mayrand, J., Leblanc, C., & Merlo, E. M. (1996). Experiment on the automatic detection of function clones in a software system using metrics. In *Proceedings of the International Conference on Software Maintenance* (pp. 244-253). IEEE. doi:10.1109/ICSM.1996.565012

Mcfadden, R. R., & Mitropoulos, F. J. (2012). Aspect mining using model-based clustering. In *Proceedings of the Southeast Conference* (pp. 1-8). IEEE.

Mens, K., Kellens, A., & Krinke, J. (2008). Pitfalls in aspect mining. In *Proceedings of the 15th Working Conference on Reverse Engineering* (pp. 113-122). IEEE.

Moldovan, G. S., & Serban, G. (2006). Aspect mining using a vector-space model based clustering approach. In *Proceedings of Linking Aspect Technology and Evolution Workshop* (pp. 36-40). Academic Press.

Mulder, F., & Zaidman, A. (2010). Identifying crosscutting concerns using software repository mining. In *Proceedings of the Joint ERCIM Workshop on Software Evolution and International Workshop on Principles of Software Evolution* (pp. 23-32). ACM. doi:10.1145/1862372.1862381

Nguyen, T. T., Nguyen, H. V., Nguyen, H. A., & Nguyen, T. N. (2011). Aspect recommendation for evolving software. In *Proceedings of the 33rd International Conference on Software Engineering* (pp. 361-370). ACM.

Nora, B., & Ghoul, S. (2006). A model-driven approach to aspect mining. In *Proceedings of the 27th International Conference on Software Engineering* (pp. 361-370). Academic Press.

Prechelt, L., Malpohl, G., & Philippsen, M. (2002). Finding plagiarisms among a set of programs with JPlag. *Journal of Universal Computer Science, 8*(11), 1016–1038.

Project Bauhaus. (2005). Retrieved from http://www.bauhaus-stuttgart.de

Qu, L., & Liu, D. (2007). Aspect mining using method call tree. In *Proceedings of the International Conference on Multimedia and Ubiquitous Engineering* (pp. 407-412). IEEE.

Rashid, A., Sawyer, P., Moreira, A., & Araújo, J. (2002). Early aspects: A model for aspect-oriented requirements engineering. In *Proceedings of the Joint International Conference on Requirements Engineering* (pp. 199-202). IEEE. doi:10.1109/ICRE.2002.1048526

Robillard, M. P., & Murphy, G. C. (2007). Representing concerns in source code. *ACM Transactions on Software Engineering and Methodology, 16*(1), 3, es. doi:10.1145/1189748.1189751

Sampaio, A., Loughran, N., Rashid, A., & Rayson, P. (2005). Mining aspects in requirements. In *Proceedings of the Early Aspects: Aspect-Oriented Requirements Engineering and Architecture Design Workshop* (held with AOSD 2005). Chicago, IL: AOSD.

Sampaio, A., & Rashid, A. (2008). *Mining early aspects from requirements with EA-Miner*. In *Proceedings of the Companion of the 30th International Conference on Software Engineering* (pp. 911-912). ACM. doi:10.1145/1370175.1370183

Serban, G., & Cojocar, G. S. (2007). A New Graph-Based Approach in Aspect Mining. In *Proceedings of the International Conference on Knowledge Engineering* (pp. 252-260). Academic Press.

Serban, G., & Moldovan, G. S. (2006). A Graph Algorithm for Identification of Crosscutting Concerns. *Studia Universitatis Babes-Bolyai. Informatica, LI*(2), 53–60.

Serban, G., & Moldovan, G. S. (2006). A new genetic clustering based approach in aspect mining. In *Proceedings of the 8th WSEAS International Conference on Mathematical Methods and Computational Techniques in Electrical Engineering* (pp. 135-140). WSEAS.

Serban, G., & Moldovan, G. S. (2006). A new k-means based clustering algorithm in aspect mining. In *Proceedings of the Eighth International Symposium on Symbolic and Numeric Algorithms for Scientific Computing* (pp. 69-74). Timisoara: IEEE. doi:10.1109/SYNASC.2006.5

Shepherd, D., Gibson, E., & Pollock, L. L. (2004). Design and Evaluation of an Automated Aspect Mining Tool. In *Proceedings of the International Conference on Software Engineering Research and Practice* (pp. 601-607). Academic Press.

Shepherd, D., & Pollock, L. (2005). Interfaces, aspects, and views. In *Proceedings of the Workshop on Linking Aspect Technology and Evolution at International Conference on Aspect Oriented Software Development* (pp. 1-6). Academic Press.

Shepherd, D., Pollock, L., & Tourwé, T. (2005). Using language clues to discover crosscutting concerns. *Software Engineering Notes, 30*(4), 1–6. doi:10.1145/1082983.1083129

Tarr, P., Ossher, H., Harrison, W., & Sutton, S. M. Jr. (1999). N degrees of separation: multi-dimensional separation of concerns. In *Proceedings of the 21st International Conference on Software Engineering* (pp. 107-119). ACM.

Tekinerdogan, B., & Aksit, M. (1998). Deriving design aspects from conceptual models. In S. Demeyer & J. Bosch (Ed.), *Object-Oriented Technology: ECOOP'98 Workshop Reader: Proceedings of the ECOOP' 98 Workshops, Demos, and Posters* (LNCS), (Vol. 1543, pp.410-413). Brussels, Belgium: Springer. doi:10.1007/3-540-49255-0_122

Tonella, P., & Ceccato, M. (2004). Aspect mining through the formal concept analysis of execution traces. In *Proceedings of the 11th Working Conference on Reverse Engineering* (pp. 112-121). IEEE. doi:10.1109/WCRE.2004.13

Tourwe, T., & Mens, K. (2004). Mining aspectual views using formal concept analysis. In *Proceedings of the 4th IEEE International Workshop on Source Code Analysis and Manipulation* (pp. 97-106). IEEE. doi:10.1109/SCAM.2004.15

Trifu, M. (2008). Using dataflow information for concern identification in object-oriented software systems. In *Proceedings of the 2008 12th European Conference on Software Maintenance and Reengineering* (pp. 193-202). Washington, DC: IEEE Computer Society. doi:10.1109/CSMR.2008.4493314

Vidal, S., Abait, E. S., Marcos, C., Casas, S., & Díaz Pace, J. A. (2009). Aspect mining meets rule-based refactoring. In *Proceedings of the 1st Workshop on Linking Aspect Technology and Evolution* (pp. 23-27). New York: ACM. doi:10.1145/1509847.1509852

Yuen, I., & Robillard, M. P. (2007). Bridging the gap between aspect mining and refactoring. In *Proceedings of the 3rd Workshop on Linking Aspect Technology and Evolution* (pp. 1-6). New York: ACM. doi:10.1145/1275672.1275673

Zhang, C., Gao, D., & Jacobsen, H. A. (2002). *Extended aspect mining tool*. Retrieved from http://www.eecg. utoronto. ca/~czhang/amtex

Zhang, C., & Jacobsen, H. A. (2004). Prism is research in aspect mining. In *Proceedings of the OOPSLA'04 Companion to the 19th Annual ACM SIGPLAN Conference on Object-Oriented Programming Systems, Languages, and Applications* (pp. 20-21). New York: ACM. doi:10.1145/1028664.1028676

Zhang, C., & Jacobsen, H. A. (2007). Efficiently mining crosscutting concerns through random walks. In *Proceedings of the 6th International Conference on Aspect-Oriented Software Development* (pp. 226-238). ACM. doi:10.1145/1218563.1218588

Zhang, C., & Jacobsen, H. A. (2012). Mining crosscutting concerns through random walks. *IEEE Transactions on Software Engineering, 38*(5), 1123–1137. doi:10.1109/TSE.2011.83

Zhang, D., Guo, Y., & Chen, X. (2008). Automated aspect recommendation through clustering-based fan-in analysis. In *Proceedings of the 23rd IEEE/ACM International Conference on Automated Software Engineering* (pp. 278-287). IEEE. doi:10.1109/ASE.2008.38

Zhu, J., Huang, J., Zhou, D., Carminati, F., Zhang, G., & He, Q. (2013). Identifying composite crosscutting concerns through semi-supervised learning. *Software, Practice & Experience, 44*(12), 1525–1545. doi:10.1002/spe.2234

KEY TERMS AND DEFINITIONS

Aspects: An *aspect* is a new modularization unit that defines a crosscutting concern. There are several different approaches to handling this functionality. One of them is Aspect Oriented Programming (AOP)- a methods where metadata is used to insert crosscutting code directly into the compiled output or during run time execution.

Code Scattering: The implementation of a concern is *scattered* if its code is spread out over multiple modules. The concern affects the implementation of multiple modules.

Code Tangling: The implementation of a concern is *tangled* if its code is intermixed with code that implements other concerns.

Crosscutting Concerns: Most software applications contain common functionalities, which are distributed over layers and tiers. These functionalities support operations such authentication, authorization, exception management, logging, and validation. Such functionalities are usually known as *crosscutting concerns* because they affect the entire application, and should be centralized in one location in the code where possible.

Maintainability: Basically, *maintainability* is defines as how easy it is to maintain the system, i.e., how easy it is to analyze, change and test the software system.

Modularity: *Modularity* is the property of being structured in modules. In other words, it is the extent to which localized changes in a system have localized effects. In Aspect-Oriented Software Development, the crosscutting concerns are modularized in the form of aspects.

Reverse Engineering: *Reverse engineering* is the process of analyzing a system (under consideration) to create representations of the system at a higher level of abstraction.

Chapter 13
A Proactive Approach to Intrusion Detection in Cloud Software as a Service

Baldev Singh
Lyallpur Khalsa College, India

Surya Narayan Panda
Chitkara University Rajpura, India

ABSTRACT

Cloud computing environment is very much malicious intrusion prone hence cloud security is very vital. Existing network security mechanisms face new challenges in the cloud such as DDOS attacks, virtual machine intrusion attacks and malicious user activities. This chapter includes brief introduction about cloud computing, concept of virtualization, cloud security, various DDOS attacks, tools to run these attacks & various techniques to detect these attacks, review of threshold methods used for detection of DDOS attacks & abnormal network behavior and proposed dynamic threshold based algorithmic approach. Although various cloud security measures are prevailing to avoid virtual machine attacks and malicious user activities but these are not foolproof. Hence, new security methods are required to increase users' level of trust in clouds. By scrubbing traffic at major Internet points and backbone connection, a defense line is created for mitigation of DDOS attacks. Dynamic threshold algorithm based approach is proposed as a proactive approach to detect DDOS attacks for achieving secure cloud environment.

INTRODUCTION TO CLOUD COMPUTING

Technology of cloud computing provides a way of using computing and storage resources by using Internet and remote servers. It presents a new way of using remote resources. The usage of computing resources is charged on usage basis where a user contracts services from a service provider by paying according to what it uses. Cloud computing makes it happen to use the applications without particular installation on personal computers, it is only by accessing and using the services by way of Internet. Cloud computing is an enabled service that may be used for various benefits to its like ease of deploying computer and information technology resources for fresh business, a lesser amount of system operating and maintenance costs and lessening of deployment time in any setup.

DOI: 10.4018/978-1-4666-8510-9.ch013

The National Institute of Standard and Technology (NIST) defines Cloud Computing as the model for enabling convenient, on-demand network access to a shared pool of configurable computing resources (e.g., Networks, servers, storage, applications, and services) that can be rapidly provisioned and released with minimal management effort or service provider interaction (Mell & Grance, 2009). Cloud Computing is one of the fastest growing service models on the Internet. Various large scale IT service providers, like Amazon and IBM, share their data centers, by using virtualization concepts, for the public usage of their computational resources. By using cloud computing, the users of cloud can minimize many startup financial overheads as well as obtain an increase in the availability and scalability for their cloud-hosted applications. In addition, cloud users can avail on-demand service with the ease of Pay-As-You-Go subscription.

VIRTUALIZATION

Virtualization is one of the crucial component being used in cloud computing. It becomes a key element to provide a set of dynamically scalable resources such as storage, software, processing power and other computing resources as services to users which could be accessed over the Internet on demand. A user needs only a browser and an Internet connection to use these resources. Virtual machines (VMs) are created within a virtualization layer (Jin et al, 2011). A cloud is built up of numerous host machines these physical machines then run multiple virtual machines, which is what are presented to the end-users.

Virtual machines are only limited in the way that their specifications cannot exceed that of their host machine. A virtual machine is a software implementation of a computing environment in which an operating system (OS) or program can be installed and run. The virtual machine typically emulates a physical computing environment, but requests for CPU, memory, hard disk, network and other hardware resources from the host machine that are managed by a virtualization layer which translates these requests to the underlying physical hardware. Researchers get the ability to test applications, their deployments and upgrades more efficiently by using VMs. They don't need to have multiple OS and installation configurations.

CLOUD SECURITY

Security is one of important issues prevailing in the cloud environment. Cyber attacks against large internet ventures keep on rising and they directly affect the cloud users. Cloud customers (organizations) are questioning the security of moving their computational assets toward the cloud. These improper operations are generally conducted for a number of reasons. Financial gain can also be a motivation to steal valuable information from sensitive organizations such as those in the banking sector. Cyber surveillance operations typically conducted to gather information about financial or industrial adversaries are some of the new trends over the internet. Existing network security mechanisms face new challenges in the cloud such as DDOS attacks (Bhuyan, Kashyap, Bhattacharyya & Kalita, 2013), virtual machine intrusion attacks and malicious user activities. Hence, new security methods (Tao, Hui, Feng & Cheng, 2012), (Subashini & Kavitha,2011) are required to increase users' level of trust in clouds. Presently, cloud service providers implement data encryption for the data centers, virtual firewalls and access control lists.

DDOS ATTACK

A DDOS attack is a malicious attempt to make the resources (a server or a network resource) unavailable to the users usually by blocking or interrupting the services of a host machine to the Internet. DDOS attack took place by using many computers and many Internet connections often distributed globally. Figure 1 shows a simple DDOS attack scenario (Bhadauria, Chaki & Sanyal, 2011), (Weiler, 2002) in which multiple attacking computers are sending streams of malicious packets to victim machine.

DDOS attacks attempt to perform the following malicious operations:

- Control legitimate network traffic by flooding the network with malicious traffic.
- Deny access to a service by way of disrupting communication between legitimate sender and receiver,
- Block the access of a particular service or an individual.

DDOS attacks lead to disruption of services in cloud and is considered as one of the important intrusions in cloud computing. Intrusion detection and prevention systems taxonomy attacks are classified as outside attacks and inside attacks (Vasanthi & Chandrasekar, 2011), (Specht & Lee, 2004). The attacks that come from external origins are called outsider attacks. Insider attacks, involve unauthorized internal users attempting to gain and misuse non-authorized access privileges. Intrusion detection is the mechanism of monitoring computers or networks for unauthorized entry, activity or file modification (Whitman & Mattord, 2011). Attacks may be treated as incidents. Although many incidents are malicious in nature, many others are not; for example, a person might mistype the address of a computer and accidentally attempt to connect to a different system without authorization.

There is an established underground cyber criminal economy which works to achieve their private individual goals best known for their keen interest in spying or for competitive monetary gains, motives that are possible by the use of disruptive technologies like DDOS attack. Thus making the science of

Figure 1. Distributed Denial-of-Service Attack Scenario

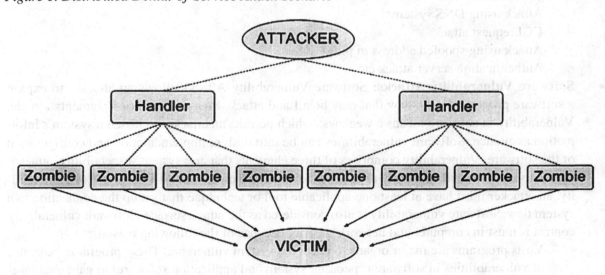

DDOS attacks ever evolving and growing in current context in such a manner that a continuous monitoring with sophisticated watchdog capabilities is required as these attacks continues to create online outrages, customer inconvenience and reputation damages across all industries and geographies. The best known victims of recent moves of these DDOS attacks (Udhayan & Anitha, 2009), (Chuiyi, Yizhi, Yuan, Shuoshan & Qin, 2011) and those who have been successfully being able to mitigate such attacks can never get a sound sleep as it is apparent from current incidences of this attack globally.

VARIOUS DDOS ATTACKS

DDOS attack results to disruption of services in cloud and is considered as one of the important intrusions in cloud computing (Simon, Rubin, Smith & Trajkovic,2000), (Gupta, Joshi & Misra, 2009). The DDOS attacks ((Mirkovic, 2013) can be classified as under:

- **Bandwidth Attacks:** The common reason of bandwidth attacks is the aspiration to create a severe problem to someone else's infrastructure by way of generating a traffic overload. Bandwidth attacks does vary. These Attacks are anticipated to overflow and consume available resources of the victim (for example: network bandwidth). Some examples of Bandwidth chocking in context of DDOS attacks are TCP SYN Flood, UDP Flood and ICMP Flood (Ning & Han, 2012),(Beardmore, 2013).
- **Protocol Attacks:** Protocol Attacks exploit a specific feature or implementation bug of some protocol installed at the victim for the purpose of consuming maximum amount of its resources to take benefit of protocol intrinsic design. All these attacks require a lot of attackers (zombies) and are mitigated by changing the protocol features. Some examples of popular protocol attacks are as under:
  - Smurf Attack
  - UDP Attack
  - ICMP Attack
  - SYN attack
  - Attack using DNS systems.
  - CGI request attack
  - Attack using spoofed address in ping
  - Authentication server attack etc.
- **Software Vulnerability Attacks:** Software Vulnerability Attacks allows an attacker to exploit a software program design flaw that may be a Land attack, Ping of Death or Fragmentation etc. Vulnerability in software means a weakness which permits an attacker to lessen a system's information assurance. Software vulnerabilities can be into design, implementation and configuration of the software. Vulnerability comprises of three elements that are: system susceptibility, attacker access to the flaw, and capability of attacker to make use of the flaw. To make use of vulnerability, an attacker must have at least one applicable tool or technique that set up the connection to a system flaw. Software vulnerability is also considered as the attack surface. Software vulnerability control is must in computer and network security because of the following reasons:
  - Virus programs are major organs to make the system vulnerable. These programs make use of vulnerabilities in software (operating system and application software) to gain unauthor-

ized access, spread and then harm the system. Intruders also make use of vulnerabilities in software (operating system and application software) to gain unauthorized access of the system, attack other systems, and harm the system. There exists some software that are itself hostile and do damage.

◦ Without software vulnerabilities, it is very difficult that viruses would exist and may gain any unauthorized access to the resources and do any harm. Following are some primary tools used for unauthorized access:

- Network sniffing.
- Trojan horse programs
- Password cracking and
- Man in the middle attacks.

- **SYN Flood Attack:** A SYN flood attack is a form of DOS attack which occurs when a host sends a flood of TCP/SYN packets, frequently with a fake sender address to target's system in an attempt to consume a huge amount of server resources to make the system unresponsive to legitimate traffic (Chuiyi,Yizhi, Yuan, Shuoshan & Qin, 2011). Each of these packets in TCP connection is handled like a connection request by sending a SYN (*synchronize*) message to the server, causing the server to spawn a half-open connection, by sending back a TCP/SYN-ACK packet (known as acknowledgement), and also waiting for a packet in response from the sender address (as a response to the ACK Packet). However, the responses never come because the sender address is fake. Due to these half-open connections, network congestion occurs that saturate the number of available connections that the server is able to make to legitimate requests of the clients.

- **Smurf Attack:** A Smurf attack is a distributed denial-of-service attack in which a system is flooded with spoofed ping messages. These flooded spoofed ping messages create high computer network traffic on the victim's network, which repeatedly make it unresponsive. In this type of attack, ICMP echo request (ping) packets addressed to an IP broadcast address that creates a large number of responses ((CERT, 2000). Hence each host on the subnet replies to the same ping request and the huge responses can consume all available network bandwidth, particularly if data is appended to the ping request. Large number of pings and the resulting echoes can make the network unresponsive for legitimate traffic and prevent legitimate traffic from being transmitted during the attack.

- **ICMP Flood:** An ICMP Flood is like the other flooding attack that sends peculiarly large number of ICMP packets (Udhayan & Anitha 2009). This flood of packets can overwhelm a target server that attempts to process every incoming ICMP request, and can be the cause of denial-of-service condition for the target server. This attack is accomplished by broadcasting a lot of ICMP packets, usually the ping packets. The main aim to send large amount of data to the target server is to slow down it so much and get disconnected due to timeouts. Mainly, Ping flood attacks causes the saturation of a network by sending a continuous series of ICMP echo requests over a high-bandwidth connection to a target system on a lower bandwidth connection.

- **Ping of Death:** A ping of death is a denial of service attack that sends a malformed or otherwise malicious ping to a computer. Normally a ping is of 32 bytes in size. This type of attack is caused by an attacker intentionally sending an IP packet larger than the 65,536 bytes allowed by the IP protocol. When such a packet is sent to a system with a vulnerable TCP/IP stack, it will cause the system to crash. Most modern day firewalls are capable of filtering such oversized packets. Now a different type of ping attack are prevailing like ping flooding that simply floods the victim with so much ping traffic that normal traffic fails to reach the system.

- **LAND Attack:** A LAND (Local Area Network Denial) attack is a kind of denial of service attack that consists of sending a special poison (spoofed packet) to a computer, causing it to lock up. A LAND attack consists of a stream of SYN attack with IP spoofing that occurs when an attacker sends spoofed SYN packets containing the IP address of the victim as both the destination and the source IP address. Therefore the receiving system responds by sending the SYN-ACK packet to itself, creating an empty connection that lasts until the idle timeout value is reached. Figure 2 shows local area network denial of service attack. If the system is flooded with such empty connections, it can overwhelm the system that may result a denial of service.
- **Teardrop:** Teardrop attack is an Operating System specific denial-of-service (DOS) attacks these attacks exploit the reassembly of fragmented IP packets. The Teardrop, though, is an old attack that relies on poor TCP/IP implementation that is still around. This kind of attack involves sending fragmented packets to a target machine. Since the machine receiving such packets cannot reassemble them due to a bug in TCP/IP fragmentation reassembly, the packets overlap one another, crashing the target network device. In an IP header, one of the fields is the "fragment offset" field, specifying the starting position, or offset, of the data enclosed in a fragmented packet relative to the data in the original packet. In case the sum of the offset and size of one fragmented packet varies from that of the next fragmented packet, the packets overlap. If this occurs, a system vulnerable to teardrop attacks is unable to reassemble the packets and results in a denial-of-service.

TOOLS FOR RUNNING DISTRIBUTED DENIAL OF SERVICE ATTACK

This section describes the distributed denial of service attack tools that are used by an attacker. These tools facilitate an attacker to coordinate and execute the attack. These kinds of tools overwhelmed the Internet in February 2000. Various distributed tools like Trinoo, TFN, Stacheldraht, Shaft, and TFN2K have become technically more advanced and that is why these are more difficult to detect (Simon et al. 2009). These are briefed below:

- **Trinoo:** Trinoo ia set of computer programs used to conduct a DDOS attack. Trinoo is well-known for permitting attackers to leave a message in a folder known as cry_baby. The file is self replicating and is modified on a regular basis as long as port 80 is active. A compromised host is used by the attacker to compile a list of machines that can be compromised. Most of this course of action is performed automatically from the compromised host, It uses TCP is used for communication between the attacker and the control master program. Master program then communicates with the attack daemons using UDP packets. Trinoo's attack daemons implement UDP Flood attacks against the target victim (Faizal, Zaki, Shahrin, Robiah & Rahayu, 2010).
- **Tribe Flood Network (TFN):** Tribe Flood Network (TFN) program causes a DDOS attack. It is a distributed denial of service tool that allows an attacker to use several hosts at once to flood a target. Tribe Flood Network supports four different types of floods. These are: ICMP Echo flood, UDP Flood, SYN Flood, and Smurf attack. With this tool, client and server use ICMP echo reply packets to communicate with each other. The attacker uses the TFN client to control the remote servers and initiate the denial of service attack. The spoofed source IP address and source ports can be randomized to make the attack more widespread victim (Faizal, Zaki, Shahrin, Robiah & Rahayu, 2010).

Figure 2. Local Area Network Denial attack

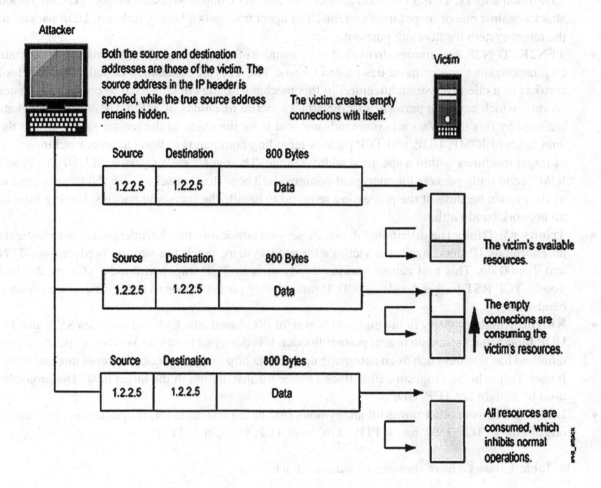

- **Stacheldraht:** Stacheldraht acts as a distributed denial of service attack and is based on the TFN attack. Stacheldraht uses an encrypted TCP connection for communication between the attacker and master control program. TCP and ICMP are used for setting up communication between the master control program and attack daemons and there exists an automatic update technique for the attack daemons. Stacheldraht tool supports four different types of floods. These are: ICMP, UDP Flood, SYN Flood, and Smurf attack.
- **Shaft:** Shaft is used in distributed denial of service (DDOS) attacks. Shaft combines well-known denial of service attacks like TCP SYN flood, smurf, and UDP flood with a distributed and coordinated approach to create a powerful program. These programs further act to slow the network communications to a crushing state. Shaft attack tool includes a handler and an agent. Here the attacker is required to install the Shaft handler and agent manually. The attacker controls the handlers through Transmission Control Protocol (TCP) port 20432 that can control many agent hosts. The handler uses User Data Protocol (UDP) port 18753, to communicate with the agents, and the agents responds by using UDP port 20433. These agents perform DDOS attacks using

UDP flood attacks, TCP SYN flood attacks and Internet Control Message Protocol (ICMP) flood attacks against one or more target systems. The agent transmits a large number of UDP packets to the target system for flooding purpose.

- **TFN2K:** TFN2K uses masters to exploit the resources of a number of agents in order to coordinate an attack against one or more designated targets. The TFN2K distributed denial of service tool consists of a client/server architecture. In this mechanism, the client is used to connect to master servers, which can then perform specific attacks victim machines. ICMP, UDP and TCP packets are used by this tool. Various commands are sent from the client to the master server within the data fields of ICMP, UDP, and TCP packets including commands to flood a target machine or set of target machines within a specified address range. The master server parses all UDP, TCP, and ICMP echo reply packets for encrypted commands. These flood attacks cause the target machine to slow down because of the processing required to handle the incoming packets, leaving little or no network bandwidth.

- **Trinity v3:** Trinity is a distributed denial-of-service attack tool that intruders can use to instigate an enormous IP flood against a victim's targeted system, much the way its predecessors TFN and Trin00 do. This tool causes various floods such as TCP fragment floods, TCP established floods, TCP RST packet floods, and TCP random flag packet floods to leave little or no network bandwidth.

- **Knight:** Knight is a very lightweight yet powerful IRC based attack tool. It provides SYN attacks, UDP Flood attacks, and an urgent pointer flooder. It is designed to run on Windows operating systems and has features such as an automatic updater via http or ftp, a checksum generator and more. It uses Trojan horse program called Back Orifice for installation in the target host. The protocols used by Knight are TCP, UDP.

- **LOIC:** LOIC is another powerful anonymous IRC based attacking tol. It operates in three methods of attack: TCP, UDP and HTTP. LOIC uses TCP, UDP, and HTTP.

The Table 1 shows a brief statistics of various attacks.

SCRUBBING CENTER

Understanding the component of a scrubbing center is important here. It is however essentially a combination of software and hardware based algorithms recipes that analyze the incoming envelop of packets and check the integrity of the outgoing envelop of data passing through multiple subnets reaching a particular set of IP addresses. By scrubbing traffic at major Internet points and backbone connection, a defense line is created for mitigation of DDOS attacks. In fact they take advantage of bandwidth density and traffic routing options with globally distributed options. They choose more to change direction of traffic and swallow the volume of data rather than just block or filter the data packet as the difference between the good and malicious packet is difficult to assess. Hence, they are able to mitigate the flood of UDP (20) or any other type of traffic artifact creating DDOS attacks.

All cloud service providers cannot afford to build their own scrubbing centers as they need to focus on their core business rather than technological issues of maintaining and defending themselves and moreover, even all cloud service providers can hire third party scrubbing solutions. Not all cloud service providers can maintain following components/processes with high quality and ensure high availability of services for themselves and their customers.

Table 1. DDOS attack statistics

Year	Attack Description
2014	114 percent increase in average peak bandwidth of DDOS attacks in Q1 vs. Q4 2013. The Media and Entertainment industry was the target of the majority of malicious attacks. (Morton, 2014)
2013	DDOS attack on stock exchange websites in London.
2012	DDOS Attack on Canadian Political Party Elections and on US and UK Government Sites
2011	DDOS attack on Sony.
2010	DDOS—December 3-5, 2010 on PayPal.
2009	DDOS flooding attacks on South Korea and the United States in July 2009 against government news media and financial websites.
2008	DDOS Attack on BBC, Amazon.com and eBuy.
2007	Estonia Cyber Attack
2006	Target US Banks for financial gain.
2004	Attack on SCO Group website to make it inaccessible to valid users.
2003	Attack on SCO and Microsoft.
2002	DDOS flooding attack thru Domain Name System (DNS) service.
2001	DNS servers attack as reflectors. DOS attack on Irish Government's Department of Finance server. The target was Register.com
2000	One of the first major DDOS flooding on Yahoo

(CSA, 2014), (Tripathi, Gupta, Mishra & Veluru, 2013)

- Detection and Monitoring Centers.
- Threat correlation services.
- Threat alert system.
- Threat identification service with false positives recognition.
- Threat rate of change.
- Threat severity analysis.
- Threat heuristics at every layer.

Hence, when a centralized data cleansing stations are deployed having all possible capabilities as mentioned above where traffic is scrutinized and mischievous traffic (DDOS, known susceptibilities and exploits) are moved or absorbed, there is normally an assumption that a volumetric attack bandwidth consumption can be overcome by adding more and more bandwidth, and swallow all data traffic thereby continuing the services, but it can happen for how much and how long is a question.

NEED OF SCRUBBING CENTERS FOR INTRUSION DETECTION

Scrubbing centers (Ted, 2013) having sophisticated processes that are often used in large enterprises, such as ISP and Cloud Service and Infrastructure Providers, and they often prefer to off-ramp traffic movement to an out of path integrated data cleansing location end-points. When under attack adversary, the whole traffic is redirected (typically using DNS or BGP) to the cleaning/scrubbing focal point where an attack mitigation system mitigates the attacks and passes clean data traffic back to the network for distribution system. The scrubbing center must be adequately equipped to sustain both low and high volumetric floods at the network and application layers, with RFC Compliance checks, with the known vulnerabilities and zero day anomalies addressed. These centers must be able to utilize a multiple diverse range of global network carriers, including Asian, American and European carriers to be really successful in building a defense line stretching beyond single set boundaries. Then, there are multiple ways in which workload management with respect to consolidation of the computing power and storage is done. Moreover, effectively partitioning of the computing capacity of the data centers into multiple tiers, which would improve the nodes utilization and responsiveness for parallel workload is a challenge more so, when there is a mix of solicited and unsolicited traffics of workload is coming into the data center, then the difficulty of realization of parallelism to monitor all ends of the data center effectively remains an issue, leading into a difficult condition in harnessing the heuristics of the scheduling algorithms in running the jobs of data center infected by malicious traffic until fully-meshed with redundancy for 100% availability is incorporated into the defense solution work to our advantage. Since, the target of the any DDOS attackers is normally to block or oversubscribe a resources in such a way that it leads to degraded service performance time, long response time matching the demand of processing the incoming workload remains a constant headache. Many methods have been evolved over a considerable time now and all these methods or technologies that claim to safeguard us from DDOS attacks also consider the various possible correlations that might be working to advantage of the attackers. The most common forces behind DDOS attacks are shown in the Figure 3 (Specht & Lee, 2004):

The following sections takes us to the point where we can now discuss the possible factors that must be observed, monitored and reported for synthesis of such attacks. However, it must be done by using multinational group of professionals with localized understanding of technical environment, cultures and practices to provide consultation and support in multiple languages to the customers so that DDOS attacks are thwarted with involvement of all the stakeholders of the network having protection scope which includes ICMP floods (Udhayan & Anitha, 2009), UDP floods, SYN floods, application level floods, CC attacks (Chuiyi, Yizhi, Yuan, Shuoshan & Qin, 2011), (CERT, 2000), reflective attack (Wang, Schulzrinne & Henning, 2004), degradation of service attacks and last but not least unintentional DDOS outrage.

Figure 3. Common Forces behind DDOS Attacks

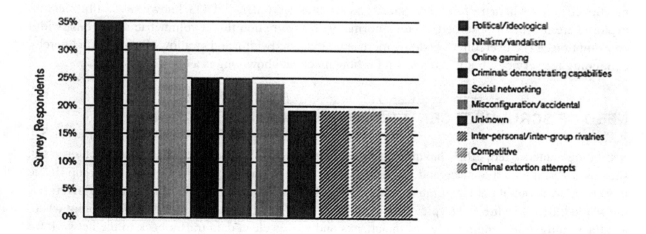

REVIEW OF TECHNIQUES USED FOR DETECTION OF ATTACKS AND ABNORMAL BEHAVIOR IN CLOUD

There are various studies that have explained the concept of solutions available for providing security with mitigation algorithms for cloud network, The Intrusion detection system (IDS) (Vasanthi & Chandrasekar, 2011), (Patel et. Al, 2012) are first to be debated and implemented as it is known fact the cloud based networks and services are prone to suffer from malicious attacks because of their inherent characteristics of being accessible globally any time and also due to the frequent changes in topology and development of Internet of things as well as because of landscape nature of Internet. Of particular concern, it is the denial of service attacks that makes the service unavailable to its intended cloud users.

As per our systematic review of related works in the field of intrusion/malicious attack detection (Jagadeeshraj, George & Thenmozhi, 2013), There are many techniques which can be used to detect intruders or malicious behavior in the cloud network are reviewed. These techniques have their own negatives and positives To comprehend this field of IDS we must look at what each technique holds in its favour and what trade-offs it must make to achieve its goals particularly to make out the abnormal behavior which seems to be DDOS attack.

Faizal et al. has used the threshold based intrusion detection system. Two techniques can be used in selecting the appropriate threshold that differentiates between the malign network traffic and abnormal network traffic. These techniques are based on the static threshold value and dynamic threshold value. Dynamic threshold based technique is more complex than the technique based on static threshold. Dynamic threshold value is based on training or priori knowledge of the network activity, after that the threshold is selected (Faizal, Zaki, Shahrind, Robiah & Rahayu, 2010). According to Faizal et al, it is time consuming process to generate priori knowledge required for generating the dynamic threshold. Their study is based on Fast attack detection mechanism. Shahrin et al. has proposed a framework of fast attack detection. The framework is based on the fast attack detection from two perspectives which are Attack Perspective and the Victim Perspective. Faizal et al. use the framework of fast attack detection at the earliest as they are more hazardous for the network. Their technique is based on the victim perspective of fast attack detection. According to Faizal et. al., fast attack can be defined as attacks that make connections within few seconds and it uses the huge volume of packet. According to Faizal et. al., the work for fast attack detection is mainly based on distributed denial of service attack. The selection of right feature selection is important for detection of attack. The features may also include some extraneous features that are to be treated as spurious features and inadvertently increase the computational issues which include memory space, time and CPU cycle and hence may cause decrease of accuracy of attack detection. The features used by (Faizal, Zaki, Shahrind, Robiah & Rahayu, 2010). in the detection of fast attack includes Timestamp (time to send the packet), Duration of connection, IP address of host, Connection protocol, Status flog of connection, Source and destination services and number of connections in Attack-Victim connection. The research work of Faizal et al. is based on static threshold to detect attacks mainly fast attack and has considered not other main protocols like UDP and ICMP for intrusion detection.

The profile based network based network IDS proposed by (Gupta, Kumar & Abraham, 2013) is based on dynamic threshold. They have proposed the concept of privileged domain in which each virtual machine is in privileged domain. In this architecture, each virtual machine in the cloud network is filtered on their IP address based in the privileged domain. The attacks are detected on the basis of profile of each virtual machine (VM) in the cloud network. VM profile is beneficial to detect attacks as traffic of

VM is not detected for each attack, only those attacks are detected which are frequent in nature. Although (Gupta, Kumar & Abraham, 2013) claimed the dynamic threshold profiling but no factor analysis for signature design is used and the proposed rank based detection is irrelevant.

Among researchers that proposed static threshold based intrusion detection system are Kim et al. (2004), Gates and Damon (2005), Leckie et al (2002) and Faizal et al (2009). Network IDS technique proposed by (Abdollah, Masud, Shahrin & Robiah, 2009) has used the concept of static threshold although dynamic threshold is better solution. The threshold is used to differentiate between normal traffic and abnormal traffic in the network. This threshold value is acquired by using observation and experimental technique and the verified by using statistical process control approach (Abdollah et al, 2009).

The research work of L. Jun-Ho et.al. has presented in the (Ho et.al, 2011) is based on intrusion detection at multiple levels. As above research work has proposed intrusion detection on basis of fast attacks and slow attacks, the later is based on security implementation at multiple levels. (Ho et.al, 2011) proposed different anomaly levels in cloud environment that are authentication, authorization and accounting (AAA). They also proposed three security levels for effective intrusion detection system that are High, Medium and Low. In case of High level of security requirement, they has suggested that- the patterns of all the known attacks are to be considered and the requisite rules for higher level security are to be implemented. They were of the opinion that when the user access the cloud environment first time, the multi level intrusion detection system (IDS) must judge the anomaly level of the user. For judgment of anomaly level, (Ho et.al, 2011) suggested various parameters like vulnerable ports attack, IP address coverage of user, attack success possibilities, attack occurrence possibilities etc. They suggested risk points for different security groups. If the risk points are greater than six, the anomaly level is of High level, risk points between 3-5 (both inclusive), the anomaly level is of medium level and for risk points 0-2, the anomaly level is of low level and accordingly IDS is required to be imposed.

A VMM based IDS has proposed by Hai Jin et al., which is based on virtual machine monitoring. This virtual machine monitor (VMM) in cloud computing environment has the concept of customizable defense system known as VMFence which is used to monitor network flow and file integrity and suggested a network defense and protection of file integrity in the cloud environment. They have implemented VMFence on Xen (open source VM platform) for intrusion detection and prevention system in cloud computing environment (Jin, Xiang & Zou, 2011). This system monitors the attack patterns coming through all VMs that are connected to the privileged machine.

TRESHHOLD ANALYSIS

As per our systematic review of related works in the field of intrusion/malicious attack detection (Jagadeeshraj, George& Thenmozhi, 2013), there are many techniques which can be used to detect intruders or malicious behavior in the cloud network. Each of these techniques/frameworks holds their own merits and demerits. In fact, there are three major techniques which are: misuse detection, anomaly detection and specific detection like DDOS attack. However, to understand this field we must look at what each technique holds in its favour and what trade-offs it must make to achieve its goals in case of using some threshold technique for identification of abnormal behavior which seems to be DDOS at first glance.

Table 2. Review of Threshold methods used for detection of DDOS attacks and abnormal behavior

Method	Merits	Demerits	Research Papers Referred
Static Threshold	Absolute threshold values easy to implement for intrusion detection. Low computational complexity	• Taken only minimum features for threshold detection. • Static Threshold. • Not applied on UDP and ICMP protocols for ID. • Fix value range is never close to real systems that changing every day, this method is not able to consider differential or cumulative threshold for giving response to adversity in real time.	Faizal, Zaki, Shahrin, Robiah & Rahayu, 2010
Dynamic Threshold	This method considers the dynamic values for detection of intrusion. This method is not having much difficulty in measurement e.g. method based on average, mode, frequency are easy to implement.	• No factor analysis for signature design. • Rank based detection irrelevant. • How signature are designed-Not clear. • Reactive, not proactive • Partial profile of VMs • Only no. of packets considered; No other parameters like bandwidth of cpu, n/w etc. • Threshhold may go wrong due to erratic behaviour of metrices used. • Statistically cannot handle extreme high and low values that may lead to wrong calculations. • May calculate wrong threshold, thereby increase the false alarm rate especially distributed change point detection.(DFA or deviation from Average)	Kumar, Ajith & Abraham, 2013
Single Threshold value based method to identify the fast attacks	Easy and Simple to implement. Clear cut demarcation of normal and abnormal behavior events. Fast attack framework with a minimum set of feature selection. Identify a fast attack at the early stage.	• Single Threshold. • Static Threshold. • Dynamic systems like cloud or adversity causing systems cannot work on such single threshold and detection decision making may be faulty. • Selecting inaccurate threshold value will cause an excessive false alarm especially if the value is too low or too high.	Faial M. A., et. al., 2009
Multilevel intrusion detection system and log management in cloud computing environment	Efficient resource utilization. Economical.	• Enormous log entries so not cost effective; • Lots of rules for Ranking of risks and file monitoring modules require high consideration for absolute solution but reduction in resources will be a question. • Each VM in one security group (H/M/L). Migration of VM from one security group to another is only judgment basis.	L. Jun-Ho et.al., 2011
VMM based IPS in cloud computing	It can monitor n/w packets and file integrity in real time. Functional for a virtualization based Cloud computing, particularly for multi core CPU	• Extra computationally complex as it monitors the attack patterns coming thru all VMs that are connected to the privileged machine. • Due to this heavy workload on privileged machine, the n/w will chock and packet drop rate increases.	Jin, Xiang & Zou, 2011.

RESEARCH GAPS

Various research gaps are identified in the review literature. These are as under:

- It is complex to detect the DDOS attacks as well as all other such kinds of attacks of every virtual machine (VM).
- Dynamic systems like cloud or adversity causing systems cannot work on such single threshold and detection decision making may be faulty.
- It cannot work on such multi-range threshold systems as the range may be discrete or continuous and may be changing with time.
- Difficult to calculate accurately as ranges may change with pattern which is difficult to realize.
- Threshold may go wrong due to erratic behavior of matrices used.
- Statistically cannot handle extreme high and low values that may lead to wrong calculations.

RESEARCH PROBLEM

Various studies have explained the concept of various solutions available for providing security and solutions in cloud network. DDOS attacks detection approaches, which are based on either anomaly based or signature based, are not robust and reliable. The cloud based networks and services are prone to suffer from malicious behavior because of their inherent characteristics of being accessible globally and due to the frequent changes in topology & development of Internet of things as well as because of landscape nature of Internet. Of particular concern, it is denial of service attacks that makes the service unavailable to its intended cloud users.

Although considerable effort has been made to understand, detect and prevent these attacks, since it is a continuously evolving as technology, new ways are found by anti development sources to compromise the Cloud based Systems, therefore methods that are based on single, multi range thresholds for detection, require constant upgradation as well refinement in terms of the algorithms for accuracy and robustness.

The threshold based algorithms for detection of DDOS attack must always numerically stable as well as must not depend on predefined thresholds.

The current intrusion detection systems mentioned in the review literature, overlooks certain aspects of calculating the threshold for identification of subspace set of abnormal behavior with the whole pattern of VM profile and this is based only frequency calculation happening in particular set of time line, which is not capable of further mathematical treatment or insight and it is more useful in qualitative cases, however, it makes more sense, if relative frequency based threshold could have been used which would have also considered the total outcome of normal and abnormal events in the VM profile. It would be more accurate to consider those methods that would fine in extreme cases when values are either too large or too small or the dataset is skewed due to particular pattern of events. Therefore, we propose variance based mechanism to overcome the demerits of existing solutions, calculate the thresholds more accurately and to achieve our objective of research. Our goal is to propose *a proactive approach to detect DDOS attacks for achieving secure cloud environment.*

In our research work we intend to analyze methods that can deal with skewed datasets (the ratio of data-row of normal behaviour (benign traffic) to abnormal behaviour (malignant traffic) rows in the profiling session of virtual machines) (trace files or profile files) for detection of DDOS attacks, since the thresholds cannot be static in nature (the statistical behaviour) in any way in cloud environment for parameters that are critical to analyse for identification of DDOS Attacks. The signature based and anomaly based DDOS mechanism is proposed which encompasses the use of dynamic and multi threshold based algorithmic approach.

Secure communication and data transmission in any distributed computing is required. Cloud computing is a shared facility and is accessed remotely, it is vulnerable to various attacks like host and network based attacks and therefore requires immediate attention. Hence there is need of secure cloud network. There is ample scope of the proposed solution in the cloud computing environment as network attacks are glaring day by day. Our research will focus on early detection of network attacks, robust and minimum complex system.

PROPOSED METHOD

For the best evaluation of proposed algorithms we shall formulate an experimental framework. This proposed experimental framework will use the Cloud simulator for experimentation purpose. Various aspects to be considered in the proposed method are discussed below:

- **Create Broker:** Once the cloud simulation setup is done, first thing is to create broker (user base). It submits tasks to the data center. A broker is responsible for mediating between users and service providers depending on users' quality of service (QoS) requirements and it also deploys service tasks across clouds. The broker may be become malicious and may cause security concerns in terms of submitting malicious workload leading to DDOS.
- **Create Datacenter:** A data center (Meng, Iyengar, Arun, Rouvellou, Liu, Lee, Palanisamy & Tang, 2012), which is home to the computation power and storage, is central to cloud computing and contains thousands of devices. Datacenter models the core infrastructure level services (hardware, software) offered by resource providers in a cloud computing environment.

The algorithm for identifying the various thresholds for each component of the cloud network is maintained by the health monitoring system, which is centralized watchdog for the network in question. The HMS maintains daily average of each parameter which represents the performance of the network and other aspects related to the degradation of the network performance, if there are too many VM migrations or too much workload deliveries and throughput is changing in erratic manner, there is huge variation which is calculated continuously by HMS using proposed algorithms.

The above method can be used for calculating the number of VM Migrations (Thresholds per day) for identification of DDOS attack (Beardmore, 2013). Migration of virtual machines improves performance, manageability and fault tolerance of systems but it may also be sign of some issue relating to DDOS attacks as unnecessary migration may occur. VM migration policy helps balance system load, which may be under threat due to adversity.

Although considerable efforts have been made to understand, detect and prevent these attacks, yet because of continuous evolving nature of cloud we have to remain on our toes and try to find out means and tools which can eliminate this malicious threat. Since it is a continuously evolving as technology, new ways are found by anti-development sources to compromise the cloud based systems, therefore methods that are based on single, multi range thresholds for detection need constant upgradation as well refinement in terms of the algorithms accuracy and robustness for identification of DDOS attacks. The threshold based algorithms for detection of DDOS attack must always numerically stable as well as must not depend on predefined thresholds.

The current DDOS attacks detection systems mentioned in the previous works (Vasanthi & Chandrasekar, 2011) overlook certain aspects of calculating the threshold for identification of subspace set of abnormal behavior with the whole pattern of VM profile and this is based on frequency calculation happening in particular set of time line, which is not capable of further mathematical treatment or insight and it is more useful in qualitative cases, however, it makes more sense, if relative frequency based threshold could have been used which would have also considered the total outcome of normal and abnormal events in the VM profile. It would be more accurate to consider those methods that would fine in extreme cases when values are either too large or too small or the dataset is skewed due to particular pattern of events.

Therefore, we propose variance based methods that can be used to overcome the demerits of existing solutions, calculate the thresholds more accurately and to achieve our objective of research. Hence, In pursuance of this research work it must be persuaded by all the stake holders to analyze methods that can deal with large skewed datasets ((benign traffic) to abnormal behaviour (malignant traffic) for detection of DDOS attacks, since the thresholds cannot be static in nature in any way in cloud environment for parameters that are critical to analyze for identification of DDOS Attacks.

CONCLUSION

From the systematic review of all the studies done in the context of the DDOS attack we can expect that there will be increase in the frequency of the DDOS attacks due to multifold increase in the online activities and wireless Internet of things. It is also apparent that the very idea of building defending lines of action against such act of destruction depends on computations coming out of the stream of the traffic at different ends of the network of networks. We have also understood that both the internal and external anatomy of the data center matters and also how to structure architecturally to measure the volume of traffic is the main critical point. If somehow the intruders are able to launch a slow attack it must be detectable or if it is a sudden flood of packets then one must be able to mitigate the flood to have clean traffic. This is not possible unless there is continuous monitoring which includes the mapping of threats cope with the understanding correlations of all the factors contributing to the adversary. Therefore, the thresholds of finding inflection points where the traffic changes to malicious is essential to successful running of data centers in cloud in thwarting the DDOS attacks.

REFERENCES

Abdollah, Masud, Shahrin, Robiah, & Siti Rahayu. (2009). Threshold verification using Statistical Approach for Fast Attack Detection. *Intl. Journal of Computer Science and Information Security, 2*(1), 1–8.

Advisory, C. E. R. T. (2010). *SYN Flooding and IP Spoofing Attacks*. CERT® Coordination Center Software Engineering Institute, Carnegie Mellon. Retrieved from http://www.cert.org/advisories/CA-1996-21.html

Beardmore, K. (2013). *The Truth about DDoS Attacks: Part 1*. Retrieved from TheCarbon60 Blog: http://www.carbon60.com/the-truth-about-DDOS-attacks-part-1/

Bhadauria, R. C. R., Chaki, N., & Sanyal, S. (2011). *A survey on security issues in cloud computing*. Retrieved December 5, 2014 from http://arxiv.org/abs/1109.5388

Chuiyi, X., Yizhi, Z., Yuan, B., Shuoshan, L., & Qin, X. (2011). *A Distributed Intrusion Detection System against flooding Denial of Services attacks*. 13th International Conference on, Advanced Communication Technology (ICACT).

Cloud Security Alliance. (2010). *Top Threats to Cloud Computing*. Retrieved from http://www.cloudsecurityalliance.org/topthreats/csathreats.v1.0.pdf

DDOS Attacks. (n.d.). Retrieved from http://www.DDOSattacks.biz/DDOS-101/glossary/scrubbing-center/

Ding & Yeung. (2002). *User Profiling for Intrusion Detection Using Dynamic and Static Behavioral Models*. Springer Berlin Heidelberg.

Faizal, M.A., Zaki, M.M., Shahrin, S., Robiah, Y., & Rahayu, S.S. (2010). Statistical Approach for Validating Static Threshold in Fast Attack Detection. *Journal of Advanced Manufacturing*.

Gupta, Joshi, & Misra (2000). Defending against Distributed Denial of Service Attacks: Issues and Challenges. *Information Security Journal: A Global Perspective, 18*(5), 224-247.

Gupta, S., Kumar, P., & Abraham, A. (2013). A Profile Based Network Intrusion Detection and Prevention System for Securing Cloud Environment. *International Journal of Distributed Sensor Networks, 2013*, 364575. doi:10.1155/2013/364575

Institute, I. S. (2015). *DDOS Attack Categorization, University of Southern California. DDOS Bechmarks*. Retrieved December 11, 2014 from http://www.isi.edu/~mirkovic/bench

Jagadeeshraj, V.S., Lijoy, C. G., & Thenmozhi, S. (2013). Attaining Pre-Eminent Cloud Security Using Intrusion Detection Systems. *International Journal of Emerging Technology and Advanced Engineering, 3*(2), 214-219.

Jin, H., Xiang, G., Zou, D., Wu, S., Zhao, F., Li, M., & Zheng, W. (2011). A VMM-based intrusion prevention system in cloud computing environment. *The Journal of Supercomputing, 66*(3), 1133–1151. doi:10.1007/s11227-011-0608-2

Jun-Ho, Min-Woo, Jung-Ho, & Tai-Myoung. (2011). Multi-level intrusion detection system and log management in cloud computing. In *Proceedings of the13th International Conf.* Academic Press.

Mell & Grance. (2009). *The NIST Definition of Cloud Computing version 15*. National Institutes of Standards and Technology (NIST), Information Technology Laboratory -Intrusion Detection. Retrieved December 5,2014 from http://en.wikipedia.org/wiki/Intrusion_detection_system

Meng, S., Iyengar, A. K., Rouvellou, I.M., Liu, Lee, Palanisamy, B., & Tang. (2012). Reliable State Monitoring in Cloud Datacenters. In *Proceedings of IEEE 5th International Conference on Cloud Computing* (CLOUD). IEEE.

Monowar,, H., Bhuyan, H. J., Kashyap, D. K., Bhattacharyya, & Kalita. (2013). Detecting Distributed Denial of Service Attacks: Methods, Tools and Future Directions. *The Computer Journal*.

Ning, S., & Han, Q. (2012). Design and implementation of DDOS attack and defense testbed. *International Conference on Wavelet Active Media Technology and Information Processing (ICWAMTIP)*, 2012, 220-223. doi:10.1109/ICWAMTIP.2012.6413478

Patel, A., Taghavi, M., & Bakhtiyari, K. (2012). An intrusion detection and prevention system in cloud computing: A systematic review. *Journal of Network and Computer Applications*. doi:10.1016/j.jnca.2012.08.007

Simon, Rubin, Smith, & Trajkovic. (2000). *Distributed Denial of Service Attacks*. Retrieved from http://www2.ensc.sfu.ca/~ljilja/papers/smc00_edited.pdf

Specht, S. M., & Lee, R. B. (2004). Distributed Denial of Service: Taxonomies of Attacks, Tools, and Countermeasures. *In Proceedings of the International Workshop on Security in Parallel and Distributed Systems*. San Francisco, CA: Academic Press.

Subashini, S., & Kavitha, V. (2011). A survey on security issues in service delivery models of cloud computing. *Journal of Network and Computer Applications*, *34*(1), 1–11. doi:10.1016/j.jnca.2010.07.006

Tripathi, S., Gupta, B., Almomani, A., Mishra, A., & Veluru, S. (2013). Hadoop Based Defense Solution to Handle Distributed Denial of Service (DDOS) Attacks. *Journal of Information Security*, *4*(03), 150–164. doi:10.4236/jis.2013.43018

Udhayan, J.; Anitha, R. 2009). *Demystifying and Rate Limiting ICMP hosted DoS/DDOS Flooding Attacks with Attack Productivity Analysis*. Advance Computing Conference IACC 2009.

Vasanthi, S., & Chandrasekar, S. (2011). A study on network intrusion detection and prevention system current status and challenging issues. *3rd International Conference on Advances in Recent Technologies in Communication and Computing (ARTCom 2011)*. doi:10.1049/ic.2011.0075

Wang, B-T., & Schulzrinne, H. (2004). An IP traceback mechanism for reflective DoS attacks. *Canadian Conference on Electrical and Computer Engineering* (vol. 2, pp. 901-904). Academic Press.

Weiler. (2002). Honeypots for Distributed Denial of Service Attacks. In *Proceedings of Eleventh IEEE International Workshops on Enabling Technologies: Infrastructure for Collaborative Enterprises*. IEEE.

Xia, Du, Cao, & Chen. (2012). *An Algorithm of Detecting and Defending CC Attack in Real Time*. International Conference on Industrial Control and Electronics Engineering (ICICEE).

KEY TERMS AND DEFINITIONS

Cloud Computing: Cloud Computing defined as a model for enabling convenient, on-demand network access to a shared pool of configurable computing resources that can be rapidly provisioned and released with minimal management effort or service provider interaction.

Cloud Computing Security: Cloud computing security is defined as a set of control-based technologies and policies that ensure the protection of data applications, information, and infrastructure used in cloud computing.

DDOS Attack: DDOS attack is a malicious attempt to make the resources of a server/network unavailable to the users usually by blocking or interrupting the services of a host machine to the Internet.

Intrusion Detection System: Intrusion Detection System is a security technology that monitors a network for any suspicious activity or policy violations and produces a report to the concerned authority.

Virtualization: Virtualization is a key element of cloud computing that provides a set of dynamically scalable resources such as storage, software, processing power and other computing resources as services to users which could be accessed over the Internet on demand.

Virtual Machine: A virtual machine emulates a physical computing environment but requests for CPU, memory, hard disk, network and other hardware resources from the underlying host machine.

Vulnerability: Vulnerability can be defined as an intrinsic weakness or absence of a protection that could be exploited by an attacker.

Compilation of References

Abdollah, Masud, Shahrin, Robiah, & Siti Rahayu. (2009). Threshold verification using Statistical Approach for Fast Attack Detection. *Intl. Journal of Computer Science and Information Security, 2*(1), 1–8.

Abdolvand, N., Albadvi, A., & Ferdowsi, Z. (2008). Assessing readiness for business process reengineering. *Business Process Management Journal, 14*(4), 497–511. doi:10.1108/14637150810888046

Abercrombie, R. K., Sheldon, F. T., & Mili, A. (2008, December). Synopsis of evaluating security controls based on key performance indicators and stakeholder mission value. In *Proceedings of High Assurance Systems Engineering Symposium, 2008. HASE 2008. 11th IEEE* (pp. 479-482). IEEE. doi:10.1109/HASE.2008.61

Abrahamsson, P., Hanhineva, A., Hulkko, H., Ihme, T., Jäälinoja, J., Korkala, M., . . . Salo, O. (2004). Mobile-D: An Agile Approach for Mobile Application Development. In *Proceedings of the 19th Annual ACM Conference on ObjectOriented Programming, Systems, Languages, and Applications, OOPSLA'04*. Vancouver, Canada: ACM.

Abrahamsson, P. (2008). *Agile processes in software engineering and eXtreme programming*. Germany: Springer. doi:10.1007/978-3-540-68255-4

Acur, N., Kandemir, D., & Boer, H. (2012). Strategic alignment and new product development: Drivers and performance effects. *Journal of Product Innovation Management, 29*(2), 304–318. doi:10.1111/j.1540-5885.2011.00897.x

Adams, B., Jiang, Z. M., & Hassan, A. E. (2010). Identifying crosscutting concerns using historical code changes. In *Proceedings of the 32nd ACM/IEEE International Conference on Software Engineering* (vol. 1, pp. 305-314). ACM/IEEE. doi:10.1145/1806799.1806846

Adeyemi, S., & Aremu, M. A. (2008). Impact assessment of business process reengineering on organizational performance. *European Journal of Soil Science, 7*(1), 115–125.

Adriansyah, A., van Dongen, B., & van der Aalst, W. (2010). Towards robust conformance checking. In M. Muehlen & J. Su (Eds.), *Business Process Management Workshops* (pp. 122–133). Berlin, Germany: Springer.

Advisory, C. E. R. T. (2010). *SYN Flooding and IP Spoofing Attacks*. CERT® Coordination Center Software Engineering Institute, Carnegie Mellon. Retrieved from http://www.cert.org/advisories/CA-1996-21.html

Ågerfalk, P. J. B. F., Holmström Olsson, H., and Ó Conchúir, E. (2008). Benefits of Global Software Development: The Known and Unknown. Lecture Notes in Computer Science, 5007, 1-9.

Agile Manifesto Group. (2001). *Manifesto for Agile Software Development*. Retrieved from http://agilemanifesto.org

Agostinho, C., Jardim-Goncalves, R., & Steiger-Garcao, A. (2011). Using neighboring domains towards setting the foundations for Enterprise Interoperability science. In Callaos, N. et al. (Eds.) *International Symposium on Collaborative Enterprises in the Context of the 15th World-Multi-Conference on Systemic, Cybernetics and Informatics* (vol. 2, pp. 258-264). Winter Garden, FL: International Institute of Informatics and Systemics.

Ahadi, H. (2004). An examination of the role of organizational enablers in business process reengineering and the impact of information technology. *Information Resources Management Journal, 17*(4), 1–19. doi:10.4018/irmj.2004100101

Ahmad, H., Francis, A., & Zairi, M. (2007). Business process reengineering: Critical success factors in higher education. *Business Process Management Journal, 13*(3), 451–469. doi:10.1108/14637150710752344

Aissa, A. B. (2013, Winter). *Vers une mesure économétrique de la sécurité des systèmes informatiques* (Unpublished doctoral dissertation). Faculty of Sciences of Tunis.

Aissa, A. B. A., Mili, A., Abercrombie, R. K., & Sheldon, F. T. (2010). Modeling stakeholder/value dependency through mean failure cost. In *Proceedings of 6th Annual Cyber Security and Information Intelligence Research Workshop* (CSI-IRW-2010). ACM.

Aissa, A. B., Abercrombie, R. K., Sheldon, F. T., & Mili, A. (2009). Quantifying security threats and their impacts, In *Proceedings of 5th Annual Cyber Security and Information Intelligence Research Workshop* (CSIIRW-2009). ACM.

Aissa, A. B., Abercrombie, R. K., Sheldon, F. T., & Mili, A. (2012). Defining and computing a value based cyber-security measure. *Information Systems and e-Business Management, 10*(4), 433-453.

Aissa, A. B., Abercrombie, R. K., Sheldon, F. T., & Mili, A. (2010). Quantifying Security Threats and Their Potential Impacts: A Case Study. *Innovations in Systems and Software Engineering, 6*(4), 269–281. doi:10.1007/s11334-010-0123-2

Aitken, A. (2014). *Lean: Concepts and Realities*. Lanner Group. Retrieved on 18.09.2014 from http://www.lanner.com/en/pdf/lean_and_lanner.pdf

Ajila, S. A., Gakhar, A. S., & Lung, C. H. (2013). Aspectualization of code clones—an algorithmic approach. *Information Systems Frontiers, 16*(5), 835–851. doi:10.1007/s10796-013-9428-7

Akbar, R., Hassan, M. F., Abdullah, A., Safdar, S., & Qureshi, M. A. (2011). Directions and Advancements in Global Software Development: A summarized review of GSD and agile methods. *Research Journal of Information Technology, 3*(2), 69–80. doi:10.3923/rjit.2011.69.80

Akhavan, P., Jafari, M., & Ali-Ahmadi, A. R. (2006). Exploring the interdependency between reengineering and information technology by developing a conceptual model. *Business Process Management Journal, 12*(4), 517–534. doi:10.1108/14637150610678104

Alenezi, M., & Magel, K. (2014). Empirical evaluation of a new coupling metric: Combining structural and semantic coupling. *International Journal of Computers and Applications, 36*(1). doi:10.2316/Journal.202.2014.1.202-3902

Al-Mashari, M., Irani, Z., & Zairi, M. (2001). Business process reengineering: A survey of international experience. *Business Process Management Journal, 7*(5), 437–455. doi:10.1108/14637150110406812

Al-Mashari, M., & Zairi, M. (1999). BPR implementation process: An analysis of key success and failure factors. *Business Process Management Journal, 5*(1), 87–112. doi:10.1108/14637159910249108

Al-Mashari, M., & Zairi, M. (2000). Revisiting BPR: A holistic review of practice and development. *Business Process Management Journal, 6*(1), 10–42. doi:10.1108/14637150010283045

Almunawar, M. N., Anshari, M., & Susanto, H. (2013). Crafting strategies for sustainability: How travel agents should react in facing a disintermediation. *Operations Research, 13*(3), 317–342. doi:10.1007/s12351-012-0129-7

Altinkemer, K., Chaturvedi, A., & Kondareddy, S. (1999). Business process reengineering and organizational performance: An exploration of issues. *International Journal of Information Management, 18*(6), 381–392. doi:10.1016/S0268-4012(98)00030-9

Al-Zoabi, Z. (2008). *Introducing discipline to XP: Applying PRINCE2 on XP projects.* Paper presented at the 3rd International Conference on Information and Communication Technologies: From Theory to Applications (ICTTA 2008), Damascus, Syria. doi:10.1109/ICTTA.2008.4530347

Ambler, S. W. (2010). *Agile Modeling. Ambysoft.* Retrieved July 26, 2010, from http://www.agilemodeling.com/

Ambler, S. W. (2013). *What Was Final Status.* Retrieved March 20, 2013, from http://www.linkedin.com/groups/What-was-final-status-most-1523.S.222770182

Ananthram, S., & Nankervis, A. (2013). Strategic agility and the role of HR as a strategic business partner: An Indian perspective. *Asia Pacific Journal of Human Resources, 51*(4), 454–470.

Andreu, R., Ricart, J., & Valor, J. (1997). Process innovation: Changing boxes or revolutionizing organizations? *Knowledge and Process Management, 4*(2), 114–125. doi:10.1002/(SICI)1099-1441(199706)4:2<114::AID-KPM90>3.0.CO;2-S

Andries, P. & Dirk, C. (2013). *Working Paper Small firm innovation performance and employee involvement.* ZEW Discussion Papers, No. 12.

Aoyama, M. (1997, August). Agile software process model. In *Proceedings of the 21st IEEE International Computer Software and Applications Conference COMPSAC '97* (pp. 454-459). IEEE.

Apache. (2011). *Apache ServiceMix.* Retrieved September 20, 2111, from http://servicemix.apache.org

Arges, C. J. (n.d.). *Linux and Lehman- Literature Review of Open Source Evolution Analysis.* Retrieved August 10, 2014 from website https://github.com/arges/chrisarges.net/blob/master/files/arges_linux_evolution.pdf

Armstrong, S. D., Brewer, W. C., & Steinberg, R. K. (2002). Usability testing. In S. G. Charlton & T. G. O'Brien (Eds.), *Handbook of human factors testing and evaluation* (pp. 403–432). Arlington, VA: Office of Naval Research.

Ashworth, C. M. (1988). Structured systems analysis and design method (SSADM). *Information and Software Technology, 30*(3), 153–163. doi:10.1016/0950-5849(88)90062-6

Asif, M., Awan, M. U., Khan, M. K., & Ahmad, N. (2013). A model for total quality management in higher education. *Quality & Quantity, 47*(4), 1883–1904. doi:10.1007/s11135-011-9632-9

Attaran, M. (2003). Information technology and business-process redesign. *Business Process Management Journal, 9*(4), 440–458. doi:10.1108/14637150310484508

Attaran, M. (2004). Exploring the relationship between information technology and business process reengineering. *Information & Management, 41*(5), 585–596. doi:10.1016/S0378-7206(03)00098-3

Aubert, J.-E. (2005). *Promoting Innovation in Developing Countries: A Conceptual Framework.* Retrieved October 14, 2014 from http://elibrary.worldbank.org/doi/pdf/10.1596/1813-9450-3554

Avison, D., & Fitzgerald, G. (1995). *Information systems development: methodologies, techniques and tools.* London, UK: McGraw-Hill Publishing.

Babu, D., & Darsi, M. (2013). A Survey on Service Oriented Architecture and Metrics to Measure Coupling. *International Journal on Computer Science and Engineering, 5*(8), 726–733.

Bae, J. S., Jeong, S. C., Seo, Y., Kim, Y., & Kang, S. H. (1999). Integration of workflow management and simulation. *Computers & Industrial Engineering, 37*(1-2), 203–206. doi:10.1016/S0360-8352(99)00055-8

Baldwin, L. P., Eldabi, T., & Paul, R. J. (2005). Business process design: Flexible modeling with multiple levels of detail. *Business Process Management Journal, 11*(1), 22–36. doi:10.1108/14637150510578700

Balter, B. (2011). Towards a more agile government: The case for rebooting federal IT procurement. *Public Contract Law Journal, 41*(1), 149–171.

Bang, T. J. (2007). An Agile Approach to Requirement Specification. In *Proceedings of the 8th international conference on Agile processes in software engineering and extreme programming.* Como. Italy: Springer-Verlag Berlin, Heidelberg. doi:10.1007/978-3-540-73101-6_35

Baniassad, E., & Clarke, S. (2004). Theme: An approach for aspect-oriented analysis and design. In *Proceedings of the 26th International Conference on Software Engineering* (pp. 158-167). Academic Press. doi:10.1109/ICSE.2004.1317438

Baniassad, E., Clements, P. C., Araujo, J., Moreira, A., Rashid, A., & Tekinerdogan, B. (2006). Discovering early aspects. *IEEE Software, 23*(1), 61–70. doi:10.1109/MS.2006.8

Bank, J., & Raza, A. (2014). *Collaborative Idea Management: A Driver of Continuous Innovation, Technology Innovation Management Review.* CaseStudy_BSTR060(2003). Retrieved from http://www.icmrindia.org/casestudies/catalogue/Business%20Strategy1/BSTR060.htm

Barlow, J., & Jashapara, A. (1998). Organisational learning and inter-firm "partnering" in the UK construction industry. *The Learning Organization, 5*(2), 86–98. doi:10.1108/09696479810212051

Bass, L., Klein, M., & Northrop, L. (2004). Identifying aspects using architectural reasoning. In *Proceedings of the Workshop on Early Aspects: Aspect-Oriented Requirements Engineering and Architecture Design* (pp. 51-57). Academic Press.

Bavota, G. (2013). An empirical study on the developers' perception of software coupling. In *International Conference on Software Engineering* (pp. 692-701). Piscataway, NJ: IEEE Computer Society Press. doi:10.1109/ICSE.2013.6606615

Baxter, I. D., Yahin, A., Moura, L., Sant'Anna, M., & Bier, L. (1998). Clone detection using abstract syntax trees. In *Proceedings of the International Conference on Software Maintenance* (pp. 368-377). Academic Press. doi:10.1109/ICSM.1998.738528

Beardmore, K. (2013). *The Truth about DDoS Attacks: Part 1.* Retrieved from TheCarbon60 Blog: http://www.carbon60.com/the-truth-about-DDOS-attacks-part-1/

Beck, K., Beedle, M., Van Bennekum, A., Cockburn, A., Cunningham, W., Fowler, M., . . . Thomas, D. (2001). Manifesto for agile software development. *Agile Alliance.* Available online: www.agilemanifesto.org

Beck, K., Beedle, M., Van Bennekum, A., Cockburn, A., Cunningham, W., Fowler, M., . . . Thomas, D. (2001). *Principles behind the agile manifesto.* Retrieved December 22, 2014 from www.agilemanifesto.org/principles.html

Belady, L. A., & Lehman, M. M. (1976). A model of large program development. *IBM Systems Journal, 15*(3), 225–252. doi:10.1147/sj.153.0225

Benbunan-Fich, R. (2001). Using protocol analysis to evaluate the usability of a commercial web site. *Information & Management, 39*(2), 151–163. doi:10.1016/S0378-7206(01)00085-4

Berczuk, S. (2007, August). Back to basics: The role of agile principles in success with an distributed scrum team. In *Proceedings of the AGILE 2007*. Washington, DC: IEEE Computer Society. doi:10.1109/AGILE.2007.17

Berger, H. (2007). Agile development in a bureaucratic arena—A case study experience. *International Journal of Information Management, 27*(6), 386–396. doi:10.1016/j.ijinfomgt.2007.08.009

Berger, H., & Beynon-Davies, P. (2009). The utility of rapid application development in large-scale, complex projects. *Information Systems Journal, 19*(6), 549–570. doi:10.1111/j.1365-2575.2009.00329.x

Bernardi, M. L., & Di Lucca, G. A. (2009). ConAn: A tool for the identification of crosscutting concerns in object oriented systems based on type hierarchy analysis. In *Proceedings of the 16th Working Conference on Reverse Engineering* (pp. 319-320). Academic Press. doi:10.1109/WCRE.2009.38

Bernardi, M. L., & Di Lucca, G. A. (2009). A role-based crosscutting concerns mining approach to evolve java systems towards AOP. In *Proceedings of the Joint International and Annual ERCIM Workshops on Principles of Software Evolution (IWPSE) and software evolution (Evol) workshops* (pp. 63-72). ERCIM. doi:10.1145/1595808.1595822

Berre, A. (2007). The ATHENA Interoperability Framework. In R. Gonçalves, J. Müller, K. Mertins, & M. Zelm (Eds.), *Enterprise Interoperability II* (pp. 569–580). London, UK: Springer. doi:10.1007/978-1-84628-858-6_62

Bhadauria, R. C. R., Chaki, N., & Sanyal, S. (2011). *A survey on security issues in cloud computing*. Retrieved December 5, 2014 from http://arxiv.org/abs/1109.5388

Bhatt, G. D. (2000). Exploring the relationship between information technology, infrastructure and business process re-engineering. *Business Process Management, 6*(2), 139–163. doi:10.1108/14637150010324085

Bieberstein, N., Laird, R. G., Jones, K., & Mitra, T. (2008). *Executing SOA: A Practical Guide for the Service-Oriented Architect*. Upper Saddle River, NJ: IBM Press.

Bin, X., Xiaohu, Y., Zhijun, H., & Maddineni, S. R. (2004). Extreme Programming in reducing the reowrk of requirements change. In *Proceeding of Canadian Conference on Electrical and Computer Engineering*. Niagara Falls, Canada: IEEE.

Bisbal, J., Lawless, D., Wu, B., Grimson, J., Wade, V., Richardson, R., & O'Sullivan, D. (1997) An overview of legacy information system migration. In *Proceedings of the Asia Pacific Software Engineering Conference and International Computer Science Conference* (pp. 529-530). Academic Press. doi:10.1109/APSEC.1997.640219

Bishop, J. (2004). The potential of persuasive technology for educating heterogeneous user groups. (Unpublished MSc). University of Glamorgan, Pontypridd.

Bishop, J. (2005). *The role of mediating artifacts in the design of persuasive e-learning systems*. Paper presented at the 1st International Conference on Internet Technologies and Applications (ITA'05), Wrexham, UK.

Bishop, J. (2007a). Ecological cognition: A new dynamic for human-computer interaction. In B. Wallace, A. Ross, J. Davies & T. Anderson (Eds.), The mind, the body and the world: Psychology after cognitivism (pp. 327-345). Exeter, UK: Imprint Academic.

Bishop, J. (2007b). *Evaluation-centred design of E-learning communities: A case study and review*. Paper presented at the 2nd International Conference on Internet Technologies and Applications (ITA'07), Wrexham, UK.

Bishop, J. (2007c). Increasing participation in online communities: A framework for human–computer interaction. *Computers in Human Behavior, 23*(4), 1881–1893. doi:10.1016/j.chb.2005.11.004

Bishop, J. (2007d). *An investigation into how the european union affects the development and provision of e-learning services. Unpublished LLM*. Pontypridd, UK: University of Glamorgan.

Bishop, J. (2011a). All's WELL that ends WELL: A comparative analysis of the constitutional and administrative frameworks of cyberspace and the United Kingdom. In A. Dudley-Sponaugle & J. Braman (Eds.), *Investigating cyber law and cyber ethics: Issues, impacts and practices*. Hershey, PA: IGI Global.

Bishop, J. (2011b). *The equatrics of intergenerational knowledge transformation in techno-cultures: Towards a model for enhancing information management in virtual worlds. (Unpublished MScEcon)*. Aberystwyth, UK: Aberystwyth University.

Bishop, J. (2012). Lessons from the emotivate project for increasing take-up of big society and responsible capitalism initiatives. In P. M. Pumilia-Gnarini, E. Favaron, E. Pacetti, J. Bishop, & L. Guerra (Eds.), *Didactic strategies and technologies for education: Incorporating advancements* (pp. 208–217). Hershey, PA: IGI Global. doi:10.4018/978-1-4666-2122-0.ch019

Bishop, J. (2013). Increasing capital revenue in social networking communities: Building social and economic relationships through avatars and characters. In J. Bishop (Ed.), *Examining the concepts, issues, and implications of internet trolling* (pp. 44–61). Hershey, PA: IGI Global. doi:10.4018/978-1-4666-2803-8.ch005

Bishop, J. (2014a). Getting to know your users for effective e-moderation. *Multimedia Information & Technology, 40*(2), 18–36.

Bishop, J. (2014b). My click is my bond: The role of contracts, social proof, and gamification for sysops to reduce pseudo-activism and internet trolling. In J. Bishop (Ed.), *Gamification for human factors integration: Social, educational, and psychological issues* (pp. 1–6). Hershey, PA: IGI Global. doi:10.4018/978-1-4666-5071-8.ch001

Bittle, S., Haller, C., & Kadlec, A. (2009). *Promising practices in online engagement No. 3*. New York, NY: Center for Advances in Public Engagement.

Blaauboer, F., Sikkel, K., & Aydin, M. N. (2007). *Deciding to adopt requirements traceability in practice*. Paper presented at the 9th International Conference on Advanced Information Systems Engineering (CAiSE'07), Trondheim. doi:10.1007/978-3-540-72988-4_21

Blight, L. K., & Ainley, D. G. (2008). Southern ocean not so pristine. *Science, 321*(5895), 1443. doi:10.1126/science.321.5895.1443b PMID:18787149

Boehm, B., and Turner, R. (2005). Management challenges to implementing agile processes in traditional development organizations. *IEEE Software, 22*(5), 30-39.

Boehm, B. (2002). Get ready for agile methods, with care. *IEEE Computer, 35*(1), 64–69. doi:10.1109/2.976920

Boldyreff, C., Lavery, J., Nutter, D., & Rank, S. (2003). Open-Source Development Processes and Tools. In *Proceedings of the 3rd Workshop on Open Source Software Engineering ICSE'03 International Conference on Software Engineering*. Portland, OR: Academic Press.

Bonet, R. (2014). High-involvement work practices and the opportunities for promotion in the organization. *Industrial Relations, 53*(2), 295–324. doi:10.1111/irel.12057

Box, G., & Luceño, A. (1997). *Statistical Control by Monitoring and Feedback Adjustment*. New York: Wiley.

Box, S., & Platts, K. (2005). Business process management: Establishing and maintaining project alignment. *Business Process Management Journal, 11*(4), 370–387. doi:10.1108/14637150510609408

Braithwaite, K., and Joyce, T. (2005). XP expanded: Distributed extreme programming. In *Proceedings of 6th International Conference on Extreme programming and agile processes in software engineering* (LNCS), (vol. 3556, pp. 1524– 1526). Springer.

Breu, S. (2004). Towards hybrid aspect mining: Static extensions to dynamic aspect mining. In *Proceedings of the 1ˢᵗ Workshop on Aspect Reverse Engineering*. Academic Press.

Breu, S., & Krinke, J. (2004). Aspect mining using event traces. In *Proceedings of the 19ᵗʰ International Conference on Automated Software Engineering* (pp. 310-315). Academic Press.

Breu, S., & Zimmermann, T. (2006). Mining aspects from version history. In *Proceedings of the 21st IEEE/ACM International Conference on Automated Software Engineering* (pp. 221-230). IEEE/ACM. doi:10.1109/ASE.2006.50

Breu, S., Zimmermann, T., & Lindig, C. (2006). Mining eclipse for crosscutting concerns. In *Proceedings of the 2006 International Workshop on Mining Software Repositories* (pp. 94-97). Academic Press. doi:10.1145/1137983.1138006

Brownbridge, D. (1990). *Using Z to develop a CASE toolset*. Paper presented at the Z User Workshop, Oxford, UK. doi:10.1007/978-1-4471-3877-8_9

Bruce, M., Daly, L., & Towers, N. (2004). Lean or agile: A solution for supply chain management in the textiles and clothing industry? *International Journal of Operations and Production Management, 24*(2), 151–170. doi:10.1108/01443570410514867

Bruntink, M. (2004). Aspect mining using clone class metrics. In *Proceedings of the 1ˢᵗ Workshop on Aspect Reverse Engineering*. Academic Press.

Bruntink, M., Van Deursen, A., Van Engelen, R., & Tourwe, T. (2005). On the use of clone detection for identifying crosscutting concern code. *IEEE Transactions on Software Engineering, 31*(10), 804–818. doi:10.1109/TSE.2005.114

Burtch, G., Ghose, A., & Wattal, S. (2011). *An empirical examination of the antecedents of contribution patterns in crowdfunded markets*. Academic Press.

Campbell, S., & Kleiner, B. H. (2001). New developments in re-engineering organizations. *Management Research News, 24*(3–4), 5–8. doi:10.1108/01409170110782531

Cam, S., Purcell, J., & Tailby, S. (2003). Contingent employment in the UK. In O. Bergström & D. W. Storri (Eds.), *Contingent employment in europe and the united states* (pp. 52–78). Cheltenham, UK: Edward Elgar Publishing. doi:10.4337/9781781008126.00010

Canfora, G., Cerulo, L., & Di Penta, M. (2006). On the use of line co-change for identifying crosscutting concern code. In *Proceedings of the 22nd IEEE International Conference on Software Maintenance* (pp. 213-222). IEEE. doi:10.1109/ICSM.2006.43

Cannizzo, F., Marcionetti, G., & Moser, P. (2008, August). Evolution of the tools and practices of a large distributed agile team. In *Proceedings of the Agile 2008 Conference, IEEE Computers and Society*. IEEE.

Carr, D., & Johansson. (1995). *Best practices in reengineering: What works and what doesn't in the reengineering process*. New York, NY: McGraw–Hill.

Carroll, J. M. (1996). Becoming social: Expanding scenario-based approaches in HCI. *Behaviour & Information Technology, 15*(4), 266–275. doi:10.1080/014492996120184

Carroll, J. M. (2000). Five reasons for scenario-based design. *Interacting with Computers, 13*(1), 43–60. doi:10.1016/S0953-5438(00)00023-0

Cataldo, M., & Ehrlich, K. (2011). The Impact of the Structure of Communication Patterns in Global Software Development: An Empirical Analysis of a Project Using Agile Methods. Pittsburgh, PA: Institute for Software. Retrieved from http://reports-archive.adm.cs.cmu.edu/anon/anon/home/ftp/isr2011/CMU-ISR-11-103.pdf

Cataldo, M., & Herbsleb, J. D. (2008). Communication patterns in geographically distributed software development and engineers' contributions to the development effort. In *Proceedings of the International Workshop on Cooperative and Human Aspects Of Software Engineering (CHASE'08)*. Leipzig,Germany: ACM.

Cataldo, M., Wagstrom, P. A., & Carley, K. M. (2006). Identification of Coordination Requirements : Implications for the Design of Collaboration and Awareness Tools. In *Proceedings of 20th anniversary conference on Computer supported cooperative work (CSCW'06)*. New York, US: ACM. doi:10.1145/1180875.1180929

Chandler, D. (2007). *Semiotics: the basics*. New York, NY: Routledge.

Chan, K. K., & Spedding, T. A. (2003). An integrated multidimensional process improvement methodology for manufacturing systems. *Computers & Industrial Engineering, 44*(4), 673–693. doi:10.1016/S0360-8352(03)00002-0

Chappell, D. (2004). *Enterprise service bus*. Sebastopol, CA: O'Reilly Media, Inc.

Chidamber, S. R., & Kemerer, C. F. (1994). A metrics suite for object oriented design. *IEEE Transactions on Software Engineering, 20*(6), 476–493. doi:10.1109/32.295895

Chi, W., Freeman, R. B., & Kleiner, M. M. (2011). Adoption and termination of employee involvement programs. *LABOUR, 25*(1), 45–62. doi:10.1111/j.1467-9914.2010.00510.x

Chow, T., & Cao, D. B. (2008). A survey study of critical success factors in agile software projects. *Journal of Systems and Software, 81*(6), 961–971. doi:10.1016/j.jss.2007.08.020

Christian. (2010). *Security Requirements Reusability and the SQUARE Methodology* (cmu/sei-2010-tn-027). Carnegie Mellon University, the Software Engineering Institute.

Christudas, B. A. (2008). *Service Oriented Java Business Integration: Enterprise Service Bus integration solutions for Java developer*. Birmingham, UK: Packt Publishing.

Chronéer, D., & Bergquist, B. (2012). Managerial complexity in process industrial R&D projects: A Swedish study. *Project Management Journal, 43*(2), 21–36. doi:10.1002/pmj.21257

Chuiyi, X., Yizhi, Z., Yuan, B., Shuoshan, L., & Qin, X. (2011). *A Distributed Intrusion Detection System against flooding Denial of Services attacks*. 13th International Conference on, Advanced Communication Technology (ICACT).

Clark, K. D., & Maggitti, P. G. (2012). TMT potency and strategic decision-making in high technology firms. *Journal of Management Studies, 49*(7), 1168–1193. doi:10.1111/j.1467-6486.2012.01060.x

Clegg, B. (2006). Business process orientated holonic (PrOH) modeling. *Business Process Management Journal, 12*(4), 410–432. doi:10.1108/14637150610678050

Clocksin, F. W., & Mellish, C. S. (2003). *Programming in Prolog*. Berlin: Springer-Verlag. doi:10.1007/978-3-642-55481-0

Cloud Security Alliance. (2010). *Top Threats to Cloud Computing*. Retrieved from http://www.cloudsecurityalliance.org/topthreats/csathreats.v1.0.pdf

Cockburn, A., & Highsmith, J. (2001). Agile software development: The people factor. *IEEE Computer, 34*(11), 131–133. doi:10.1109/2.963450

Cockrill, A., & Goode, M. M. H. (2010). Perceived price fairness and price decay in the DVD market. *Journal of Product and Brand Management, 19*(5), 367–374. doi:10.1108/10610421011068603

Cohn, M. (n.d.a). *Daily Scrum Meeting*. Retrieved December 21, 2014, from http://mountaingoatsoftware.com/agile/scrum/daily-scrum

Cohn, M. (n.d.b). *Sprint Planning Meeting*. Retrieved December 21, 2014, from http://mountaingoatsoftware.com/agile/scrum/sprint-planning-meeting

Cohn, M. (2003). *User Stories Applied For Agile Software Development*. Addison Wesley.

Cohn, M. (2004). *User stories applied: For agile software development*. Addison-Wesley Professional.

Cohn, S. (2013). *A Firm-Level Innovation Management Framework and Assessment Tool for Increasing Competitiveness*. Technology Innovation Management Review.

Coleman, J. P. (2013). Data flow sequences: A revision of data flow diagrams for modelling applications using XML. *International Journal of Advanced Computer Science & Applications*, *4*(5).

Combs, J. G., Ketchen, D. J. Jr, Ireland, R. D., & Webb, J. W. (2011). The role of resource flexibility in leveraging strategic resources. *Journal of Management Studies*, *48*(5), 1098–1125. doi:10.1111/j.1467-6486.2009.00912.x

Comella-Dorda, S., Wallnau, K., Seacord, R. C., & Robert, J. (2000). *A survey of legacy system modernization approaches, (No. CMU/SEI-2000-TN-003)*. Carnegie-Mellon University Pittsburgh Pa Software Engineering Institute.

Conboy, K., & Fitzgerald, B. (2004). Toward a Conceptual Framework of Agile Methods. In *Proceedings of the 2004 ACM Workshop on Interdisciplinary Software Engineering Research*. Newport Beach, CA: ACM. doi:10.1145/1029997.1030005

Cook, S., Harrison, R., Lehman, M. M., & Wernick, P. (2006). Evolution in software systems: Foundations of the SPE classification scheme. *Journal of Software Maintenance and Evolution: Research and Practice*, *18*(1), 1–35. doi:10.1002/smr.314

Coombs, R., Knights, D., & Willmott, H. (1992). Culture, control, and competition: Towards a conceptual framework for study of information technology in organization. *Organization Studies*, *13*(1), 51–72. doi:10.1177/017084069201300106

Cottmeyer, M. (2008, August). The good and bad of Agile offshore development. In *Proceedings Agile 2008* (pp. 362–367). Academic Press.

Coyle-Shapiro, J. A., & Kessler, I. (2002). Contingent and Non-Contingent working in local government: Contrasting psychological contracts. *Public Administration*, *80*(1), 77–101. doi:10.1111/1467-9299.00295

Cristini, A., Eriksson, T., & Pozzoli, D. (2013). High-performance management practices and employee outcomes in Denmark. *Scottish Journal of Political Economy*, *60*(3), 232–266. doi:10.1111/sjpe.12010

Crowe, T. J., Fong, P. M., & Zayas-Castro, J. L. (2002). Quantitative risk level estimation of business process reengineering efforts. *Business Process Management Journal*, *8*(5), 490–511. doi:10.1108/14637150210449148

Cunha, R., Cunha, M., Morgado, A., & Brewster, C. (2003). Market forces, strategic management, HRM practices and organizational performance, A model based in a european sample. *Management Research*, *1*(1), 79–91. doi:10.1108/15365430380000519

Cunliffe, D. (2000). Developing usable web sites–a review and model. *Internet Research*, *10*(4), 295–308. doi:10.1108/10662240010342577

Cunliffe, D., Kritou, E., & Tudhope, D. (2001). Usability evaluation for museum web sites. *Museum Management and Curatorship*, *19*(3), 229–252. doi:10.1080/09647770100201903

Cunliffe, D., Morris, D., & Prys, C. (2013). Young bilinguals' language behaviour in social networking sites: The use of welsh on facebook. *Journal of Computer-Mediated Communication*, *18*(3), 339–361. doi:10.1111/jcc4.12010

Cusumano, M., MacCormack, A., Kemerer, C. F., & Crandall, W. (2003). A global survey of software development practices. *eBusiness@ MIT, 178*, 1-17.

Cypress, H. (1994). Reengineering. *OR/MS Today, 21*(1), 18–29.

D'Ambros, M., & Lanza, M. (2006). Reverse engineering with logical coupling. In *Proceedings of the 13th Working Conference on Reverse Engineering*. Washington, DC: IEEE Computer Society.

Dabholka r, V., & Krishnan, R. T. (2013). *8 Steps to innovation: Going from jugaad to excellence*. Harper Collins Publishers.

Damian, D., Kwan, I., & Marczak, S. (2010). Requirements-Driven Collaboration : Leveraging the Invisible Relationships Between Requirements and People. In A. Finkelstein, J. Grundy, A. van der Hoek, I. Mistrik, & J. Whitehead (Eds.), *Collaborative Software Engineering, Computer Science Editorial Series* (pp. 1–24). Berlin, Germany: Springer-Verlag. doi:10.1007/978-3-642-10294-3_3

Damian, D., Marczak, S., & Kwan, I. (2007). Collaboration Patterns and the Impact of Distance on Awareness in Requirements-Centred Social Networks. In *Proceedings of 15th International Requirements Engineering Conference (RE'07)*. Delhi, India: IEEE. doi:10.1109/RE.2007.51

Darmani, A., & Hanafizadeh, P. (2013). Business process portfolio selection in re-engineering projects. *Business Process Management Journal, 19*(6), 892–916. doi:10.1108/BPMJ-08-2011-0052

Davenport, T. H. (1993). Need radical innovation and continuous improvement? Integrated process reengineering and TQM. *Planning Review, 21*(3), 6–12. doi:10.1108/eb054413

Davenport, T. H. (2008). Business process management-foreword. In V. Grover & M. L. Markus (Eds.), *Business process transformation* (pp. 41–46). Armonk, NY: M.E. Sharpe.

Davenport, T. H., & Short, J. (1990). The new industrial engineering: Information technology and business process redesign. *Sloan Management Review, 31*(4), 11–27.

Davidson, W. (1993). Beyond re-engineering: The three phases of business transformation. *IBM Systems Journal, 32*(1), 65–79. doi:10.1147/sj.321.0065

Davis, C. (2000). Maintaining a balance? In A. Scammell (Ed.), *I in the sky: Visions of the information future* (pp. 18–29). London: Routledge.

Dawson, C., & Dawson, R. (2014). Software development process models: A technique for evaluation and Decision-Making. *Knowledge and Process Management, 21*(1), 42–53. doi:10.1002/kpm.1419

DDOS Attacks. (n.d.). Retrieved from http://www.DDOSattacks.biz/DDOS-101/glossary/scrubbing-center/

de Beer, E., & Rensburg, R. (2011). Towards a theoretical framework for the governing of stakeholder relationships: A perspective from South Africa. *Journal of Public Affairs, 11*(4), 208–225. doi:10.1002/pa.414

De Bruyn, P., Van Nuffel, D., Verelst, J., & Mannaert, H. (2012). Towards Applying Normalized Systems Theory Implications to Enterprise Process Reference Models. In A. Albani, D. Aveiro, & J. Barjis (Eds.), *Advances in Enterprise Engineering VI* (pp. 31–45). Berlin, Germany: Springer. doi:10.1007/978-3-642-29903-2_3

de Fortuny, E. J., Martens, D., & Provost, F. (2013). Predictive modeling with big data: Is bigger really better? *Big Data*, de Souza, C. S., & Preece, J. (2004). A framework for analyzing and understanding online communities. *Interacting with Computers, 16*(3), 579–610.

De Nicola, A., Missikoff, M., & Smith, F. (2012). Towards a method for business process and informal business rules compliance. *Journal of Software: Evolution and Process, 24*(3), 341–360.

Dearden, A., & Light, A. (2009). *Designing for e-social action an application taxonomy*. Sheffield, UK: Communication & Computing Research Centre.

Debela, T. (2010). Business process reengineering in Ethiopian public organizations: The relationship between theory and practice. *Journal of Business and Administrative Studies*, *1*(2), 20–59. doi:10.4314/jbas.v1i2.57348

Delgado, J. (2012). Structural interoperability as a basis for service adaptability. In G. Ortiz & J. Cubo (Eds.), *Adaptive Web Services for Modular and Reusable Software Development: Tactics and Solutions* (pp. 33–59). Hershey, PA: IGI Global.

Delgado, J. (2013). Architectural Styles for Distributed Interoperability.[IRMJ]. *Information Resources Management Journal*, *26*(4), 40–65. doi:10.4018/irmj.2013100103

Ding & Yeung. (2002). *User Profiling for Intrusion Detection Using Dynamic and Static Behavioral Models*. Springer Berlin Heidelberg.

Dingsøyr, T., Nerur, S., Balijepally, V., & Moe, N. (2012). A decade of agile methodologies: Towards explaining agile software development. *Journal of Systems and Software*, *85*(6), 1213–1221. doi:10.1016/j.jss.2012.02.033

Dixon, N. M. (2000). *Common knowledge: How companies thrive by sharing what they know*. Boston: Harvard Business Press.

DNA Correspondent. (2013). Retrieved from http://www.dnaindia.com/academy/report-indian-varsities-account-for-5-of-patents-1853811

Doherty, M. J. (2011). *Examining Project Manager Insights of Agile and Traditional Success Factors for Information Technology Projects: A Q-Methodology Study*. (PhD Dissertation). Marian University.

Dongjin, Y. U., Xiang, S. U., & Yunlei, M. U. (2014). Towards the Identification of Crosscutting Concerns: A Comprehensive Dynamic Approach Based on Execution Relations. *IEICE Transactions on Information and Systems*, *97*(5), 1235–1243.

Doomun, R., & Jungum, N. V. (2008). Business process modelling, simulation and reengineering: Call centres. *Business Process Management Journal*, *14*(6), 838–848. doi:10.1108/14637150810916017

Drummond, B., and Unson, J. F. (2008, August). Yahoo! Distributed Agile: Notes from the world over. In *Proceedings of the Conference on Agile 2008*. IEEE Computer Society. doi:10.1109/Agile.2008.21

Dustdar, S., & Schreiner, W. (2005). A survey on web services composition. *International Journal of Web and Grid Services*, *1*(1), 1–30. doi:.10.1504/IJWGS.2005.007545

Dyer, J., & Gregersen, H. (n.d.). *The secret of innovative companies isn't RD*. Retrieved from http://www.innovation-management.se/2013/04/18/the-secret-of-innovative-compa-nies-it-isnt-rd/

Eardley, A., Shah, H., & Radman, A. (2008). A model for improving the role of IT in BPR. *Business Process Management Journal*, *14*(5), 629–653. doi:10.1108/14637150810903039

Eberlein, A., & Julio Cesar, S. do P. L. (2002). Agile Requirements Definition : A View from Requirements Engineering. In *Proceedings of the International Workshop on Time Constrained Requirements Engineering*. Essen, Germany: IEEE.

Ehrig, M. (2007). Ontology alignment: bridging the semantic gap (Vol. 4). New York, NY: Springer Science+Business Media, LLC.

Ehrlich, K., Cataldo, M., & York, N. (2014). The Communication Patterns of Technical Leaders : Impact on Product Development Team Performance. In *Computer Supported Cooperative Work* (pp. 733–744). Baltimore, MD, US: ACM. doi:10.1145/2531602.2531671

Ehrlich, K., & Chang, K. (2006). Leveraging expertise in global software teams: Going outside boundaries. In *Proceedings of International Conference on Global Software Engineering (ICGSE'06)*. Florianopolis, Brazil: IEEE. doi:10.1109/ICGSE.2006.261228

EIF. (2010). *European Interoperability Framework (EIF) for European Public Services, Annex 2 to the Communication from the Commission to the European Parliament, the Council, the European Economic and Social Committee and the Committee of Regions 'Towards interoperability for European public services'*. Retrieved July 21, 2014 from http://ec.europa.eu/isa/documents/isa_annex_ii_eif_en.pdf

El-Aziz, R. M. A., Aboutabl, A. E., & Mostafa, M. S. (2012). Clone Detection Using DIFF Algorithm for Aspect Mining. *International Journal of Advanced Computer Science & Applications*, *3*(8), 137–140.

Elkins, D. A., Huang, N., & Alden, J. M. (2004). Agile manufacturing systems in the automotive industry. *International Journal of Production Economics*, *91*(3), 201–214. doi:10.1016/j.ijpe.2003.07.006

Engeström, Y., & Miettinen, R. (1999). *Perspectives on activity theory*. Cambridge, UK: Cambridge University Press. doi:10.1017/CBO9780511812774

Erdil, K., Finn, E., Keating, K., Meattle, J., Park, S., & Yoon, D. (2003). *Software Maintenance As Part of the Software Life Cycle*. Comp180: Software Engineering Project.

Erl, T. (2008). *SOA: Principles of Service Design*. Upper Saddle River, NJ: Prentice Hall PTR.

Erl, T., Utschig, C., Maier, B., Normann, H., & Trops, B. (2013). *Next Generation SOA: A Real-World Guide to Modern Service-Oriented Computing*. Upper Saddle River, NJ: Prentice Hall PTR.

Esmaeili, A. (2012). Strategic human-resource management in a dynamic environment. *Scientific and Technical Information Processing*, *39*(2), 85–89. doi:10.3103/S0147688212020037

Euzenat, J., & Shvaiko, P. (2007). *Ontology matching*. Berlin, Germany: Springer.

Faison, T. (2006). *Event-Based Programming*. Berkeley, CA: Apress.

Faizal, M.A., Zaki, M.M., Shahrin, S., Robiah, Y., & Rahayu, S.S. (2010). Statistical Approach for Validating Static Threshold in Fast Attack Detection. *Journal of Advanced Manufacturing*.

FDRsafty. (2014). *Seven forms of Waste*. Retrieved on 21.11.2014 from http://www.fdrsafety.com/LS-7FormsOfWaste.pdf

Fernando Cardoso de Sousa. (2012). Creativity, innovation and collaborative organizations. *The International Journal of Organization Innovation*, *5*(1).

Fielding, R. (2000). *Architectural Styles and the Design of Network-based Software Architectures*. (Doctoral dissertation). University of California at Irvine, CA.

Figallo, C. (1998). *Hosting web communities: Building relationships, increasing customer loyalty, and maintaining a competitive edge*. New York, NY: John Wiley & Sons, Inc.

Firesmith, D. (2004). Prioritizing Requirements. *Journal of Object Technology*, *3*(8), 35–48. doi:10.5381/jot.2004.3.8.c4

Flight Gear source code available (Parent Directory). (n.d.). Retrieved February15,2014 from FGS website http://fgfs.physra.net/ftp/Source

FlightGear Flight Simulator. (1996). *Flight Gear Revision details*. Retrieved February 20, 2014 from website: http://www.flightgear.org

Fogg, B. J. (2002). *Persuasive technology: Using computers to change what we think and do.* San Francisco, CA: Morgan Kaufmann.

Fox, A. (n.d.). *Working on Multiple Agile Teams.* Retrieved December 20, 2014, from http://techwhirl.com/working-multiple-agile-teams/

Fricke, E., & Schulz, A. (2005). Design for changeability (DfC): Principles to enable changes in systems throughout their entire lifecycle. *Systems Engineering, 8*(4), 342–359. doi:10.1002/sys.20039

Frishammar, J., Lichtenthaler, U., & Richtnér, A. (2013). Managing process development: Key issues and dimensions in the front end. *R & D Management, 43*(3), 213–226. doi:10.1111/radm.12011

Fuhr, A., Winter, A., Erdmenger, U., Horn, T., Kaiser, U., Riediger, V., & Teppe, W. (2012). Model-Driven Software Migration: Process Model, Tool Support, and Application. In A. D. Ionita, M. Litoiu, & G. Lewis (Eds.), *Migrating Legacy Applications: Challenges in Service Oriented Architecture and Cloud Computing Environments.* Hershey, PA: Information Science Publishing.

Fuks, H., Rapsoso, A., Gerosa, M. A., Pimental, M., & Lucena, C. J. P. (2008). The 3C Collaboration Model. In K. K. K. Roth, J. N. S. Reed, & K. P. B. Shore (Eds.), Encyclopedia of E-Collaboration (pp. 637–344). UK: Information Science Reference (an imprint of IGI Global).

Ganguly, A., Nilchiani, R., & Farr, J. (2009). Evaluating agility in corporate enterprises. *International Journal of Production Economics, 118*(2), 410–423. doi:10.1016/j.ijpe.2008.12.009

Ganter, B., & Wille, R. (1999). *Formal concept analysis: Mathematical foundations.* Berlin: Springer-Verlag Berlin Heidelberg. doi:10.1007/978-3-642-59830-2

Garrett, R. P. Jr, & Neubaum, D. O. (2013). Top management support and initial strategic assets: A dependency model for internal corporate venture performance. *Journal of Product Innovation Management, 30*(5), 896–915. doi:10.1111/jpim.12036

Geetika, R., & Singh, P. (2014). Dynamic coupling metrics for object oriented software systems: A survey. *Software Engineering Notes, 39*(2), 1–8. doi:10.1145/2579281.2579296

George, C. (n.d.). *Why Limiting Your Work-in-Progress Matters.* Retrieved December 20, 2014, from http://leankit.com/blog/2014/03/limiting-work-in-progress/

Georgsson, A. (2011). *Introducing story points and user stories to perform estimations in a software development organisation. A case study at Swedbank IT.* (Unpublished master's thesis). Umeå University, Umeå, Sweden.

Giaglis, G. M., Hlupic, V., de Vreede, G. J., & Verbraeck, A. (2005). Synchronous design of business processes and information systems using dynamic process modeling. *Business Process Management Journal, 11*(5), 488–500. doi:10.1108/14637150510619849

Gibb, A. A. (1997). Small firms' training and competitiveness. building upon the small business as a learning organisation. *International Small Business Journal, 15*(3), 13–29. doi:10.1177/0266242697153001

GLE Source Code. (n.d.). Retrieved March 13, 2014 from SourceForge website: http://sourceforge.net/projects/glx/files/gle3.3h%20(old%20version)/source%20code/

Godfrey, M. W., & Tu, Q. (2000). Evolution in open source software: A case study. In *Proceedings of IEEE International Conference on Software Maintenance (ICSM'00).* IEEE Computer Society Press.

Goldman, S. L., Nagel, R. N., & Preiss, K. (1995). *Agile Competitors and Virtual Organizations: Strategies for Enriching the Customer*. Van Nostrand Reinhold.

Goldstein, I. (2011). *Sprint issues – When sprints turn into crawls*. Retrieved December 18, 2014, from http://axisagile.com.au/blog/planning-and-metrics/sprint-issues-when-sprints-turn-into-crawls/

Gorard, S. (2003). Patterns of work-based learning. *Journal of Vocational Education and Training*, *55*(1), 47–64. doi:10.1080/13636820300200218

Grachev, V. M., Esin, V. I., Polukhina, N. G., & Rassomakhin, S. G. (2014). Technology for developing databases of information systems. *Bulletin of the Lebedev Physics Institute*, *41*(5), 119–122. doi:10.3103/S1068335614050017

Grant, D. (2002). A wider view of business process reengineering. *Communications of the ACM*, *45*(2), 84–92. doi:10.1145/503124.503128

Graphics Layout Engine. (2012). *GLE revision details*. Retrieved March12, 2014 from GLE website, http://www.gle-graphics.org

Green Suplier Netwrok. (2014). *Lean and clean value stream mapping*. Retrieved on 10.06.2014 from http://gsn.nist.gov/pubs/VSM.pdf

Green, F., & Wayhan, V. (1996). Reengineering: Clarifying the confusion. *SAM Advanced Management Journal*, *61*(3), 37–40.

Green, P., & Roseman, M. (2000). Integrated process modeling: An ontological evaluation. *Information Systems*, *25*(2), 73–87. doi:10.1016/S0306-4379(00)00010-7

Green, S. D. (2011). *From business process re-engineering to partnering, in making sense of construction improvement*. Oxford, UK: Wiley-Blackwell. doi:10.1002/9781444341102

Grieves, J. (2000). Introductions: The origins of organizational development. *Journal of Management Development*, *19*(5), 345–447. doi:10.1108/02621710010371865

Grinys, A. (2012). *Agile Project Estimation*. Retrieved from http://skemman.is/stream/get/1946/11973/30239/4/AG_MSthesis.pdf

Griswold, W. G., Kato, Y., & Yuan, J. J. (1999). *Aspect Browser: Tool support for managing dispersed aspects*. In *First Workshop on Multi-Dimensional Separation of Concerns in Object-Oriented Systems*.

Grover, V., Jeong, S. R., Kettinger, W., & Teng, J. T. (1995). The implementation of business process reengineering. *Journal of Management Information Systems*, *12*(1), 109–144.

Grover, V., & Malhotra, M. (1997). Business process re-engineering: A tutorial on the concept, evolution, method, technology and application. *Journal of Operations Management*, *15*(3), 193–213. doi:10.1016/S0272-6963(96)00104-0

Grover, V., Teng, J., & Fiedler, K. (1993). Information technology enabled business process redesign: An integrated planning framework. *Omega: The International Journal of Management Science*, *21*(4), 433–447. doi:10.1016/0305-0483(93)90076-W

Groznik, A., & Maslaric, M. (2012). A process approach to distribution channel re-engineering. *Journal of Enterprise Information Management*, *25*(2), 123–135. doi:10.1108/17410391211204383

Guimaraes, T. (1999). Field testing of the proposed predictors of BPR success in manufacturing firms. *Journal of Manufacturing Systems*, *18*(1), 53–65. doi:10.1016/S0278-6125(99)80012-0

Guimaraes, T., & Paranjape, K. (2013). Testing success factors for manufacturing BPR project phases. *International Journal of Advanced Manufacturing Technology, 68*(9–12), 1937–1947. doi:10.1007/s00170-013-4809-0

Gulden, G., & Reck, R. (1992). Combining quality and re-engineering efforts for process excellence. *Information Strategy: The Executive's Journal, 10*(1), 10–16.

Gunasekaran, A. (1998). Agile manufacturing: Enablers and an implementation framework. *International Journal of Production Research, 36*(5), 1223–1247. doi:10.1080/002075498193291

Gunasekaran, A. (1999). Agile manufacturing: A framework for research and development. *International Journal of Production Economics, 62*(1), 87–105. doi:10.1016/S0925-5273(98)00222-9

Gunasekaran, A. (1999). Editorial: Design and implementation of agile manufacturing systems. *International Journal of Production Economics, 62*(1-2), 1–6. doi:10.1016/S0925-5273(98)00216-3

Gunasekaran, A., Chung, W. W. C., & Kan, K. (2000). Business process reengineering in British company: A case study. *Logistics Information Management, 13*(5), 271–285. doi:10.1108/09576050010378496

Gupta, Joshi, & Misra (2000). Defending against Distributed Denial of Service Attacks: Issues and Challenges. *Information Security Journal: A Global Perspective, 18*(5), 224-247.

Gupta, V. K. (2008). Retrieved October 13, 2014 from http://www.nistads.res.in/indiasnt2008/t5output/t5out9.htm

Gupta, S., Kumar, P., & Abraham, A. (2013). A Profile Based Network Intrusion Detection and Prevention System for Securing Cloud Environment. *International Journal of Distributed Sensor Networks, 2013*, 364575. doi:10.1155/2013/364575

Gutwin, C., & Greenberg, S. (2004). The Importance of Awareness for Team Cognition in Distributed Collaboration. In E. Salas & S. Fiore (Eds.), *Team Cognition: Understanding the Factors That Drive Process and Performance* (pp. 177–201). doi:10.1037/10690-009

Gybels, K., & Kellens, A. (2004). An experiment in using inductive logic programming to uncover pointcuts. *European Interactive Workshop on Aspects in Software.*

Gybels, K., & Kellens, A. (2005). *Experiences with identifying aspects in smalltalk using 'unique methods'.* In *Workshop on Linking Aspect Technology and Evolution.*

Ha, B. H., Bae, J., Park, Y. T., & Kang, S. H. (2006). Development of process execution rules for workload balancing on agents. *Data & Knowledge Engineering, 56*(1), 64–84. doi:10.1016/j.datak.2005.02.007

Hagen, M., & Gavrilova Aguilar, M. (2012). The impact of managerial coaching on learning outcomes within the team context: An analysis. *Human Resource Development Quarterly, 23*(3), 363–388. doi:10.1002/hrdq.21140

Hammer, M. (1990). Reengineering work: Don't automate, obliterate. *Harvard Business Review, 68*(4), 104–112.

Hammer, M. (2010). What is business process management? In J. vom Brocke & M. Rosemann (Eds.), *Handbook on business process management 1: Introduction, methods, and information systems* (pp. 3–16). Berlin, Germany: Springer–Verlag. doi:10.1007/978-3-642-00416-2_1

Hammer, M., & Champy, J. (1993). *Reengineering the corporation: A manifesto for business revolution.* New York, NY: HarperBusiness.

Hannemann, J., & Kiczales, G. (2001). Overcoming the prevalent decomposition in legacy code. In *Proceedings of Workshop on Advanced Separations of Concerns, 23rd International Conference on Software Engineering (ICSE).* Toronto, Canada: Academic Press.

Harland, C. M. (1997). Supply chain operational performance roles. *Integrated Management Systems, 8*(2), 6–14.

Harmon, P. (2010). The scope and evolution of business process management? In J. vom Brocke & M. Rosemann (Eds.), *Handbook on business process management 1: Introduction, methods, and information systems* (pp. 37–81). Berlin, Germany: Springer–Verlag. doi:10.1007/978-3-642-00416-2_3

Hauglum, J. (n.d.). Retrieved October 15, 2014 from http://www.mixprize.org/story/ensuring-innovation-through-autonomy-work

Hawryszkiewycz, I. (2008). Supporting complex adaptive processes with lightweight platforms. In L. M. Camarinha-Matos & W. Picard (Eds.), *Pervasive collaborative networks* (pp. 381–388). Wien, Austria: Springer. doi:10.1007/978-0-387-84837-2_39

He, L., Bai, H., Zhang, J., & Hu, C. (2005). AMUCA algorithm for aspect mining. In *Proceedings of the 17ᵗʰ International Conference on Software Engineering and Knowledge Engineering* (SEKE, 2005), (pp. 520-524). SEKE.

Hebeler, J., Fisher, M., Blace, R., Perez-Lopez, A., & Dean, M. (2009). *Semantic Web Programming*. New Jersey: John Wiley & Son.

Heizer, J., & Render, B. (2011). *Operations management*. Upper Saddle River, NJ: Printice–Hall.

Heraclitus., & Patrick, G. (Eds.). (2013). The Fragments of Heraclitus. New York, NY: Digireads.com Publishing.

Herazo, B., Lizarralde, G., & Paquin, R. (2012). Sustainable development in the building sector: A Canadian case study on the alignment of strategic and tactical management. *Project Management Journal, 43*(2), 84–100. doi:10.1002/pmj.21258

Herzog, N. V., Polajnar, A., & Tonchia, S. (2007). Development and validation of business process reengineering (BPR) variables: A survey research in Slovenian companies. *International Journal of Production Research, 45*(24), 5811–5834. doi:10.1080/00207540600854992

Hesson, M. (2007). Business process reengineering in UAE public sector: A naturalization and residency case study. *Business Process Management Journal, 13*(5), 707–727. doi:10.1108/14637150710823174

He, X. J. (2005). A comparative study of business process reengineering in China. *Communication of the IIMA, 5*(2), 25–30.

Heygate, R. (1993). Immoderate redesign. *The McKinsey Quarterly*, (1): 73–87.

Highsmith. (2000). *Adaptive Software Development: A Collaborative Approach to Managing Complex Systems*. New York: Dorset House.

Hinds, P., & Mcgrath, C. (2006). Structures that Work : Social Structure, Work Structure and Coordination Ease in Geographically Distributed Teams. In *Proceedings of Computer Supported Cooperative Work (CSCW'06)*. Alberta, Canada: ACM. doi:10.1145/1180875.1180928

Hinterhuber, H. (1995). Business process management: The European approach. *Business Change & Re-engineering, 2*(4), 63–73.

Hirzinger, G., and Bauml, B. (2006, October). Agile robot development (aRD): A pragmatic approach to robotic software. In *Proceedings of IEEE/RSJ International Conference on Intelligent Robots and Systems* (pp. 3741–3748). IEEE.

Hix, D., & Hartson, H. R. (1993). *Developing user interfaces: Ensuring usability through product & process*. New York, NY: John Wiley & Sons, Inc.

Hock-Koon, A., & Oussalah, M. (2010). Defining metrics for loose coupling evaluation in service composition. In *International Conference on Services Computing* (pp. 362-369). Piscataway, NJ: IEEE Computer Society Press. doi:10.1109/SCC.2010.17

Hohpe, G., & Woolfe, B. (2004). *Enterprise Integration Patterns: Designing, Building, and Deploying Messaging Solutions*. Reading, MA: Addison-Wesley.

Hoyrup, S., Bonnafous-Boucher, M., Hasse, C., Lotz, M., & Moller, K. (2012). *Employee-Driven Innovation: A New Approach*. Palgrave Macmillan. doi:10.1057/9781137014764

Huang, J., Lu, Y., & Yang, J. (2010). Aspect mining using link analysis. In *Proceedings of the 5th International Conference on Frontier of Computer Science and Technology* (pp. 312-317). Academic Press.

Hunt, J. W., & McIlroy, M. D. (1976). *An algorithm for differential file comparison*. Computing Science Technical Report 41. Bell Laboratories.

Hutchins, E. (1995). Cognition in the wild. MIT Press.

Hwang, S., & Yang, W. (2002). On the discovery of process models from their instances. *Decision Support Systems*, *31*(1), 41–57. doi:10.1016/S0167-9236(02)00008-8

Iacocca Institute. (1991). 21st Century Manufacturing Enterprise Strategy. An Industry-Led View (2 vols.). Iacocca Institute.

Inayat, I., Marczak, S., & Salim, S. S. (2013). Studying Relevant Socio-technical Aspects of Requirements-Driven Collaboration in Agile Teams. In *Proceedings of 3rd International Workshop on Empirical Requirements Engineering*. Rio de Janeiro, Brazil: IEEE. doi:10.1109/EmpiRE.2013.6615213

Inayat, I., Salim, S. S., Marczak, S., & Kasirun, Z. M. (2014). Identifying and Reviewing the Most Relevant Socio-technical Aspects of Requirements- Driven Collaboration in Agile Teams. In *Proceedings of International Conference on Advancements in Engineering and Technology (ICAET'14)*. Singapore: IIENG.

India Today Online. (2014). Retrieved from http://indiatoday.intoday.in/education/story/iit-bombay-leads-with-400-percent-growth-in%20patentfiling/1/341476.html

Infosys Lodestone. (2014). *Using Lean IT to do more with less*. Retrieved on 11.11.2014 from http://www.lodestonemc.com/files/pdf/white%20papers/WP_LeanIT_web_271112.pdf

Institute, I. S. (2015). *DDOS Attack Categorization, University of Southern California. DDOS Bechmarks*. Retrieved December 11, 2014 from http://www.isi.edu/~mirkovic/bench

Ishio, T., Miyake, T., & Inoue, K. (2008). Mining coding patterns to detect crosscutting concerns in java programs. In *Proceedings of the 15th Working Conference on Reverse Engineering* (pp. 123-132). IEEE. doi:10.1109/WCRE.2008.28

ISO. (2011). *CEN EN/ISO 11354-1, Advanced Automation Technologies and their Applications, Part 1: Framework for Enterprise Interoperability*. Geneva, Switzerland: International Standards Office.

ISO/IEC. (1994). *ISO/IEC 7498-1, Information technology – Open Systems Interconnection – Basic Reference Model: The Basic Model, 2nd edition*. Geneva, Switzerland: International Standards Office. Retrieved July 21, 2014 from http://standards.iso.org/ittf/PubliclyAvailableStandards/index.html

ISO/IEC/IEEE. (2010). *Systems and software engineering – Vocabulary. International Standard ISO/IEC/IEEE 24765:2010(E)* (1st ed., p. 186). Geneva, Switzerland: International Organization for Standardization.

Iyer, V. N. (2008). *Legacy Modernization- Modernize and Scale. View point*. Infosys.

Jagadeeshraj, V.S., Lijoy, C. G., & Thenmozhi, S. (2013). Attaining Pre-Eminent Cloud Security Using Intrusion Detection Systems. *International Journal of Emerging Technology and Advanced Engineering, 3*(2), 214-219.

Jain, R., Erol, O., & Chandrasekaran, A. (2007). *Designing a course on business process reengineering (BPR): Bridging the gap between business operations and engineering of systems.* Paper presented at the 2007 ASEE Annual Conference, Honolulu, HI.

Jain, R., Chandrasekaran, A., & Gunasekaran, A. (2010). Benchmarking the redesign of "business process reengineering" curriculum: A continuous process improvement (CPI). *Benchmarking: An International Journal, 17*(1), 77–94. doi:10.1108/14635771011022325

Jain, R., Gunasekaran, A., & Chandrasekaran, A. (2009). Evolving role of business process reengineering: A perspective of employers. *Industrial and Commercial Training, 41*(7), 382–390. doi:10.1108/00197850910995782

Jalim, S. (2010). Green IT and collective action. In T. Tomlinson (Ed.), *Information technology for environmental sustainability* (pp. 147–170). Cambridge, MA: MIT Press.

Janzen, D., & De Volder, K. (2003). Navigating and querying code without getting lost. In *Proceedings of the 2nd International Conference on Aspect-Oriented Software Development* (pp. 178-187). ACM. doi:10.1145/643603.643622

Janzen, D., & Saiedian, H. (2005). Test-driven development: Concepts, taxonomy, and future direction. *Computer, 38*(9), 43–50. doi:10.1109/MC.2005.314

Jeong, B., Lee, D., Cho, H., & Lee, J. (2008). A novel method for measuring semantic similarity for XML schema matching. *Expert Systems with Applications, 34*(3), 1651–1658. doi:10.1016/j.eswa.2007.01.025

Jin, H., Xiang, G., Zou, D., Wu, S., Zhao, F., Li, M., & Zheng, W. (2011). A VMM-based intrusion prevention system in cloud computing environment. *The Journal of Supercomputing, 66*(3), 1133–1151. doi:10.1007/s11227-011-0608-2

Johansson, H., McHugh, P., Pendlebury, J., & Wheeler, W. (1993). *Business process reengineering: Break point strategies for market dominance.* Chichester, UK: John Wiley & Sons.

Johari, K., & Kaur, A., (2011). Effect of software evolution on software metrics: An open source case study. *ACM SIGSOFT Software Engineering Notes, 36*(5), 1-8. DOI: 10.1145/2020976.2020987

Josuttis, N. M. (2007). SOA in Pratice. Sebastopol, CA: O'Reilly Media.

Jun-Ho, Min-Woo, Jung-Ho, & Tai-Myoung. (2011). Multi-level intrusion detection system and log management in cloud computing. In *Proceedings of the13th International Conf.* Academic Press.

Juric, M., & Pant, K. (2008). *Business Process Driven SOA using BPMN and BPEL: From Business Process Modeling to Orchestration and Service Oriented Architecture.* Birmingham, UK: Packt Publishing.

Kamhawi, E. M. (2008). Determinants of Bahraini managers' acceptance of business process reengineering. *Business Process Management Journal, 14*(2), 166–187. doi:10.1108/14637150810864916

Kamiya, T., Kusumoto, S., & Inoue, K. (2002). CCFinder: A multilinguistic token-based code clone detection system for large scale source code. *IEEE Transactions on Software Engineering, 28*(7), 654–670. doi:10.1109/TSE.2002.1019480

Kasemsap, K. (2015a). The role of total quality management practices on quality performance. In A. Moumtzoglou, A. Kastania, & S. Archondakis (Eds.), *Laboratory management information systems: Current requirements and future perspectives* (pp. 1–31). Hershey, PA: IGI Global. doi:10.4018/978-1-4666-6320-6.ch001

Kasemsap, K. (2015b). Developing a framework of human resource management, organizational learning, knowledge management capability, and organizational performance. In P. Ordoñez de Pablos, L. Turró, R. Tennyson, & J. Zhao (Eds.), *Knowledge management for competitive advantage during economic crisis* (pp. 164–193). Hershey, PA: IGI Global. doi:10.4018/978-1-4666-6457-9.ch010

Kasemsap, K. (2015c). The role of data mining for business intelligence in knowledge management. In A. Azevedo & M. Santos (Eds.), *Integration of data mining in business intelligence systems* (pp. 12–33). Hershey, PA: IGI Global. doi:10.4018/978-1-4666-6477-7.ch002

Kasemsap, K. (2015d). The role of information system within enterprise architecture and their impact on business performance. In M. Wadhwa & A. Harper (Eds.), *Technology, innovation, and enterprise transformation* (pp. 262–284). Hershey, PA: IGI Global. doi:10.4018/978-1-4666-6473-9.ch012

Kassahun, A. E., & Molla, A. (2013). BPR complementary competence: Definition, model and measurement. *Business Process Management Journal, 19*(3), 575–596. doi:10.1108/14637151311319950

Kaur, P., & Singh, H. (2011). Measurement of Processes in Open Source Software Development. In Proc. Trends in Information Management (vol. 7). Academic Press.

Kaur, T., Ratti, N., & Kaur, P. (2014). A Review of Lehman's Laws in Open Source Software Systems. *International Journal of Computer Science and Communication Engineering, 3*(2).

Keen, P. (1991). *Shaping the future: Business design through information technology.* Boston, MA: Harvard Business School Press.

Kelada, J. (1994). Is reengineering replacing total quality? *Quality Progress, 27*(12), 79–85.

Kellens, A., Mens, K., & Tonella, P. (2007). A survey of automated code-level aspect mining techniques. In A. Rashid & M. Akshit (Eds.), Transactions on Aspect-Oriented Software Development IV (LNCS), (vol. 4640, pp. 143–162). Berlin: Springer-Verlag. doi:10.1007/978-3-540-77042-8_6

Kerrigan, F., & Graham, G. (2010). Interaction of regional news-media production and consumption through the social space. *Journal of Marketing Management, 26*(3), 302–320. doi:10.1080/02672570903566334

Kettinger, W., Teng, J., & Guha, S. (1997). Business process change: A study of methodologies, techniques, and tools. *Management Information Systems Quarterly, 21*(1), 55–80. doi:10.2307/249742

Khadka, R., Batlajery, B. V., Saeidi, A., Jansen, S., & Hage, J. (2014). How do professionals perceive legacy systems and software modernization? In *Proceedings of the 36th International Conference on Software Engineering* (pp. 36-47). ACM New York. doi:10.1145/2568225.2568318

Khalil, O. E. M. (1997). Implications for the role of information systems in a business process reengineering environment. *Information Resources Management Journal, 10*(1), 36–42. doi:10.4018/irmj.1997010103

Khandwalla, P. A. (1985). *Management of Corporate Greatness: Blending Goodness with Greed.* Pearson Education in South Asia.

Kim, A. J. (2000). *Community building on the web: Secret strategies for successful online communities.* Berkeley, CA: Peachpit Press.

Kim, D., & Shen, W. (2007). An Approach to Evaluating Structural Pattern Conformance of UML Models. In *ACM Symposium on Applied Computing* (pp. 1404-1408). New York, NY: ACM Press. doi:10.1145/1244002.1244305

Klein, M. (1994). Reengineering methodologies and tools: A prescription for enhancing success. *Information Systems Management, 11*(2), 30–35. doi:10.1080/10580539408964633

Kober, R., Subraamanniam, T., & Watson, J. (2012). The impact of total quality management adoption on small and medium enterprises' financial performance. *Accounting and Finance, 52*(2), 421–438. doi:10.1111/j.1467-629X.2011.00402.x

Kokash, N., & Arbab, F. (2009). Formal Behavioral Modeling and Compliance Analysis for Service-Oriented Systems. In F. Boer, M. Bonsangue, & E. Madelaine (Eds.), *Formal Methods for Components and Objects* (pp. 21–41). Berlin, Germany: Springer-Verlag. doi:10.1007/978-3-642-04167-9_2

Komondoor, R., & Horwitz, S. (2001). Using slicing to identify duplication in source code. Static Analysis. In *Proceeding of the 8th International Symposium on Static Analysis SAS '01* (pp. 40-56). London, UK: Springer-Verlag.

Kooijmans, A. L., Chiang, R., Litman, I., Pettersson, M., Seubert, B., & Wendelboe, J. E. (2007). *SOA Transition Scenarios for the IBM z/OS Platform*. Upper Saddle River, NJ: IBM Redbooks.

Koskela, teknillinen tutkimuskeskus, V. (2003). *Software configuration management in agile methods*. VTT Technical Research Centre of Finland.

Kotnour, T. (2001). Building knowledge for and about large-scale organizational transformations. *International Journal of Operations & Production Management, 21*(8), 1053–1075. doi:10.1108/EUM0000000005585

Krinke, J., & Breu, S. (2004). *Control-flow-graph-based aspect mining*. 1st*Workshop on Aspect Reverse Engineering*.

Kruchten, P. (2001). *Common misconceptions about Software Architecture*. The Rational Edge.

Kruchten, P. (2004). *The rational unified process: an introduction*. Boston, MA: Pearson Education Inc.

Kull, T. J., Narasimhan, R., & Schroeder, R. (2012). Sustaining the benefits of a quality initiative through cooperative values: A longitudinal study. *Decision Sciences, 43*(4), 553–588. doi:10.1111/j.1540-5915.2012.00359.x

Kumar, S., & Dutta, K. (2011). Investigation on Security in Lms Moodle. *International Journal of Information Technology and Knowledge Management, 4*(1), 233–238.

Kuutti, K. (1996). Activity theory as a potential framework for human-computer interaction research. In Context and consciousness: Activity theory and human-computer interaction (pp. 17-44). Academic Press.

Kwan, I., & Damian, D. (2011). Extending Socio-technical Congruence with Awareness Relationships. In *Proceedings of 4th international workshop on Social Software Engineering*. Szeged, Hungary: ACM.

Kwee, Z., Van Den Bosch, F. A. J., & Volberda, H. W. (2011). The influence of top management team's corporate governance orientation on strategic renewal trajectories: A longitudinal analysis of Royal Dutch Shell plc, 1907–2004. *Journal of Management Studies, 48*(5), 984–1014. doi:10.1111/j.1467-6486.2010.00961.x

Lagerberg, L., Skude, T., Emanuelsson, P., & Sandahl, K. (2013). The Impact of Agile Principles and Practices on Large-Scale Software Development Projects: A Multiple-Case Study of Two Projects at Ericsson. In *International Symposium on Empirical Software Engineering and Measurement*. Baltimore, MD, US: IEEE. doi:10.1109/ESEM.2013.53

Lalonde, W. (1994). *Discovering Smalltalk*. Redwood City, CA: Benjamin Cummings.

Larman, C. (2004). *Agile and iterative development: a manager's guide*. Boston: Addison-Wesley Professional.

Larman, C., & Basili, V. R. (2003). Iterative and incremental development: A brief history. *IEEE Computer, 36*(6), 47–56. doi:10.1109/MC.2003.1204375

Laszenwski, T., & Williamson, J. (2008). *Oracle Modernization Solutions*. Birmingham, UK: Packt Publishing.

Laudon, K. C., & Laudon, J. P. (2006). *Management information system: Managing the digital firm*. Upper Saddle River, NJ: Prentice–Hall.

Lean Manufacturing Junction. (2014).*Key Lean Manufacturing Principle*. Retrieved on 15.10.2014 from http://www. lean-manufacturing-junction.com/lean-manufacturing-principles.html

Lee, S. M., & Asllani, A. (1997). TQM and BPR: Symbiosis and a new approach for integration. *Management Decision, 35*(6), 409–416. doi:10.1108/00251749710173788

Lehman, M. M. (1974). Programs, Cities, Students, Limits to Growth? Inaugural Lecture, May 1974. Imp. Col of Sc. Tech. Inaug. Lect. Ser., 9, 211 - 229.

Lehman, M. M. (1978). Laws of Program Evolution - Rules and Tools for Programming Management. In *Proc. Infotech State of the Art Conf., Why Software Projects Fail*. Academic Press.

Lehman, M. M., Ramil, J., Wernick, P., Perry, D., & Turski, W. (1997), Metrics and laws of software evolution - the nineties view. In *Proceedings of the Fourth Intl Software Metrics Symposium*. Portland, OR: Academic Press. doi:10.1109/METRIC.1997.637156

Lehman, M. M. (1980). On Understanding Laws, Evolution and Conservation in the Large Program Life Cycle. *Journal of Systems and Software, 1*(3), 213–221.

Lehman, M. M. (1980). Programs, life cycles and the laws of software evolution. *Proceedings of the IEEE, 68*(9), 1060–1076. doi:10.1109/PROC.1980.11805

Lehman, M. M., & Belady, L. A. (Eds.). (1985). *Program Evolution. Processes of Software Change*. San Diego, CA: Academic Press Professional, Inc.

Lewis, G., Morris, E., Simanta, S., & Wrage, L. (2008). Why Standards Are Not Enough To Guarantee End-to-End Interoperability. In C. Ncube, & J. Carvallo (Eds.) *Seventh International Conference on Composition-Based Software Systems* (pp. 164-173). Piscataway, NJ: IEEE Computer Society Press. doi:10.1109/ICCBSS.2008.25

Lientz, B. P., & Swanson, E. B. (1980). *Software Maintenance Management, A Study Of The Maintenance Of Computer Application Software In 487 Data Processing Organizations*. Reading, MA: Addison-Wesley.

Linden, R. M. (1994). *Seamless government: A practical guide to re-engineering in the public sector*. San Francisco, CA: Jossey–Bass.

Lindsay, A., Downs, D., & Lunn, K. (2003). Business processes: Attempts to find a definition. *Information and Software Technology, 45*(15), 1015–1019. doi:10.1016/S0950-5849(03)00129-0

Linthicum, D. (1999). *Enterprise application integration*. Massachusetts, USA: Addison-Wesley.

Liskov, B. (1988). Keynote address-data abstraction and hierarchy. *ACM Sigplan Notices, 23*(5), 17–34. doi:10.1145/62139.62141

Loonam, J., McDonagh, J., Kumar, V., & O'Regan, N. (2014). Top managers and information systems: "Crossing the Rubicon! *Strategic Change, 23*(3–4), 205–224. doi:10.1002/jsc.1971

Lowenthal, J. (1994). Reengineering the organization: A step-by-step approach to corporate revitalization. *Quality Progress, 27*(2), 61–63.

Luftman, J., & Ben-Zvi, T. (2009). Key issues for IT executives 2009: Difficult economy's impact on IT. *MIS Quarterly Executive, 9*(1), 203–213.

Luftman, J., & Zadeh, H. S. (2011). Key information technology and management issues 2010–11: An international study. *Journal of Information Technology*, *26*(3), 193–204. doi:10.1057/jit.2011.3

Luminita, D. C. (2011). Information security in E-learning Platforms. *Procedia Social and Behavioral Sciences, Elsevier*, *15*, 2689–2693. doi:10.1016/j.sbspro.2011.04.171

Mabin, V. J., Forgeson, S., & Green, L. (2001). Harnessing resistance: Using the theory of constraints to assist change management. *Journal of European Industrial Training*, *25*(2–4), 168–191. doi:10.1108/EUM0000000005446

MacIntosh, R. (2003). BPR: Alive and well in the public sector. *International Journal of Operations & Production Management*, *23*(3), 327–344. doi:10.1108/01443570310462794

Magutu, P. O., Nyamwange, S. O., & Kaptoge, G. K. (2010). Business process reengineering for competitive advantage: Key factors that may lead to the success or failure of the BPR implementation (The Wrigley Company). *African Journal of Business & Management*, *1*, 135–150.

Maisikeli, S. G., & Mitropoulos, F. J. (2010). Aspect mining using self-organizing maps with method level dynamic software metrics as input vectors. In *Proceedings of the 2nd International Conference on Software Technology and Engineering* (Vol. *1*, pp. V1-212 - V1-217). IEEE. doi:10.1109/ICSTE.2010.5608880

Malhotra, M., Grover, V., & Desilvio, M. (1996). Reengineering the new product development process: A framework for innovation and flexibility in high technology firms. *Omega: International Journal of Management Science*, *24*(4), 425–441. doi:10.1016/0305-0483(96)00007-2

Malik, N. (2009). Toward an Enterprise Business Motivation Model. *The Architecture Journal*, *19*, 10–16.

Malinova, A. (2010). *Approaches and techniques for legacy software modernization*. Plovdiv: Bulgaria Scientific Works.

Manganelli, R. L., & Klein, M. M. (1994). Your reengineering toolkit. *Management Review*, *83*(8), 26–29.

Mannaert, H., Verelst, J., & Ven, K. (2011). The transformation of requirements into software primitives: Studying evolvability based on systems theoretic stability. *Science of Computer Programming*, *76*(12), 1210–1222. doi:10.1016/j.scico.2010.11.009

Mannaert, H., Verelst, J., & Ven, K. (2012). Towards evolvable software architectures based on systems theoretic stability. *Software, Practice & Experience*, *42*(1), 89–116. doi:10.1002/spe.1051

Mansar, S. L., Marir, F., & Reijers, H. A. (2003). Case-based reasoning as a technique for knowledge management in business process redesign. *Electronic Journal of Knowledge Management*, *1*(2), 113–124.

Mansar, S. L., & Reijers, H. A. (2005). Best practices in business process redesign: Validation of a redesign framework. *Computers in Industry*, *56*(5), 457–471. doi:10.1016/j.compind.2005.01.001

Marchi, G., Giachetti, C., & De Gennaro, P. (2011). Extending lead-user theory to online brand communities: The case of the community Ducati. *Technovation*.

Marczak, S., & Damian, D. (2011). How interaction between roles shapes the communication structure in requirements-driven collaboration.*InProceeding of 19th International Requirements Engineering Conference*. Trento, Italy: IEEE. doi:10.1109/RE.2011.6051643

Marczak, S., Inayat, I., & Salim, S. S. (2013). Expanding Empirical Studies to Better Understand Requirements-driven Collaboration. In *Proceedings of Requirements Engineering in Brazil*. Rio de Janerio, Brazil: Springer-Verlag.

Marin, M., Deursen, A. V., & Moonen, L. (2007). Identifying crosscutting concerns using fan-in analysis. *ACM Transactions on Software Engineering and Methodology*, *17*(1), 3. doi:10.1145/1314493.1314496

Marin, M., Van Deursen, A., & Moonen, L. (2004). Identifying aspects using fan-in analysis. In *Proceedings of the 11th Working Conference on Reverse Engineering* (pp. 132-141). IEEE. doi:10.1109/WCRE.2004.23

Marin, M., van Deursen, A., Moonen, L., & van der Rijst, R. (2009). An integrated crosscutting concern migration strategy and its semi-automated application to JHotDraw. *Automated Software Engineering, 16*(2), 323–356. doi:10.1007/s10515-009-0051-2

Marir, F., & Mansar, S. L. (2004). *An adapted framework and case-based reasoning for business process redesign*. Paper presented at the IEEE 2nd International Conference on Information Technology: Research and Education, London, UK. doi:10.1109/ITRE.2004.1393671

Martin, R. (2003). *Agile software development: principles, patterns, and practices*. Upper Saddle River, NJ: Prentice Hall PTR.

Martinsuo, M., & Killen, C. P. (2014). Value management in project portfolios: Identifying and assessing strategic value. *Project Management Journal, 45*(5), 56–70. doi:10.1002/pmj.21452

Matthews, J. H. (2003). *Knowledge management and organizational learning: strategies and practices for innovation, Organizational Learning and Knowledge*. Paper presented at the 5th International Conference.

Maull, R. S., Tranfield, D. R., & Maull, W. (2003). Factors characterizing the maturity of BPR programmes. *International Journal of Operations & Production Management, 23*(6), 596–624. doi:10.1108/01443570310476645

Maull, R. S., Weaver, A. M., Childe, S. J., Smart, P. A., & Bennet, J. (1995). Current issues in business process re-engineering. *International Journal of Operations & Production Management, 15*(11), 37–52. doi:10.1108/01443579510102882

Mayrand, J., Leblanc, C., & Merlo, E. M. (1996). Experiment on the automatic detection of function clones in a software system using metrics. In *Proceedings of the International Conference on Software Maintenance* (pp. 244-253). IEEE. doi:10.1109/ICSM.1996.565012

Mbakwe, C., & Cunliffe, D. (2003). Conceptualising the process of hypermedia seduction. In *Proceedings of the 1st International Meeting of Science and Technology Design: Senses and Sensibility – Linking Tradition to Innovation through Design*. Lisbon, Portugal: Academic Press.

Mbakwe, C., & Cunliffe, D. (2007). Hypermedia seduction: Further exploration of the process of "seductive" online user interaction. In B. Ganor & K. von Knop (Eds.), *Hypermedia seduction for terrorist recruiting* (p. 207). New York, NY: Ios Pr Inc.

Mcfadden, R. R., & Mitropoulos, F. J. (2012). Aspect mining using model-based clustering. In *Proceedings of the Southeast Conference* (pp. 1-8). IEEE.

McHugh, M., McCaffery, F., & Casey, V. (2012). Barriers to adopting agile practices when developing medical device software. In *Software Process Improvement and Capability Determination* (pp. 141–147). Springer Berlin Heidelberg. doi:10.1007/978-3-642-30439-2_13

Melé, D. (2014). "Human quality treatment": Five organizational levels. *Journal of Business Ethics, 120*(4), 457–471. doi:10.1007/s10551-013-1999-1

Mell & Grance. (2009). *The NIST Definition of Cloud Computing version 15*. National Institutes of Standards and Technology (NIST), Information Technology Laboratory -Intrusion Detection. Retrieved December 5,2014 from http://en.wikipedia.org/wiki/Intrusion_detection_system

Meng, S., Iyengar, A. K., Rouvellou, I.M., Liu, Lee, Palanisamy, B., & Tang. (2012). Reliable State Monitoring in Cloud Datacenters. In *Proceedings of IEEE 5th International Conference on Cloud Computing* (CLOUD). IEEE.

Mens, K., Kellens, A., & Krinke, J. (2008). Pitfalls in aspect mining. In *Proceedings of the 15th Working Conference on Reverse Engineering* (pp. 113-122). IEEE.

Mens, T., Guehéneuc, Y. G., Ramil, J. F., & D'Hondt, M. (2010, July-August). Guest Editors' Introduction: Software Evolution. *IEEE Software*, 27(4), 22–25. doi:10.1109/MS.2010.100

Merritt, D. (1989). *Building Expert Systems in Prolog*. New York, NY: Springer-Verlag. doi:10.1007/978-1-4613-8911-8

Mertins, K., & Jochem, R. (2005). Architectures, methods and tools for enterprise engineering. *International Journal of Production Economics*, 98(2), 179–188. doi:10.1016/j.ijpe.2004.05.024

Metzler, T. (2011). *Venture financing by crowdfunding*. Munich: GRIN Verlag.

Middleware School. (2013) *Mule ESB*. Retrieved July 23, 2114, from http://training.middlewareschool.com/mule/category/mule/mule-esb/

Mihalache, O. R., Jansen, J. J. P., Van den Bosch, F. A. J., & Volberda, H. W. (2014). Top management team shared leadership and organizational ambidexterity: A moderated mediation framework. *Strategic Entrepreneurship Journal*, 8(2), 128–148. doi:10.1002/sej.1168

Mili, A., & Sheldon, F. T. (2009). Challenging the Mean Time to Failure: Measuring Dependability as a Mean Failure Cost. In *Proceedings of 42nd Hawaii International Conference on System Sciences (HICSS-42)*. Waikoloa, HI: IEEE.

Miranda, E., & Bourque, P. (2010). Agile monitoring using the line of balance. *Journal of Systems and Software*, 83(7), 1205–1215. doi:10.1016/j.jss.2010.01.043

Mitchell, R., Obeidat, S., & Bray, M. (2013). The effect of strategic human resource management on organizational performance: The mediating role of high-performance human resource practices. *Human Resource Management*, 52(6), 899–921. doi:10.1002/hrm.21587

MohdAlwi, N. H., & Fan, I. S. (2010). e-Learning and information security management. *International Journal of Digit Society, 1*(2), 148-156.

Moldovan, G. S., & Serban, G. (2006). Aspect mining using a vector-space model based clustering approach. In *Proceedings of Linking Aspect Technology and Evolution Workshop* (pp. 36-40). Academic Press.

Monfelt, Y., Pilemalm, S., Hallberg, J., & Yngström, L. (2011). The 14-layered framework for including social and organizational aspects in security management. *Information Management & Computer Security, 19*(2), 124–133. doi:10.1108/09685221111143060

Monowar,, H., Bhuyan, H. J., Kashyap, D. K., Bhattacharyya, & Kalita. (2013). Detecting Distributed Denial of Service Attacks: Methods, Tools and Future Directions. *The Computer Journal*.

Moonsamy, V., & Singh, S. (2014). Using factor analysis to explore principal components for quality management implementation. *Quality & Quantity, 48*(2), 605–622. doi:10.1007/s11135-012-9790-4

Moran, J. W., & Brightman, B. K. (2000). Leading organizational change. *Journal of Workplace Learning, 12*(2), 66–74. doi:10.1108/13665620010316226

Morris, E., ... (2004). *System of Systems Interoperability (SOSI): final report. Report No. CMU/SEI-2004-TR-004*. Carnegie Mellon Software Engineering Institute. Retrieved July 21, 2014 from http://www.sei.cmu.edu/reports/04tr004.pdf

Morris, D., Cunliffe, D., & Prys, C. (2012). Social networks and minority languages speakers: The use of social networking sites among young people. *Sociolinguistic Studies, 6*(1), 1–20. doi:10.1558/sols.v6.i1.1

Motwani, J., Subramanian, R., & Gopalakrishna, P. (2005). Critical factors for successful ERP implementation: Exploratory findings from four case studies. *Computers in Industry, 56*(6), 529–544. doi:10.1016/j.compind.2005.02.005

Mulder, F., & Zaidman, A. (2010). Identifying crosscutting concerns using software repository mining. In *Proceedings of the Joint ERCIM Workshop on Software Evolution and International Workshop on Principles of Software Evolution* (pp. 23-32). ACM. doi:10.1145/1862372.1862381

Mule, E. S. B. (2013). Retrieved September 28, 2113, from http://www.mulesoft.org

Mule, E. S. B. (2014). *Basic Studio and Tutorial.* Retrieved July 23, 2114, from http://www.mulesoft.org/documentation/display/current/Basic+Studio+Tutorial

Murauskaite, A., & Adomauskas, V. (2008). *Bottlenecks in Agile Software Development using Theory of Constraints (TOC) Principles* (Doctoral dissertation, Master's Thesis, Gothenburg, Sweden). (Report No. 2008:014)

Naaji, A., & Herman, C. (2011). Implementation of an e-learning system: Optimization and security Aspects. In *Proceedings of the 15th WSEAS International Conference on Computers, Part of the 15th WSEAS CSCC Multiconference.* WSEAS.

Nell, J. G., & Kosanke, K. (1997). Enterprise engineering and integration: building international consensus.*Proceedings of ICEIMT 97, International Conference on Enterprise Integration and Modeling Technology.* Springer.

Nerur, S., & Balijepally, V. (2007). Theoretical reflections on agile development methodologies. *Communications of the ACM, 50*(3), 79–83. doi:10.1145/1226736.1226739

Nerur, S., Mahapatra, R., & Mangalaraj, G. (2005). Challenges of migrating to agile methodologies. *Communications of the ACM, 48*(5), 72–78. doi:10.1145/1060710.1060712

Ng, J. K. C., Ip, W. H., & Lee, T. C. (1999). A paradigm for ERP and BPR integration. *International Journal of Production Research, 37*(9), 2093–2108. doi:10.1080/002075499190923

Nguyen, T. T., Nguyen, H. V., Nguyen, H. A., & Nguyen, T. N. (2011). Aspect recommendation for evolving software. In *Proceedings of the 33rd International Conference on Software Engineering* (pp. 361-370). ACM.

Nickolova, M., & Nickolov, E. (2007). Threat model for user security in e-learning systems. *International Journal Information Technologies and Knowledge, 1,* 341–347.

Nielsen, J. (2000). *Designing web usability.* New York, NY: New Riders.

Ning, S., & Han, Q. (2012). Design and implementation of DDOS attack and defense testbed.*International Conference on Wavelet Active Media Technology and Information Processing (ICWAMTIP)*, 2012, 220-223. doi:10.1109/ICWAMTIP.2012.6413478

Nisar, M. F., and Hameed, T. (2004, December). Agile methods handling offshore software development issues. In *Proceedings of INMIC 2004, 8th International Multitopic Conference.* INMIC.

Nora, B., & Ghoul, S. (2006). A model-driven approach to aspect mining. In *Proceedings of the 27ᵗʰ International Conference on Software Engineering* (pp. 361-370). Academic Press.

OASIS. (2007). *Web Services Business Process Execution Language Primer Version 2.0.* Retrieved September 28, 2113, from https://www.oasis-open.org/committees/download.php/23964/

Object Management Group. (2011). *Business Process Model and Notation Version 2.0.* Retrieved September 28, 2113, from http://www.omg.org/spec/BPMN/2.0/PDF

Oguz, F., & Sengün, A. (2011). Mystery of the unknown: Revisiting tacit knowledge in the organizational literature. *Journal of Knowledge Management, 15*(3), 445–461. doi:10.1108/13673271111137420

Ongaro, E. (2004). Process management in the public sector: The experience of one-stop shops in Italy. *International Journal of Public Sector Management, 17*(1), 81–107. doi:10.1108/09513550410515592

Ooi, K. B., Cheah, W. C., Lin, B., & Teh, P. L. (2012). TQM practices and knowledge sharing: An empirical study of Malaysia's manufacturing organizations. *Asia Pacific Journal of Management, 29*(1), 59–78. doi:10.1007/s10490-009-9185-9

Ordanini, A., Miceli, L., Pizzetti, M., & Parasuraman, A. (2011). Crowd-funding: Transforming customers into investors through innovative service platforms. *Journal of Service Management, 22*(4), 443–470. doi:10.1108/09564231111155079

O'Rourke, C., Fishman, N., & Selkow, W. (2003). *Enterprise architecture using the Zachman framework.* Boston, MA: Course Technology.

Ostadzadeh, S., & Fereidoon, S. (2011). An Architectural Framework for the Improvement of the Ultra-Large-Scale Systems Interoperability. In H. Arabnia, H. Reza, & L. Deligiannidis (Eds.) *International Conference on Software Engineering Research and Practice* (pp. 212-219). Athens, GA: CSREA Press.

Ovenden, T. (1994). Business process reengineering: Definitely worth considering. *The TQM Magazine, 6*(3), 56–61. doi:10.1108/09544789410057917

Ozcelik, Y. (2009). Do business process reengineering projects payoff? Evidence from the United States. *International Journal of Project Management, 28*(1), 7–13. doi:10.1016/j.ijproman.2009.03.004

Page-Jones, M. (1992). Comparing techniques by means of encapsulation and connascence. *Communications of the ACM, 35*(9), 147–151. doi:10.1145/130994.131004

Page-Jones, M. (1995). *What every programmer should know about object-oriented design.* New York, NY: Dorset House Publishing.

Palm, J., Anderson, K., & Lieberherr, K. (2003). Investigating the relationship between violations of the law of demeter and software maintainability. *Paper presented at the Workshop on Software-Engineering Properties of Languages for Aspect Technologies.* Retrieved July 21, 2014 from http://www.daimi.au.dk/~eernst/splat03/papers/Jeffrey_Palm.pdf

Palmer, B. (2004). Overcoming resistance to change. *Quality Progress, 37*(4), 35–40.

Pang, C.Y. (2001). A Design Pattern Type Extension with Facets and Decorators. *Journal of Object-Oriented Programming, 13.*

Pang, C. Y. (2012). Improve Business Agility of Legacy IT System. In V. Valverde & M. R. Talla (Eds.), *Information Systems Reengineering for Modern Business Systems: ERP, SCM, CRM, E-Commerce Management Solutions* (pp. 1–29). Hershey, PA: Information Science Publishing. doi:10.4018/978-1-4666-0155-0.ch001

Pang, C. Y. (2014). Legacy Software Integration in Service-driven Ecosystems: An Intelligent Agent-based Approach. In R. Ramanathan & K. Raja (Eds.), *Handbook of Research on Architectural Trends in Service-driven Computing.* Hershey, PA: Information Science Publishing.

Papazoglou, M. (2008). *Web services: principles and technology.* Harlow, England: Pearson Education Limited.

Parker, R. E. (2002). The global economy and changes in the nature of contingent work. In *Labor and Capital in the Age of Globalization: The Labor Process and the Changing Nature of Work in the Global Economy* (pp. 107-123). Academic Press.

Patel, A., Taghavi, M., & Bakhtiyari, K. (2012). An intrusion detection and prevention system in cloud computing: A systematic review. *Journal of Network and Computer Applications*. doi:10.1016/j.jnca.2012.08.007

Pathak, K., & Saha, A. (2013). Review of Agile Software Development Methodologies. *International Journal of Advanced Research in Computer Science and Software Engineering, 3*(2), 270–276.

Pathfinder. (2013). *Agile in an FDA Regulated Environment*. Retrieved from http://himss.files.cms-plus.com/FileDownloads/2013-1101%20Agile%20in%20FDA%20Environment%20Pathfinder%20White%20Paper_1387316073933_4.pdf

Patten, K., Whitworth, B., Fjermestad, J., & Mahinda, E. (2005). Leading IT flexibility: anticipation, agility and adaptability. In N. Romano (Ed.) *11th Americas Conference on Information Systems* (11–14). Red Hook, NY: Curran Associates, Inc.

Patwardhan, B. (2014). *Fixing innovation ecosystem*. Retrieved October 10, 2014 from, http://www.financialexpress.com /news/fixing-innovation-ecosystem/1280202

Paul, T. (1994). *Kidd Manufacturing Knowledge Inc. Agile manufacturing: forging new frontiers*. Boston, MA: Addison-Wesley Longman Publishing Co., Inc.

Pautasso, C., Zimmermann, O., & Leymann, F. (2008). Restful web services vs. "big"' web services: making the right architectural decision. In *International conference on World Wide Web* (pp. 805-814). ACM Press.

Peck, J., & Theodore, N. (2001). Contingent Chicago: Restructuring the spaces of temporary labor. *International Journal of Urban and Regional Research, 25*(3), 471–496. doi:10.1111/1468-2427.00325

Pérez-Castillo, R., García-Rodríguez de Guzmán, I., Piattini, M., & Places, Á. S. (2012). A case study on business process recovery using an e-government system. *Software, Practice & Experience, 42*(2), 159–189. doi:10.1002/spe.1057

Peristeras, V., & Tarabanis, K. (2006). The Connection, Communication, Consolidation, Collaboration Interoperability Framework (C4IF) For Information Systems Interoperability. *International Journal of Interoperability in Business Information Systems, 1*(1), 61-72.

Pettersen, J. (2009). Defining lean production: Some conceptual and practical issues. *The TQM Journal, 21*(2), 127–142. doi:10.1108/17542730910938137

Piening, E. P., Baluch, A. M., & Ridder, H. G. (2014). Mind the intended-implemented gap: Understanding employees' perceptions of HRM. *Human Resource Management, 53*(4), 545–567. doi:10.1002/hrm.21605

Poduval, A., & Todd, D. (2011). *Do More with SOA Integration*. Birmingham, UK: Packt Publishing.

Polack, F., & Mander, K. C. (1994). *Software quality assurance using the SAZ method*. Paper presented at the Z User Workshop, Cambridge, UK. doi:10.1007/978-1-4471-3452-7_13

Powazek, D. M. (2002). *Design for community: The art of connecting real people in virtual places*. Upper Saddle River, NJ: New Riders.

Prechelt, L., Malpohl, G., & Philippsen, M. (2002). Finding plagiarisms among a set of programs with JPlag. *Journal of Universal Computer Science, 8*(11), 1016–1038.

Preece, J. (2001). *Designing usability, supporting sociability: Questions participants ask about online communities*. Paper presented at the Human-Computer Interaction: INTERACT'01: IFIP TC. 13 International Conference on Human-Comupter Interaction, Tokyo, Japan.

Preece, J. (2000). *Online communities: Designing usability, supporting sociability*. Chichester, UK: John Wiley & Sons.

Pressman, R. S. (2005). *Software engineering: a practitioner's approach*. New York, NY: McGraw-Hill.

Project Bauhaus. (2005). Retrieved from http://www.bauhaus-stuttgart.de

Putnik, G., & Sluga, A. (2007). Reconfigurability of manufacturing systems for agility implementation, part I: requirements and principles. In Digital Enterprise Technology: Perspectives and Future Challenges (pp. 91-98). New York, NY: Springer Science+Business Media.

Qu, L., & Liu, D. (2007). Aspect mining using method call tree. In *Proceedings of the International Conference on Multimedia and Ubiquitous Engineering* (pp. 407-412). IEEE.

Rabai, L. B. A., Rjaibi, N., & Aissa, A. B. (2012). Quantifying Security Threats for E-learning Systems. In *Proceedings of IEEE International Conference on Education & E-Learning Innovations- Infrastructural Development in Education* (ICEELI 2012). IEEE. doi:10.1109/ICEELI.2012.6360592

Radhakrishnan, R., & Balasubramanian, S. (2008). *Business process reengineering: Text and cases.* New Delhi, India: Phi Learning.

Rahimian, V., and Ramsin, R. (2008). Designing an agile methodology for mobile software development: a hybrid method engineering approach. In *Proceedings of International Conference on Research Challenges in Information Science (RCIS).* Academic Press. doi:10.1109/RCIS.2008.4632123

Ranganathan, C., & Dhaliwal, J. (2001). A survey of business process reengineering practices in Singapore. *Information & Management, 39*(2), 125–134. doi:10.1016/S0378-7206(01)00087-8

Rao, K. N., Naidu, G. K., and Chakka, P. (2011). A study of the agile software development methods, applicability and implications in industry. *International Journal of Software Engineering and its Applications, 5*(2), 35-45.

Rashid, A., Sawyer, P., Moreira, A., & Araújo, J. (2002). Early aspects: A model for aspect-oriented requirements engineering. In *Proceedings of the Joint International Conference on Requirements Engineering* (pp. 199-202). IEEE. doi:10.1109/ICRE.2002.1048526

Reijers, H. A. (2006). Implementing BPM systems: The role of process orientation. *Business Process Management Journal, 12*(4), 389–409. doi:10.1108/14637150610678041

Revere, L. (2004). Re-engineering proves effective for reducing courier costs. *Business Process Management Journal, 10*(4), 400–414. doi:10.1108/14637150410548074

Rigby, D. (1993). The secret history of process reengineering. *Planning Review, 21*(2), 24–27. doi:10.1108/eb054408

Rigby, D., & Bilodeau, B. (2005). The Bain 2005 management tool survey. *Strategy and Leadership, 33*(4), 4–12. doi:10.1108/10878570510607997

Rjaibi, N. (2013). *Questionnaire MFC.* Retrieved Jan, 2013, from https://docs.google.com/forms/d/1NPT64kSdJhXaWDeBhXft5WQiPYZNHutW5WL2CpU7Fmw/edit?usp=sharing

Rjaibi, N., & Aissa, A. B. (2013). *The empirical data base for quantifying security threats.* Retrieved Jan, 2013, from https://docs.google.com/file/d/0B0Z2laATxEo7Tlk2TGd4elJjNFk/edit

Rjaibi, N., & Rabai, L. B. A. (2011). Toward A New Model For Assessing Quality Teaching Processes In E-learning. In *Proceedings of 3rd International Conference on Computer Supported Education, CSEDU'2011* (Vol. 2, pp. 468-472). SciTePress.

Rjaibi, N., & Rabai, L. B. A. (2012). Modeling The Assessment of Quality Online Course: An empirical Investigation of Key Factors Affecting Learner's Satisfaction. *IEEE Technology and Engineering Education, 7*(1), 6-13.

Rjaibi, N., Rabai, L. B. A., & Aissa, A. B. (2013). A basic security requirements taxonomy to quantify security threats: an e-learning application. In *Proceedings of The Third International Conference on Digital Information Processing and Communications* (ICDIPC2013), Session: Information security, Islamic Azad University (IAU),Dubai, United Arab Emirates (UAE). SDIWC. Retrieved from http://www.sdiwc.net/conferences/2013/Dubai/

Rjaibi, N., Rabai, L. B. A., Aissa, A. B., & Louadi, M. (2012). Cyber Security Measurement in Depth for E-learning Systems. *International Journal of Advanced Research in Computer Science and Software Engineering,2*(11), 107-120.

Rjaibi, N., Rabai, L. B. A., Aissa, A. B., & Mili, A. (2013). Mean failure Cost as a Measurable Value and Evidence of Cybersecurity: E-learning Case Study. *International Journal of Secure Software Engineering, 4*(3), 64-81. doi:10.4018/jsse.2013070104

Robert Mitchell, J., & Shepherd, D. A. (2012). Capability development and decision incongruence in strategic opportunity pursuit. *Strategic Entrepreneurship Journal, 6*(4), 355–381. doi:10.1002/sej.1145

Robert Mitchell, J., Shepherd, D. A., & Sharfman, M. P. (2011). Erratic strategic decisions: When and why managers are inconsistent in strategic decision making. *Strategic Management Journal, 32*(7), 683–704. doi:10.1002/smj.905

Robillard, M. P., & Murphy, G. C. (2007). Representing concerns in source code. *ACM Transactions on Software Engineering and Methodology, 16*(1), 3, es. doi:10.1145/1189748.1189751

Robinson, A., & Stern, S. (1998). *Corporate Creativity: How Innovation and Improvement Actually Happens*. Berret-Kohler Publishers.

Robles, G., Amor, J., Barahona, G. J., & Herrariz, I. (2013). The evolution of the laws of software evolution. A discussion based on a systematic literature review. *ACM Computing Surveys, 1*(1).

Roets, R., Minnaar, M., & Wright, K. (2007). Towards Successful Systems Development Projects in Developing Countries. In *Proceedings of the 9th International Conference on Social Implications of Computers in Developing Countries*. São Paulo, Brazil: Academic Press.

Roshen, M., Lublinsky, B., Smith, K. T., & Balcer, M. J. (2008). *Applied SOA: Service-Oriented Architecture and Design Strategies*. New Jersey: John Wiley & Son.

Roshen, W. (2009). *SOA-Based Enterprise Integration*. New York, NY: McGraw-Hill.

Rowley, J. (1998). Creating a learning organisation in higher education. *Industrial and Commercial Training, 30*(1), 16–19. doi:10.1108/00197859810197708

Roy, S. (2014). *5 Lean Tools and Principles to Integrate into Six Sigma*. Retrieved on 16.10.2014 from http://www.isixsigma.com/methodology/lean-methodology/5-lean-tools-and-principles-integrate-six-sigma/

Runeson, P. (2006). A survey of unit testing practices. *Software, IEEE, 23*(4), 22–29. doi:10.1109/MS.2006.91

Rüping, A. (2003). *Agile documentation: a pattern guide to producing lightweight documents for software projects*. New York: John Wiley and Sons.

Salmon, G. (2003). E-moderating: The key to teaching & learning online. London: Taylor & Frances Books Ltd.

Sampaio, A., Loughran, N., Rashid, A., & Rayson, P. (2005). Mining aspects in requirements. In *Proceedings of the Early Aspects: Aspect-Oriented Requirements Engineering and Architecture Design Workshop* (held with AOSD 2005). Chicago, IL: AOSD.

Sampaio, A., & Rashid, A. (2008). *Mining early aspects from requirements with EA-Miner*. In *Proceedings of the Companion of the 30th International Conference on Software Engineering* (pp. 911-912). ACM. doi:10.1145/1370175.1370183

Sanyal, B. C., & Varghese, N. V. (2007). *Knowledge for the future: Research capacity in developing countries.* Retrieved October 14, 2014 from www.unesco.org/iiep/en/publications/pubs.htm

Sarathy, P. S. (2013). TQM practice in real-estate industry using AHP. *Quality & Quantity, 47*(4), 2049–2063. doi:10.1007/s11135-011-9641-8

Saravanan, G. (2013). *Why Software Engineering Fails! (Most of the Time).* Retrieved March 9, 2013 from https://www.linkedin.com/groups/Why-Software-Engineering-Fails-Most-1523.S.221165656

Saxena, V., & Kumar, S. (2012). Impact of Coupling and Cohesion in Object-Oriented Technology. *Journal of Software Engineering and Applications, 5*(09), 671–676. doi:10.4236/jsea.2012.59079

Scacchi, W. (2001). Software Development Practices in Open Software Development Communities: A Comparative Case Study. In *Proceedings of the First Workshop on Open Source Software Engineering.* Toronto, Canada: Academic Press.

Schniederjans, M. J., & Kim, G. C. (2003). Implementing enterprise resource planning systems with total quality control and business process reengineering: Survey results. *International Journal of Operations & Production Management, 23*(4), 418–429. doi:10.1108/01443570310467339

Schnitt, D. (1993). Reengineering the organization using information technology. *Journal of Systems Management, 44*(1), 14–20.

Schoenherr, T., Power, D., Narasimhan, R., & Samson, D. (2012). Competitive capabilities among manufacturing plants in developing, emerging, and industrialized countries: A comparative analysis. *Decision Sciences, 43*(1), 37–72. doi:10.1111/j.1540-5915.2011.00341.x

Schubert, L. (2011). *The Keys To Distributed and Agile Application Development.* White Paper. CollabNet Inc. Retrieved from http://visit.collab.net/rs/collabnet/images/keys_to_distributed_agile_app_dev_in_cloud.pdf

Sealey, R. (2010). Logistics workers and global logistics: The heavy lifters of globalisation. *Work Organisation, Labour & Globalisation, 4*(2), 25–38.

Seethamraju, R. (2012). Business process management: A missing link in business education. *Business Process Management Journal, 18*(3), 532–547. doi:10.1108/14637151211232696

Selvi, R. T., Balasubramanian, N. V., & Manohar, G. T. (2008). Framework and Architectural Style Metrics for Component Based Software Engineering. In *Proceedings of the International MultiConference of Engineers and Computer Scientists* (vol. 1, pp. 19-21). Hong Kong: Academic Press.

Serban, G., & Cojocar, G. S. (2007). A New Graph-Based Approach in Aspect Mining. In *Proceedings of the International Conference on Knowledge Engineering* (pp. 252-260). Academic Press.

Serban, G., & Moldovan, G. S. (2006). A Graph Algorithm for Identification of Crosscutting Concerns. *Studia Universitatis Babes-Bolyai. Informatica, LI*(2), 53–60.

Serban, G., & Moldovan, G. S. (2006). A new genetic clustering based approach in aspect mining. In *Proceedings of the 8th WSEAS International Conference on Mathematical Methods and Computational Techniques in Electrical Engineering* (pp. 135-140). WSEAS.

Serban, G., & Moldovan, G. S. (2006). A new k-means based clustering algorithm in aspect mining. In *Proceedings of the Eighth International Symposium on Symbolic and Numeric Algorithms for Scientific Computing* (pp. 69-74). Timisoara: IEEE. doi:10.1109/SYNASC.2006.5

Shadbolt, N., Hall, W., & Berners-Lee, T. (2006). The semantic web revisited. *IEEE Intelligent Systems, 21*(3), 96–101. doi:10.1109/MIS.2006.62

Shankararaman, V., & Megargel, A. (2013). Enterprise Integration: Architectural Approaches. In R. Ramanathan & K. Raja (Eds.), *Service-Driven Approaches to Architecture and Enterprise Integration*. Hershey, PA: Information Science Publishing. doi:10.4018/978-1-4666-4193-8.ch003

Sharp, J. H., & Ryan, S. D. (2011). Best Practices for Configuring Globally Distributed Agile Teams. *Journal of Information Technology Management, 22*(4), 56.

Shepherd, D., & Pollock, L. (2005). Interfaces, aspects, and views. In *Proceedings of the Workshop on Linking Aspect Technology and Evolution at International Conference on Aspect Oriented Software Development* (pp. 1-6). Academic Press.

Shepherd, D., Gibson, E., & Pollock, L. L. (2004). Design and Evaluation of an Automated Aspect Mining Tool. In *Proceedings of the International Conference on Software Engineering Research and Practice* (pp. 601-607). Academic Press.

Shepherd, D., Pollock, L., & Tourwé, T. (2005). Using language clues to discover crosscutting concerns. *Software Engineering Notes, 30*(4), 1–6. doi:10.1145/1082983.1083129

Sheth, A., Gomadam, K., & Lathem, J. (2007). SA-REST: Semantically interoperable and easier-to-use services and mashups. *IEEE Internet Computing, 11*(6), 91–94. doi:10.1109/MIC.2007.133

Shin, N., & Jemella, D. F. (2002). Business process reengineering and performance improvements: The case of Chase Manhattan Bank. *Business Process Management Journal, 8*(4), 351–363. doi:10.1108/14637150210435008

Shrivastava, S. V., & Date, H. (2010). A Framework for Risk Management in Globally Distributed Agile Software Development (Agile GSD). *Interscience Management Review, 2*(1), 32–41.

Shuster, L. (2013). Enterprise Integration: Challenges and Solution Architecture. In R. Ramanathan & K. Raja (Eds.), *Service-Driven Approaches to Architecture and Enterprise Integration*. Hershey, PA: Information Science Publishing. doi:10.4018/978-1-4666-4193-8.ch002

Sia, S. K., & Neo, B. S. (2008). Business process reengineering, empowerment and work monitoring: An empirical analysis through the Panopticon. *Business Process Management Journal, 14*(5), 609–628. doi:10.1108/14637150810903020

Siegelaub, J. M. (2004). *How PRINCE2 can complement PMBOK and your PMP*. Paper presented at the PMI Global Congress, Anaheim, CA.

Simms, M., & Dean, D. (2014). Mobilising contingent workers: An analysis of two successful cases. *Economic and Industrial Democracy*.

Simon, Rubin, Smith, & Trajkovic. (2000). *Distributed Denial of Service Attacks*. Retrieved from http://www2.ensc.sfu.ca/~ljilja/papers/smc00_edited.pdf

Singh, A., Singh, K., & Sharma, N. (2012). Managing Knowledge in Agile Software Development. In *IJCA Proceedings on International Conference on Recent Advances and Future Trends in Information Technology* (iRAFIT 2012) (pp. 33-37). IJCA.

Singh, A., Singh, K., & Sharma, N. (2013). Knowledge Management: the agile way. Information and Knowledge Management, 3(3), 143-152.

Singh, A., & Singh, K. (2010). Agile Adoption – Crossing the Chasm. In *Proceedings of the International Conference on Applied Computer Science*. ACS.

Singh, A., Singh, K., & Sharma, N. (2014). Agile knowledge management: A survey of Indian perceptions. *Innovations in Systems and Software Engineering, 10*(4), 297–315. doi:10.1007/s11334-014-0237-z

Sirén, C. A., Kohtamäki, M., & Kuckertz, A. (2012). Exploration and exploitation strategies, profit performance, and the mediating role of strategic learning: Escaping the exploitation trap. *Strategic Entrepreneurship Journal, 6*(1), 18–41. doi:10.1002/sej.1126

Slack, N., Chambers, S., & Johnston, R. (2007). *Operations management*. Harlow, UK: Financial Times/Prentice–Hall.

Slocombe, M. (2001). Max hits: Building successful websites (1st ed.). Hove, UK: Rotovision.

Smith, M. (2003). Business process design: Correlates of success and failure. *The Quality Management Journal, 10*(2), 38–49.

Sneed, H. M. (2012). Reengineering and Wrapping Legacy Modules for Reuse as Web Services: Motivation, Method, Tools, and Case Studies. In A. D. Ionita, M. Litoiu, & G. Lewis (Eds.), *Migrating Legacy Applications: Challenges in Service Oriented Architecture and Cloud Computing Environments*. Hershey, PA: Information Science Publishing.

Soltani, E., Chau, V. S., & Liao, Y. Y. (2012). A learning organization perspective of service quality operations in the IT industry. *Strategic Change, 21*(5-6), 275–284. doi:10.1002/jsc.1909

Sommerville, I., & Sawyer, P. (1997). *Requirements engineering: A good practice guide*. John Wiley and Sons, Inc.

Spackman, D., & Speaker, M. (2004). *Enterprise Integration Solution*. Microsoft Press.

Specht, S. M., & Lee, R. B. (2004). Distributed Denial of Service: Taxonomies of Attacks, Tools, and Countermeasures. *In Proceedings of the International Workshop on Security in Parallel and Distributed Systems*. San Francisco, CA: Academic Press.

Stapié, Z., Orehovacki, T., & Danié, M. (2008). Determination of optimal security settings for LMS Moodle. In *Proceedings of 31st MIPRO International Convention on Information Systems Security*. MIPRO.

Stein, E. (2003). *Re-Engineering the Manufacturing System: Applying the Theory of Constraints*. New York, NY: Marcel Dekker, Inc. doi:10.1201/9780203912508

Steinmacher, I., Chaves, A. P., & Gerosa, M. A. (2012). Awareness Support in Distributed Software Development: A Systematic Review and Mapping of the Literature. *Computer Supported Cooperative Work, 22*(3), 113–158.

Steinmacher, I., Chaves, A. P., & Gerosa, M. A. (2010). Awareness Support in Global Software Development : A Systematic Review Based on the 3C Collaboration Model. In L. G. Kolfschoten & T. Herrmann (Eds.), *Collaboration and Technology* (pp. 185–201). Berlin, Germany: Springer-Verlag. doi:10.1007/978-3-642-15714-1_15

Stollberg, M., & Strang, T. (2005). Integrating Agents, Ontologies, and Semantic Web Services for Collaboration on the Semantic Web. In *Proc. of the First International Symposium on Agents and the Semantic Web*. AAAI.

Subashini, S., & Kavitha, V. (2011). A survey on security issues in service delivery models of cloud computing. *Journal of Network and Computer Applications, 34*(1), 1–11. doi:10.1016/j.jnca.2010.07.006

Sungau, J., Ndunguru, P. C., & Kimeme, J. (2013). Business process re-engineering: The technique to improve delivering speed of service industry in Tanzania. *Independent Journal of Management & Production, 4*(1), 208–227. doi:10.14807/ijmp.v4i1.68

Sun, P. C., Ray, J. T., Finger, G., Chen, Y. Y., & Yeh, D. (2008). What drives a successful e-learning? an empirical investigation of the critical factors influencing learner satisfaction. *Computers and Education, Elsevier, 50*(4), 1183–1202. doi:10.1016/j.compedu.2006.11.007

Suttapong, K., Srimai, S., & Pitchayadol, P. (2014). Best practices for building high performance in human resource management. *Global Business and Organizational Excellence*, *33*(2), 39–50. doi:10.1002/joe.21532

Sweeny, R. (2010). *Achieving Service-Oriented Architecture*. Hoboken, NJ: John Wiley & Son.

Talwar, R. (1993). Business reengineering: A strategy-driven approach. *Long Range Planning*, *26*(6), 22–40. doi:10.1016/0024-6301(93)90204-S

Tapscott, D., & Caston, A. (1993). *Paradigm shift: The new promise of information technology*. New York, NY: Mc-Graw–Hill.

Tarokh, M., Sharifi, E., & Nazemi, E. (2008). Survey of BPR experiences in Iran: Reasons for success and failure. *Journal of Business and Industrial Marketing*, *23*(5), 350–362. doi:10.1108/08858620810881629

Tarr, P., Ossher, H., Harrison, W., & Sutton, S. M. Jr. (1999). N degrees of separation: multi-dimensional separation of concerns. In *Proceedings of the 21st International Conference on Software Engineering* (pp. 107-119). ACM.

Tatroe, K., MacIntyre, P., & Lerdorf, R. (2013). *Programming PHP* (3rd ed.). Sebastopol, CA: O'Reilly.

Tatsiopoulos, I. P., & Panayiotou, N. (2000). The integration of activity based costing and enterprise modeling for reengineering purposes. *International Journal of Production Economics*, *66*(1), 33–44. doi:10.1016/S0925-5273(99)00080-8

Tekinerdogan, B., & Aksit, M. (1998). Deriving design aspects from conceptual models. In S. Demeyer & J. Bosch (Ed.), *Object-Oriented Technology: ECOOP'98 Workshop Reader: Proceedings of the ECOOP' 98 Workshops, Demos, and Posters* (LNCS), (Vol. 1543, pp.410-413). Brussels, Belgium: Springer. doi:10.1007/3-540-49255-0_122

Tennant, C., & Wu, Y. C. (2005). The application of business process reengineering in the UK. *The TQM Magazine*, *17*(6), 537–545. doi:10.1108/09544780510627633

Terziovski, M. E., Fitzpatrick, P., & O'Neill, P. (2003). Successful predictors of business process reengineering (BPR) in financial services. *International Journal of Production Economics*, *84*(1), 35–50. doi:10.1016/S0925-5273(02)00378-X

Thakur, S., & Kaur, A. (2013). Role of Agile Methodology in Software Development. *International Journal of Computer Science and Mobile Computing*, *2*(10), 86–90.

Thomas, K., & Allen, S. (2006). The learning organisation: A meta-analysis of themes in literature. *The Learning Organization*, *13*(2), 123–139. doi:10.1108/09696470610645467

Tonella, P., & Ceccato, M. (2004). Aspect mining through the formal concept analysis of execution traces. In *Proceedings of the 11th Working Conference on Reverse Engineering* (pp. 112-121). IEEE. doi:10.1109/WCRE.2004.13

Tourwe, T., & Mens, K. (2004). Mining aspectual views using formal concept analysis. In *Proceedings of the 4th IEEE International Workshop on Source Code Analysis and Manipulation* (pp. 97-106). IEEE. doi:10.1109/SCAM.2004.15

Trevor, J., & Brown, W. (2014). The limits on pay as a strategic tool: Obstacles to alignment in non-union environments. *British Journal of Industrial Relations*, *52*(3), 553–578. doi:10.1111/bjir.12004

Trifu, M. (2008). Using dataflow information for concern identification in object-oriented software systems. In *Proceedings of the 2008 12th European Conference on Software Maintenance and Reengineering* (pp. 193-202). Washington, DC: IEEE Computer Society. doi:10.1109/CSMR.2008.4493314

Tripathi, S., Gupta, B., Almomani, A., Mishra, A., & Veluru, S. (2013). Hadoop Based Defense Solution to Handle Distributed Denial of Service (DDOS) Attacks. *Journal of Information Security*, *4*(03), 150–164. doi:10.4236/jis.2013.43018

Trist, E., & Bamforth, K. (1951). Some social and psychological consequences of the longwall method of coal getting. *Human Relations, 4*, 3–38. doi:10.1177/001872675100400101

Tugui, O., Funar, S., & Cofari, A. (2008). Trends of Integrating the E-Learning Platform in the Graduate Agronomic Educational System in Romania. *Bulletin of the University of Agricultural Sciences & Veterinary, 65*(2), 621–626.

Udhayan, J.; Anitha, R. 2009). *Demystifying and Rate Limiting ICMP hosted DoS/DDOS Flooding Attacks with Attack Productivity Analysis.* Advance Computing Conference IACC 2009.

Umar, A., & Zordan, A. (2009). Reengineering for service oriented architectures: A strategic decision model for integration versus migration. *Journal of Systems and Software, 82*(3), 448–462. doi:10.1016/j.jss.2008.07.047

Vakola, M., & Rezgui, Y. (2000). Critique of existing business process re-engineering methodologies: The development and implementation of a new methodology. *Business Process Management Journal, 6*(3), 238–250. doi:10.1108/14637150010325453

Vakola, M., Rezgui, Y., & Wood-Harper, T. (2000). The Condor business process re-engineering model. *Managerial Auditing Journal, 15*(1–2), 42–46. doi:10.1108/02686900010304623

Valentine, S., Hollingworth, D., & Francis, C. A. (2013). Quality-related HR practices, organizational ethics, and positive work attitudes: Implications for HRD. *Human Resource Development Quarterly, 24*(4), 493–523. doi:10.1002/hrdq.21169

Vasanthi, S., & Chandrasekar, S. (2011). A study on network intrusion detection and prevention system current status and challenging issues.*3rd International Conference on Advances in Recent Technologies in Communication and Computing (ARTCom 2011).* doi:10.1049/ic.2011.0075

Venkatraman, N. (1994). IT-enabled business transformation: From automation to business scope redefinition. *Sloan Management Review, 35*(2), 73–87.

Verginadis, Y., & Mentzas, G. (2008). Agents and workflow engines for inter-organizational workflows in e-government cases. *Business Process Management Journal, 14*(2), 188–203. doi:10.1108/14637150810864925

Vernadat, F. (1996). *Enterprise Modeling and Integration: Principles and Applications.* London: Chapman & Hall.

VersionOne. (2012). *7ᵗʰ Annual State of Agile Development Survey.* Retrieved from http://www.versionone.com/pdf/7th-Annual-State-of-Agile-Development-Survey.pdf

Vidal, S., Abait, E. S., Marcos, C., Casas, S., & Díaz Pace, J. A. (2009). Aspect mining meets rule-based refactoring. In *Proceedings of the 1st Workshop on Linking Aspect Technology and Evolution* (pp. 23-27). New York: ACM. doi:10.1145/1509847.1509852

Villanova University. (2014). *Six Sigma vs. Lean Six Sigma.* Retrived on 12.10.2014 from http://www.villanovau.com/resources/six-sigma/six-sigma-vs-lean-six-sigma/

Vixie, P. (1999). Software Engineering. In M. Stone, S. Ockman, & C. Dibona (Eds.), *Open sources: Voices from the open source revolution.* Sebastopol, CA: O'Reilly & Associates.

Volberda, H. W., Van Den Bosch, F. A. J., & Heij, C. V. (2013). Management innovation: Management as fertile ground for innovation. *European Management Review, 10*(1), 1–15. doi:10.1111/emre.12007

W3C. (2004). *Resource Description Framework Primer.* Retrieved September 28, 2113, from http://www.w3.org/TR/rdf-primer/

W3C. (2012). *Web Ontology Language (OWL) Primer* (2nd Ed.). W3C. Retrieved September 28, 2113, from http://www.w3.org/TR/owl2-primer/

Wähner, K. (2013). Choosing the Right ESB for Your Integration Needs. *InfoQ Articles*. Retrieved June 11, 2014, from http://www.infoq.com/articles/ESB-Integration

Wang, B-T., & Schulzrinne, H. (2004). An IP traceback mechanism for reflective DoS attacks. *Canadian Conference on Electrical and Computer Engineering* (vol. 2, pp. 901-904). Academic Press.

Wang, W., Tolk, A., & Wang, W. (2009). The levels of conceptual interoperability model: Applying systems engineering principles to M&S. In *Spring Simulation Multiconference* (article no.: 168). San Diego, CA: Society for Computer Simulation International.

Wang, C. L., & Ahmed, P. K. (2003). Organisational learning: A critical review. *The Learning Organization*, *10*(1), 8–17. doi:10.1108/09696470310457469

Waters, K. (2007). *Sprint Planning (Tasks)*. Retrieved December 20, 2014, from http://www.allaboutagile.com/how-to-implement-scrum-in-10-easy-steps-step-4-sprint-planning-tasks/

Weaver, P. L., Lambrou, N., & Walkley, M. (2002). *Practical business systems development using SSADM: A complete tutorial guide*. London: Pearson Education.

Webber, J., Parastatidis, S., & Robinson, I. (2010). *REST in Practice: Hypermedia and Systems Architecture*. Sebastopol, CA: O'Reilly Media, Inc. doi:10.1007/978-3-642-15114-9_3

Wegner, P. (1989). *Concepts and Paradigms of Object-Oriented Programming*. Expansion of Oct. 4 OOPSLA-89 Keynote Talk.

Weiler. (2002). Honeypots for Distributed Denial of Service Attacks. In *Proceedings of Eleventh IEEE International Workshops on Enabling Technologies: Infrastructure for Collaborative Enterprises*. IEEE.

Wells, D. (2009). *Agile Software Development: A gentle introduction*. Retrieved December 20, 2014, from http://agile-process.org

Wells, M. G. (2000). Business process re-engineering implementations using Internet technology. *Business Process Management Journal*, *6*(2), 164–184. doi:10.1108/14637150010321303

Wells, R., O'Connell, P., & Hochman, S. (1993). What's the difference between reengineering and TQEM? *Total Quality Environmental Management*, *2*(3), 273–282. doi:10.1002/tqem.3310020307

Whitworth, E., and Biddle, R. (2007, August). The social nature of agile teams. In *Proceedings of Agile Conference (AGILE)* (pp. 26-36). Academic Press.

Winter, R. (2002). An executive MBA program in business engineering: A curriculum focusing on change. *Journal of Information Technology Education*, *1*(4), 279–288.

Wolak, R., Kalafatis, S., & Harris, P. (1998). An investigation into four characteristics of services. *Journal of Empirical Generalisations in Marketing Science*, *3*(2), 22–43.

Womack, J. (2005). *A Lean Walk Through History*. Saatavissa. Retrieved from http://www. superfactory. com/articles/featured/2005/pdf/0501-womack-lean-walkhistory. pdf

Womack, J. P. (2004). *An action plan for Lean services*. Amsterdam: Lean Service Summit.

Womack, J. P., & Jones, D. T. (2010). *Lean thinking: Banish waste and create wealth in your corporation*. Simon and Schuster.

WRONG. R. (2009). *Increasing membership in online communities: The five principles of managing virtual club economies.* Paper presented at the 3rd International Conference on Internet Technologies and Applications (ITA'09), Wrexham, UK.

Wu, I. (2003). Understanding senior management's behavior in promoting the strategic role of IT in process reengineering: Use of the theory of reasoned action. *Information & Management, 41*(1), 1–11. doi:10.1016/S0378-7206(02)00115-5

Wyke, R., & Watt, A. (2002). *XML Schema Essentials.* John Wiley & Sons.

Xia, Du, Cao, & Chen. (2012). *An Algorithm of Detecting and Defending CC Attack in Real Time.* International Conference on Industrial Control and Electronics Engineering (ICICEE).

Xiao, H., Zou, Y., Ng, J., & Nigul, L. (2010). An Approach for Context-Aware Service Discovery and Recommendation. In *Proceedings of the IEEE International Conference on Web Services* (pp. 63-170). IEEE. doi:10.1109/ICWS.2010.95

Xiaoli, L. (2011). Correlation between business process reengineering and operation performance of National Commercial Banks. *Journal of Innovation and Management, 7,* 981–985.

Yitmen, I. (2013). Organizational cultural intelligence: A competitive capability for strategic alliances in the international construction industry. *Project Management Journal, 44*(4), 5–25. doi:10.1002/pmj.21356

Ylimannela, V. (2011). *A Model for Risk Management in Agile Software Development. Communications of Cloud Software.* Tampere: Tampere University of Technology.

Young, M. L., & Levine, J. R. (2000). *Poor richard's building online communities: Create a web community for your business, club, association, or family.* Top Floor Pub.

Yourdon, E., & Contantine, L. (1979). *Structured Design: Fundamentals of a Discipline of Computer Program and Systems Design.* Yourdon Press.

Yuen, I., & Robillard, M. P. (2007). Bridging the gap between aspect mining and refactoring. In *Proceedings of the 3rd Workshop on Linking Aspect Technology and Evolution* (pp. 1-6). New York: ACM. doi:10.1145/1275672.1275673

Yung, W. K. C., & Chan, D. T. H. (2003). Application of value delivery system (VDS) and performance benchmarking in flexible business process reengineering. *International Journal of Operations & Production Management, 23*(3), 300–315. doi:10.1108/01443570310462277-6

Yusuf, Y., Sarhadi, M., & Gunasekaran, A. (1999). Agile manufacturing: The drivers, concepts and attributes. *International Journal of Production Economics, 62*(1/2), 33–43. doi:10.1016/S0925-5273(98)00219-9

Zairi, M., & Sinclair, D. (1995). Business process reengineering and process management: A survey of current practice and future trends in integrated management. *Management Decision, 33*(3), 3–16. doi:10.1108/00251749510085021

Zatzick, C. D., Moliterno, T. P., & Fang, T. (2012). Strategic (MIS)FIT: The implementation of TQM in manufacturing organizations. *Strategic Management Journal, 33*(11), 1321–1330. doi:10.1002/smj.1988

Zhang, C., & Jacobsen, H. A. (2004). Prism is research in aspect mining. In *Proceedings of the OOPSLA'04 Companion to the 19th Annual ACM SIGPLAN Conference on Object-Oriented Programming Systems, Languages, and Applications* (pp. 20-21). New York: ACM. doi:10.1145/1028664.1028676

Zhang, C., Gao, D., & Jacobsen, H. A. (2002). *Extended aspect mining tool.* Retrieved from http://www. eecg. utoronto. ca/~czhang/amtex

Zhang, C., & Jacobsen, H. A. (2007). Efficiently mining crosscutting concerns through random walks. In *Proceedings of the 6th International Conference on Aspect-Oriented Software Development* (pp. 226-238). ACM. doi:10.1145/1218563.1218588

Zhang, C., & Jacobsen, H. A. (2012). Mining crosscutting concerns through random walks. *IEEE Transactions on Software Engineering, 38*(5), 1123–1137. doi:10.1109/TSE.2011.83

Zhang, D., Guo, Y., & Chen, X. (2008). Automated aspect recommendation through clustering-based fan-in analysis. In *Proceedings of the 23rd IEEE/ACM International Conference on Automated Software Engineering* (pp. 278-287). IEEE. doi:10.1109/ASE.2008.38

Zhang, G. P., & Xia, Y. (2013). Does quality still pay? A reexamination of the relationship between effective quality management and firm performance. *Production and Operations Management, 22*(1), 120–136. doi:10.1111/j.1937-5956.2012.01341.x

Zhu, J., Huang, J., Zhou, D., Carminati, F., Zhang, G., & He, Q. (2013). Identifying composite crosscutting concerns through semi-supervised learning. *Software, Practice & Experience, 44*(12), 1525–1545. doi:10.1002/spe.2234

About the Contributors

Amitoj Singh is working as Assistant Director at the Center for Advance Computing Research in Chitkara University, India. He has more that 10 years of teaching/ reserach experience. He earned his doctorate dehree in 2013 from Punajbi University, Patiala, India. His research interests include development of language resources for differently-abled persons and resources for under resourced languages. He is working on speech and sign language technologies and is guiding students for developing technological resources of software industry. He is working also in Agile software development methodologies and integration of these methodologies in different domains.

* * *

Sachin Ahuja obtained his Ph.D. (C.S.E.) in the year 2013. He completed his Master of Technology in the year 2010. He has over 10 years of experience in teaching and research at UG and PG levels of Computer Science & Engineering. His research interests include Data Mining, Educational Data Mining, Prediction using Fuzzy Logic and Fuzzy Time series, Association Rule Mining. Presently, Dr. Ahuja is working as coordinator of Office of Patent Facilitation & Licensing at Chitkara University and guiding two PhD scholars in the areas of Data Mining in Education.

Jonathan Bishop is an information technology executive, researcher and writer. He is the founder of the companies that form part of the Crocels Community Media Group, and founded the Centre for Research into Online Communities and E-Learning Systems in 2005 from which the group is named. Jonathan's research generally falls within human-computer interaction, and he has numerous publications in this area, such as on Internet trolling, gamification, Classroom 2.0, and multimedia forensics. In addition to his BSc(Hons) in Multimedia Studies and various postgraduate degrees, including in law, economics and computing, Jonathan has served in local government as a councillor and school governor, as well as having contested numerous elections. He is also a fellow of numerous learned bodies, including BCS - The Chartered Institute for IT, the Royal Anthropological Institute, and the Royal Society of Arts. Jonathan has won prizes for his literary skills and been a finalist in national and local competitions for his environmental, community and equality work, which often form part of action research studies. In his spare time Jonathan enjoys listening to music, swimming and chess.

José C. Delgado is an Associate Professor at the Computer Science and Engineering Department of the Instituto Superior Técnico (University of Lisbon), in Lisbon, Portugal, where he earned the Ph.D. degree in 1988. He lectures courses in the areas of Computer Architecture, Information Technology and

Service Engineering. He has performed several management roles in his faculty, namely Director of the Taguspark campus, near Lisbon, and Coordinator of the B.Sc. and M.Sc. in Computer Science and Engineering at that campus. He has been the coordinator of and researcher in several research projects, both national and European. As an author, his publications include one book, several book chapters and more than 50 papers in international refereed conferences and journals.

Noopur Goel is serving as Assistant Professor with the Department of Computer Applications of the U.N.S. Institute of Engineering and Technology, V.B.S. Purvanchal University, Jaunpur, India. She has her Master of Computer Applications Degree from National Institute of Technology, Jamshedpur, India and a Ph.D. in Computer Science from Banaras Hindu University, Varanasi, India. She has been engaged in teaching for the last 15 years and the areas of her research interest include Software Reuse, Software Testing, Design Patterns, and Cloud Computing. She has to her credit publications in international and national journals as well as research papers in proceedings of international and national level conferences.

Irum Inayat received here PhD from the University of Malaya, Malaysia. Her degree in Computer Science from Comsats University of Science and Technology and degree from Pakistan Institute of Engineering and Applied Sciences, Pakistan. Her research interest lies in requirements engineering, agile software development methods, social software engineering, computer supported cooperative work, and collaborative e-learning. She has published in to a number of international conferences and ISI journals.

Kijpokin Kasemsap received his BEng degree in Mechanical Engineering from King Mongkut's University of Technology Thonburi, his MBA degree from Ramkhamhaeng University, and his DBA degree in Human Resource Management from Suan Sunandha Rajabhat University. He is a Special Lecturer at Faculty of Management Sciences, Suan Sunandha Rajabhat University based in Bangkok, Thailand. He is a Member of International Association of Engineers (IAENG), International Association of Engineers and Scientists (IAEST), International Economics Development and Research Center (IEDRC), International Association of Computer Science and Information Technology (IACSIT), International Foundation for Research and Development (IFRD), and International Innovative Scientific and Research Organization (IISRO). He also serves on the International Advisory Committee (IAC) for International Association of Academicians and Researchers (INAAR). He has numerous original research articles in top international journals, conference proceedings, and book chapters on business management, human resource management, and knowledge management published internationally.

Deepinder Kaur is an IT Professional working as Senior Quality Analyst in IBM India Pvt Ltd. She acquired her MS in Software Systems from BITS, Pilani and completed her B.tech from Baba Banda Singh Bahadur Engg College, Punjab. Her research areas are Lean, Six Sigma and various quality assurance methodologies used in Software industries.

Parminder Kaur is working as Assistant Professor in the Department of Computer Science & Engineering, Guru Nanak Dev University, Amritsar. She has published around 45 research papers in International/National journals as well as Conferences. Her research area includes Component-based Software Engineering, Open Source Systems, Web Engineering and Software Security.

Vinay Kukreja works as Assistant professor in Chitkara University for the last 8 and a half years. Kukreja is also pursuing a Phd from Chitkara Univeristy. His research areas are Agile development, Cloud computing and Algorithms.

Karun Madan works as Assistant Professor in SD College, Ludhiana. Madan has around 9 years of teaching experience, has published 2 books and approximately 21 research papers in International Journals and conferences.

Archana Mantri obtained her PhD in Education Technology in the year 2010. Prior to that she did her Master of Technology from NIT, Bhopal, MP, India in the year 1994. She has over 25 years of experience in teaching and research at UG and PG levels of Electronics Engineering. Her research interests include: Project and Problem based Learning, Augmented reality for Teaching Aids and Learning Analytics. At present she is guiding two PhD scholars in the areas of Augmented Reality Teaching Aids.

Sabrina Marczak is a Professor at Pontifícia Universidade Católica do Rio Grande do Sul University (PUCRS), Porto Alegre, Brazil. She holds a PhD degree in Computer Science from Victoria University, Canada. Her research interests lies in requirements engineering, collaborative engineering, and social aspects in software development, and agile development. She has published in to a number of international conferences and ISI journals such as RE, ICGSE, and IST.

Ali Mili holds a PhD from the University of Illinois and a Doctorat es Sciences d'Etat from the Joseph Fourier University of Grenoble. He has authored ten books (four of which are in Arabic), twelve book chapters, and 200 papers in journals and conference proceedings. One of his current projects, planned in conjunction with Arabic speaking researchers, involves the design and implementation of a programming language, a specification language, an architectural description language, and a design and modeling language, all in Arabic.

Chung-Yeung Pang received his Ph.D. degree from Cambridge University, England. He has over 25 years' experience in software development in various areas, ranging from device driver to large enterprise IT systems. He has experience in many programming languages including low level languages like assembler and C, high level languages like COBOL, Java and Ada, and AI languages such as LISP and Prolog. For the past 20 years, he has been working as a consultant in different enterprise software projects. He has been engaged in architecture design, development, coaching and managing IT projects. At one time, he was one of the lead architects in a project with a budget for over 1 billion USD. In the last years, he has led many projects to completion within time and budgets despite the limited resources and high pressure in some of the projects.

Latifa Ben Arfa Rabai is a University Associate Professor in the Department of Computer Science at the Tunis University in the Higher Institute of Management (ISG). She received the computer science Engineering diploma in 1989 from the sciences faculty of Tunis and the PhD, from the sciences faculty of Tunis in 1992. Her research interest includes software engineering trends quantification, quality assessment in education and e-learning, and security measurement and quantification. She has published in information sciences Journal and IEEE Technology and Engineering Education magazine. She has participated in several international conferences covering topics related to computer science, E-learning, quality assessment in education, and cyber security.

Nisha Ratti is an Assistant Professor in Rayat Institute of Engg. & Information Technology, Ropar, Punjab. She has done her M.Tech.(IT) from GNDU, Amritsar, India. She is presently pursuing the Ph.D. degree in Computer Science from GNDU, Amritsar. She has approx. 20 papers published in various national and International Journals. Her research areas include Component based systems, version control systems. Special thanks to Taranjeet Kaur for her contribution in practical work.

Neila Rjaibi is a University Common Core Professor of Computer Science at the Higher Institute of Commerce and Accountancy of Bizerte (ISCCB), University of Carthage, Tunisia, since September 2008. Neila graduated from the University of Tunis, High Institute of Management, Computer Science in 2007. She holds a Master Diploma in Applied Informatics to management in 2010 from High Institute of Management. She is presently pursuing the Ph.D. degree in Informatics at the University of Tunis. Her areas of interests are: software engineering, Cyber Security measurement, Security Risk Management, and E-learning Systems.

Siti Salwa Salim is a Professor in University of Malaya, Malaysia. She holds a PhD degree in software engineering from Manchester University, UK. Her research interest lies in requirements engineering, human computer interaction, computer supported cooperative work, component based software development, and affective computing.

Baldev Singh works as Asst. Prof. in the Department of Computer Science & IT and has more than 18 years of teaching experience. Singh attended and presented papers in International Conferences in India and abroad (USA & UK) and worked on UGC, Govt. of India sponsored Research Project.

Index

Information Resources Management Association

Become an IRMA Member

Members of the **Information Resources Management Association (IRMA)** understand the importance of community within their field of study. The Information Resources Management Association is an ideal venue through which professionals, students, and academicians can convene and share the latest industry innovations and scholarly research that is changing the field of information science and technology. Become a member today and enjoy the benefits of membership as well as the opportunity to collaborate and network with fellow experts in the field.

IRMA Membership Benefits:

- **One FREE Journal Subscription**

- **30% Off Additional Journal Subscriptions**

- **20% Off Book Purchases**

- Updates on the latest events and research on Information Resources Management through the IRMA-L listserv.

- Updates on new open access and downloadable content added to Research IRM.

- A copy of the Information Technology Management Newsletter twice a year.

- A certificate of membership.

IRMA Membership $195

Scan code to visit irma-international.org and begin by selecting your free journal subscription.

Membership is good for one full year.

Printed in the United States
By Bookmasters